Empire State Railway Museum's

Tourist
Trains

41st Annual Guide to
Tourist Railroads and Museums

KALMBACH
BOOKS

Copyright © 2006 Empire State Railway Museum, Inc., P.O. Box 455, Phoenicia, NY 12464. All Rights
Reserved. Printed in Canada.

This book may not be reproduced in part or in whole without written permission from the publisher, except in
the case of brief quotations used in reviews. Published by Kalmbach Publishing Co., 21027 Crossroads Circle,
P.O. Box 1612, Waukesha, WI 53187-1612.

Cover Design: Tom Ford, Mike Soliday   ISSN: 1546-2730
Editor: Tea Benduhn

To the Museums and Tourist Railroads

Listings: We would like to consider for inclusion every tourist railroad, trolley
operation, railroad museum, live-steam railroad, model railroad, and toy train exhibit
in the United States and Canada that is open to the public and has regular hours and
about which reliable information is available.

2007 Directory: To be published in February 2007. A packet containing all pertinent
information needed for inclusion in *Tourist Trains* will be mailed to all organizations
listed in this book. New listings are welcomed. For information, please write to:

> Editor—Tourist Trains 2007
> Books Division
> Kalmbach Publishing Co.
> P.O. Box 1612
> Waukesha, WI 53187–1612

On the web go to www.kalmbach.com/books

Photos: We're always looking for cover images; if you have any high-quality images
that might be available for a cover, please send it to the above address.

Advertising: Advertising space for *Tourist Trains 2007* must be reserved by
November 15, 2006. Please contact Mike Yuhas at 1-888-558-1544, extension 625 or
Lori Schneider at 1-888-558-1544, extension 472.

Publisher's Cataloging in Publication
(Provided by The Donahue Group, Inc.)

Empire State Railway Museum's tourist trains. -- 41st ed. (2006)-

   v. ; cm.
   Annual
   ISSN: 1546-2730

1.   Railroad museums--United States--Periodicals.   2. Railroad museums--
Canada--Periodicals.   I. Empire State Railway Museum.   II. Title:
Tourist trains.   III. Title: Empire State Railway Museum's . . . annual tourist trains guide.

TF6.U5 S75
385

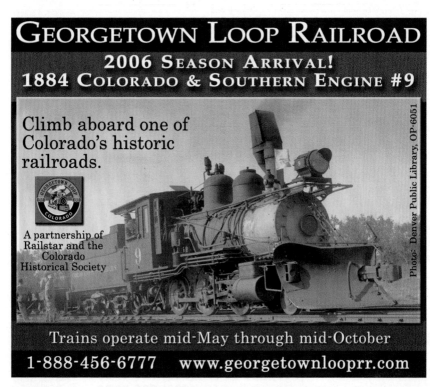

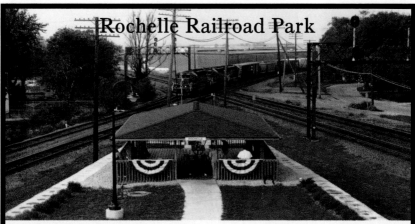

Rochelle Railroad Park

Visit the Rochelle Railroad Park in Illinois and enjoy the more than 80 trains that pass through Rochelle, Illinois each day. Bring the family. Watch from the hobo jungle. Walk through the gift shop. Enjoy a picnic. Whatever choice you make, be sure to include the Rochelle Railroad Park in your next vacation or weekend getaway!

For more information about the Railroad Park and Rochelle

call **815-562-7031**

or visit **www.rochelletourism.com**

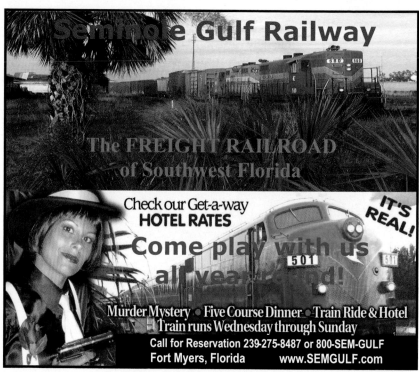

RIDE THE RAILS OF THE HISTORIC BUTTE, ANACONDA AND PACIFIC RAILROAD.

Incorporated in 1892, the B.A. & P. operated between the mining and smelting communities of Butte and Anaconda, Montana. The B.A. & P. was the first railroad in the country to electrify at 2400 volts.

The Copper King Express

The Copper King Express is a 52 mile round trip passenger excursion train over the former B.A. & P. rail line. The excursion train operates through scenic Durant Canyon and near many of the area's historic attractions:

- The Anaconda Smelter
- The Historic B.A. & P. Roundhouse
- The Largest Open Pit Copper Mine in the World
- The World Museum of Mining
- The Washoe Park Fish Hatchery
- Our Lady of the Rockies

Each car has been retrofitted with video monitors that provide information on the numerous area attractions along the historic rail route. You can also enjoy a drink while riding in our refurbished 100 seat passenger cars.

As part of the Copper King Express, a museum has been established showcasing our area's rich history in mining, smelting and railroading. The museum and passenger depot is located at 300 West Commercial Avenue in Anaconda, Montana.

RESERVATIONS ARE STRONGLY SUGGESTED.

To purchase tickets, either visit
WWW.COPPERKINGEXPRESS.COM
or phone **406-563-7121.**

McCLOUD RAILWAY OPEN-AIR TRAIN RIDES

Bring the whole family for a delightful, inexpensive, excursion trip featuring either diesel locomotives or historic steam locomotive No.25. Try our new "double deck" car for incomparable views of unspoiled northern California.

Hear the "clickety clack" as your trains winds its way around the base of Mt. Shasta. Open Air Excursion Trains depart McCloud, California. Call for schedule details.

ALL ABOARD! SHASTA SUNSET DINNER TRAIN

A nostalgic train ride through spectacular scenery in the shadow of Mt. Shasta featuring elegant four-course dining aboard restored vintage rail cars. A memorable evening riding the rails into yesterday!

Experience true luxury in our 1916-vintage rail cars amid surroundings of mahogany and brass. Shasta Sunset Dinner Train departs McCloud, California, weekends year round, Thursday through Saturday June through September. Reservations are required.

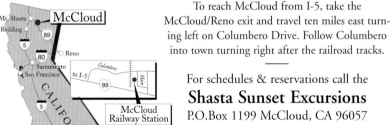

To reach McCloud from I-5, take the McCloud/Reno exit and travel ten miles east turning left on Columbero Drive. Follow Columbero into town turning right after the railroad tracks.

For schedules & reservations call the

Shasta Sunset Excursions
P.O.Box 1199 McCloud, CA 96057
(800) 733-2141 (530) 964-2142
www.shastasunset.com
Email: info@shastasunset.com

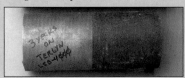

Yreka, CA

Yreka Western Railroad

Train ride, Museum, Static display, Model railroad layout

SITE ADDRESS: Rocky Mountain Railway and Mining Museum
300 E Miner St. Yreka, CA 96097
MAILING ADDRESS: PO Box 660 Yreka, CA 96097
TELEPHONE: (800) YREKARR or (530) 842-4146
E-MAIL: yrekawesternrr@snowcrest.net
WEBSITE: www.yrekawesternrr.com

DESCRIPTION: A 15-mile, 3½-hour round-trip to Montague, CA. Lunch is available, though not included in ticket price. Museum and gift shop in Yreka Depot.

SCHEDULE: May, September, and October: weekends only, two round trips per day, 9 a.m. and 1 p.m. June through August: weekdays, one round trip per day, 11 a.m.

ADMISSION/FARE: Steam excursions: adults, $16.50; children, $7; seniors, $10, group and party discounts: 15% for 10 or more; cab rides: adults, $25; children, $15; seniors, $10. Private car and caboose fares available. Charter train and special event rates are also available; call for estimate.

LOCOMOTIVES/ROLLING STOCK: 1915 Baldwin no. 19, 2-8-2 Mikado; 1959 EMD SW-8 nos. 20 and 21; 1953 ALCO, MRS-1 no. 244; 1912 Pullman, private car, "Great Northern;" Milwaukee coaches no. 30 and 31; Ex-SP commuter coaches no. 32 and 33; Ex-McCloud River RR Work Caboose, "Yreka" no. 001.

SPECIAL EVENTS: Wild Goose Chase 2-mile and 10K race, Hot Air Balloon Fair, Pumpkin Train, dinner trains.

DIRECTIONS: Take central Yreka exit from I-5 and follow sign.

TRAVEL TIP: *Best place to ride*

What's the best place to ride on a tourist train? It all depends on what you like. Many lines offer open-air cars so you can enjoy the scenery, but remember, these are subject to the whim of weather. Closed-window cars offer climate control. And some railroads offer an open car with no top, where all can enjoy the scenery. Be sure and ask what's available before you make your reservations.

SPECIAL EVENTS: Great Train Robberies, sunset dinners, murder mysteries, Great Pumpkin Express, party trains, picnic trains, winter Fog Cutter, and Christmas trains.

NEARBY ATTRACTIONS: Hayes Truck and Tractor Museum, Southern Pacific Depot (under restoration), Woodland Opera House.

DIRECTIONS: I-5 or Hwy. 113, take Main St. east to E St., turn right into parking lot. Twenty miles north of Sacramento.

Photo courtesy of Chris Hart.
Coupon available, see insert.

Yermo, CA
Calico & Odessa Railroad
Train ride
Narrow gauge

ADDRESS: 36600 Ghost Town Rd., PO Box 638 Yermo, CA 92398
TELEPHONE: (760) 254-2117
E-MAIL: calico@mscomm.com
WEBSITE: www.calicotown.com

DESCRIPTION: An 8- to 10-minute amusement ride in Calico Ghost Town. The town was settled in 1881, at the beginning of one of the largest silver strikes in California history. A narrow gauge railroad operates within town limits. In addition to serving as a living history museum, there are camping opportunities nearby.

SCHEDULE: 364 days a year, 9 a.m. to 5 p.m.; closed Christmas day.

ADMISSION/FARE: Adults, $2.50; special rate for schoolchildren, $1.

SPECIAL EVENTS: Presidents' weekend in February, Civil War; Mother's Day weekend, Spring Festival; October, Calico Days, Halloween weekend; November, Harvest Festival.

NEARBY ATTRACTIONS: Calico Ghost Town, regional parks in San Bernardino County, original 1890s silver mine town.

DIRECTIONS: Take I-15 to Ghost Town Rd. exit just 10 minutes north of Barstow, California. Main St. to sign for C&O Railroad.

Photo courtesy of Richard Jones.

LEADERSHIP IN CREATIVE RAILROADING

Tourist Railway Association INC

TRAIN, Inc., the Tourist Railway Association, Inc. was formed in 1972 to foster the tourist railway and museum industry. Full or Associate membership is open to all interested persons.

Members receive the organization's bi-monthly publication **TrainLine**, which includes comprehensive information and news from the industry. Our members are identified in **Tourist Trains** by the **TRAIN** logo.

Our 2006 Spring Meeting is in East Ely, NV. Our 2006 Annual Convention will be a joint meeting with ARM, Nov. 8–12, 2006 in Sacramento, CA. Please visit our Website for additional information.

TRAIN, Inc. is a leader and serves as a voice on all issues, which affect the operation and display of vintage and historic railway equipment and the industry.

If you are not currently a member… **GET ON TRACK NOW** or if you are a member **STAY ON TRACK** by renewing your membership!

For More Information Contact:

TOURIST RAILWAY ASSOCIATION, INC.

P.O. Box 1245
Chama, NM 87520-1245
1-800-67TRAIN (1-800-678-7246)
(505) 756-1240 • FAX (505) 756-1238
Email address: train@cvn.com
Visit our website at *http://www.traininc.org*

Bowie Train Station Museum

- *Restored 1910 Pennsylvania Railroad Station and Interlocking Tower*

- *1922 Norfolk & Western Caboose*

- *Alongside Amtrak/MARC Rail Lines*

8614 Chestnut Avenue, in historic Old Bowie.

Open Wednesday through Sunday, 12-4 p.m. Free admission. Groups of 10 or more by appointment at other times.

301-809-3089 • museums@cityofbowie.org

Operate this **Locomotive!**

Train Rides Memorial Day to Labor Day (weekends only)

Museum open daily 10:00am – 5:00pm • March 1 – October 31

- *150 Pieces of Equipment*

- *Hands-on Museum*

- *Snack Bar*

- *Gift Shop*

www.WPLives.org

Operate a Locomotive (530) 832-4532
Museum Information (530) 832-4131
Portola Railroad Museum
Operated by the Feather River Rail Society

WESTERN PACIFIC
"The Feather River Route"

Photo By: Scott Chandler

A-39

Empire State Railway Museum's

Tourist Trains

2 0 0 6

41ˢᵗ Annual Guide to Tourist Railroads and Museums

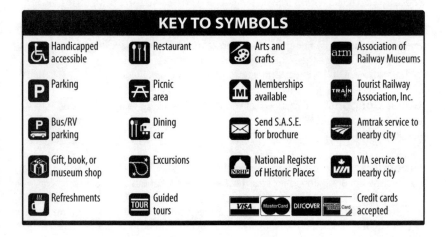

KEY TO SYMBOLS			
Handicapped accessible	Restaurant	Arts and crafts	Association of Railway Museums
Parking	Picnic area	Memberships available	Tourist Railway Association, Inc.
Bus/RV parking	Dining car	Send S.A.S.E. for brochure	Amtrak service to nearby city
Gift, book, or museum shop	Excursions	National Register of Historic Places	VIA service to nearby city
Refreshments	Guided tours	VISA MasterCard DISCOVER AMERICAN EXPRESS Card	Credit cards accepted

For our foreign visitors:
This year Memorial Day is Monday, May 29;
Labor Day is Monday, September 4; and
Thanksgiving is Thursday, November 23.

To the Reader

In 1966, railroad enthusiasts Marvin Cohen and Steve Bogen produced, and the Empire State Railway Museum published, the first *Steam Passenger Service Directory* (now titled *Tourist Trains: Empire State Railway Museum's Annual Guide to Tourist Railroads and Museums*). At that time, tourist railroading was in its infancy, and the book featured 62 tourist railroads and steam excursion operations. Four years later, in 1970, the Museum and *Directory* sponsored a tourist railroad conference, and the Tourist Railroad Association, Inc. (TRAIN) was founded.

The tourist railroad industry has flourished over the past three and a half decades, with local groups of rail enthusiasts and preservationists banding together to return to service locomotives and rolling stock that have sat dormant and neglected for too many years. The mission of these organizations includes educating and entertaining the general public. That's where the Empire State Railway Museum and this book fit in. Through the foresight and perseverance of the Museum, this book continues to be published so that rail enthusiasts, as well as those who are only casually interested in trains, can become aware of the hundreds of wonderful tourist railroads and railroad attractions available for them to enjoy and learn from. Kalmbach Publishing Co. is pleased and proud to be able to produce this book on behalf of the Empire State Railway Museum.

Editor's Choice: Attractions marked with the "Editor's choice" emblem are especially noteworthy. They're chosen for many reasons, but all are "not-to-be-missed" museums or tourist trains that are among the best in North America. Selections are chosen by the editors of TRAINS magazine based on field visits, reports, and extensive experience in visiting historical railroad sites. Some locations offer extensive artifact, document, or rolling stock collections. Others provide a look at spectacular scenery that is only available by riding the train. Many are one-of-a-kind venues that provide an experience like no other. All are capable of taking the curious visitor to a new plane in the enjoyment and appreciation of our rich railroading heritage.

Guest Coupons: The reduced-rate coupons provided by many operations in this edition of *Tourist Trains* will be honored by the museums. Be sure to present them when purchasing tickets.

Brochures: Many operations offer brochures and/or timetables. Please see the symbol sections in the listings for those operations that provide brochures.

Every effort has been made to ensure the accuracy of the contents. However, we depend on the information supplied by each operation. Internet addresses, business office locations, and phone numbers are subject to change. We cannot assume responsibility for errors, omissions, or fare and schedule changes. Be sure to write or phone ahead to confirm hours and prices.

If you know of an operation that is not included in the book, please send information to the publisher. See page ii.

ALABAMA

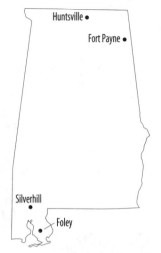

Huntsville •

Fort Payne •

Silverhill •

Foley •

Calera, AL
Heart of Dixie Railroad Museum
Train ride, Museum

ADDRESS: 1919 9th St., PO Box 727 Calera, AL 35040
TELEPHONE: (800) 943-4490 or (205) 668-3435
E-MAIL: csrr_gm@bellsouth.net
WEBSITE: www.heartofdixierrmuseum.org

DESCRIPTION: The museum features operating standard and narrow gauge trains, two restored depots, railroad artifacts, memorabilia, locomotives, and rolling stock.

SCHEDULE: Museum: Monday to Saturday, 9 a.m. to 4 p.m.; train rides: late March to mid-November, Saturday.

ADMISSION/FARE: Museum: free; donations appreciated; train: adults, $3-$12; seniors, $3-$10; children, $3-$9; babies, free; locomotive: $25-$27; caboose: $15-$17.

LOCOMOTIVES/ROLLING STOCK: Nine diesel locomotives, including three rare Fairbanks-Morse H12-44s, a Whitcomb 25-tonner, and two EMD SW-8 locomotives, 195; four steam locomotives, including two 0-4-0s, an 0-6-0 and former Woodward Iron 2-8-0 No. 38; 65 freight, passenger, and special cars.

SPECIAL EVENTS: Day Out with Thomas™; Pumpkin Patch Express; website for more.

NEARBY ATTRACTIONS: American Village, Oak Mountain State Park; 30 miles to Birmingham.

DIRECTIONS: Exit 228 off I-65, go ⁶⁄₁₀ mile on SR25 S, left on 9th St., 2 blocks to museum.

Photo courtesy of Jeff Hartz.

Foley, AL
Foley Railway Museum
Train ride

ADDRESS: 125 E Laurel Ave. Foley, AL 36536
TELEPHONE: (251) 943-1818
E-MAIL: foleymuseum@gulftel.com

DESCRIPTION: The Foley Railway Museum houses L&N Railroad artifacts, as well as artifacts representing the history of Foley and Baldwin County.

SCHEDULE: Monday through Friday, 10 a.m. to 4 p.m.

ADMISSION/FARE: Free.

LOCOMOTIVES/ROLLING STOCK:
Louisville & Nashville SW1 diesel switch engine No. 13; two boxcars; one caboose.

SPECIAL EVENTS: Mother's Day weekend, Art in the Park; October, Annual Shrimp Festival, German Sausage Festival; November, Heritage Harbor Days.

NEARBY ATTRACTIONS: Ten miles from the white sandy beaches on the Gulf of Mexico; Tanger Mall is one of the largest outlet malls in the Southeast; all types of restaurants and several antique stores are also nearby.

DIRECTIONS: From I-10, take the Gulf Shores Pkwy./Hwy. 59 south to Foley. The museum is one block east of the intersection of Hwy. 59 and Hwy. 98.

Fort Payne, AL

Fort Payne Depot Museum, Inc.

Museum

ADDRESS: 105 5th St. NE Ft. Payne, AL 35967
TELEPHONE: (256) 845-5714
WEBSITE: www.fortpaynedepotmuseum.org

DESCRIPTION: The Fort Payne Depot Museum is free and open to the public. Exhibits include a large American Indian artifact collection, early Dekalb county history items, a caboose with railroad memorabilia, and 95 dioramas. Located in Northeast Alabama, the museum is a former train depot circa late 1800s and contains railroad and historical artifacts from every war since the Civil War and much more.

SCHEDULE: Monday, Wednesday, and Friday, 10 a.m. to 4 p.m.; Sunday, 2 p.m. to 4 p.m. Special tours by appointment.

ADMISSION/FARE: Free.

LOCOMOTIVES/ROLLING STOCK: Caboose X246, Gant SCV, SOV CT.

NEARBY ATTRACTIONS: DeSoto State Park, Little River Canyon National Reserve.

DIRECTIONS: Located in downtown Fort Payne, at US11 and Alabama Hwy. 35, across from Fort Payne City Park.

Huntsville, AL

Historic Huntsville Depot
Museum

ADDRESS: 320 Church St. Huntsville, AL 35801
TELEPHONE: (256) 564-8100
WEBSITE: www.earlyworks.com

DESCRIPTION: Built circa 1860, the depot is one of the nation's oldest remaining railroad structures. A tour includes a one-hour guided experience of the original three-story building.

SCHEDULE: September through December: Wednesday through Saturday, 10 a.m. to 4 p.m.; January and February: closed; March through August: Wednesday through Saturday, 10 a.m. to 4 p.m.

ADMISSION/FARE: Adults, $7; seniors, $6; children 4-17, $6; children 3 and under, free.

SPECIAL EVENTS: Rocket City BBQ and Whistle Stop Festival May 5-6.

NEARBY ATTRACTIONS: EarlyWorks Museum Complex includes Alabama Constitution Village and the EarlyWorks Children's Museum.

DIRECTIONS: I-565 east, exit 19c, Washington/Jefferson St. exit, right to Monroe St., right to Church St., Depot on right.

Huntsville, AL

North Alabama Railroad Museum
Train Ride, Museum
Standard gauge
Radio frequency: 452.325, 457.325

ADDRESS: 694 Chase Rd., PO Box 4163 Huntsville, AL 35815-4163
TELEPHONE: (256) 851-6276
E-MAIL: fredrrman@aol.com
WEBSITE: www.northalabamarailroadmuseum.com

DESCRIPTION: Display passenger train, excursion train, historic watchman's hut, exhibits, self-guided walking tour, 10-mile, round-trip excursion on Mercury and Chase Railroad.

SCHEDULE: Viewing: daily with tour sheets available; staff present Wednesday and Saturday, 8:30 a.m. to 2 p.m.; train rides: some Saturdays; call for schedule.

ADMISSION/FARE: Museum, parking, and self-guided walking tour: free; 1½-hour train ride: adults, $12; children under 12, $8; children under 2 not requiring a seat, free.

LOCOMOTIVES/ROLLING STOCK: NC&St.L-painted Alco S-2 No. 484; former Army Alco RSD-1 No. 8652; rare 1926 Alco/GE/Ingersoll-Rand boxcab; 40 passenger and freight cars.

SPECIAL EVENTS: April 8, Open House; October 28, Goblin Train; November 18 & 25 and December 2 & 3, Santa Train.

NEARBY ATTRACTIONS: Alabama Space & Rocket Center, Monte Sano State Park, Huntsville Depot Museum, Museum of Art, Botanical Garden, Dogwood Manor B&B.

DIRECTIONS: East of I-565 in Huntsville, go east on US72 for 2 miles, left on Moores Mill Rd. for 1 mile, cross second railroad track, left on Chase Rd. for ¹/₂ mile.

Photo courtesy of Hugh Dudley.

Silverhill, AL

Wales West Light Railway
Miniature/ Park train

ADDRESS: 13650 Smiley St. Silverhill, AL 36576
TELEPHONE: (888) 569-5337
WEBSITE: www.waleswest.com

DESCRIPTION: Authentic steam-powered Welsh 2'-gauge railway with Victorian-era station, gift shop, and tea room. This 7¹/₂" gauge railway is located next to an RV resort.

SCHEDULE: Steam: weekends, 1 to 5 p.m.; diesel: weekdays, 10 a.m. to 4 p.m.; parties, groups, field trips by reservation; steam train anytime by reservation.

ADMISSION/FARE: Diesel, weekdays: adults, $4; children, $3; children 2 and under, free. Steam, weekends: adults, $6; children, $4; children under 2, free. Group rates by request.

LOCOMOTIVES/ROLLING STOCK: 2' 0-4-2 Hunslet coal-burning steam locomotive, 2' 0-4-0 Simplex 540 diesel, six 2' 4-wheel "bread box" coaches, 7¹/₂" 0-4-0 Hunslet steam locomotive, riding cars, and brake wagons.

SPECIAL EVENTS: April, Spring and Fall Steam-Up Benefit, Easter Bunny Express; September, Bluegrass Festival; October, Pumpkin Patch; December, Arctic Express.

NEARBY ATTRACTIONS: Gulf of Mexico beaches, golf courses, battleship, air & space museum.

DIRECTIONS: CR9 to the resort and station. See website for map.

ALASKA

Anchorage, AK
Alaska Railroad Corporation
Train ride

ADDRESS: 411 W First Ave., PO Box 107500 Anchorage, AK 99510
TELEPHONE: (800) 544-0552
E-MAIL: reservations@akrr.com
WEBSITE: www.alaskarailroad.com

DESCRIPTION: The best way to see Alaska is from the railroad. The great service, comfortable seating, and knowledgeable tour guides are part of the rail experience. With world-class scenery, passengers can begin a tour in Anchorage, Seward, or Fairbanks. The Alaska Railroad covers more than 500 miles. Day trips and overnight excursions are available.

SCHEDULE: See website for updated schedule.

ADMISSION/FARE: See website for current fares.

NEARBY ATTRACTIONS: Hotel accommodations and popular attractions available at all rail stops.

DIRECTIONS: See website for complete directions.

Photo courtesy of Caloin Hall.
See ad on page A-7.

Skagway, AK
White Pass & Yukon Route
Train ride

SITE ADDRESS: 2nd & Spring St. Skagway, AK 99840
MAILING ADDRESS: PO Box 435 Skagway, AK 99840
TELEPHONE: (800) 343-7373 or (907) 983-2217
E-MAIL: info@whitepass.net
WEBSITE: www.wpyr.com

DESCRIPTION: Built in 1898, the 3-foot-gauge White Pass & Yukon is a spectacular mountain railroad. The WP&YR offers round-trip excursions from Skagway to the White Pass Summit, Lake Bennett, and through rail/bus connections to Whitehorse, Yukon.

SCHEDULE: May to September: daily diesel-powered trains; Summit Excursion: depart Skagway 8:15 a.m. and 12:45 p.m., 3-hour round trip. Through service with bus transfer northbound from Skagway to Whitehorse, Yukon: depart 8 a.m. and 12:30 p.m. Through service with bus transfer southbound from Whitehorse, Yukon to Skagway: depart 8 a.m. and 1:30 p.m. June to August, steam train: Saturday, 8 a.m. 8-hour round trip with lunch.

ADMISSION/FARE: Summit Excursion: adults, $89; children, $44.50. Steam train: adults, $160; children, $80. Skagway to Whitehorse Rail/coach connection: adults, $95; children, $47.50. Reservations.

LOCOMOTIVES/ROLLING STOCK: Original WP&Y 1947 Baldwin 2-8-2 no. 73, and 2-8-0 no. 69; Alco and GE diesels; 69 passenger cars; 1898 rotary snowplow no. 1.

NEARBY ATTRACTIONS: Klondike Gold Rush National Historical Park.

Photo courtesy of Dedman's Photo.

Wasilla, AK

Museum of Alaska Transportation & Industry

Museum, Display, and Model train layout

SITE ADDRESS: Mile 47 Parks Hwy. Dr., 3800 W Museum Dr. Wasilla, AK
MAILING ADDRESS: PO Box 870646 Wasilla, AK 99687
TELEPHONE: (907) 376-1211
WEBSITE: www.museumofalaska.org

DESCRIPTION: 2-mile train ride, $1/25$ scale antique trains, planes, autos, tractors, boats.

SCHEDULE: Year-round: Tuesday through Sunday, 10 a.m. to 5 p.m.

ADMISSION/FARE: Adults, $8; seniors and children, $5; family, $18.

LOCOMOTIVES/ROLLING STOCK: EMD MRS-1 no. 1718; GE 80-ton switcher no. 1604; Baldwin S-12 no. 1841; Baldwin S-12 no. 1842; former Alaska Railroad F7A no. 1500; former Alaska Railroad Alco RS1 no. 1000.

SPECIAL EVENTS: June, Transportation Expo; December weekends, Historic Holiday Bazaars.

NEARBY ATTRACTIONS: Denali National Park.

DIRECTIONS: Parks Hwy. from Anchorage, left at mile post 47 (Neuser Dr.), follow signs.

Photo courtesy of Museum of Alaska.

ARIZONA

Chandler, AZ
Arizona Railway Museum
Museum, Display

ADDRESS: 399 N Delaware St., PO Box 842
Chandler, AZ 85224
TELEPHONE: (480) 821-1108
WEBSITE: www.azrymuseum.org

DESCRIPTION: The museum was founded
and incorporated in 1983 as a non-profit
educational and historical organization
dedicated to the railways of Arizona and
the Southwest.

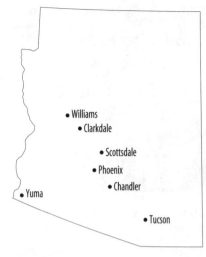

- Williams
- Clarkdale
- Scottsdale
- Phoenix
- Chandler
- Yuma
- Tucson

SCHEDULE: Labor Day to Memorial Day: Saturday and Sunday, 12 to 4 p.m. Tours available.

ADMISSION/FARE: Free; donations accepted.

LOCOMOTIVES/ROLLING STOCK: Magma
Arizona Baldwin DRS-6-1500 No. 10; SP
2-8-0 No. 2562; ARM 30-ton Plymouth
no. 1; SP 7130 and 7131, a steam derrick
and tool car; Pullman sleeper "Imperial
Manor;" Santa Fe coach 2870; Southern
Pacific horse car 5984; Southern Railway
business car "Desert Valley;" US Army
locomotive crane C-45; Santa Fe wood
coach 580, built in 1910; Santa Fe observation car "Denehotso;" and 14 other cars.

NEARBY ATTRACTIONS: Historic downtown Chandler, Chandler Fashion Center, San
Marcos Resort & Country Club.

DIRECTIONS: From US60: south on SR 87 (Arizona Ave.), approximately 5 miles. From I-10:
east on Chandler Blvd., approximately 8 miles.

Clarkdale, AZ
Verde Canyon Railroad
Train ride, Dinner train, Museum
Standard gauge

ADDRESS: 300 N Broadway Clarkdale, AZ 86324-2602
TELEPHONE: (800) 293-7245, reservations or (928) 639-0010
E-MAIL: info@verdecanyonrr.com
WEBSITE: www.verdecanyonrr.com

DESCRIPTION: The four-hour scenic ride includes views of bald and golden eagles, Sinagua Indian ruins, waterfowl, wildlife, a 680-foot tunnel, and the upper Verde River.

SCHEDULE: Year-round, schedule varies. Most trains depart at 1 p.m. and return at 5 p.m. Fall and spring: Thursday and Sunday morning and afternoon; May through September: starlight ride, 5:30 to 9:30 p.m.

ADMISSION/FARE: Adults, $54.95; seniors 65+, $49.95; children 12 and under, $34.95; all first-class, $79.95.

LOCOMOTIVES/ROLLING STOCK: EMD FP7 unit nos. 1510 and 1512, built 1953.

SPECIAL EVENTS: February 11-12, Chocolate Lovers' Festival; March through May, Spring in Bloom; March 17, St. Patrick's Day; April, Easter Bunny Express; May, Cinco de Mayo and Throw Mama on the Train; May through September, Starlight Trains; June, Throw Papa on the Train; July 4, Firecracker Express; September, Grandparents Day; October, Oktoberfest Beer Garden; October 31, Haunted Halloween Express; October through November, Fall Colors; November through December, Holiday Parties; December, Santa Claus Express; December through March, Eagle Watch in the Canyon.

DIRECTIONS: From I-17 take Hwy. 260 north to Cottonwood. Turn left onto Historic Hwy. 89A and proceed through Cottonwood to Clarkdale depot.

Phoenix, AZ

Maricopa Live Steamers
Miniature/ Park train

ADDRESS: 22822 N 43rd Ave. Phoenix, AZ 85310
TELEPHONE: (623) 925-1811
E-MAIL: pmccully1811@msn.com
WEBSITE: www.maricopalivesteamers.com

DESCRIPTION: 1½" scale with 40,000 feet of track running on 150 acres of desert. The MLS is a club for those who enjoy preserving the heritage of railroading. Club members research and build scale steam locomotives and modern diesels, and enjoy running, track switching, hauling, and doing maintenance.

SCHEDULE: September through May: Sunday, 12 to 5 p.m.

ADMISSION/FARE: Free.

DIRECTIONS: Left off I-17 at Pinnacle Peak Rd., 2 miles west to 43rd Ave., left ½ mile.

Scottsdale, AZ

McCormick-Stillman Railroad Park
Train ride, Museum, Display, Model railroad layout

ADDRESS: 7301 E Indian Bend Rd. Scottsdale, AZ 85250
TELEPHONE: (480) 312-2312
WEBSITE: www.therailroadpark.com

DESCRIPTION: A 30-acre theme park offers train rides, carousel rides, railroad museum, retail shops, picnic area, two playgrounds, snack stop, Hartley's General Store, and model railroad displays.

SCHEDULE: Year-round: seven days a week, 10 a.m. to sunset; Summer: June through August, weekdays, 9 a.m. to 1 p.m. and 4 to 9 p.m.; weekends, 9 a.m. to 9 p.m.

ADMISSION/FARE: Train or carousel: anyone 3 and up, $1; Museum: anyone 13 and up, $1.

DIRECTIONS: Southeast corner of Scottsdale Rd. and Indian Bend Rd.

Tucson, AZ

Gadsden-Pacific Division Toy Train Operating Museum
Museum
Standard, G, O, S, HO, N, & Z scales

ADDRESS: 3975 N Miller Ave., PO Box 85425 Tucson, AZ 85754
TELEPHONE: (520) 888-2222
WEBSITE: http://hometown.aol.com/ienglish/index.htm

DESCRIPTION: Seven multiple-gauge layouts with 16 or more toy trains running. Includes push button operating accessories and a rug layout for small kids to play with wooden and electric trains. Also static displays, pictures, and other railroad memorabilia.

SCHEDULE: Second and fourth Sunday each month, 12:30 to 4:30 p.m.; December, some Saturdays; July and August, closed. Call for exact dates/times.

ADMISSION/FARE: Free. Donations accepted.

SPECIAL EVENTS: January 21, 2006, Winter Toy Train Show; June 3, Summer Toy Train Show.

NEARBY ATTRACTIONS: Old Tucson Studios, Sonora Desert Museum, weekend trolley car rides, Pima Air & Space Museum, Kartchner Caverns State Park, San Xavier del Bac Mission, Southern Arizona Transportation Museum and Historic SP Depot.

DIRECTIONS: Travel I-10 to Prince Rd. exit, east on Prince to Romero Rd., then north on Romero, turn left on Price St. to Miller Ave.

Photo courtesy of Ivan English.

Tucson, AZ

Karrels' Double K Ranch Bed & Breakfast

Model railroad layout, Bed & breakfast inn

ADDRESS: 3930 N Smokey Topaz Ln. Tucson, AZ 85749
TELEPHONE: (520) 749-5345
E-MAIL: kmkarrels@yahoo.com
WEBSITE: www.doublekranch.com

DESCRIPTION: This railroader's B&B has a "Depot" room, railroad memorabilia, HO- and O-gauge layouts, and a garden railway. There's also a restored caboose that has been converted into a private room complete with double bed nestled into a bay window, railroader's bunk for children, claw-footed tub, lounging area, and more.

SCHEDULE: B&B open year-round; garden railway by appointment.

ADMISSION/FARE: B&B, $95 to $125 per room; layout, free admission.

DIRECTIONS: From Houghton & Tanque Verde, go east two miles to Soldier Trail, north two miles to Roger Rd., east ¼ mile to Smokey Topaz, south.

Photo courtesy of Dean Bennett.

Tucson, AZ

Sierra Madre Express

Train ride

SITE ADDRESS: 4415 S Contractors Way Tucson, AZ 85726
MAILING ADDRESS: PO Box 26381 Tucson, AZ 85726
TELEPHONE: (800) 666-0346 or (520) 757-0346
E-MAIL: adventure@sierramadreexpress.com
WEBSITE: www.sierramadreexpress.com

DESCRIPTION: Deluxe, private train vacations to Mexico's magnificent Copper Canyon. Vintage Pullman sleepers and dome and observation car.

SCHEDULE: September through May: round-trip from from Tuscon, AZ; off-season dates by request.

ADMISSION/FARE: Contact sales office for fares and availability for individuals, groups, or charters.

SPECIAL EVENTS: December 27 through January 3, New Year's Tour; incentive travel, special interest groups, executive retreats, charters, and custom.

NEARBY ATTRACTIONS: Old Tucson Studios, Sonora Desert Museum, weekend trolley car rides, Pima Air & Space Museum, Kartchner Caverns State Park, San Xavier del Bac Mission.

Photo courtesy of Gerald French, 2004.
Coupon available, see page insert.

Tucson, AZ
Southern Arizona Transportation Museum
Museum

ADDRESS: Historic Downtown Depot, 414 N Toole Ave. Tucson, AZ 85701
TELEPHONE: (520) 623-2223
E-MAIL: contactus@tucsonhistoricdepot.org
WEBSITE: www.TucsonHistoricDepot.org

DESCRIPTION: Interprets the history of railroads and railroading in Southern Arizona with a focus on Tucson, the restored 1941 historic depot, and the displayed historic locomotive no. 1673. Tours available by appointment or self-guided.

SCHEDULE: Tuesday through Thursday, 12 to 3 p.m.; Friday and Saturday, 10 a.m. to 4 p.m.

ADMISSION/FARE: No fee, suggested donation, $2.

LOCOMOTIVES/ROLLING STOCK: Southern Pacific 2-6-0 steam locomotive no. 1673.

NEARBY ATTRACTIONS: Old Pueblo Trolley.

DIRECTIONS: Interstate 10, to Congress St., East to 5th Ave., turn left. The street ends at the Depot. Turn right on Toole Ave. to access parking.

Photo courtesy of Southern Arizona Transportation Museum.

Williams, AZ

Grand Canyon Railway

Train Ride, Museum
Standard gauge

SITE ADDRESS: 233 N Grand Canyon Blvd. Williams, AZ 86046
MAILING ADDRESS: 1201 W Route 66, Ste. 200 Flagstaff, AZ 86001
TELEPHONE: (800) THE TRAIN (843-8724)
E-MAIL: info@thetrain.com
WEBSITE: www.thetrain.com

DESCRIPTION: Relive the excitement of the Old West aboard a historic train to America's national treasure, the Grand Canyon. After a 2¼-hour journey, passengers have 3¼ hours to explore the canyon before the train returns to Williams. Many passengers spend the night at Grand Canyon National Park.

SCHEDULE: Year-round, daily except December 24 and 25; Williams departure, 10 a.m., arrives Grand Canyon National Park 12:15 p.m., departs Grand Canyon 3:30 p.m., returns to Williams at 5:45 p.m.

ADMISSION/FARE: Adults, $60; youth 11-16, $35; children 2-10, $25. Additional park entrance fee and tax. Upgrades available.

LOCOMOTIVES/ROLLING STOCK: Steam locomotives: no. 29, a 1906 Alco 2-8-0; no. 4960, a 1923 Baldwin 2-8-2. Diesel: Alco-MLW FPA4s nos. 6762, 6768, 6773, 6788, 6793, 6860, 6871; EMD GP7 no. 2134. Many historic coach and other passenger cars.

SPECIAL EVENTS: December, Polar Express.

NEARBY ATTRACTIONS: Grand Canyon Railway Hotel, Max & Thelma's Restaurant, historic downtown Williams, Route 66, golf. Amtrak now stops in Williams for an all-rail trip to the Grand Canyon. Grand Canyon Railway RV Park opening in 2005.

DIRECTIONS: I-40 exit 163 (Williams), Grand Canyon Blvd. to Williams depot.

Photo courtesy of Grand Canyon Railway.
See ad on page A-9.

TRAVEL TIP: *Dining cars*

While many tourist railroads offer food and beverage services on site or nearby, some still equip their trains with authentic dining cars. This gives visitors the chance to experience a real "dinner in the diner," as it was prepared and served on board a moving train.

Yuma Valley Railway
Train ride

SITE ADDRESS: 100 N Second Ave. Yuma, AZ 85364
MAILING ADDRESS: PO Box 10305 Yuma, AZ 85366-8305
TELEPHONE: (928) 783-3456
E-MAIL: timnlorene@adelphia.net

DESCRIPTION: Passengers can ride back through time aboard the Yuma Valley Railway. For two hours the train travels along the Colorado River Route while a historian provides a detailed narration. Local wildlife is visible at the West Wetlands Park. Riders can travel in comfort aboard the Jersey Lil, a 1922 Pullman coach featured in the movie *The Life and Times of Judge Roy Bean*, starring Paul Newman. During the cool months (October through May), trains move at a leisurely pace of 15 mph, though the trips aren't uneventful. The Yuma Vigilantes have "discovered" the train, and take a fiendish delight in robbing the passengers at the slightest provocation. Riders, therefore, may wish to leave all valuables with their next of kin. Pulling out of Olde Town Yuma, the train departs from 100 N Second Ave. all winter.

SCHEDULE: January through March, Saturday and Sunday, 1 p.m.; April through May and October through December, Sunday, 1 p.m.

ADMISSION/FARE: Adults, $17; seniors 55+, $16; children 4-16, $8.

LOCOMOTIVES/ROLLING STOCK: US Marine Corps 1943 and 1957 GE center-cab diesels; US Army 1952 Davenport-Besler; Apache Railway 1922 Pullman chair car; 1923 Pullman club car built from a former US Army ambulance car;1950 Pullman chair car.

SPECIAL EVENTS: Last weekend of February, Yuma Crossing Day; available for holidays, weddings, family reunions, company picnics, and more.

NEARBY ATTRACTIONS: Next to the West Wetlands Park (the only National Heritage Area west of the Mississippi); the Yuma Crossing Park; Olde Town Yuma; the Arizona Territorial Prison; the mostly Main St. Block Parties; the annual Yuma Lettuce Days; both of the Paradise Casinos (owned and operated by the Quechan Indian Nation); Fort Yuma, home to St. Thomas Mission; the Territorial Mall; the Colorado and Gila Rivers; and the Imperial Sand Dunes.

DIRECTIONS: On the north end of town, just off the first exit from Interstate 8. Next to the Yuma Crossing Park. 100 North Second Ave., behind the Old City Hall.

Photo courtesy of Randy Smith, P&R Photography.
Coupon available, see insert.

ARKANSAS

Fort Smith, AR

Fort Smith Trolley Museum

Museum
Standard gauge

ADDRESS: 100 S 4th St.
Fort Smith, AR 72901
TELEPHONE: (479) 783-0205 or
(479) 783-1237
E-MAIL: bmartin@ipa.net
WEBSITE: www.fstm.org

Mammoth Spring •

• Springdale

• Fort Smith

• Pine Bluff
• Hot Springs

DESCRIPTION: Restored Fort Smith Light & Traction Birney Safety Car travels over ⅔ mile of track in the downtown area.

SCHEDULE: May through October: Monday through Saturday, 10 a.m. to 5 p.m.; Sunday, 1 to 5 p.m.; November through April: Saturday, 10 a.m. to 5 p.m.; Sunday, 1 to 5 p.m.

ADMISSION/FARE: Adults, $2; children, $1.

LOCOMOTIVES/ROLLING STOCK: Fort Smith Light & Traction streetcars 205, 224, 10; Hot Springs St. Railway no. 50; Frisco 2-8-2 steam locomitve no. 4003; USAF no. 1246; August Railroad no. 6; ARR no. 7; diner MKT no. 100162; troop sleeper (power car) MKT no. 100186; cabeese BN 12240, UP 25139, MKT 126, and more.

SPECIAL EVENTS: First May Sunday: open house, 1 to 5 p.m., free rides and refreshments.

NEARBY ATTRACTIONS: Fort Smith Historic Site, Fort Smith Museum of History, Civic Center, Fort Smith National Cemetery.

DIRECTIONS: From west Hwy. 64 to Garrison Ave., Garrison to S 4th St., south four blocks. From east I-540 to Rogers exit, west on Rogers to S 4th St., south three blocks.

Photo courtesy of Bradley Martin.

Hot Springs, AR

Reader Railroad

Train ride

SITE ADDRESS: 320 Ouachita Ste. 312 Hot Springs, AR 71901
MAILING ADDRESS: PO Box 507 Hot Springs, AR 71902
TELEPHONE: (501) 624-6881
WEBSITE: www.movietrains.com

DESCRIPTION: Reader Railroad, one of the oldest all-steam standard gauge carriers to operate in the United States, offers a 7-mile, one-hour round trip. Open-platform wooden coaches are drawn by veteran logging engines.

SCHEDULE: Write or call for information.

ADMISSION/FARE: Adults, $6; children 4-11, $3.60; children under 4, free with parent; group rates available; fares may be slightly higher for special events.

LOCOMOTIVES/ROLLING STOCK: No. 7, 1907 Baldwin 2-6-2, former Victoria, Fisher & Western; open-platform wooden coaches; open-air car; caboose.

DIRECTIONS: Off SR24 between Camden and Prescott on Hwy. 368.

Mammoth Spring, AR

Frisco Depot Museum

Museum

ADDRESS: Mammoth Spring State Park, PO Box 36 Mammoth Spring, AR 72554
TELEPHONE: (870) 625-7364
E-MAIL: mammothspring@arkansas.com
WEBSITE: www.arkansasstateparks.com

DESCRIPTION: This restored Victorian depot was built in 1885/1886 and operated by the Frisco Railroad from 1901 to 1968. On the self-guided tour, there are nine exhibits depicting 13 life-size figures dressed in historical costumes, each with an audio unit telling their stories. Two videos are shown about the history of the railroad in Mammoth Spring.

SCHEDULE: Year-round; Tuesday through Saturday, 8 a.m. to 5 p.m.; Sunday, 1 to 5 p.m.; closed Monday, except Monday holidays.

ADMISSION/FARE: Adults, $2.50; children 6-12, $1.50; children 5 and under, free; special rates for groups of 15 or more with two weeks' notice; season passes.

LOCOMOTIVES/ROLLING STOCK: Wooden Frisco caboose no. 1176.

SPECIAL EVENTS: March through October, Mammoth Spring Park offers events and programs; call for information.

NEARBY ATTRACTIONS: Mammoth Spring State Park, Mammoth Spring Federal Fish Hatchery, camping, canoeing, trout fishing on Spring River, museums, antique stores.

DIRECTIONS: Located in Mammoth Spring State Park on Hwy. 63. Twenty-seven miles south of West Plains, Missouri, and 16 miles north of Hardy, Arkansas.

Pine Bluff, AR

Arkansas Railroad Museum
Display

ADDRESS: 1700 Port Rd., PO Box 2044 Pine Bluff, AR 71613
TELEPHONE: (870) 535-8819

DESCRIPTION: Located in the 1½-acre former Cotton Belt erecting and machine shop. It contains the last two Cotton Belt steam engines and several big Alco diesel locomotives.

SCHEDULE: Year-round; Monday through Saturday, 9 a.m. to 3 p.m.; closed during periods of extremely cold weather; call before a visit during hottest summer weather.

ADMISSION/FARE: Free; donations.

LOCOMOTIVES/ROLLING STOCK: SSW 4-8-4 no. 819; SSW 2-6-0 no. 336; Alco RSD-12; Alco RSD-15; Alco C-630; SSW GP-30; SSW cabooses; passenger cars; ex-US Army snow plow and guard car; SSW relief crane and outfit train; railroad artifacts.

SPECIAL EVENTS: First Saturday in April, annual show and sale.

NEARBY ATTRACTIONS: Jefferson County Museum, Band Museum, Delta Rivers Nature Center.

DIRECTIONS: Take Business US65 and follow hwy. signs to museum at Port Rd. exit.

Photo courtesy of Barry Robinson.

TRAVEL TIP: *Special events*

Most tourist and museum railroads offer a regular train trip, and many put on extra trains with a special flair during holidays like Easter, Mother's Day, Father's Day, Independence Day, Veterans Day, and Christmas. These themed events offer a way to combine the railroad experience with holiday flavor.

Springdale, AR

Arkansas & Missouri Railroad

Train ride, Dinner train, Museum, Layout

ADDRESS: 306 E Emma Springdale, AR 72764
TELEPHONE: (800) 687-8600 or (479) 751-8600
WEBSITE: www.arkansasmissouri-rr.com

DESCRIPTION: Excursion train through the Boston Mountains over a working freight railroad. Burrow through a quarter-mile tunnel and enjoy views from three high trestles over 100 feet from the ground.

SCHEDULE: April through September, Friday through Sunday; October through November, Wednesday and Friday through Sunday. Specials throughout the year.

ADMISSION/FARE: $15-$80 (depending on excursion type).

SPECIAL EVENTS: Valentine Special, Spring Fest, Feather Fest, Frisco Festival, Air Show, Annual Christmas Train.

NEARBY ATTRACTIONS: Fayetteville Air Museum, Ft. Smith Trolley Museum, Daisy Bee Bee Museum, National Historic Site.

Photo courtesy of JP Bell.
Coupon available, see insert.

KEY TO SYMBOLS

♿ Handicapped accessible	🍴 Restaurant	🎨 Arts and crafts	arm Association of Railway Museums
P Parking	⛩ Picnic area	M Memberships available	TRAIN Tourist Railway Association, Inc.
P Bus/RV parking	Dining car	✉ Send S.A.S.E. for brochure	Amtrak service to nearby city
Gift, book, or museum shop	Excursions	National Register of Historic Places	VIA service to nearby city
Refreshments	TOUR Guided tours	VISA MasterCard DISCOVER AMERICAN EXPRESS Card	Credit cards accepted

CALIFORNIA

Alpine, CA
Descanso, Alpine & Pacific Railway
Train ride, Display
24"

ADDRESS: 1266 Alpine Heights Rd. Alpine, CA 91901
TELEPHONE: (619) 445-4781
E-MAIL: dapry@juno.com

DESCRIPTION: Passengers ride a 2'-gauge industrial railway to yesteryear among 100-year-old Engelman oaks in San Diego County's foothills. The train leaves Shade Depot and makes a ½-mile round trip, climbing the 6½-percent grade to High Pass/Lookout and crossing a 112'-long wooden trestle. Railroad artifacts are on display at Shade Depot and Freight Shed. Mail service and mailer's postmark permit canceling are available.

SCHEDULE: June through August: Sunday, 1 to 3 p.m., every ½ hour; September through May: intermittent Sunday operation. Please call for rides and tours at other times.

ADMISSION/FARE: Free.

LOCOMOTIVES/ROLLING STOCK:
No. 2, 1935 2¹⁄₂-ton Brookville, powered by original McCormick-Deering 22¹⁄₂-hp P-12 gasoline engine, former Carthage (Missouri) Crushed Limestone Company.

NEARBY ATTRACTIONS: Located 2¹⁄₂ miles off I-8; almost midway between San Diego and the Pacific Southwest Railway Museum; US Forest Service camp grounds, and the historic gold mining and apple growing community of Julian, CA.

DIRECTIONS: 30 miles east of San Diego. I-8 exit Tavern Rd., travel south on Tavern 1.9 miles, turn right on South Grade Rd. and travel .6 miles, turn left onto Alpine Heights Rd.; the DA&P is the fifth driveway on the right.

Photo courtesy of Miran Flores.

Anaheim, CA
Disneyland Railroad
Train ride
Narrow gauge

ADDRESS: 1313 S. Harbor Blvd., PO Box 3232 Anaheim, CA
TELEPHONE: (714) 781-4565
WEBSITE: www.disneyland.com

DESCRIPTION: Twenty-minute train ride that circles the perimeter of Disneyland and makes four stops. Also takes guests through major Grand Canyon Diorama and Primeval World. Steam trains pull open-air cars.

SCHEDULE: Daily: Disneyland Park hours.

ADMISSION/FARE: Included with admission.

LOCOMOTIVES/ROLLING STOCK: 4-4-0 C.K. Holliday (1955 Disney), 4-4-0 E.P. Ripley (1955 Disney), 2-4-4 Fred G. Gurley (1894 Baldwin), 2-4-0 Ernest S. Marsh (1925 Baldwin). Various open-air cars used to transport guests.

NEARBY ATTRACTIONS: Inside Disneyland Park. Disneyland Resort is located in Anaheim, which offers Anaheim Angels baseball, Mighty Ducks ice hockey, Disney's California Adventure park and the Downtown Disney shopping, dining, and entertainment district.

DIRECTIONS: Disneyland is located about 35 miles east of downtown Los Angeles. Take the 5 freeway south, exit at Disneyland Dr. in Anaheim, and turn right to the Disneyland entrance.

Barstow, CA

Western America Railroad Museum

Museum, Display, Model train layout, Harvey House
HO scale & Standard gauge

ADDRESS: 685 N First St., PO Box 703 Barstow, CA 92311
TELEPHONE: (760) 256-WARM
WEBSITE: www.barstowrailmuseum.org

DESCRIPTION: Non-profit railroad museum featuring railroad art, artifacts, memorabilia, rolling stock, HO layout, tours of Barstow Harvey House, gift shop.

SCHEDULE: Friday through Sunday, 11 a.m. to 4 p.m. and by appointment for groups.

ADMISSION/FARE: Free. Donations appreciated.

LOCOMOTIVES/ROLLING STOCK: Diesel engines FP45, SD40-2, UP Class CA-8 caboose, Santa Fe "Horse Car" circa 1938, Canadian National Business Car Tioga Pass.

SPECIAL EVENTS: Second week in November, Barstow Rail & Craft Fest.

NEARBY ATTRACTIONS: Historic Harvey House, next to the Santa Fe Barstow Yard.

DIRECTIONS: From Hwy. US15, follow the freeway signs to the Harvey House.

Berkeley, CA

Golden Gate Live Steamers Inc.

Model train layout
7¹/₂″, 4³/₄″, 3¹/₂″, and 2¹/₂″

SITE ADDRESS: 2501 Grizzly Park Blvd. Berkeley, CA
MAILING ADDRESS: 130 Pereira Ave. Tracy, CA 95376
TELEPHONE: (209) 835-0263

DESCRIPTION: Membership club builds and runs scale model steam locomotives and offers a ¹/₂ mile train ride on Sundays.

SCHEDULE: Public train: year-round, Sunday, 12 to 3 p.m., weather permitting.

ADMISSION/FARE: Donations appreciated.

LOCOMOTIVES/ROLLING STOCK: Numerous steam and diesel locomotives and cars.

SPECIAL EVENTS: First Sunday of May and first Sunday of August the public is invited to observe displayed models, both complete and under construction.

NEARBY ATTRACTIONS: Redwood Valley Railway, 1920s carousel, pony rides, little farm.

DIRECTIONS: Hwy. 24, exit Fish Ranch Rd., then follow the signs.

Photo courtesy of Jim Mason.

Bishop, CA

Laws Railroad Museum & Historical Site
Museum

SITE ADDRESS: Silver Canyon Rd. Bishop, CA
MAILING ADDRESS: PO Box 363 Bishop, CA 93515
TELEPHONE: (760) 873-5950
E-MAIL: lawsmuseum@aol.com
WEBSITE: www.thesierraweb.com/bishop/laws/

DESCRIPTION: Original 1883 depot and agent's house, including more than 20 historic buildings with exhibits, and 11 acres of mining, farming, and railroad equipment. Located on the original location of the Carson-Colorado and later the Southern Pacific site.

SCHEDULE: Year-round, daily, 10 a.m. to 4 p.m. except New Year's Day, Easter, Thanksgiving, and Christmas.

ADMISSION/FARE: Suggested donation: $3 per person.

LOCOMOTIVES/ROLLING STOCK: Southern Pacific 3-foot gauge 4-6-0 No. 9, built in 1909 by Baldwin; Brill motor car, 1927; 12 boxcars; A-frame gondola; stock car; combination caboose; postal caboose.

NEARBY ATTRACTIONS: Fishing, skiing, hunting, camping.

DIRECTIONS: From Bishop, follow Hwy. 6 north 5 miles, then right on Silver Canyon Rd.

Photo courtesy of Bob Hayden.

Buena Park, CA

Knott's Berry Farm®, a Cedar Fair L.P. Park

Train ride, Display
3' narrow gauge

ADDRESS: 8039 Beach Blvd. Buena Park, CA 90620
TELEPHONE: (714) 220-5200
E-MAIL: pr@knotts.com

DESCRIPTION: The Ghost Town & Calico Railway is a narrow gauge passenger service that operates on a daily, year-round schedule. Located within Knott's Berry Farm theme park, the railway has authentic Colorado narrow-gauge equipment.

SCHEDULE: Daily, except Christmas. Please call or check website for operating hours.

ADMISSION/FARE: Admission: adults, $45; seniors 60+, $35; children 3-11, $14.95. Parking: autos, $9; bus/RV, $15.

LOCOMOTIVES/ROLLING STOCK: GT&C motive power includes two Baldwin C-19 Consolidations, former Denver & Rio Grande Western no. 340 and Rio Grande Southern no. 41, and diesel-powered RGS Galloping Goose no. 3. The GT&C employs four closed-vestibule wooden coaches from the D&RGW, including ex-parlor-buffet car "Chama;" and 4 freight cars, including a rare 8 short caboose, RGS no. 0402. Two fully restored special cars round out the collection: Otto Mears' personal car, RGS no. B-20, "Edna" (formerly "San Juan"); and parlor-buffet car "Durango." Static displays of mining equipment throughout the park include a 2'-gauge Vulcan 0-4-0 saddletank.

NEARBY ATTRACTIONS: Historic Los Angeles Union Station, the hub of the city's revitalized light-rail system; equipment collections in LA's Griffith Park, the Los Angeles County Fair grounds in Pomona, and the Orange Empire Railway Museum in Perris; Amtrak services the nearby Fullerton Railroad Plaza, which features three historic depots. In addition to the Santa Fe (now Amtrak) depot, there are the former Union Pacific and Pacific Electric depots. Both of these restored depots currently house Italian restaurants.

DIRECTIONS: Please call or check website for directions.

Photo courtesy of Don Conner, Sr.

TRAVEL TIP: *Engineer for an hour.*

Many tourist railroads and museums offer the chance to take the throttle and run a locomotive under supervision. These programs are often scheduled during the "off" season and include instruction, classroom training, and the chance to get to know the crews at the railroads. Many offer the chance to operate a real diesel locomotive, and some even offer the same for steam.

Campo, CA

Campo Railroad Museum

Train ride, Museum, Display
Standard gauge

SITE ADDRESS: State Hwy. 94 at Forrest Gate Rd. Campo, CA
MAILING ADDRESS: Pacific Southwest Railway Museum Association, Inc. 4695 Nebo Dr.
La Mesa, CA 91941-5259
TELEPHONE: (619) 465-7776
WEBSITE: www.psrm.org

DESCRIPTION: This 12-acre museum and train operation center is on the historic San Diego & Arizona Eastern Railway, completed in 1919. Vintage trains, using steam or early-diesel locomotives, operate over 12 miles of the common-carrier SD&AE Ry. in the US and the Tijuana & Tecate Ry. in Mexico with tunnels, trestles, and a ruling grade of 1.4%. Operating semaphore-type train order signal at Campo railway station.

SCHEDULE: Year-round, weekends and some major holidays, 9 a.m. to 5 p.m. Regular trains depart Campo Depot 11 a.m. and 2:30 p.m. for a 1- to 1½-hour round trip. Third Saturday of each month, trains to Tecate, Mexico depart 10:30 a.m. and return 4 p.m.

ADMISSION/FARE: Museum: $3; train rides (with museum): adults, $15; children, $5; children under 6, free; diesel locomotive cab rides, $35; discounts for AAA, seniors, groups 15+.

LOCOMOTIVES/ROLLING STOCK: More than 80 pieces: vintage steam and diesel locomotives including Oregon & Northwestern Baldwin AS-616 no. 1 and Southern Pacific Alco RS32 no. 7304; Weyerhauser Timber Co. 2-6-6-2 Mallet no. 110; Southern Pacific 4-6-0 no. 2353; 1886 all-wood "Jim Crow" combination car, used in many Western movies; 1927 Railway Post Office car; 1927 Pullman "Robert Peary," used by President Franklin D. Roosevelt 1934-36; John Spreckles' 1910 wooden business car "Carriso Gorge," an 1875 Southern Pacific wood coach; large caboose collection; 1931 nine-passenger gasoline railbus; 1920 Brownhoist locomotive crane; more.

SPECIAL EVENTS: Santa trains, children's trains, Mexico specials, Valentine's Day trains, Father's/Mother's Day trains, Postal Heritage Days, Run-a-Locomotive program, Railfan specials, movie trains and other charters available at any time; call or write for details.

NEARBY ATTRACTIONS: 200 ft. Upper Campo Creek Viaduct railroad bridge, Carriso Gorge, Anza-Borrego Desert State Park, Campo Old Stone Store Museum, Campo Motor Transport Museum, Camp Lockett (last US mounted cavalry base), southern terminus of 1400-mile Pacific Crest Hiking Trail, Indian gaming casino, RV parks, campgrounds, restaurants.

DIRECTIONS: I-8 east from San Diego, 50 miles to Buckman Springs Rd. Go south 10 miles to SR94, turn right. 1.6 miles to Forrest Gate Rd. (at railroad crossing). Turn left and follow signs.

Photo courtesy of R.E. Pennick.
Coupon available, see insert.

Colma, CA

Colma's Historic Train Depot

Museum, Display

ADDRESS: Colma Historical Association 1500 Hillside Blvd. Colma, CA 94014
TELEPHONE: (650) 757-1676
E-MAIL: colmahist@sbcglobal.net

DESCRIPTION: Former Southern Pacific depot, built 1865. There are four museum buildings: History of Colma Museum, Colma Railroad Depot, a freight shed displaying the history of shipping vehicles, and a blacksmith shop.

SCHEDULE: Six days a week, 10 a.m. to 3 p.m., closed Mondays and holidays.

NEARBY ATTRACTIONS: Famous underground residents in 17 cemeteries in 2.2 square miles: Wyatt Earp, Joe DiMaggio, William Randolph Hearst, and many others.

DIRECTIONS: Two blocks east of Freeway 280 off Sierra Monte Blvd. Up to Hillside Blvd. and left two blocks to museum.

Costa Mesa, CA

Orange County Model Engineers, Inc.

Miniature/park train

ADDRESS: 2480 Placentia Ave., PO Box 3216 Costa Mesa, CA 92628-3216
TELEPHONE: (949) 54-TRAIN or (949) 548-7246
E-MAIL: kevtol1@gte.net
WEBSITE: link "Orange County Model Engineers" at www.livesteamclubs.com

DESCRIPTION: The Orange County Model Engineers have 20,000 feet of track and offer guided tours of the roundhouse and facilities. The train rides are 12 to 20 minutes long. This is a non-profit club of train enthusiasts operating a small-scale railroad on over 40 acres of open park.

SCHEDULE: Public run: third full Saturday and Sunday each month, 10 a.m. to 3:30 p.m.

ADMISSION/FARE: Free; donations accepted.

LOCOMOTIVES/ROLLING STOCK: Various 1½"-scale locomotives: steam, diesel, and electric.

SPECIAL EVENTS: Third full weekend in September, Fall Meet; camping available.

NEARBY ATTRACTIONS: Beach two miles away, Disneyland, Knotts Berry Farm, Wild Rivers, Amtrak station, Santa Ana, hundreds of restaurants, numerous hotels and motels.

DIRECTIONS: From north, 405 to Brookhurst South, turn left on Adams, turn right on Placentia. From south, 405 to Harbor South, turn right on Adams, turn left on Placentia. Station is located on the left side, across from Estancia High School.

Dunsmuir, CA

Railroad Park Resort
Display, Resort

ADDRESS: 100 Railroad Park Rd. Dunsmuir, CA 96025
TELEPHONE: (530) 235-4440
E-MAIL: rrp@rrpark.com
WEBSITE: www.rrpark.com

DESCRIPTION: Since 1968, the Railroad Park Resort has been reliving the romantic days of railroading with a 28-room caboose motel and restaurant in refurbished rail cars. RV park and campground on site. Visitors can live the life of a railroader in the caboose motel, find a nostalgic treasure in the gift shop, or explore relics like the gear-driven steam logging locomotive, the 1893 Wells Fargo car, or the wooden snow plow and flanger.

SCHEDULE: Year-round.

ADMISSION/FARE: Rooms $70 to $75 per night. Dinner average $15 per person.

LOCOMOTIVES/ROLLING STOCK: Ed Hines Willamette geared steam locomotive No. 7, snowplow, flanger, cabooses, speeders.

NEARBY ATTRACTIONS: Golfing, skiing, camping, hiking, lakes, fishing, boating, and state park.

DIRECTIONS: I-5, Railroad Park exit. Forty miles north of Redding, just south of Dunsmuir.

Photo courtesy of C. Murphy.

Eureka

Eureka, CA

Fort Humboldt State Historic Park

Train ride, Museum

SITE ADDRESS: 3431 Fort Ave., PO Box 6399 Eureka, CA 95502
TELEPHONE: (707) 445-6567
WEBSITE: www.timberheritage.org

DESCRIPTION: Historic steam redwood logging equipment on site with several artifacts that have been restored to operating condition and are demonstrated by the Timber Heritage Association. Two small steam locomotives provide short rides during summer.

SCHEDULE: Museum: daily, 9 a.m. to 4 p.m.; steam trains and equipment: April 29 and 30 (Donkey Days), May 20, June 17, July 15, August 19, and September 16, 11 a.m. to 4 p.m.

ADMISSION/FARE: Free.

LOCOMOTIVES/ROLLING STOCK: Bear Harbor Lumber Co., Marshutz & Cantrell, 1892, 12-ton 0-4-0, no. 1 "Gypsy;" Elk River Mill and Lumber Co., Marshutz & Cantrell, 1884, 9-ton 0-4-0, no. 1 "Falk;" more.

SPECIAL EVENTS: April 29 and 30, Dolbeer Steam Donkey Days.

NEARBY ATTRACTIONS: Historic military fort and national and state redwood parks.

DIRECTIONS: Off Hwy. 101 at the southern end of Eureka, opposite Bayshore Mall.

Photo courtesy of Michael Kellogg.

Eureka, CA

Humboldt Bay & Eureka Model Railroad Club

Model train layout
HO gauge

ADDRESS: 10 W 7th St., Ste. C Eureka, CA 95501
TELEPHONE: (707) 825-7689
E-MAIL: dougtrain@cox.net

DESCRIPTION: This 855-square-foot HO gauge layout with 2,000 feet of track goes through and over mountains, valleys, trestles, towns, and railyards. Visitors who keep a close eye on the layout can find hidden tongue-in-cheek humor on the fronts of businesses, in the mountains, in the valleys, and wherever the fancy strikes!

SCHEDULE: Saturday night, 7:30 to 9 p.m.

ADMISSION/FARE: Free; donations gladly accepted.

SPECIAL EVENTS: Open house in conjunction with Eureka Rhody Festival, and weekend near Veteran's day.

NEARBY ATTRACTIONS: Redwood National/State Parks.

DIRECTIONS: Off Hwy. 101 at 7th and A Sts. in Eureka, on the second floor.

Felton, CA

Roaring Camp Railroads
Train ride

SITE ADDRESS: Grahman Hill Rd. Felton, CA 95018
MAILING ADDRESS: PO Box G-1 Felton, CA 95018
TELEPHONE: (831) 335-4484
E-MAIL: depot@roaringcamp.com
WEBSITE: www.roaringcamp.com

DESCRIPTION: Visitors can see California's towering redwood forests from two historic railroads near the San Francisco and Monterey Bay Areas. A narrow-gauge steam train travels through the Big Trees to Bear Mountain, while a standard-gauge beach train travels down the scenic San Lorenzo River to the sunny beaches of Santa Cruz.

SCHEDULE: Roaring Camp: year-round; Santa Cruz: schedule varies; check website.

ADMISSION/FARE: Roaring Camp: adults, $18; children, $12; Santa Cruz: adults, $20; children, $15; Parking, $6.

LOCOMOTIVES/ROLLING STOCK: Roaring Camp narrow gauge: 1912 Lima 2-truck Shay, 2-truck Heisler, 3-truck Shay, former West Side Lumber; Santa Cruz beach line: former Santa Fe CF7 diesels 2600 and 2641; no. 20, 50-ton center-cab Whitcomb; passenger cars.

SPECIAL EVENTS: December, Holiday Lights; call, write, or check website for dates of this and several other events.

DIRECTIONS: Off SR17/880 to Santa Cruz, Mt. Hermon exit, 3.5 miles to left on Graham Hill Rd., ¼ mile to Roaring Camp.

See ad on page A-19.

Fillmore, CA

Fillmore & Western Railway

Train ride, Dinner train
Standard gauge

ADDRESS: Santa Clara St., PO Box 960 Fillmore, CA 93016
TELEPHONE: (805) 524-2546
WEBSITE: www.fwry.com

DESCRIPTION: Day and evening diner car service, 2½- to 3-hour rides; Murder Mystery dinners on Saturday evenings; school field trips; Pumpkinliner; Christmas Tree excursion trains; North Pole Express; dance car (with dinner); special events, holiday themed trains.

SCHEDULE: Year-round, weekends. Group excursions by prior arrangement.

ADMISSION/FARE: Day excursions: adults, $20; seniors 60+, $18; children 4-12, $10; babies, $6.

LOCOMOTIVES/ROLLING STOCK: 1891 0-4-0 Porter no. 1 Sespe; 1949 F7 engines nos. 100 and 101; more.

SPECIAL EVENTS: March, Railroad Days festival, Fillmore town festival; April and August, Day Out with Thomas™; Fourth of July, festival, classic car show; October, Pumpkinliner; December, Christmas Tree Trains, North Pole Express.

NEARBY ATTRACTIONS: Six Flags Magic Mountain, Ventura County Beaches, Santa Barbara.

DIRECTIONS: I-5 to Hwy. 126 (Ventura County, California) and Central Ave. in Fillmore. Two blocks north to Main St. Or, I-101 from Ventura, Hwy. 126 east to Central Ave. Two blocks north to Main St. Free parking.

Fish Camp, CA

Yosemite Mountain Sugar Pine Railroad

Train ride, Dinner train, Museum, Display

ADDRESS: 56001 Hwy. 41 Fish Camp, CA 93623
TELEPHONE: (559) 683-7273
WEBSITE: www.ymsprr.com

DESCRIPTION: The railroad, founded in 1965, operates a one-hour narrated, steam-powered excursion over a restored section of the Madera Sugar Pine Lumber Co. The 4-mile trip runs through the Sierra Nevada at an elevation of 5,000 feet, winds down a 4% grade into Lewis Creek Canyon, passes Horseshoe Curve and Cold Spring Crossing, and stops at Lewis Creek Loop. Ex-Westside Lumber Co. Shays provide the motive power for the train. Converted logging cars using sectioned logs are used for passenger cars.

SCHEDULE: Railcars: April through October, daily. Steam train: May through September, daily; April and October, weekends.

ADMISSION/FARE: Steam train: adults, $16; children 3-12, $8; railcars: adults, $11.50; children 3-12, $5.75; moonlight special: adults, $42; children, $23.

LOCOMOTIVES/ROLLING STOCK: 1928 Lima 3-truck Shay, no. 10; 1913 Lima 3-truck Shay, no. 15; Vulcan 1935 10-ton switcher; four model-A powered railcars; logging cars; covered and open converted flat cars, more.

SPECIAL EVENTS: Summer: Saturday and Wednesday nights, Moonlight Special with steak barbeque and music. Gold panning, group tours, theme events, and private charters.

NEARBY ATTRACTIONS: Sierra National Forest, Yosemite National Park, Narrow Gauge Inn.

Folsom, CA
Folsom Valley Railway/Folsom City Zoo

ADDRESS: 121 Dunstable Way Folsom, CA 95630
TELEPHONE: (916) 983-1873
E-MAIL: Goldtown@juno.com

DESCRIPTION: A $\frac{1}{3}$-scale steam locomotive pulls vintage freight cars for $\frac{3}{4}$-mile.

SCHEDULE: February through October: Tuesday through Friday, 11 a.m. to 2 p.m.; Saturday, Sunday, and holidays, 11 a.m. to 4 p.m.; November and January: Saturday, Sunday, and school holidays, 11 a.m. to 2 p.m.; December 26 through January 1: 11 a.m. to 2 p.m.

ADMISSION/FARE: $1.50 per person.

LOCOMOTIVES/ROLLING STOCK: 1950 Ottoway Locomotive, truss rod style freight cars, cattle car, hopper car, five open gondola cars, bobber caboose.

SPECIAL EVENTS: 4th of July, until 10 p.m.

NEARBY ATTRACTIONS: Folsom Zoo.

DIRECTIONS: Folsom is about 25 miles east of Sacramento off US50.

Photo courtesy of Terry Gold.

Fort Bragg, CA

Sierra Railroad/Skunk Train/Fort Bragg

Train ride

ADDRESS: Foot of Laurel St. Fort Bragg, CA 95437
TELEPHONE: (866) 45-SKUNK or (707)964-6371
E-MAIL: skunk@skunktrain.com or info@sierrarailroad.com
WEBSITE: www.skunktrain.com

DESCRIPTION: Rides from the Mendocino Coast into the mountains. The 3½-hour trip goes along the Noyo River canyon to the California Redwoods.

SCHEDULE: Spring through Fall, daily; winter, weekends.

ADMISSION/FARE: Check website for price.

LOCOMOTIVES/ROLLING STOCK: 1924 Baldwin 2-8-2 no. 45; 1955 EMD GP9 diesels nos. 64, 65, 66.

NEARBY ATTRACTIONS: Logging museum, deep sea fishing, Mendocino, beaches.

DIRECTIONS: Hwy. 1 and Laurel St. in Fort Bragg.

Fremont, CA

Niles Depot Museum

Museum, Model train layout
HO & N scale

SITE ADDRESS: 36997 Mission Blvd. Fremont, CA 94536
MAILING ADDRESS: PO Box 2716 Fremont, CA 94536
TELEPHONE: (510) 797-4449
E-MAIL: nilesdepot@railfan.net
WEBSITE: www.nilesdepot.railfan.net

DESCRIPTION: Exhibits in 1901 Southern Pacific depot include: photographs, track equipment, signals, locomotive artifacts and uniforms, many other local area items, and an N scale and HO scale layout. The primary focus is the early railroads of Fremont, Newark, and Union City with an emphasis on the Niles District of Fremont—mainly the Southern Pacific and Western Pacific.

SCHEDULE: First and third Sunday of each month, 10 a.m. to 4 p.m.

ADMISSION/FARE: Donation.

LOCOMOTIVES/ROLLING STOCK: WP caboose no. 467.

NEARBY ATTRACTIONS: The Niles District, home to the first Hollywood.

DIRECTIONS: Between Nursery Ave. and the Sullivan underpass.

Fremont, CA
Society for the Preservation of Carter Railroad Resources
Museum

SITE ADDRESS: 34600 Ardenwood Blvd. Fremont, CA 94555
MAILING ADDRESS: PO Box 783 Newark, CA 94560
TELEPHONE: (510) 797-9557
E-MAIL: rkhill@worldnet.att.net

DESCRIPTION: The museum is close to the original Carter Shops in Newark. They restore equipment representative of bygone days. The collection contains over 17 wooden cars from the 1870s and 1920s. Most of the cars were built by the Carter Brothers in Newark or the West Side Lumber Company. The SPCRR has 1½ miles of track and operates a recreation of the original Centerville Branch at Ardenwood. They use draft horses to pull an 1885 North Pacific Coast RR flatcar set up as a picnic car on scheduled runs through farm fields and eucalyptus groves. The restoration efforts are usually performed in front of the park visitors using hand tools and 19th century techniques.

SCHEDULE: Tuesday through Sunday; park closed Monday; some days allow more access than others. Check website for details.

ADMISSION/FARE: $1 to $8.

DIRECTIONS: Fremont (formerly Washington Township) is located between San Jose and Oakland, California, on I-880.

Goleta, CA
South Coast Railroad Museum
Train ride, Museum
7½″

ADDRESS: 300 N Los Carneros Rd. Goleta, CA 93117-1502
TELEPHONE: (805) 964-3540
E-MAIL: museum@goletadepot.org
WEBSITE: www.goletadepot.org

DESCRIPTION: The museum's centerpiece is the historic Goleta Depot, a Victorian-styled Southern Pacific country station. The museum features refurnished rooms and station grounds, and a variety of informative displays, including a 300-square-foot HO scale model railroad exhibit. Other attractions include miniature train and handcar rides, Gandy Dancer Theater, picnic grounds, and a museum store and gift shop.

CALIFORNIA

Goleta – Grass Valley

SCHEDULE: Museum, Wednesday through Sunday, 1 to 4 p.m.; miniature train, 1:15 to 3:45 p.m.; handcar, third Saturday of each month, 1:15 to 3:45 p.m.

ADMISSION/FARE: Museum, donations appreciated; handcar, free; miniature train, $1.

LOCOMOTIVES/ROLLING STOCK: 1960s Southern Pacific bay window caboose no. 4023.

SPECIAL EVENTS: Fourth Sunday in September, 11 a.m. to 4 p.m., Depot Day.

DIRECTIONS: Seven miles west of Santa Barbara, US101 north exit Los Carneros Rd.

Photo courtesy of South Coast Railroad Museum.

Grass Valley, CA

Nevada County Narrow Gauge Project
Display, Layout
On3 gauge

SITE ADDRESS: Nevada County Fair Grounds, McCourtney Rd. Grass Valley, CA 95949
MAILING ADDRESS: NCNG Project, PO Box 2258 Nevada City, CA 95949
WEBSITE: www.ncngproject.org

DESCRIPTION: The On3 model railroad display is a historically accurate depiction of 1932-1942, and located in its own building on the Nevada County Fair grounds. The exhibit has models of the three major towns served by the NCNGRR—Nevada City, Grass Valley, and Colfax, as well as historic points in between.

SCHEDULE: 4th of July; August, 5-day summer County Fair; September, Draft Horse Classic; Thanksgiving weekend, 3-day Christmas Craft Fair. Operating hours consistent with fair events.

ADMISSION/FARE: County Fair: adults, $1; children, free with adult admission.

LOCOMOTIVES/ROLLING STOCK: Various scale models of NCNG motive power and rolling stock in use during 1930s.

SPECIAL EVENTS: First Saturday, 1 to 3 p.m.

NEARBY ATTRACTIONS: County Fair, Gold Country State Parks, Northern California mining towns, new historical society railroad museums.

DIRECTIONS: Exhibit located at Nevada County Fairgrounds, Grass Valley, CA.

34

Jamestown, CA

Railtown 1897 State Historic Park

Train ride, Museum
Standard gauge

ADDRESS: 5th Ave. & Reservoir Rd., PO Box 1250 Jamestown, CA 95327
TELEPHONE: (209) 984-3953
E-MAIL: railtowninfo@parks.ca.gov
WEBSITE: www.railtown1897.org

DESCRIPTION: Operated by the California State Railroad Museum, the former Sierra Railroad property is a popular filming location. The Historic Jamestown Shops and Roundhouse at Railtown 1897 have been in operation as a steam locomotive maintenance facility for over a century. The six-mile, 40-minute round-trip passes through Gold Country.

SCHEDULE: Daily, 9:30 a.m. to 4:30 p.m., except Thanksgiving, Christmas, and New Year's Day. Steam trains: April through October, weekends, departing hourly, 11 a.m. to 3 p.m.; roundhouse tours: daily.

ADMISSION/FARE: Roundhouse tours: adults, $2; children 6-12, $1; train rides: adults, $6; children 6-12, $3; children 5 and under, free.

LOCOMOTIVES/ROLLING STOCK: Sierra Railroad 2-8-0 no. 28, 4-6-0 no. 3, combine no. 5, coach no. 6, former Feather River Shay no. 2, former Southern Pacific commuter coaches.

SPECIAL EVENTS: April through May, Spring Wildflower Trains; September, Wine & Cheese Special; October, Halloween Trains; November through December, Santa Trains.

NEARBY ATTRACTIONS: Columbia State Historic Park, Yosemite National Park, Sierra Foothills wine region, Gold Rush heritage towns.

DIRECTIONS: Located three blocks east of downtown Jamestown on Hwys. 49/107, just west of the Hwy. 120 junction.

Photo courtesy of California State Railroad Museum.

TRAVEL TIP: *Photo outings*

Many railroads offer a railfan event that includes special trains, unusual equipment, and the chance to get great photos of your favorite railroad. Be sure to check the special events listings of your favorite line to see if they schedule a photography weekend or a photo freight that will provide a glimpse into the past.

La Mesa, CA

La Mesa Depot Museum

Museum, Display

SITE ADDRESS: 4695 Nebo Dr. La Mesa, CA 91941
MAILING ADDRESS: Pacific Southwest Railway Museum Association,
4695 Nebo Dr. La Mesa, CA 91941-5259
TELEPHONE: (619) 465-7776
WEBSITE: www.psrm.org

DESCRIPTION: Restored original 1894 train station, complete with train order board, furniture, telegraph and telephone equipment, pot-belly coal stove, and more. Steam locomotive and caboose on display. The depot is the second-oldest commercial building in La Mesa still on its original site.

SCHEDULE: Saturday, 1 to 4 p.m.; other selected days, year-round; groups by appointment.

ADMISSION/FARE: Admission is free. Donations are accepted.

LOCOMOTIVES/ROLLING STOCK: 1923 Davenport 0-6-0ST steam locomotive, an ice-type refrigerator car, and 1941 Southern Pacific class C-40-3 caboose.

SPECIAL EVENTS: Classic Car Show, Oktoberfest, Christmas in the Village.

NEARBY ATTRACTIONS: San Diego Trolley light-rail line, McKinney House Museum, Reed's Model Train Shop, and antique stores.

DIRECTIONS: I-8, SR94, or Orange Line trolley east from San Diego 12 miles to La Mesa. Located in La Mesa village on Nebo Dr. at La Mesa Blvd., ½ block south of light-rail station.

Photo courtesy of PSMRA Photo.

Lomita, CA

Lomita Railroad Museum

Museum

ADDRESS: 250th & Woodward Ave. Lomita, CA 90717
TELEPHONE: (310) 326-6255
WEBSITE: www.lomita-rr.org

DESCRIPTION: A replica of the Boston & Maine station at Wakefield, MA. On display are lanterns of the steam era, chinaware, and silverware of the period, scale model live steam engines, spikes, tie date nails, insulators, prints, photographs, postcards, clocks, and a wooden water tower.

SCHEDULE: Year-round: Thursday through Sunday, 10 a.m. to 5 p.m.; closed all holidays.

ADMISSION/FARE: Adults, $4; children under 12, $2.

LOCOMOTIVES/ROLLING STOCK: 1902 Baldwin 2-6-0 (Mogul) no. 1765 with a whale-back tender, former Southern Pacific; 1910 yellow caboose, UP OWR&N; 1913 UP boxcar; 1923 oil tank car, Union Oil Co.; Santa Fe red caboose no. 999531.

NEARBY ATTRACTIONS: South Coast Botanical Gardens, Torrance Cabrillo Museum, San Pedro, Banning House and Drum Barracks, Wilmington.

DIRECTIONS: Hwy. 110 (Harbor Freeway) south to Pacific Coast Hwy. off ramp. Right (west) to Narbonne Ave. Right to second signal. Right (east) one block. Parking on 250th St.

Los Angeles, CA
Griffith Park & Southern Railroad
Miniature/park train
18 1/2" gauge

ADDRESS: 4400 Crystal Springs Dr. Los Angeles, CA 90027
TELEPHONE: (323) 664-6788
E-MAIL: webmaster@gprah.com
WEBSITE: www.gprah.com

DESCRIPTION: The 18 1/2" gauge trains travel along one mile of track that runs over several bridges, including a 60' long wood and steel box girder bridge. They also go though an 80' tunnel and past several attractions, including the Western Old Town.

SCHEDULE: Weather permitting, 364 days per year; closed Christmas.

LOCOMOTIVES/ROLLING STOCK: The Colonel Griffith, a 1983 Severn Lamb Ltd. 2-8-0 locomotive; the Freedom Train, an All American Streamliner Co. of Los Angeles streamliner; the Stanley Diamond, a 1993 Gerry Bowden 2-6-0; ten Pullman style, five-seat steel coaches built by All American Streamliner of Los Angeles; three six-seat wood gondolas built by Skeets Simpson in 1993 after a design by Erik Thomsen of Redwood Valley Railway.

TRAVEL TIP: *Volunteers*

Many museum and tourist railroads rely on volunteers for their restoration and operating workers. If you like what you see at a railroad, inquire about volunteer opportunities. You might find yourself working on your favorite locomotive one day, or even better, running it!

Los Angeles, CA

Los Angeles Live Steamers Railroad Museum

Miniature/Park train, Museum
7¹/₂"

SITE ADDRESS: Griffith Park Los Angeles, CA
MAILING ADDRESS: PO Box 2156 Toluca Lake, CA 91610

DESCRIPTION: Founded in 1956 by train enthusiasts to educate the public about railroad history and to advance railroad technology. Has about 20,000 feet of 7¹/₂" gauge track and layouts for 4³/₄" and 3¹/₂" gauge model trains.

SCHEDULE: Sunday, 11 a.m. to 3 p.m., weather permitting; except Sunday before Memorial Day and first Sunday in October.

ADMISSION/FARE: Free.

NEARBY ATTRACTIONS: Travel Town.

DIRECTIONS: Ventura Freeway (134) exit Forest Lawn Dr., left on Zoo Dr.

Photo courtesy of Donald Frozina.

Los Angeles, CA

Travel Town Museum

Museum

SITE ADDRESS: 5200 Zoo Dr. Los Angeles, CA 90039
MAILING ADDRESS: 3900 W Chevy Chase Dr., Mail Stop 656/3 Los Angeles, CA 90039
TELEPHONE: (323) 662-5874
E-MAIL: TravelTown@rap.lacity.org
WEBSITE: www.laparks.org/grifmet/tt/index.htm

DESCRIPTION: An outdoor transportation museum celebrating the history of railroading in the western United States, concentrating on California and, specifically, Los Angeles.

SCHEDULE: Year-round: weekdays, 10 a.m. to 4 p.m.; weekends, 10 a.m. to 5 p.m.

ADMISSION/FARE: Free.

LOCOMOTIVES/ROLLING STOCK: 14 steam locomotives, numerous freight cars, cabooses, interurbans, and motorcars.

NEARBY ATTRACTIONS: Griffith Park, Los Angeles Zoo, Autry Museum of Western Heritage, Griffith Observatory, Greek Theatre.

DIRECTIONS: Ventura Fwy. exit 134 (Forest Lawn Dr.), located at Griffith Park and Zoo Drs.

Los Gatos, CA

Billy Jones Wildcat Railroad
Train ride
18" gauge

SITE ADDRESS: 110 Blossom Hill Rd. Los Gatos, CA 95032
MAILING ADDRESS: PO Box 234 Los Gatos, CA 95031-0234
TELEPHONE: (408) 395-7433
E-MAIL: bjwrr1@aol.com
WEBSITE: www.bjwrr.org

DESCRIPTION: A 7-minute train ride through Vasona and Oak Meadow Park. A 1905 steam engine and a diesel engine pull open air cars over two bridges and about a mile of track.

SCHEDULE: November 1 to March 14: weekends, 11 a.m. to 3 p.m.; March 15 to June 14: weekends, 10:30 a.m. to 4:30 p.m.; June 15 to Labor Day: daily, 10:30 a.m. to 4:30 p.m.; Labor Day to October 31: weekends, 10:30 a.m. to 4:30 p.m. All times weather permitting.

ADMISSION/FARE: $1.50; children 2 and under, free with adult; 50 or more tickets, $1 each; handicapped people, free.

LOCOMOTIVES/ROLLING STOCK: 1905 2-6-2 locomotive no. 2; 1992 diesel hydraulic locomotive no. 2502.

SPECIAL EVENTS: Last three weeks of December, Thursday through Sunday, 6 to 9 p.m., Fantasy Train of Lights, light displays in Vasona Park.

NEARBY ATTRACTIONS: W.E. Bill Mason Carousel, an antique, English-style carousel; Oak Meadow Town Park; Vasona Lake and County Park.

DIRECTIONS: From Hwy. 17 in Los Gatos, Hwy. 9 to Saratoga, right onto University, right onto Blossom Hill Rd., left into Oak Meadows Park. BJWRR is at the back of the park.

Photo courtesy of Jim Koski.

McCloud, CA

Shasta Sunset Dinner Train

Train ride, Dinner train
Standard gauge

SITE ADDRESS: 801 Industrial Way, PO Box 1500 McCloud, CA 96057
MAILING ADDRESS: PO Box 1199 McCloud, CA 96057
TELEPHONE: (800) 733-2141
WEBSITE: www.shastasunset.com

DESCRIPTION: Four-course gourmet meal served aboard 1916 Illinois Central dining cars, and diesel-powered open-air excursion trains.

SCHEDULE: Dinner: year-round; excursion: summer.

ADMISSION/FARE: Varies, call for information.

LOCOMOTIVES/ROLLING STOCK: SD38 diesels nos. 36, 37, and 38; 1916 IC refurbished cars, open-air and double-decker cars.

SPECIAL EVENTS: 4th of July, Fireworks Special; first weekend in August, Civil War Days.

NEARBY ATTRACTIONS: Burney Falls, McCloud Historic Museum, Mt. Shasta.

DIRECTIONS: I-5 to Hwy. 89 exit to McCloud, left on Colombero, right on Main St. at station.

See ad on page A-24.

Millbrae, CA

Millbrae Train Museum

Museum

SITE ADDRESS: California and Murchison drives, adjacent to the Caltrain parking lot southwest of the BART/Caltrain station Millbrae, CA 94030
MAILING ADDRESS: PO Box 511 Millbrae, CA 94030
TELEPHONE: (650) 333-1136
WEBSITE: www.millbraehs.org

DESCRIPTION: The Millbrae Historical Society got its start in the early 1970s, when a group of citizens prevented the destruction of the Southern Pacific train station, and created a museum in the building they saved. The museum is dedicated to railroad history of Millbrae, the Peninsula, and the Bay Area.

SCHEDULE: Saturday, 10 a.m. to 2 p.m.

ADMISSION/FARE: Adults, $2; children under 7 and Millbrae Historical Society members, free.

NEARBY ATTRACTIONS: Walking distance from Caltrain, BART, and numerous restaurants.

Photo courtesy of Randy Sahae.
Coupon available, see insert.

Napa, CA
Napa Valley Wine Train
Train ride, Dinner train, Museum
Standard gauge

ADDRESS: 1275 McKinstry St. Napa, CA 94559
TELEPHONE: (800) 427-44124 or (707) 253-2111
WEBSITE: www.winetrain.com

DESCRIPTION: Year-round gourmet dining excursions during a three-hour, 36-mile round trip. The Napa Valley Railroad was founded in 1864. The current chairman, Vincent DeDomenico, is a 50-year veteran of the food industry who received the Parisian Gold Medal of Honor for his efforts to promote the marriage of good food with great wines.

SCHEDULE: Daily, 8 a.m. to 10 p.m.

ADMISSION/FARE: $47.50 to $150.

LOCOMOTIVES/ROLLING STOCK: Four Alco-MLW FPA-4 diesels, nos. 70, 71, 72, and 73; seven Pullman dining and lounge cars, circa 1915-1917; one 1952 Pullman dome car; one Pullman coach converted to professional viewing kitchen.

SPECIAL EVENTS: Murder mystery dinner theatre, family fun, vintners luncheons, appellation dinners, dinner concert series, Moonlight Escapades.

NEARBY ATTRACTIONS: American Center for Wine, Food & the Arts (COPIA), and Napa Valley Opera House.

DIRECTIONS: One hour north of San Francisco in downtown Napa off Soscol Ave. and First St.

See ad on page A-11.

41

National City, CA

San Diego Electric Railway Association Inc./ National City Depot

Museum, Display, Model train layout

SITE ADDRESS: 922 W 23rd St. National City, CA 91950
MAILING ADDRESS: PO Box 89068 San Diego, CA 92138-9068
TELEPHONE: (619) 474-4400
E-MAIL: ncd@trainweb.com
WEBSITE: www.sdera.org

DESCRIPTION: California registered historical landmark no. 1023 depicts the Santa Fe and San Diego Electric Railway Company, and houses an operating three-rail toy train layout.

SCHEDULE: Saturday and Sunday, 12 to 4 p.m.; major holidays, 12 to 4 p.m., except Thanksgiving and Christmas (closed).

ADMISSION/FARE: Free. Donations accepted.

LOCOMOTIVES/ROLLING STOCK: Three trolley cars from the 1920s, Vienna and Australia.

NEARBY ATTRACTIONS: National City and Otay (NC&O) no. 1 Car Plaza, San Diego Zoo and wild animal park, Sea World, Knott's Soak City, Arco Olympic Training Center, San Diego Trolley, Coaster Commuter Rail, San Diego Model Railroad Museum, and Tijuana, Mexico.

DIRECTIONS: Five miles south of San Diego. Take I-5 south to Bay Marina Dr. exit in National City and turn right. Go west two blocks and the museum is on the right.

Photo courtesy of Jim Papulas.

Nevada City, CA

Nevada County Narrow Gauge Railroad and Transportation Museum

Museum, Display

ADDRESS: 5 Kidder Ct. Nevada City, CA 95959
TELEPHONE: (530) 470-0902
E-MAIL: contact@ncngrrmuseum.org
WEBSITE: www.ncngrrmuseum.org

DESCRIPTION: The collection of railroad and transportation artifacts includes NCNGRR Engine 5. The 1875 Baldwin hauled timber, passengers, and freight, before being sent to Hollywood to become a working prop. Narrow gauge locomotives and rolling stock are on display in the restoration shop and switch yard. Also on display is a 1901 steam-powered carriage and other examples of Nevada County's early transportation history.

SCHEDULE: May to October: Friday to Tuesday, 10 a.m. to 4 p.m.; November to April: Tuesday and Saturday, 10 a.m. to 4 p.m.

ADMISSION/FARE: Free admission; donations appreciated.

LOCOMOTIVES/ROLLING STOCK: 1875 Baldwin 2-6-0 (display); 1889 Porter 0-4-0 (operational); 1911 Heisler 2-truck (restoration); NCNGRR Tank 187; NCNGRR Caboose 1, and more.

SPECIAL EVENTS: 2nd Saturday in May, Anniversary Steam-up; 1st Saturday in December, Children's Christmas Party.

NEARBY ATTRACTIONS: Nevada County Historical Society–Firehouse Museum, North Star Mining Museum, Searls Historical Library, Nevada County Traction Co., three state parks.

DIRECTIONS: Hwy. 20/49 to Gold Flat exit. Look for sign at Hollow Way. Hollow Way to Bost. Right on Bost to Kidder Court.

Photo courtesy of Al Dittmann.

Nevada City, CA

Nevada County Traction Company
Train ride, Display, Model railroad layout
Narrow gauge

ADDRESS: 402 Railroad Ave. Nevada City, CA 95959
TELEPHONE: (800) 226-3090 x262 or (530) 265-0896
E-MAIL: depotpeople@stardustweb.net
WEBSITE: northernqueeninn.com

DESCRIPTION: The four-car train switcher holds up to 90 people on a 90-minute, three-mile round trip. Tour includes a short walk through an 1860s Chinese cemetery and gardens. Cars are open-top, so tours run weather-permitting.

SCHEDULE: June to September: Thursday to Monday, 9:30 a.m. to 4:30 p.m.; Monday, Thursday, and Friday departures, 12 and 2 p.m.; Saturday departures, 10 a.m., 12, 2, and 4 p.m.; Sunday departures: 10 a.m., 12, and 2 p.m.

ADMISSION/FARE: Adults, $10; children 2-12, $7.

LOCOMOTIVES/ROLLING STOCK: 1959 12-ton Plymouth switcher, no. 7; Argent Lumber Co. 1910 Lima 2-6-2, a 26-ton wood burner; 1939 coal-burning Henshel 0-4-0.

SPECIAL EVENTS: June through August, Sunday Sno Cone Social and Medicine Man Show; October, Halloween events all month, train departs at 10 a.m., 12, 2, and 4 p.m. daily for Haunted Forest of Terror, Poltergeist Express, and Night Train rides.

NEARBY ATTRACTIONS: Nevada County Narrow Gauge Railroad Transportation Museum, Historical Nevada City, Empire Mine, NorthStar Palton Wheel Museum, Yuba River.

DIRECTIONS: On Hwy. 49/20, 55 miles northeast of Sacramento. Take Sacramento St. exit, right on Railroad Ave., 1/8 mile on right. Located at Northern Queen Inn upper parking lot.

Oakdale, CA

Sierra Railroad Dinner Train

Dinner train
Standard gauge

ADDRESS: 220 S Sierra Ave. Oakdale, CA 95361
TELEPHONE: (800) 866-1690 or (209) 848-2100
E-MAIL: info@sierrarailroad.com
WEBSITE: www.sierrarailroad.com

DESCRIPTION: The Sierra Railroad Dinner Train offers a variety of romantic, family, and tourist trips with a memorable combination of fine dining, excellent food, entertainment, and scenery on this luxurious train.

SCHEDULE: Year-round, every week.

ADMISSION/FARE: Brunch and lunch, $59; dinner, $69.

LOCOMOTIVES/ROLLING STOCK: Baldwin S-12 Sierra no. 42.

SPECIAL EVENTS: January, Robert Burns Scottish Dinner; Valentine's Day; 3rd weekend in May, Oakdale Chocolate Festival; Little Engine That Could; Summertime Rail & Raft trips; Christmas Trains; New Year's Eve.

NEARBY ATTRACTIONS: Yosemite National Park, Hershey's Chocolate, Gold Country, rafting.

DIRECTIONS: From San Francisco, take 580 and 120 east to Oakdale (100 miles). From Sacramento, 99 south to Manteca, and 120 east to Oakdale (70 miles). From Los Angeles, 99 to Turlock and J14 north to Oakdale (300 miles).

Photo courtesy of Chris Hart.
Coupon available, see insert.

Orange, CA

Irvine Park Railroad

Train ride
24" gauge

ADDRESS: 1 Irvine Park Rd. Orange, CA 92862
TELEPHONE: (714) 997-3968
WEBSITE: www.irvineparkrr.com

DESCRIPTION: Irvine Park Railroad is located on 500 acres in the oldest county park in California. The train makes a scenic one-mile journey around the park during which riders can view two lakes complete with waterfalls and fountains, a grove of oak trees, and the Orange County Zoo. The 12-minute ride is narrated by the engineer.

SCHEDULE: Daily: summer, 10 a.m. to 4:30 p.m.; winter, 10 a.m. to 4 p.m.; closed Thanksgiving and Christmas.

ADMISSION/FARE: $3; children under 1, free; school group rates are available.

LOCOMOTIVES/ROLLING STOCK: A ⅓ scale replica of 1863 C.P. Huntington; four coaches.

SPECIAL EVENTS: Four weeks prior to Christmas, Christmas train. Call for times.

NEARBY ATTRACTIONS: Bicycle and paddleboat rentals, Orange County Zoo, pony rides.

DIRECTIONS: From State Hwy. 55 take the Chapman Ave. exit and drive east to Jamboree Rd. Turn left into the park entrance.

Phot courtesy of John Ford.
Coupon available, see insert.

Perris, CA

Orange Empire Railway Museum   EDITOR'S CHOICE

Train ride, Museum

ADDRESS: 2201 S A St., PO Box 548 Perris, CA 92572-0548
TELEPHONE: (951) 943-3020
E-MAIL: oerm@juno.com
WEBSITE: www.oerm.org

DESCRIPTION: Trolley and train rides on weekends and during special events, lasting approximately 15 minutes. Selected on a rotating basis from the historic collection, the train and trolleys can be: an electric or diesel-powered freight train (with multiple cabooses), a consist of passenger cars, an early Los Angeles streetcar, more modern PCC on the Loop Line, caboose, or open gondola. Steam locomotive operation is scheduled for certain special events and one major holiday.

SCHEDULE: Museum: every weekend and most major holidays, 11 a.m. to 5 p.m.; weekdays, charters and other special events; museum grounds: daily, 9 a.m. to 5 p.m.; closed Thanksgiving and Christmas.

ADMISSION/FARE: Free. Special events may have additional fees, ranging from $5 to $15.

LOCOMOTIVES/ROLLING STOCK: More than 180 locomotives, freight cars, passenger cars, and streetcars.

SPECIAL EVENTS: See website or call for details.

NEARBY ATTRACTIONS: Perris Valley Skydiving Center, Perris Auto Speedway, Lake Perris Recreation Area, March Field Air Museum, Temecula Wineries.

DIRECTIONS: 17 miles south of Riverside on I-215 to Perris.

Photo courtesy of Orange Empire Railway Museum.
Coupon available, see insert.

Point Richmond, CA
Golden State Model Railroad Museum
Museum, Display, Model train layout
O, HO, N scales

SITE ADDRESS: 900 Dornan Dr. Point Richmond, CA 94801
MAILING ADDRESS: PO Box 71244 Point Richmond, CA 94807-1244
TELEPHONE: (510) 234-4884
E-MAIL: info@gsmrm.org
WEBSITE: www.gsmrm.org

DESCRIPTION: A 10,000-square-foot display area features large layouts with historic scenery in three scales, static displays, and railroad artifacts.

SCHEDULE: Operating layouts: April through December, Sunday, 12 to 5 p.m.; December 23 and 30, 12 to 5 p.m.; viewing only: Wednesday and Saturday, 12 to 5p.m.; work evenings: all year, Friday, 7 to 10 p.m., public welcome. Also open and operating on Independence, Memorial, and Labor Days.

ADMISSION/FARE: Sunday only: Adults, $3; seniors and children under 12, $2; family maximum, $7.

SPECIAL EVENTS: Christmas season, holiday decorations; weekends before and after December 25, layouts operate on Saturday and Sunday.

NEARBY ATTRACTIONS: In Miller-Knox Regional Park, S.S. Red Oak Victory, Rosie the Riveter (NPS) site.

DIRECTIONS: See website.

Photo courtesy of John Edington.

Pomona, CA

Railway & Locomotive Historical Society, Southern California Chapter
Museum, Display

ADDRESS: Los Angeles County Fairplex, PO Box 2250 Pomona, CA 91769
TELEPHONE: (909) 623-0190
E-MAIL: rlhs-pomona@rrmail.com
WEBSITE: www.trainweb.org/rlhs

DESCRIPTION: Former 1885 ATSF Arcadia Depot houses exhibits and a gift shop. There is an outside display of locomotives and rolling stock, including motor cars, ice refrigerator car, caboose, berth and galley section of business car, and horse car showing stable.

SCHEDULE: Second Saturday weekend of every month, 10 a.m. to 3 p.m.

ADMISSION/FARE: Free, except during fair.

LOCOMOTIVES/ROLLING STOCK: Santa Fe 4-6-2 no. 3450; Union Pacific 4-12-2 no. 9000, 4-8-8-4 "Big Boy" no. 4014, and DDA40X "Centennial" no. 6915; Southern Pacific 4-10-2 no. 5021; and more.

SPECIAL EVENTS: September, Los Angeles County Fair.

NEARBY ATTRACTIONS: Disneyland, Knott's Berry Farm, Orange Empire Railroad Museum.

DIRECTIONS: Enter the Fairplex at Gate 1, or Main Gate, Pomona, CA.

Photo courtesy of Ted Liddle.

Portola, CA

Portola Railroad Museum

Train ride, Museum

EDITOR'S CHOICE

ADDRESS: 700 Western Pacific Way, PO Box 608 Portola, CA 96122
TELEPHONE: (530) 832-4131
WEBSITE: www.WPLives.org

DESCRIPTION: This 37-acre diesel servicing facility displays 160 pieces of equipment. Visitors can ride in a caboose through a pine forest on a one-mile loop of track or climb into a locomotive and sit in the engineer's seat. For the ultimate thrill, personal instructors offer a one-hour "run-a-locomotive" test drive for $95 per hour. Reservations required.

SCHEDULE: Museum: March through October: daily, 10 a.m. to 5 p.m.;train rides: Memorial Day through Labor Day: weekends.

ADMISSION/FARE: Adults, $5; children, $2.

LOCOMOTIVES/ROLLING STOCK: Western Pacific SW1 501; WP NW2 608; WP F7As 921 and 917; WP GP20 2001; WP GP7s 705, 707, 708, and 712; WP GP9 725 and 731; WP U30B 3051; O&NW AS616s 3 and 4; UP GP30 849; UP DDA40X 6946; Quincy Railroad GE 44-tonner no. 3, Quincy S1 no. 4; WP FP7 805; SP GP9 2873, SP SD9 4404; WP S4 563; Kennecott Copper RS2 908; Kennecott Copper RS3 no. 2 and no. 3; Milwaukee Road U25B no. 5057.

SPECIAL EVENTS: May 20, Rail Photographer's Day, $20; August 25-27, Railroad Days.

NEARBY ATTRACTIONS: UP/BNSF train watching in the beautiful Feather River Canyon.

DIRECTIONS: SR70, south on CRA-15 (Gulling). West on Commercial to Pacific. West on 1st.

Photo courtesy of John Walker.
See ad on page A-36.

Poway, CA

Poway-Midland Railroad

Train ride
3'6" Narrow gauge

SITE ADDRESS: Old Poway Park, 14134 Midland Rd., between Aubrey and Temple
MAILING ADDRESS: PO Box 1244 Poway, CA 92074
TELEPHONE: (858) 486-4063
E-MAIL: pmrrweb@powaymidlandrr.org
WEBSITE: www.powaymidlandrr.org

DESCRIPTION: Visitors can see restored historic buildings and rolling stock, a gallows turntable, and an expanded train barn that call up the Old West of 100 years ago.

SCHEDULE: Year-round except Christmas/New Year and second Sunday of each month; Saturday, 10 a.m. to 4 p.m.; Sunday, 11 a.m. to 2 p.m.

ADMISSION/FARE: Adults, $1-2 (depending on ride); children, $0.50.

LOCOMOTIVES/ROLLING STOCK: 1907 Baldwin 0-4-0 steam locomotive no. 3; replica 1880s passenger car no. 325; 1894 Los Angeles Railway Yellow Line no. 57; 1950 Fairmont speeder no. 38; four 1880s ore cars; 1906 San Francisco California Street cable car no. 17 (in restoration).

SPECIAL EVENTS: May, Rendezvous in Poway; July, old-fashioned Fourth of July; October, Train Song Festival; December, Christmas in the Park.

NEARBY ATTRACTIONS: San Diego Zoo, San Diego Wild Animal Park, Sea World, Legoland, San Diego Model Railroad Museum.

DIRECTIONS: 5 miles east of I-15 on Midland Rd. in Poway. From Los Angeles, exit Camino del Norte, south on Midland. From San Diego, exit Poway Rd., turn north on Midland.

Photo courtesy of Poway-Midland Railroad.

Riverside, CA
Riverside Live Steamers
Miniature/Park train

SITE ADDRESS: 1496 Columbia Ave. Riverside, CA 92507
MAILING ADDRESS: PO Box 5512 Riverside, CA 92517
TELEPHONE: (951) 779-9024
WEBSITE: www.steamonly.org

DESCRIPTION: The ⅛-size trains are all steam and run on a 6,800-foot track in Hunter Park. For the past 30 years, RLS has expanded the original railroad and built three buildings and the station. RLS is pleased to offer thousands of people an opportunity to see, hear, and smell what steam locomotion is all about.

SCHEDULE: Second and fourth Sunday, 10 a.m. to 3 p.m., Christmas excluded.

DIRECTIONS: Corner of Columbia and Iowa, approximately one mile northeast of the junction of California 60/91 and I-215.

Sacramento, CA

California State Railroad Museum *EDITOR'S CHOICE*

Museum
Standard and 3'0" gauge

SITE ADDRESS: 2nd & "I" Sts. Sacramento, CA
MAILING ADDRESS: 111 I St. Sacramento, CA 95814
TELEPHONE: (916) 445-6645
E-MAIL: rrmuseuminfo@parks.ca.gov
WEBSITE: www.californiastaterailroadmuseum.org

DESCRIPTION: CSRM's 11-acre complex in Old Sacramento includes the 100,000-square-foot Railroad History Museum, the reconstructed Central Pacific Railroad Passenger Station, and an extensive library and archive. Comprehensive toy trains exhibit, reinstalled galleries, and exhibits highlighting the human face of railroading.

SCHEDULE: Year-round: daily, 10 a.m to 5 p.m.; closed Thanksgiving, Christmas, New Year's.

ADMISSION/FARE: Adults, $6; youth 6-17, $2; children 5 and under, free.

LOCOMOTIVES/ROLLING STOCK: Over 30 restored locomotives and passenger and freight cars on display, dating from the 1860s to present. A Pullman sleeper, streamlined Santa Fe dining car, 1870s Victorian coaches, Great Northern Railway Post Office, and Southern Pacific Cab-Forward No. 4294 are favorites.

SPECIAL EVENTS: February, Sacramento Museum Day; Memorial Day weekend, Sacramento Jazz Jubilee; Labor Day weekend, Gold Rush Days; Thanksgiving weekend, Train Time for Santa; also regular changing exhibits throughout the year.

NEARBY ATTRACTIONS: Old Sacramento (California's largest concentration of restored 19th-century commercial structures), state capitol, Sutter's Fort, Crocker Art Museum, dining, shopping, and lodging.

DIRECTIONS: Directions: In Old Sacramento, adjacent to I-5 exit J St.

Photo courtesy of California State Railroad Museum.

Sacramento, CA

Sacramento Southern Railroad

EDITOR'S CHOICE

Train ride
Standard gauge

SITE ADDRESS: Front & K Sts. Sacramento, CA 95814
MAILING ADDRESS: 111 I St. Sacramento, CA 95814
TELEPHONE: (916) 445-6645
E-MAIL: rrmuseuminfo@parks.ca.gov
WEBSITE: www.californiastaterailroadmuseum.org

DESCRIPTION: The excursion railroad of the California State Railroad Museum was built as a subsidiary of the Southern Pacific at the turn of the century. A 6-mile, 40-minute round trip takes passengers along the Sacramento River in vintage 1920s coaches and open-air cars.

SCHEDULE: Steam: April through September: weekends, hourly from 11 a.m. to 5 p.m.; October through December: selected weekends. Diesel-powered school trains: February through May and October through November, Tuesday and Friday by reservation.

ADMISSION/FARE: Adults, $6; youth 6-17, $3; children 5 and under, free.

LOCOMOTIVES/ROLLING STOCK: No. 10 1942 Porter 0-6-0T, former Granite Rock Company; more.

SPECIAL EVENTS: Memorial Day weekend, Sacramento Jazz Jubilee; Labor Day weekend, Gold Rush Days; October, "Spookmotive" Halloween Trains; Thanksgiving weekend and December, Santa Trains.

NEARBY ATTRACTIONS: Old Sacramento (California's largest concentration of restored 19th-century commercial structures), state capitol, Sutter's Fort, Crocker Art Museum, dining, shopping, and lodging.

DIRECTIONS: Northern terminus is the reconstructed Central Pacific Railroad Freight Depot at Front and "K" Sts. in Old Sacramento.

Photo courtesy of California State Railroad Museum.

TRAVEL TIP: *Bring safety goggles, wear smart shoes*

Ready to go? When riding a tourist train, it's a great idea to bring along a pair of safety glasses so you can ride the open Dutch door. Smart shoes are a must too—wear sturdy, closed-toe shoes, and watch your step!

San Diego, CA

San Diego Model Railroad Museum

Museum
HO, O, N, and Toy scales

ADDRESS: 1649 El Prado San Diego, CA 92101
TELEPHONE: (619) 696-0199
WEBSITE: www.sdmrm.org

DESCRIPTION: One of the largest permanent operating model railroad train exhibitions in North America, with over 27,000 square feet of exhibit space. Features five layouts, toy train gallery, railroad-themed gift shop.

SCHEDULE: Saturday and Sunday, 11 a.m. to 5 p.m.; Tuesday to Friday, 11 a.m. to 4 p.m.

ADMISSION/FARE: Adults $5; students, $3; seniors 65+, $4; active military, $2.50; children under 15, free.

NEARBY ATTRACTIONS: San Diego Zoo, Balboa Park.

DIRECTIONS: Hwy. 163 south to Park Blvd. North on Park Blvd., left on Space Theater Way.

Coupon available, see insert.

San Francisco, CA

San Francisco Cable Car Museum

Trolley ride, Museum

ADDRESS: 1201 Mason St. San Francisco, CA 94108
TELEPHONE: (415) 474-1887
WEBSITE: www.cablecarmuseum.org

DESCRIPTION: Visitors can learn about the inventor, technologies, builders, rapid expansion, near loss, and the ongoing efforts to save and rebuild the cable cars of San Francisco. The museum houses a collection of historic cable cars, photographs, mechanical displays, and gift shop run by the Friends of the Cable Car Museum.

SCHEDULE: Year-round: daily, except New Year's, Easter, Thanksgiving, and Christmas; April 1 through September 30, 10 a.m. to 6 p.m.; October 1 through March 31, 10 a.m. to 5 p.m.

ADMISSION/FARE: Museum: free; cable car: adults and youth 5-17, $5 each way; seniors 65+ and disabled before 7 a.m. and after 9 p.m., $1 each way; 7 a.m. to 9 p.m., $5 each way; one day cable car pass, $10.

LOCOMOTIVES/ROLLING STOCK: 28 Powell St. cars and 12 California St. Cars.

San Francisco Municipal Railway

Train ride
Standard gauge

SITE ADDRESS: 1145 Market St., 3rd Floor San Francisco, CA 94103
MAILING ADDRESS: 949 Presidio Ave. #243 San Francisco, CA 94115
TELEPHONE: (415) 673-6864, trip or (415) 474-1881, museum

DESCRIPTION: The San Francisco Municipal Railway operates city transit services. Along with buses, they operate historic street cars and cable cars (F-Market and Wharves line).

SCHEDULE: Buses, street cars, and cable cars run on a regular schedule throughout the year. Please visit website for details.

ADMISSION/FARE: Adults, $1.50; seniors 65+ and youth 5-17, $.50; children under 4, free. Check website for other rates.

NEARBY ATTRACTIONS: All of San Francisco, Cable Car Museum at Washington and Mason.

DIRECTIONS: The F line operates on Market St., the central thoroughfare. Volunteers' site: Market & Dubcoe (near the US Mint).

Photo courtesy of Carmen Magaña/S.F.P.U.C.

San Jose, CA

History San Jose Trolley Barn

Train ride, Museum
Standard gauge

ADDRESS: 1650 Senter Rd. San Jose, CA 95112-2599
TELEPHONE: (408) 293-2276
WEBSITE: www.historysanjose.org

DESCRIPTION: The wooden shelter of the trolley barn recaptures the form of early California barns of the 1900-1930 era. Constructed in 1984, the structure houses the trolley restoration projects of the California Trolley and Railroad Corporation. Six historic trolley cars have been restored and refurbished. Two of them operate for rides on ½ mile of track on park grounds.

SCHEDULE: Year-round: Saturday and Sunday, 1 to 5 p.m.

ADMISSION/FARE: Free museum and trolley rides.

LOCOMOTIVES/ROLLING STOCK: Trolley car no. 124 ex-San Jose; no. 143 Birney; 168 ex-Porto; horse car no. 7 ex-San Francisco.

NEARBY ATTRACTIONS: Many attractions within a radius of 40 miles.

DIRECTIONS: Located in Kelley Park, which is a short distance from Hwys. 280, 680, and 101. Take the no. 73 bus from downtown.

San Pedro, CA

Port of Los Angeles Waterfront Red Car Line
Trolley ride
Standard gauge

ADDRESS: 425 S Palos Verdes St., PO Box 151 San Pedro, CA 90731
TELEPHONE: (310) 732-3473
E-MAIL: rhenry@portla.org
WEBSITE: www.portoflosangeles.org

DESCRIPTION: A 1½-mile trolley line connects the Port of Los Angeles Cruise Center with waterfront attractions. The line uses restored and replica rolling stock designed to recreate a segment of the Pacific Electric Railway, which once had more than 1,000 miles of rail lines in the Los Angeles area. Rubber-tired trolley-style vehicles connect with downtown San Pedro and Cabrillo Beach.

SCHEDULE: Friday through Monday, 10 a.m. to 6 p.m., every 20 minutes.

ADMISSION/FARE: $1 all day with unlimited transfers between the Red Cars and the rubber-tired trolleys.

LOCOMOTIVES/ROLLING STOCK: Restored Pacific Electric Red Car no. 1058. Replica Red Cars nos. 500 and 501.

NEARBY ATTRACTIONS: Lane Victory-WWII Victory ship, Los Angeles Maritime Museum, Cabrillo Marine Aquarium, Los Angeles Fire Department Harbor Museum.

DIRECTIONS: 110 Harbor Fwy. to Harbor Blvd.

Photo courtesy of Port of Los Angeles Waterfront Red Car Line.

Santa Clara, CA

Rail Journeys West, Inc.

Train ride, Dinner train

ADDRESS: 3770 Flora Vista Ave. #404 Santa Clara, CA 95051
TELEPHONE: (408) 241-7807
WEBSITE: www.railjourneyswest.com

DESCRIPTION: Luxury private rail travel in the US and Canada aboard private railcars.

SCHEDULE: Year-round, by charter or prior arrangement.

ADMISSION/FARE: Varies depending on destination and duration of trip.

LOCOMOTIVES/ROLLING STOCK: California Zephyr dome observation car "Silver Solarium"; SP 3105 Baggage-Sleeper; Dome-Business car "Sierra Hotel."

Santa Clara, CA

South Bay Historical Railroad Society

Museum, Model train layout
HO & N scale

ADDRESS: 1005 Railroad Ave. Santa Clara, CA 95050
TELEPHONE: (408) 243-3969
E-MAIL: information@sbhrs.org
WEBSITE: www.sbhrs.org

DESCRIPTION: The restored historic former Southern Pacific Santa Clara Depot (built 1863) houses a collection of artifacts and memorabilia that highlights the work and lives of local railroaders, with operational HO and N-scale model railroad displays. The depot and a restored tower are adjacent to the Caltrain commute and Union Pacific rail lines, where observers can view railroad operations of peninsula commute trains, Amtrak and Altamont Corridor Express (ACE) passenger trains, and UP freight traffic.

SCHEDULE: Tuesday, 6 p.m. to 9 p.m.; Saturday, 10 a.m. to 3 p.m.

ADMISSION/FARE: Donations accepted, except for special events with fixed fee.

SPECIAL EVENTS: April and November, Model Train Show and Open House; see website for exact dates, times, and admission fees.

NEARBY ATTRACTIONS: Great America Theme Park, Tech Museum of Innovation, Children's Discovery Museum, and San Jose Sharks Hockey.

DIRECTIONS: Across from Santa Clara University, one block east of CA SR 82 (El Camino Real). From I-880, take the Alameda exit west, until it becomes El Camino Real. From US101, take the De La Cruz Blvd. exit to Lafayette St. Turn right on Lafayette, right on El Camino Real, then left on Benton St., to Railroad Ave. The website includes a map link.

Sonoma, CA

Sonoma Train Town Railroad
Miniature train ride

ADDRESS: 20264 Broadway Hwy. 12, PO Box 656 Sonoma, CA 95476
TELEPHONE: (707) 938-3912
WEBSITE: www.traintown.com

DESCRIPTION: Fifteen-inch-gauge live steam locomotives and diesel replicas pull passenger trains on 1¼ miles of track over 5 bridges and trestles and through 2 tunnels. Railroad shops and a complete miniature town are built to the same ¼ scale as the railroad. The 47-foot clock tower and station are modeled after Oakland's 16th St. Depot. Train Town also includes three full-sized cabooses, dating from the 1930s and 40s.

SCHEDULE: June 1 through Labor Day, daily; year-round, Friday through Sunday; closed Christmas and Thanksgiving, open.

ADMISSION/FARE: Adults and children 15 months to 15, $3.75; seniors, $3.25.

LOCOMOTIVES/ROLLING STOCK: SW 600 Custom Locomotive, 1995; SW 1200 Custom Locomotive 1992; 2-6-0 Mogul-Winton 1960 Engr.; plus 20 assorted railcars.

NEARBY ATTRACTIONS: Napa Valley Wine Train.

DIRECTIONS: Broadway (Hwy. 12), one mile south of Sonoma Town Square.

Western Railway Museum

Train ride, Museum, and Display
Standard gauge

EDITOR'S CHOICE

ADDRESS: 5848 State Hwy. 12 Suisun City, CA 94585
TELEPHONE: (707) 374-2978
E-MAIL: info@wrm.org
WEBSITE: www.wrm.org

DESCRIPTION: A 9.5-mile interurban round trip over re-electrified historic Sacramento Northern Railway in rural Solano County.

SCHEDULE: Year-round, weekends, 10:30 a.m. to 5 p.m.; June to Labor Day, Wednesday to Sunday, 10:30 a.m. to 5 p.m.

ADMISSION/FARE: Adults, $8; seniors 65+, $7; children 14 and under, $5.

LOCOMOTIVES/ROLLING STOCK: Wood interurbans: Peninsular Railway no. 52; Petaluma & Santa Rosa no. 63; Sacramento Northern no. 1005. Steel interurbans: Napa Valley no. 63; Key System units 182 and 187. Steel locomotives: CCT no. 7; SN nos. 652, 654; many streetcars.

SPECIAL EVENTS: April, special Montezuma Hills Trains; October, Pumpkin Patch Trains.

NEARBY ATTRACTIONS: Marine World, Jelly Belly, and Anheuser-Busch factory tours.

DIRECTIONS: I-80, 12 miles from Suisan/Rio Vista; or I-5, 23 miles from Rio Vista/Fairfield.

Photo courtesy of Bart Nadeau.

KEY TO SYMBOLS

♿ Handicapped accessible	🍴 Restaurant	🎨 Arts and crafts	arm Association of Railway Museums
P Parking	🪑 Picnic area	IMI Memberships available	TRAIN Tourist Railway Association, Inc.
P Bus/RV parking	🚃 Dining car	✉ Send S.A.S.E. for brochure	AMTRAK Amtrak service to nearby city
🎁 Gift, book, or museum shop	✨ Excursions	NRHP National Register of Historic Places	VIA VIA service to nearby city
☕ Refreshments	TOUR Guided tours	VISA MasterCard DISCOVER AMERICAN EXPRESS Card	Credit cards accepted

Sunol, CA

Niles Canyon Railway
(Pacific Locomotive Association, Inc.)

Train ride, Museum
Standard gauge

SITE ADDRESS: Sunol Depot 6, Kilkare Rd. Sunol, CA 94586
MAILING ADDRESS: PO Box 2247, Niles Station Fremont, CA 94536-0247
TELEPHONE: (925) 862-9063
WEBSITE: www.ncry.org

DESCRIPTION: A 70-minute ride through scenic Niles Canyon, over the final leg of the original transcontinental railroad. Steam locomotives pulled trains through Niles Canyon for eighty years before diesels took over in the 1950s. Train rides are now available to the public year-round from the 1880s depot in Sunol. The rare and unusual railroad equipment has been collected since the early 1960s.

SCHEDULE: Year-round: first and third Sunday; summer: every Sunday. Check website.

ADMISSION/FARE: Adults, $10; seniors, $8; children 3-12, $5; children under 3, free.

LOCOMOTIVES/ROLLING STOCK: 10 diesels, eight steam locomotives, 12 passenger coaches, one dome car, six cabooses. Check website for equipment roster.

SPECIAL EVENTS: December, Train of Lights. Check website for speeder rides.

NEARBY ATTRACTIONS: Southeast corner of the San Francisco Bay Area, restored Essanay film studio (studio of Charlie Chaplin), antique stores and restaurants.

DIRECTIONS: One mile west of I-680 on route 84. Check website for map.

Photo courtesy of Alan Frank.

Thousand Oaks, CA

Walt Disney's Carolwood Barn and Museum

Museum

ADDRESS: 1032 Amberton Ln. Thousand Oaks, CA 91320-3514
TELEPHONE: (805) 498-2336
E-MAIL: scbroggie@msn.com
WEBSITE: www.carolwood.com

DESCRIPTION: Walt Disney was one of America's greatest railfans; he used his personal financial resources to preserve real steam railroading. He also helped build, and enjoyed sharing, an intricately detailed miniature live steam home railroad, which provided the launching point for his vision of family-oriented, themed amusement parks.

SCHEDULE: Third Sunday, 11 a.m. to 3 p.m.; Labor Day and Memorial Day weekends.

ADMISSION/FARE: Free.

NEARBY ATTRACTIONS: East of Traveltown on Zoo Drive, Griffith Park.

DIRECTIONS: Interstate 5 and 134, exit Forest Lawn Dr. to Zoo Dr.

Coupon available, see insert.

Tilden Regional Park, CA

Redwood Valley Railway
Train ride
15" gauge, 5" scale, Narrow gauge

SITE ADDRESS: Tilden Regional Park, CA 94705
MAILING ADDRESS: 2950 Magnolia St. Berkeley, CA 94705
TELEPHONE: (510) 548-6100
WEBSITE: www.redwoodvalleyrailway.com

DESCRIPTION: A 1¼-mile ride in the East Bay Hills through redwood groves. Authentic scale narrow gauge steam equipment and trackwork. Everyone is welcome to ride the trains, even dogs.

SCHEDULE: Year-round: weekends and holidays, 11 a.m. to 6 p.m., weather permitting; weekdays, mid-June through Labor Day, 12 to 5 p.m.

ADMISSION/FARE: Single ticket, $1.75; family ticket (5), $7; children under 2, free.

LOCOMOTIVES/ROLLING STOCK: 2-4-2 "Laurel" no. 4, 4-4-0 "Fern" no. 5, 4-6-0 "Sequoia" no. 11, 2-6-2 "Oak" no. 7, gondolas and stock cars.

DIRECTIONS: Off Hwy. 24 at Fish Ranch Rd.

Willits, CA

Sierra Railroad/Skunk Train/Willits

Train ride

EDITOR'S CHOICE

ADDRESS: 299 E Commercial St. Willits, CA 95490
TELEPHONE: (866) 45-SKUNK or (707) 964-6371
E-MAIL: info@sierrarailroad.com
WEBSITE: www.skunktrain.com

DESCRIPTION: A 90-minute ride to Wolf Tree in the mountains. Along this scenic trip, passengers will see the California Redwoods.

SCHEDULE: Daily service in Spring and Fall. Weekend service in Winter.

ADMISSION/FARE: Adults, $20; kids, $10.

LOCOMOTIVES/ROLLING STOCK: 1955 EMD GP 9 nos. 64, 65, 66 M100, M300 motorcars.

SPECIAL EVENTS: Frontier Days, Christmas Train.

NEARBY ATTRACTIONS: Home of the famous racehorse, Seabiscuit; camping; Roots of Motive Power-Antique Steam Logging Equipment Display.

Woodland, CA

Sacramento RiverTrain

Dinner train

SITE ADDRESS: East and Main St. Woodland, CA 95776
MAILING ADDRESS: 220 S Sierra Ave. Oakdale, CA 95361
TELEPHONE: (800) 942-6387
E-MAIL: info@sierrarailroad.com
WEBSITE: www.sacramentorivertrain.com

DESCRIPTION: Train travels 28 miles from Woodland to West Sacramento, over one of the longest wooden trestles in the west, along the Sacramento River, and through wildlife refuge and scenic farmland. A common carrier railroad company, the Yolo Shortline Railroad Company began rail operations in February 1991 and purchased two branch lines from the Union Pacific Railroad.

SCHEDULE: Year-round, every week.

ADMISSION/FARE: Most trips include trip, meal, and entertainment; price range: $30 to $65.

LOCOMOTIVES/ROLLING STOCK: Nos. 131, 132, and 133 GP-9 EMD diesels, former Southern Pacific.

NEARBY ATTRACTIONS: Soldier Field, Navy Pier, Shedd Aquarium, Field Museum, Adler Planetarium, Art Institute, Wrigley Field, USCellular Field.

DIRECTIONS: By car: Lake Shore Dr. south to 57th St. By train: Metra trains stop at the 55th/56th/57th St. station, two blocks from the Museum's north exit. Turn left as you exit the station. Chicago South Shore & South Bend trains stop at the 59th St. station.

Downers Grove, IL

American Orient Express
Train ride

ADDRESS: 5100 Main St., Ste. 300 Downers Grove, IL 60515
TELEPHONE: (800) 320-4206 or (630) 663-4550
E-MAIL: info@americanorientexpress.com
WEBSITE: www.americanorientexpress.com

DESCRIPTION: The American Orient Express offers deluxe 7- to 10-night rail journeys throughout the United States and Mexico. Tours include Copper Canyon and Colonial Mexico, Antebellum South, Antebellum South and the Civil War, Coastal Culinary Explorer, Great Northwest and Rockies, National Parks of the West, Rockies and Sierras, American Southwest and Great Transcontinental Rail Journey.

SCHEDULE: Tours: January to November; office hours, 8 a.m. to 5 p.m., CST.

ADMISSION/FARE: Prices based on tour and accommodations. Fares start at $1,695 per person, Vintage Pullman, based on double occupancy.

Elizabeth, IL

Elizabeth Depot Museum EDITOR'S CHOICE
Museum

SITE ADDRESS: Myrtle St. Elizabeth, IL 61028-0115
MAILING ADDRESS: PO Box 115 Elizabeth, IL 61028-0115
TELEPHONE: (815) 858-3355

DESCRIPTION: This depot museum displays artifacts of the Chicago Great Western and other railroads. The depot serviced the nearby Winston Tunnel, the longest railroad tunnel in Illinois. The museum features a working telegraph, operating HO-scale and G-scale model railroads, and a Milwaukee Road caboose.

SCHEDULE: May through October: weekends, 1 to 4 p.m.

ADMISSION/FARE: Adults, $2; children under 18, free.

Chicago, IL
Historic Pullman Foundation
Museum

ADDRESS: 11141 S Cottage Grove Ave. Chicago, IL 60628
TELEPHONE: (773) 785-8901
E-MAIL: foundation@pullmanil.org
WEBSITE: www.pullmanil.org

DESCRIPTION: The Historic Pullman Foundation operates the Pullman Visitor Center, which gives an overview of George Pullman, the Pullman Company, and Mr. Pullman's 1880s town.

SCHEDULE: Year-round: Tuesday through Sunday, 11 a.m. to 3 p.m.

ADMISSION/FARE: Call for prices.

NEARBY ATTRACTIONS: Ridge Historic District, Downtown Chicago, Museum of Science and Industry, riverboat casinos, Sandridge Nature Center, International Harborside Golf Course, River Oaks Mill, Calumet Park Beach, East Side Historical Society, Wolf Lake, South Suburban Genealogy Society.

DIRECTIONS: I-94 to 111th St. (exit 66A), travel west four blocks. Metra Electric stops at 111th St./Pullman, 115th St./Kensington, and downtown Chicago.

Chicago, IL
Museum of Science and Industry **EDITOR'S CHOICE**
Museum, Display, Model railroad layout type
Standard gauge

ADDRESS: 57th St and Lake Shore Dr. Chicago, IL 60637
TELEPHONE: (877) GO-TO-MSI
WEBSITE: www.msichicago.org

DESCRIPTION: The Great Train Story, the museum's new model railroad exhibit, is a 3,500-square-foot layout that depicts the BNSF Railway's winding journey between Chicago and Seattle. Historic steam and diesel trains are also on display.

SCHEDULE: Year-round, except December 25; hours vary; check website for detailed schedule.

ADMISSION/FARE: Adults, $9; seniors 65+, $7.50; children 3-11, $5; Chicago residents receive a discount.

LOCOMOTIVES/ROLLING STOCK: New York Central 4-4-0 no. 999, the first locomotive to exceed 100 mph; Burlington Route Pioneer Zephyr, first streamlined diesel train.

COLORADO

Boulder, CO

Boulder County Railway Historical Society

Display

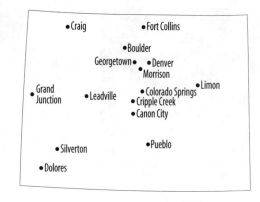

- •Craig
- •Fort Collins
- •Boulder
- Georgetown• •Denver
- Morrison
- •Grand Junction
- •Leadville
- •Colorado Springs •Limon
- •Cripple Creek
- •Canon City
- •Silverton
- •Pueblo
- •Dolores

ADDRESS: Valmont & Indian Rds.
PO Box 149 Boulder, CO 80544
TELEPHONE: (303) 809-6105
E-MAIL: amjm@indra.com
WEBSITE: www.boulderrail.org

DESCRIPTION: Display of railroad equipment from the Boulder County area. Formed in 1997, the Society assists the City of Boulder in the restoration of three pieces of narrow gauge railroad equipment and educates the public about the regional history of railroads.

SCHEDULE: Daily, self-guided tours.

ADMISSION/FARE: Free.

LOCOMOTIVES/ROLLING STOCK: Great Western GP9 no. 296; Public Service Co. of Colorado GE 80-ton locomotive no. 14; Colorado & Southern coach no. 543 and boxcar; Burlington Northern caboose 12300 D&RGW track panel car AX3219; Denver, South Park & Pacific boxcar no. 608, plus other D&RGW narrow gauge cars.

SPECIAL EVENTS: Work day: third Saturday, 10 a.m. to 2 p.m.; volunteers welcome.

DIRECTIONS: Take Pearl St. east from Boulder. After 55th St., Pearl becomes Valmont Rd. Turn left on 61st St. and then left on Indian Rd. Follow Indian Rd. to site.

Photo courtesy of Jason Midyette.

Cañon City, CO

Royal Gorge Route Railroad

Train ride, Dinner train
Standard gauge

SITE ADDRESS: 410 Water St. Cañon City, CO 81212
MAILING ADDRESS: PO Box 859 Georgetown, CO 80444
TELEPHONE: (888) RAILS-4-U or (303) 569-1000
WEBSITE: www.royalgorgeroute.com

DESCRIPTION: Passengers can experience the grandeur of traveling by train through the spectacular Royal Gorge. The train operates alongside the Arkansas River from Cañon City, traveling over the famous "Hanging Bridge" where the canyon rim towers 1,000 feet. This is a 24-mile, 2-hour round trip ride.

SCHEDULE: Mid-May through mid-October, daily departures, coach, club, and lunch service available; mid-October through mid-May, Saturday and Sunday (except Christmas), 12:30 p.m.; March through December, Saturday evening dinner trains; call for more information, reservations required.

ADMISSION/FARE: Round trip coach: adults, $28.95; children 3-12, $18.50; children under 3, no charge if carried on lap. Dinner train and lunch service: call for pricing information.

LOCOMOTIVES/ROLLING STOCK: EMD F7A nos. 402, 403; VIA Rail CC&F passenger car nos. 3225, 5497, 5541, 5562, 5580, 5586, club car 650; three super domes, Milwaukee Road nos. 50 and 56, and Santa Fe no. 507. EMD SD9 no. 5305 and EMD GP7 no. 2238.

SPECIAL EVENTS: Year-round, Murder Mystery Dinner Trains; call for schedule.

NEARBY ATTRACTIONS: Royal Gorge Bridge, Manitou & Pikes Peak Railway, rafting, horseback riding, camping.

DIRECTIONS: Located at the Santa Fe Depot, 401 Water St. (one block south on Third St. off Hwy. 50). Cañon City is 45 miles southwest of Colorado Springs.

Photo courtesy of Ron Ruhoff.
See ad on page A-6.

Colorado Springs, CO
Pikes Peak Historical Street Railway
*Car ride, Museum, Display, Model train layout,
Working restoration shop*

SITE ADDRESS: 2333 Steel Dr. Colorado Springs, CO 80901
MAILING ADDRESS: PO Box 544 Colorado Springs, CO 80901
TELEPHONE: (719) 475-9508 or (719) 471-2619
WEBSITE: http://colospringstrolleys.home.att.net

DESCRIPTION: Museum with guided tours, working restoration shop, and a large equipment storage yard. Car ride is currently 650 feet long.

SCHEDULE: Saturday, 10 a.m. to 4 p.m., excludes Christmas and New Year's weeks; Tuesday through Friday, appointments available; closed Sunday and Monday; all holidays except Thanksgiving and Christmas, 10 a.m. to 4 p.m.

ADMISSION/FARE: Adults, $3; children 12 and under, $1.50.

LOCOMOTIVES/ROLLING STOCK: PCC SEPTA 2093, 2102, 2107, 2097, 2109, 2114, 2119, 2131, 2722; LARY 3101; Birney FCMR 22; CS&I 59, 48; DTC box motor 724 & 770; DRGW Caboose 1501; SP baggage 6777; DRGW 40-foot box 60294; D&RGW Bulk Head Flat Car no. 22446.

SPECIAL EVENTS: Annual Rock Island Days Festival held in conjunction with the annual meeting of the Rock Island Technical Society.

NEARBY ATTRACTIONS: Union Pacific & BNSF joint line on west side; see 30 to 35 trains per day.

DIRECTIONS: I-25 to Fillmore St. (exit 145). Exit east (½ block) to first traffic light, then south on Steel Dr. Road ends in yard (½ mile).

Photo courtesy of PPHSRF.
Coupon available, see insert.

Craig, CO
Moffat County Visitors Center
Museum

ADDRESS: 360 E Victory Way Craig, CO 81625
TELEPHONE: (970) 824-5689
E-MAIL: craigcoc@craig-chamber.com
WEBSITE: www.craig-chamber.com

DESCRIPTION: Tours of private Pullman railcar of railroad magnate David Moffat. The car was named for his only child, Marcia.

SCHEDULE: Memorial to Labor Day: Monday through Friday, 9 a.m. to 5 p.m.

ADMISSION/FARE: Donations accepted.

LOCOMOTIVES/ROLLING STOCK: Private Pullman car of David Moffat, founder of the famed Moffat Railroad.

NEARBY ATTRACTIONS: Adjacent to City Park and the wave pool.

DIRECTIONS: Directly across from Moffat County Visitor's Center.

Photo courtesy of Patricia Stauffer.

Craig, CO
Museum of Northwest Colorado
Museum

ADDRESS: 590 Yampa Ave. Craig, CO 81625
TELEPHONE: (970) 824-6360
E-MAIL: musnwco@moffatcounty.net
WEBSITE: www.museumnwco.org

DESCRIPTION: Moffat Road memorabilia was carefully collected over many years by a local collector, and is now a permanent exhibit. In 1903, David Moffat began construction on the Denver Northwestern & Pacific Railroad; it began in Denver, continued northwesterly, and ended in Craig. In 1913, the name was changed to the Denver & Salt Lake Railroad but was changed again in 1947, when it was reorganized and merged with the Denver & Rio Grande Western.

SCHEDULE: Monday through Friday, 9 a.m. to 5 p.m.; Saturday, 10 a.m. to 4 p.m.

ADMISSION/FARE: Free.

Photo courtesy of Museum of Northwest Colorado.

Cripple Creek, CO
Cripple Creek & Victor Narrow Gauge Railroad
Train ride

ADDRESS: 520 E Carr, PO Box 459 Cripple Creek, CO 80813
TELEPHONE: (719) 689-2640
E-MAIL: www.cripplecreekrailroad.com

DESCRIPTION: The four-mile, round trip tour lasts 45 minutes and goes over a portion of the old Midland Terminal Railroad. The train runs south from Cripple Creek past the old MT wye, over a reconstructed trestle, and past many historic mines to the deserted mining town of Anaconda.

SCHEDULE: Mid-May to mid-October: daily, 9:30 a.m. to 5:30 p.m., every 45 minutes.

ADMISSION/FARE: Adults, $10; seniors, $9; children 3-12, $5; children under 3, free.

LOCOMOTIVES/ROLLING STOCK: No. 1 1902 Orenstein & Koppel 0-4-4-0, no. 2 1936 Henschel 0-4-0, no. 3 1927 Porter 0-4-0T, no. 13 1946 Bagnall 0-4-0T.

NEARBY ATTRACTIONS: Cripple Creek District Museum, Mueller State Park.

DIRECTIONS: From Colorado Springs west on Hwy. 24 to Hwy. 67 south to Cripple Creek. Trains leave from former Midland Terminal Railroad Bull Hill Depot.

Photo courtesy of James Birmingham.

Denver, CO

Forney Museum of Transportation

Museum

ADDRESS: 4303 Brighton Blvd. Denver, CO 80216
TELEPHONE: (303) 297-1113
E-MAIL: museum@forneymuseum.com
WEBSITE: www.forneymuseum.com

DESCRIPTION: The transportation museum features over 500 exhibits relating to historical transportation. Included is the Forney tank type locomotive, which was designed and patented by Mathhias Nace Forney. It was built by several manufacturers and used on elevated railways. Called "Little Giants," over 500 were in service at the turn of the century.

SCHEDULE: Year-round: Monday through Saturday, 9 a.m. to 5 p.m.

ADMISSION/FARE: Adults, $7; seniors, $6; youth 11-15, $4.50; children 5-10, $3.50; children under 5, free.

LOCOMOTIVES/ROLLING STOCK: Union Pacific "Big Boy" steam locomotive no. 4005; Rotary snowplow; C&NW 4-6-0 steam locomotive no. 444; Pikes Peak Diner 804; Forney locomotive; CBQ Business car; 2 cabooses; 2 wooden coaches; crane; German locomotive no. 7.

NEARBY ATTRACTIONS: Minutes from downtown, Ocean Journey, the Children's Museum, Six Flags, Elitch Gardens, and Coors Field.

DIRECTIONS: From I-25 exit on I-70 east, then exit on Brighton Blvd. and go southwest two blocks. Turn right into the museum driveway when you see the sign.

Coupon available, see insert.

Denver, CO
Platte Valley Trolley
Trolley ride

SITE ADDRESS: Water St. Denver, CO 80211
MAILING ADDRESS: PO Box 1348 Denver, CO 80201
TELEPHONE: (303) 458-6255
E-MAIL: mail@denvertrolley.org
WEBSITE: www.denvertrolley.org

DESCRIPTION: The Denver Sightseeing route, about four miles round trip, lasts 30 minutes. The Route 84 Excursion includes an additional five miles and many trestles.

SCHEDULE: April 1 to May 31: Friday to Sunday; June 1 to September 5: Thursday to Sunday; September 6 to October 31: Friday to Sunday. Riverfront Ride trips, every 30 minutes from 12 to 3:30 p.m.; Route 84 Excursion, 12:30 p.m.

ADMISSION/FARE: Sightseeing route: adults, $3; children and seniors, $1. Route 84 Excursion: adults, $4; seniors, $3; children, $2.

LOCOMOTIVES/ROLLING STOCK: Reproduction Brill open trolley, diesel-powered, no. 1977.

NEARBY ATTRACTIONS: Children's Museum, Colorado's Ocean Journey Aquarium, Six Flags.

DIRECTIONS: I-25 exit 211, 23rd St. Turn east to Water St. and follow the signs.

Photo courtesy of John Hammond.

Denver, CO
Ski Train **EDITOR'S CHOICE**
Train ride
Standard gauge

ADDRESS: 555 17th St. Ste. 2400 Denver, CO 80202
TELEPHONE: (303) 296-4754
WEBSITE: www.skitrain.com

DESCRIPTION: Begun in 1940, this 130-mile round trip runs on the historic Moffat Line. There are 14 passenger cars that leave Denver's Union Station, travel west, climb about 4,000 feet, and pass through 28 tunnels before reaching the 6.2-mile-long Moffat Tunnel. It is the highest railroad tunnel in the United States and passes under the Continental Divide. The train stops near the ski lifts of Winter Park.

SCHEDULE: January, Saturday and Sunday; February, Friday through Sunday; March, Thursday through Sunday; Summer, Saturday.

ADMISSION/FARE: $44.

LOCOMOTIVES/ROLLING STOCK: Three leased Amtrak F40PHs and 17 passenger cars: 9 coach cars, 2 cafe-lounge cars, 3 club cars, and 3 private luxury cars.

DIRECTIONS: Train departs from Denver Union Station.

Dolores, CO

Galloping Goose
Historical Society of Dolores, Inc.

Train ride, Museum, Display, Model train layout

SITE ADDRESS: 421 Railroad Ave. Dolores, CO 81323
MAILING ADDRESS: PO Box 297 Dolores, CO 81323
TELEPHONE: (970) 882-4767
E-MAIL: gghs5@fone.net

DESCRIPTION: The ride is 320 feet. By request, it travels up and back, 640 feet.

SCHEDULE: May 15 through October 15: Monday through Saturday, 9 a.m. to 5 p.m.

ADMISSION/FARE: Free, donations welcome.

LOCOMOTIVES/ROLLING STOCK: RGS Galloping Goose motor no. 5.

SPECIAL EVENTS: Memorial Day, Raft Days, Escalante Days, Railfest, June Cumbres & Toltec, August D&SNGR.

NEARBY ATTRACTIONS: Mesa Verde, Anasazi Heritage Center, McPhee Reservoir.

DIRECTIONS: Southwest Colorado, 45 miles west of Durango, Hwy. 145 north.

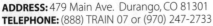

Durango, CO

Durango & Silverton Narrow Gauge Railroad

Train ride, Museum
Narrow gauge

ADDRESS: 479 Main Ave. Durango, CO 81301
TELEPHONE: (888) TRAIN 07 or (970) 247-2733
E-MAIL: info@durangotrain.com
WEBSITE: www.durangotrain.com

DESCRIPTION: Coal-fired, steam-powered scenic train excursions go through the remote San Juan wilderness.

SCHEDULE: Summer excursions: Silverton, 90-mile round trip, full day; winter excursions: Cascade Canyon, half day. Call or visit website for updated schedule.

ADMISSION/FARE: Fares vary from $22 through $89; check website for details.

LOCOMOTIVES/ROLLING STOCK: K-28 nos. 473, 476, 478; K-36 nos. 480, 481, 482, 486. Luxury cars B-2 "Cinco Animas," B-3 "Nomad," B-7 "General Palmer," and caboose 0500 are available for private charter.

SPECIAL EVENTS: Winter photo special, Narrow Gauge Day, opening day to Silverton, 8th annual Durango & Silverton Narrow Gauge RAILFEST, Cascade Canyon Winter Train, Polar Express™, annual New Year's Eve midnight train.

NEARBY ATTRACTIONS: Durango is a quaint boom mining town in Southwest Colorado, three hours north of Albuquerque and one hour west of Mesa Verde National Park.

DIRECTIONS: At the intersection of US Hwys. 550 and 160 in Southwest Colorado. Depot located at the far south end of Main Ave.

Photo courtesy of D & S.
See ad on page A-16.

Fort Collins, CO

Fort Collins Municipal Railway

Trolley ride

ADDRESS: Roosevelt St. and Oak St., PO Box 635 Fort Collins, CO 80522
TELEPHONE: (970) 224-5372
WEBSITE: www.fortnet.org/trolley

DESCRIPTION: The 3-mile, round trip trolley ride travels in a peaceful residential setting on its original right-of-way. The restored Fort Collins Birney safety car no. 21 was one of four cars purchased by the City in 1919. Along with additional Birneys, they provided daily service until 1951. It now operates along the rebuilt line on West Mountain Ave.

SCHEDULE: May through September: weekends and holidays, 12 to 5 p.m.

ADMISSION/FARE: Adults, $1; seniors, $.75; children under 12, $0.50.

LOCOMOTIVES/ROLLING STOCK: 1919 Birney single-truck streetcar no. 21.

SPECIAL EVENTS: Mother's Day, Father's Day, Fourth of July.

NEARBY ATTRACTIONS: Rocky Mountain National Park, Colorado State University, and Poudre Canyon.

DIRECTIONS: From I-25 take exit 269 (Colorado 14, Mulberry St.) west to Jackson St. Right on Jackson St. to Oak St. Left on Oak St. to Depot at Roosevelt St. in City Park.

Golden, CO
Colorado Railroad Museum
Museum
36" and Standard gauge

SITE ADDRESS: 17155 W 44th Ave. Golden, CO 80402
MAILING ADDRESS: PO Box 10 Golden, CO 80402
TELEPHONE: (800) 365-6263 or (303) 279-4591
E-MAIL: mail@crrm.org
WEBSITE: www.crrm.org

DESCRIPTION: An extensive collection of Colorado railroad memorabilia and more than 70 historic cars and locomotives, both standard and narrow gauge. It is the home of the Denver HO Model Railroad Club and the Denver Garden Railway Society. "Galloping Goose" motorcars operate on selected weekends.

SCHEDULE: Museum: daily, 9 a.m. to 5 p.m.; closed Thanksgiving, Christmas, and New Year's; call for hours on Easter, Christmas Eve, and New Year's Eve. Museum, library, gift store: Thursday, until 9 p.m.; museum grounds close at 5 p.m.; June, July, and August: until 6 p.m.

ADMISSION/FARE: Adults, $7; seniors 60+, $6; children 2-16, $4; children under 2 and museum members, free; family, $16.

LOCOMOTIVES/ROLLING STOCK: Three Rio Grande Southern "Galloping Goose" motorcars; D&RGW 2-8-0 no. 683; Rio Grande Zephyr EMD F9s 5771 and 5762; Chicago Burlington & Quincy 4-8-4 no. 5629; Santa Fe Super Chief 1937 observation car "Navajo;" more.

NEARBY ATTRACTIONS: Coors Brewery, Buffalo Bill Museum, Blackhawk and Central City casinos.

DIRECTIONS: Twelve miles west of downtown Denver. I-70 westbound exit 265 or eastbound exit 266 to W 44th Ave.

Photo courtesy of Bob Jensen.
See ad on page A-19.

Grand Junction, CO
Grand Valley Model Railroad Club
Museum, Display, Model train layout

SITE ADDRESS: 3073 F Rd. Grand Junction, CO 81504
MAILING ADDRESS: PO Box 4101 Grand Junction, CO 81502-4101
TELEPHONE: (970) 523-5900
E-MAIL: waynek9240@aol.com

DESCRIPTION: Depicting railroading in western Colorado, the model railroad layout is located in Cross Orchards Living History Farm, a part of The Museum of Western Colorado.

SCHEDULE: Tuesday, 7 p.m.; fourth Saturday of each month, 9 a.m.

ADMISSION/FARE: Donations welcome.

SPECIAL EVENTS: Open for all museum special events and the last three weekends in December.

NEARBY ATTRACTIONS: NRHS, Rio Grande Chapter, Uintah Railcar display.

DIRECTIONS: On F Rd. between 30 and 31 Rds.

Photo courtesy of Mickey Nuttall.

Leadville, CO
Leadville Colorado & Southern Railroad **EDITOR'S CHOICE**
Train ride

ADDRESS: 326 E 7th St. Leadville, CO 80461
TELEPHONE: (866) 386-3936 or (719) 486-3936
E-MAIL: info@leadville-train.com
WEBSITE: www.leadville-train.com

DESCRIPTION: The 22.5-mile, 2½-hour train trip follows the headwaters of the Arkansas River to an elevation of 11,120 feet, over an old narrow gauge roadbed converted to standard gauge in the 1940s. The train leaves from the restored 1894 railroad depot (formerly Colorado & Southern, built originally for the Denver, South Park & Pacific) in Leadville. It stops at the French Gulch water tower to view Mt. Ebert. Enclosed, open, and sun cars are available along with snacks, souvenirs, and restrooms in the boxcars.

ADMISSION/FARE: Adults, $26.50; children 4-12, $15; children 3 and under, free.

LOCOMOTIVES/ROLLING STOCK: 1955 EMD GP9 no. 1714, former Burlington Northern; EMD GP-9 no. 1918; Burlington Route 2-8-0 no. 641, built by Brooks in 1906.

NEARBY ATTRACTIONS: National Mining Hall of Fame Museum, Tabor Opera House, Matchless Mine Heritage Museum, Healy House and Dexter Cabin, Tabor Home.

DIRECTIONS: 3 blocks east of Harrison Ave.

Photo courtesy of Barbara Mallette, The Leadville Picture Company.

Limon, CO

Limon Heritage Museum & Railroad Park
Museum

ADDRESS: 899 First St. Limon, CO 80828
TELEPHONE: (719) 775-8605
E-MAIL: limonmuseum@hotmail.com

DESCRIPTION: A Rock Island/Union Pacific museum with 5 rail cars and an N-scale model train. The museum focuses on the local history of the Colorado high plains, the Union Pacific and Rock Island Railroads, ranching, and farming. Located in the restored Union Depot, the display includes a saddle boxcar, a lunch counter-diner, a working N scale model of Limon's bustling 1940s yard, and more.

SCHEDULE: June 1 through August 31: Monday through Saturday, 1 to 8 p.m.

ADMISSION/FARE: Free.

LOCOMOTIVES/ROLLING STOCK: 1880 wooden box car; Rock Island/Union Pacific snow plow; Union Pacific steel caboose; 1914 rail lunch counter diner; Milwaukee combination car.

SPECIAL EVENTS: First Saturday in June, Western Festival and Parade; First Saturday in August, Limon Heritage Festival.

NEARBY ATTRACTIONS: 75 miles from Colorado Railroad Museum, Golden.

DIRECTIONS: One mile off I-70, exits 359-361. Located in downtown Limon on 1st St.

Photo courtesy of Limon Heritage Museum.

Manitou Springs, CO

Manitou & Pikes Peak Railway

Train ride
Standard gauge

EDITOR'S CHOICE

ADDRESS: 515 Ruxton Ave. Manitou Springs, CO 80829
TELEPHONE: (719) 685-5401
WEBSITE: www.cograilway.com

DESCRIPTION: Opened in 1891, the Pikes Peak Cog Railway has taken millions of people to the 14,110-foot summit of Pikes Peak. Amid cascading streams and forests of aspen and pine, this railway takes riders in comfort and safety past panoramas that inspired "America the Beautiful." Views extend from the Great Plains to the Continental Divide.

ADMISSION/FARE: Adults, $29; children 3-12, $17.

LOCOMOTIVES/ROLLING STOCK: Swiss Locomotive Works: nos. 25, 24, 18, and 19 (216-passenger railcars); nos. 17, 16, 15, 14 (80-passenger railcars); no. 22 snow plow; no. 23 work car; no. 12 coach, 1955; nos. 9 and 11 GE diesel-electric locomotives; no. 4 Baldwin steam locomotive, Vauclain Compound, 1896.

NEARBY ATTRACTIONS: The Pikes Peak region is home to more than 30 attractions.

DIRECTIONS: 6 miles west of Colorado Springs.

Photo courtesy of M & PP Railway.

Morrison, CO

Tiny Town Railroad

Train ride, Display

ADDRESS: 6249 S Turkey Creek Rd. Morrison, CO 80465
TELEPHONE: (303) 697-6829
WEBSITE: www.tinytownrailroad.com

DESCRIPTION: A ¼ to ½ scale live steam railroad takes passengers on a one-mile loop around Tiny Town, the oldest miniature (⅙-sized) town in the U.S.

SCHEDULE: Memorial Day through Labor Day, daily; May, September, and October, weekends, 10 a.m. to 5 p.m.

ADMISSION/FARE: Display: adults, $3; children 3-12, $2. Train: $1.

LOCOMOTIVES/ROLLING STOCK: Two live steam, two diesel locomotives, passenger cars.

DIRECTIONS: About 30 minutes southwest of Denver, off Hwy. 285.

Pueblo, CO

Pueblo Railway Museum
Train ride, Museum, Display
Standard gauge
Radio frequency: 160.485

ADDRESS: 132 W B St. Pueblo, CO 81003
TELEPHONE: (719) 251-5024, tours or (719) 544-1773, office
E-MAIL: info@pueblorailway.org
WEBSITE: www.pueblorailway.org

DESCRIPTION: This museum concentrates on the golden age of railroading between 1900 and 1960. There are static steam, static and operating diesel and traction, freight & passenger cars in the coach yard behind Union Depot. Artifacts and rotating displays can be viewed in Southeastern Colorado Heritage Center, 201 W B St. Locomotive cab, caboose, and coach rides are offered during special events.

SCHEDULE: Gift shop and visitors center: Saturday, 10 a.m. to 4 p.m.; Rail yard: daily, unguided tours; guided tours by appointment. See website for calendar.

ADMISSION/FARE: Free admission. Donations are appreciated.

LOCOMOTIVES/ROLLING STOCK: Three operating GP-7s, GE U30C, Santa Fe 4-8-4 no. 2912 under restoration, various passenger, freight, M.O.W. cars and cabooses. Collection of Colorado & Wyoming CF&I equipment.

SPECIAL EVENTS: Easter, Hippity Hop Express; October 1 & 2, Depot Daze (train rides, music, food, etc.); last three weekends in December, Pueblo Express, Santa Train.

NEARBY ATTRACTIONS: Pueblo Union Depot, National Historical Landmark, 1889; HARP, Riverwalk and El Pueblo Museum within ½ mile; Canon City & Royal Gorge Scenic Railway, Cañon City, 30 miles west of Pueblo, shopping and restaurants.

DIRECTIONS: At B St. and Victoria. Take 1st St. from I-25 exit 98B three blocks west to Union Ave., left 6 blocks to B St., just before Arkansas River Bridge, right to museum.

Photo courtesy of Gerald Dandurand.

Ridgway, CO

Ridgway Railroad Museum

Museum, Railyard

ADDRESS: PO Box 588 Ridgway, CO 81432
TELEPHONE: (970) 626-5181
WEBSITE: www.ridgwayrailroadmuseum.org

DESCRIPTION: Historical, restored rolling stock plus artifacts, pictures, models, and tools. The museum also has a collection of DVDs, videos, books, and other documents.

LOCOMOTIVES/ROLLING STOCK: Motor no. 1, stock car no. 5574, box car no. 3130, plow flanger no. 02, coach no. 254, Butch Cassidy Car, drop bottom gondola no. 702.

SPECIAL EVENTS: Picnic in the Trainyard, Fourth of July Parades, Ridgway Arts and Crafts Show, Ouray County Railroad Days, Western Colorado Train Extravaganza, Motor no. 1 runs.

Silver Plume, CO

Georgetown Loop Railroad

Train ride
Narrow gauge

ADDRESS: Devils Gate Station Silver Plume, CO and PO Box 249 Georgetown, CO 80444
TELEPHONE: (888) 456-6777
E-MAIL: info@railstarusa.com
WEBSITE: www.georgetownlooprr.com

DESCRIPTION: Visitors will be astounded by the Devil's Gate High Bridge, the beautiful Rocky Mountain views, and the engineering marvel.

SCHEDULE: Nine daily departures between the Devil's Gate and Silver Plume locations.

ADMISSION/FARE: Train: adults, $17.50; children 3-15, $12.50; Lebanon Silver Mine Tours: adults, $8; children 3-15, $6. Mine tour accessible only by train; train ticket required in addition to mine tour fee.

LOCOMOTIVES/ROLLING STOCK: 1929 2-6-2 no. 12 former Kahului R.R., 1884 2-6-0 no. 9 former Colorado & Southern, no. 21 GE 44 Ton Center Cab Diesel, various 1900s D & RGW gondolas and boxcars converted for passenger service. On display: C&S Baggage/Mail car no. 13, C&S coach no. 76, C&S Business car no. 911.

NEARBY ATTRACTIONS: Historic Landmark District and Silver Plume and Georgetown, CO.

DIRECTIONS: 45 miles west of Denver on I-70.

See ad on page A-35.

Old Hundred Gold Mine Tour

Train ride, Mine tour
24" gauge

SITE ADDRESS: 721 CR4-A Silverton, CO 81433
MAILING ADDRESS: PO Box 316 Montrose, CO 81402-0316
TELEPHONE: (800) 872-3009 or (970) 387-5444
E-MAIL: old100@minetour.com
WEBSITE: www.minetour.com

DESCRIPTION: A ⅔-mile mine train ride and one-hour underground guided mine tour with mining demonstrations. Gold panning included with tour purchase. Mining artifact and rail equipment displays.

SCHEDULE: Mid-May through mid-October, daily; tours depart hourly, 10 a.m. to 4 p.m.

ADMISSION/FARE: Adults, $16; seniors 60+, $15; children 5-12, $8.

LOCOMOTIVES/ROLLING STOCK: Ex-Sunnyside Mine-Greensburg 4-ton battery electric; ex N.J. Zinc-Greensburg 6-ton battery electric; various mine cars and rail-mounted mining equipment.

SPECIAL EVENTS: Second weekend in August, Hardrocker's Holidays mining contests.

NEARBY ATTRACTIONS: Durango & Silverton Narrow Gauge Railroad, Mayflower Gold Mill National Historic Landmark.

DIRECTIONS: 5 miles east of Silverton on CR2 & CR4-A, follow signs.

KEY TO SYMBOLS

♿ Handicapped accessible	🍴 Restaurant	🎨 Arts and crafts	arm Association of Railway Museums
P Parking	🪑 Picnic area	🏛 Memberships available	TRAIN Tourist Railway Association, Inc.
P Bus/RV parking	🍽 Dining car	✉ Send S.A.S.E. for brochure	AMTRAK Amtrak service to nearby city
🎁 Gift, book, or museum shop	🔄 Excursions	NRHP National Register of Historic Places	VIA VIA service to nearby city
☕ Refreshments	TOUR Guided tours	VISA MasterCard DISCOVER AMERICAN EXPRESS Card	Credit cards accepted

Windsor, CO

Windsor Museum

Museum

SITE ADDRESS: North 6th St. Windsor, CO 80550
MAILING ADDRESS: Division of Cultural Affairs and Museums, Town of Windsor
301 Walnut St. Windsor, CO 80550
TELEPHONE: (970) 674-2439
E-MAIL: jarosd@digis.net

DESCRIPTION: This 1882 Colorado & Southern depot houses an exhibit of steam-era railroading history. There is a heavy emphasis on local operations of the Colorado & Southern and Great Western Railway. Visitors can view an REA platform baggage truck, artifacts, signals, lighting, photos, operating telegraph display, and documents.

SCHEDULE: May 13 through September 10: Tuesday through Saturday, 10 a.m. to 4 p.m.; Sunday 12 to 4 p.m.

ADMISSION/FARE: Free.

LOCOMOTIVES/ROLLING STOCK: Colorado & Southern 1906 Pullman coach no. 543; Great Western 1925 caboose no. 1010; C&S 1926 boxcar no. 30787; c. 1905 Kalamazoo velocipede; Fairmont speeder.

DIRECTIONS: From I-25 north or south bound, exit 262, Colorado Hwy. 392. Follow 392 (Main St., Windsor) eastbound five miles to downtown Windsor. Turn left at 6th St., cross GW railroad tracks, and immediately turn right for depot parking.

Photo courtesy of Great Western Railway caboose, Windsor Museum. Photo by Cindy Harris.

KEY TO SYMBOLS

♿ Handicapped accessible	🍴 Restaurant	🎨 Arts and crafts	arm Association of Railway Museums
P Parking	🎋 Picnic area	M Memberships available	TRAIN Tourist Railway Association, Inc.
P Bus/RV parking	🍴 Dining car	✉ Send S.A.S.E. for brochure	Amtrak service to nearby city
🎁 Gift, book, or museum shop	Excursions	National Register of Historic Places	VIA service to nearby city
Refreshments	TOUR Guided tours	VISA MasterCard DISCOVER AMERICAN EXPRESS Card	Credit cards accepted

CONNECTICUT

Danbury, CT

Danbury Railway Museum

Train ride, Museum, Model train layout

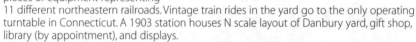

• East Windsor

• Thomaston   • Willimantic

• Kent

• Danbury   • East Haven

South Norwalk

ADDRESS: 120 White St.
Danbury, CT 06810
TELEPHONE: (203) 778-8337
E-MAIL: info@danburyrail.com
WEBSITE: www.danbury.org/drm

DESCRIPTION: There are over 50 pieces of equipment representing 11 different northeastern railroads. Vintage train rides in the yard go to the only operating turntable in Connecticut. A 1903 station houses N scale layout of Danbury yard, gift shop, library (by appointment), and displays.

SCHEDULE: November through March: Wednesday through Saturday, 10 a.m. to 4 p.m.; Sunday, 12 to 4 p.m.; April through October: Tuesday through Saturday, 10 a.m. to 5 p.m.; Sunday, 12 to 5 p.m. Train rides: April through December, Saturday and Sunday.

ADMISSION/FARE: Adults, $6; seniors, $5; children 5-12, $4. Train ride, add: coach, $3; caboose, $4; locomotive cab, $10.

LOCOMOTIVES/ROLLING STOCK: New Haven RS1 0673; NH Budd RDC1 32; 7589, former New Haven RS11 1402; B&M Alco 2-6-0 1455; New York Central E9 4096; NYC Alco FPA 1390; NYC EMD FL9 2013; NH EMD FL9 2006; LIRR Alco FA 617, former NH 0428; CDOT RS3m 605; more.

SPECIAL EVENTS: April 1-2, 8-9, 14-15, Bunny Trains; October 14-15, 21-22, 28-29, Pumpkin Patch Trains; December 2-3, 9-10, 16-17, Santa Trains.

NEARBY ATTRACTIONS: Military Museum, Danbury Historical Society Museum, Danbury Fair Mall, many international cuisine restaurants.

DIRECTIONS: I-84 exit 5, right on Main St., left on White St.

Photo courtesy of Charlie Albanetti.
Coupon available, see insert.

East Haven, CT

Shore Line Trolley Museum

Museum
Standard gauge
Radio frequency: 466.900/461.900

ADDRESS: 17 River St. East Haven, CT 06512-2519
TELEPHONE: (203) 467-6927 or (203) 467-7635, group sales
E-MAIL: sltmbera@sbcglobal.net
WEBSITE: www.bera.org

DESCRIPTION: The sole remaining segment of the historic Branford Electric Railway. The 3-mile round trip passes woods, salt marshes, and meadows along the scenic shore.

SCHEDULE: April: Sunday; May, September, and October: Saturday, Sunday, and holidays; November: Sunday and first Saturday; Memorial Day through Labor Day: daily; first trolley leaves at 10:30 a.m.; trolleys run frequently until 4:30 p.m.

ADMISSION/FARE: Unlimited rides and guided tours: adults, $6; seniors, $5; children 2-15, $3; children under 2, free.

LOCOMOTIVES/ROLLING STOCK: Connecticut Co. suburban no. 775; Connecticut Co. no. 1602; Montreal no. 2001; Johnstown no. 357; Brooklyn (New York) convertible no. 4573; 3rd Ave. no. 629.

SPECIAL EVENTS: Thanksgiving through Christmas on weekends, Santa Days.

NEARBY ATTRACTIONS: Valley Railroad in Essex, CT; Yale University in New Haven, CT; Foxwoods and Mohegan Sun Casinos.

DIRECTIONS: I-95 exits 51 north or 52 south and follow signs.

Photo courtesy of G. Boucher.
Coupon available, see insert.

East Windsor, CT

Connecticut Trolley Museum

Train ride, Museum

ADDRESS: 58 North Rd., Route 140, PO Box 360 East Windsor, CT 06088
TELEPHONE: (860) 627-6540
WEBSITE: www.ceraonline.org

DESCRIPTION: A 3-mile, round trip trolley ride through the countryside. Founded in 1940, the museum houses passenger and freight street cars, interurban cars, elevated railway cars, service cars, locomotives, passenger and freight railroad cars, and a variety of other rail equipment. The streetcar ride includes an educational narrative at the museum.

SCHEDULE: April to Memorial Day: Saturday, 10 a.m. to 4 p.m.; Sunday, 12 to 4 p.m.; Memorial to Labor Day: Monday and Wednesday to Saturday, 10 a.m. to 4 p.m.; Sunday, 12 to 4 p.m.; Labor Day to December: Saturday, 10 a.m. to 4 p.m.; Sunday, 12 to 4 p.m. Closed Thanksgiving, Christmas Eve, and Christmas Day.

ADMISSION/FARE: Adults, $7; seniors 62+, $6; youth 2-12, $4; children under 2, free; group rates.

LOCOMOTIVES/ROLLING STOCK: Trolleys: No. 1326, ex-Connecticut Co.; nos. 4, 2056, and 2600, ex-Montreal Tramways; no. 1850, ex-Rio de Janeiro; no. 451, ex-Illinois Terminal PCC car.

SPECIAL EVENTS: Last three weekends in October, Saturday 11 a.m. to 4 p.m., Sunday 12 to 4 p.m., Halloween program "Little Pumpkin Patch" includes trolley rides, games, and a pumpkin for each child. Day after Thanksgiving through December, Friday through Sunday, 5 to 9 p.m., Winterfest, a 3-mile trolley ride through tunnel of lights.

NEARBY ATTRACTIONS: Six Flags Park, Agawan, Massachusetts; Air Museum, Bradley Field, Connecticut; Mark Twain House, Hartford, Connecticut.

DIRECTIONS: Near Hartford, CT, and Springfield, MA. I-91, exit 45, ¾ mile east on Route 140.

Photo courtesy of William E. Wood.

Essex, CT
Essex Steam Train & Riverboat
Train ride, Dinner train, display
Standard gauge

ADDRESS: One Railroad Ave., PO Box 452 Essex, CT 06426
TELEPHONE: (800) 377-3987 or (860) 767-0103
E-MAIL: valley.railroad@snet.net
WEBSITE: www.valleyrr.com

DESCRIPTION: A 1½-hour excursion through the scenic Connecticut River Valley with views of the river and wetlands. The passenger trains consist of restored 1920s-era coaches. Passengers can connect with a riverboat ride for a 2½-hour train-boat combination excursion.

SCHEDULE: Call or check website for updated schedule.

ADMISSION/FARE: Train and boat: adults, $24; children 3-11, $12; train ride only: adults, $16; children 3-11, $8; parlor car and caboose: adults and children 3-11, $5; open car: adults and children 3-11, $3; all rides: children under 3, free; train and boat family pass: $80; train only family pass: $50. Fares are seasonal and exclude special events.

LOCOMOTIVES/ROLLING STOCK: No. 40, Alco 2-8-2; no. 97, Alco 2-8-0; more.

SPECIAL EVENTS: A Day Out with Thomas™, Your Hand on the Throttle, Polar Express Santa Special. Call for more information and to learn about additional events.

DIRECTIONS: From New York and Boston, I-95 to exit 69, north on SR9 to exit 3. From Hartford, I-91 south to exit 22S, south on SR9 to exit 3. Follow signs.

Kent, CT

Connecticut Antique Machinery Assoc., Inc.
Museum
36" gauge

ADDRESS: Route 7, PO Box 425 Kent, CT 06757
TELEPHONE: (860) 927-0050
WEBSITE: www.ctamachinery.com

DESCRIPTION: Exhibits show the development of the country's agricultural and industrial technology from the mid-1800s to the present. Holdings include a collection of large stationary steam engines, large internal combustion engines, an oil field pump house, mining museum, agricultural displays of tractors and farm implements, and the reconstructed Cream Hill Agricultural School buildings, which served as the forerunner to the University of Connecticut. A stretch of 3-foot gauge track is in operation during the Fall Festival.

SCHEDULE: Memorial to Labor Day: Wednesday to Sunday, 10 a.m. to 4 p.m.

ADMISSION/FARE: Adults, $4; children 5-12, $2; children under 5, free.

LOCOMOTIVES/ROLLING STOCK: No. 4 Argent Lumber Co. Porter 2-8-0; no. 5 Hawaii Railway Co. Baldwin 2-4-2; no. 16 Hutton Brick Co. DL Plymouth; no. 18 Wickwire Spencer Vulcan limited clearance 0-4-0-T; no. 6 Waynesburg & Washington 1894 coach; nos. 1132 and 1331 Denver & Rio Grande 1902 high-side gondolas; no. 111 Tionesta Valley Railway 1917 caboose.

SPECIAL EVENTS: First May Sunday, Spring Gas Up; last September weekend, Fall Festival.

DIRECTIONS: One mile north of Village of Kent on Route 7, adjacent to Housatonic Railroad.

Photo courtesy of Jim Anderson.

South Norwalk, CT

The Sono Switch Tower Museum

Museum, Display

ADDRESS: 77 Washington St. South Norwalk, CT 06854
TELEPHONE: (203) 246-6958
E-MAIL: info@westctnrhs.org
WEBSITE: www.sonotower.org

DESCRIPTION: Restored New Haven Railroad 1896 switch tower complete with original 68 Armstrong lever mechanical machine located next to the Northeast Corridor Mainline.

SCHEDULE: May through October: Saturday and Sunday, 12 to 5 p.m., and by appointment.

ADMISSION/FARE: Donations are appreciated.

SPECIAL EVENTS: Norwalk Harbor Splash Festival, Arts Festival, Oyster Festival.

NEARBY ATTRACTIONS: IMAX Theater, Stepping Stones Museum for Children, Norwalk Museum, Lockwood Mansion Museum, Norwalk Maritime Museum, Harbor Cruises.

DIRECTIONS: I-95, exit 14 (north) or exit 15 (south).

Photo courtesy of Robert Gambling.
Coupon available, see insert.

Thomaston, CT

Naugatuck Railroad/
Railroad Museum of New England

Train ride, Museum
Standard gauge

ADDRESS: PO Box 400 Thomaston, CT 06787
TELEPHONE: (860) 283-7245 (RAIL)
E-MAIL: naugatuck.railroad@snet.net
WEBSITE: www.rmne.org

DESCRIPTION: This 17.5-mile round trip goes over a former New Haven Railroad line, which was opened in 1849. The train runs from the 1881 Thomaston Station along Naugatuck River, past 100-year-old New England brass mills, on to the Thomaston Dam.

SCHEDULE: Early May: groups of 45 or more; May 27 to October 29: weekends, 12 and 2 p.m.; May 30 to October 24: Tuesday, 10 a.m.; first three weekends in December: 12 and 2 p.m. No trains Memorial Day, July 4, Labor Day. Detailed schedule available on website.

ADMISSION/FARE: Adults, $12; seniors, $10; children 3-12, $8. Ask for group rates & charters.

LOCOMOTIVES/ROLLING STOCK: New Haven Alco RS-3 no. 529; Naugatuck GE U23B no. 2203; Canadian National open-window heavyweight coaches from 1920s.

SPECIAL EVENTS: Some excursions over 19.6-mile route between Waterbury and Torrington; Engineer-for-an-Hour program; early August, A Day Out with Thomas™.

NEARBY ATTRACTIONS: Amusement parks, vineyards, state parks.

DIRECTIONS: I-84, exit 20 to north on Route 8, exit 38 Thomaston.

Photo courtesy of Howard Pincus.
Coupon available, see insert.

Willimantic, CT
Connecticut Eastern Railroad Museum
Museum, Display

ADDRESS: 55 Bridge St., PO Box 665 Willimantic, CT 06226
TELEPHONE: (860) 456-9999
WEBSITE: www.cteastrrmuseum.org

DESCRIPTION: The museum is on the original site of the Columbia Junction Freight Yard. The collection includes locomotives and rolling stock, vintage railroad buildings, and a six-stall roundhouse reconstructed on the original foundation. Visitors can operate a replica 1850s-style pump car on a section of rail that once was part of the New Haven Railroad's "Air Line."

SCHEDULE: May to October: Saturday and Sunday, 10 a.m. to 4 p.m., weekdays by appointment only.

ADMISSION/FARE: Adults and seniors, $5; children, $1.

LOCOMOTIVES/ROLLING STOCK: CERR no. 0800 44-ton; CERR 25-ton; CV S-4 no. 8081; MEC railbus no. 10; Pfizer SW8 no. 2; New Haven baggage no. 3841; New Haven coach no. 4414; New Haven coaches nos. 8673 and 8695; CV boxcar no. 43022; CV flatcar no. 4287; CV cabooses nos. 4029 and 4052; New Haven caboose C618; CDOT FL9 no. 2023 and Metro-North SPV 2000 no. 293; Trackmobile car mover.

NEARBY ATTRACTIONS: Windham Textile and History Museum, Jillson House Museum.

DIRECTIONS: Located off Route 32 (Bridge St.) in downtown Willimantic.

Photo courtesy of Robert A. LaMay.
Coupon available, see insert.

DELAWARE

Wilmington •

Wilmington, DE

Wilmington & Western Railroad

Train ride, Dinner train, Museum
Standard gauge

SITE ADDRESS: 2201 Newport Gap Pike (Route 41)
Wilmington, DE 19808
MAILING ADDRESS: PO Box 5787 Wilmington, DE 19808
TELEPHONE: (302) 998-1930
E-MAIL: schedule@wwrr.com
WEBSITE: www.wwrr.com

DESCRIPTION: Delaware's only steam tourist railroad operates
over a portion of the former Baltimore & Ohio Landenberg
branch for 5- and 10-mile excursions to Mt. Cuba, Picnic Grove,
Yorklyn, and Hockessin.

SCHEDULE: March through December: Saturday and/or Sunday, one- and two-hour
excursions along the Red Clay Valley. Call or write for timetable.

ADMISSION/FARE: Varies; please call or write for information. Caboose rentals, group rates,
and private charters available.

LOCOMOTIVES/ROLLING STOCK:
Two EMD SW1 switchers; 1909 Alco
4-4-0 no. 98; 1907 Baldwin 0-6-0 no. 58;
1910 Canadian National 2-6-0 no. 92;
1929 PRR railcar.

SPECIAL EVENTS: Easter Bunny Special,
Santa Claus Express, Dinner and/or
Murder Mystery Trains, Civil War Weekend.

NEARBY ATTRACTIONS: Longwood
Gardens, Hagley Museum, Kalmar Nyckel,
Winterthur Museum.

DIRECTIONS: I-95, exit 5, follow Route 141 north to Route 2 west, then Route 41 north.
Greenbank Station is on Route 41 north of Route 2, 4 miles southwest of Wilmington.

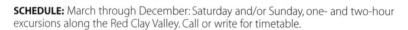

Photo courtesy of David S. Ludlow.
Coupon available, see insert.

DISTRICT OF COLUMBIA

Washington, DC

Smithsonian Institution, National Museum of American History

Museum

Washington D.C.

SITE ADDRESS: National Mall 14th St. and Constitution Ave., NW Washington, DC 20013
MAILING ADDRESS: Room 5004, MRC 628, PO Box 37012 Washington, DC 20013
TELEPHONE: (202) 633-1000
E-MAIL: info@si.edu
WEBSITE: www.si.edu

DESCRIPTION: The National Museum of American History dedicates its collections and scholarship to inspiring a broader understanding of the nation and its many peoples. They create learning opportunities, stimulate imaginations, and present challenging ideas about the country's past. The museum collects and preserves more than 3 million artifacts. The collections form a vast and fascinating mosaic of American life, while the exhibitions explore major themes in American history and culture, from the War of Independence to the present day. In the transportation collections, railroad objects range from tools, tracks, and many train models to the massive 1401, a 280-ton locomotive built in 1926. The library houses an extensive collection of information about railroads and their important link to the nation's history.

SCHEDULE: Daily, 10 a.m. to 5:30 p.m.; closed December 25.

ADMISSION/FARE: Museum: free.

KEY TO SYMBOLS

♿ Handicapped accessible	🍴 Restaurant	🎨 Arts and crafts	arm Association of Railway Museums
P Parking	🏕 Picnic area	Ⓜ Memberships available	TRAIN Tourist Railway Association, Inc.
P Bus/RV parking	🍴 Dining car	✉ Send S.A.S.E. for brochure	AMTRAK Amtrak service to nearby city
🎁 Gift, book, or museum shop	➰ Excursions	NRHP National Register of Historic Places	VIA VIA service to nearby city
☕ Refreshments	TOUR Guided tours	VISA MasterCard DISCOVER AMERICAN EXPRESS Card	Credit cards accepted

FLORIDA

Altamonte Springs, FL
Altamonte Pass Railroad

*Live steam train ride
7½" gauge*

SITE ADDRESS: 300 Broadview Ave.
Barclay Woods Subdivision
Altamonte Springs, FL 32715-0672
MAILING ADDRESS: PO Box 150672
Altamonte Springs, FL 32715-0672
TELEPHONE: (407) 650-2546
E-MAIL: altamontepass@gmail.com
WEBSITE: www.aprr.info

DESCRIPTION: This private facility railroad is located at the residence of Jerry and Diana Selwyn, about 10 miles north of downtown Orlando. The APRR features a mainline loop (30-foot radius) approximately 700 feet long with 800 additional feet of double tracks, passing sidings, storage tracks, and a reversing wye which takes the train right through the house. Florida Live Steam members are encouraged to bring equipment to run, and are invited to enjoy the G-gauge railroad.

SCHEDULE: Please call ahead to ensure availability and yard access.

LOCOMOTIVES/ROLLING STOCK: Two diesel electric engines; electric "galloping goose;" police speeder; 2-6-0 steamer; eight rider cars; four specialty cars, three MOW Utility cars; two cabooses.

NEARBY ATTRACTIONS: Bob and Betty Zuckerman's Lockhart & Lakewood Forest Railroad.

DIRECTIONS: 10 miles north of downtown Orlando (just over a mile from I-4).

Fort Myers, FL

Murder Mystery Dinner Train on Seminole Gulf Railway

Train ride, Dinner train
Standard gauge

ADDRESS: 4110 Centerpointe Dr., Ste. 207 Fort Myers, FL 33916
TELEPHONE: (800) SEM-GULF or (239) 275-8487
E-MAIL: rsvp@semgulf.com
WEBSITE: www.semgulf.com

DESCRIPTION: This freight railroad serves southwest Florida and offers excursion trains (20-mile, 2-hour round trip) and dinner trains (30-mile, 3½-hour round trip).

SCHEDULE: Excursion trains: mid-December through Labor Day; murder mystery dinner train with five-course meal: Wednesday through Saturday, 6:30 p.m.; Sunday, 5:30 p.m.

ADMISSION/FARE: Excursion train: adults, $13.95+tax and up; children 3-12, $8.95+tax and up; dinner train theater, $49.98 and up.

LOCOMOTIVES/ROLLING STOCK: GP9s; Alco C-425; EMD F7 and F9.

SPECIAL EVENTS: Valentine's weekend, Easter dinner, Mother's and Father's Days, Halloween, Thanksgiving, Christmas rail/boat, New Year's party.

NEARBY ATTRACTIONS: Edison and Ford winter homes, Edison lab and museum, Red Sox and Minnesota Twins spring training, former ACL City Station (Fort Myers Historical Museum), beaches (Sanibel Island) and water attractions.

DIRECTIONS: Trains depart from Colonial Station near Colonial Blvd. (SR884) and Metro Pkwy. intersection in Fort Myers, 3 miles west of I-75 exit 136.

See ad on page A-23.

TRAVEL TIP: *Come early, ride one, photograph one*

A great way to enjoy a tourist railroad is to make a day of it. Ride one trip and use it as an opportunity to look for great photo locations. Have lunch. Visit with the crews. Then enjoy taking photographs of the train on a following trip.

Fort Myers, FL

Southwest Florida Museum of History

Museum

ADDRESS: 2300 Peck St. Fort Myers, FL 33901
TELEPHONE: (239) 332-5955
E-MAIL: museuminfo@cityftmyers.com
WEBSITE: www.cityftmyers.com/attractions/historical.htm

DESCRIPTION: Relive the rich history of southwest Florida. Housed in the former Atlantic Coast Line Railroad depot, the Museum showcases exhibits from prehistoric times to modern day. Ever wonder how Thomas Edison traveled there? Visitors can experience it firsthand via a tour of the "Esperanza," a private Pullman railcar. There are also a variety of traveling exhibits.

SCHEDULE: Tuesday to Saturday, 10 a.m. to 5 p.m.; Sunday 12 to 4 p.m., in season.

ADMISSION/FARE: Adults, $9.50; seniors, $8.50; children 3-12, $4; children under 3, free.

LOCOMOTIVES/ROLLING STOCK: Pullman Standard Car & Manufacturing Co. 1929/30 "Esperanza" no. 6242.

NEARBY ATTRACTIONS: Thomas A. Edison winter home, Henry Ford winter home, Burroughs home, baseball spring training camps for Boston Red Sox and Minnesota Twins, and Sanibel Island beaches.

DIRECTIONS: Take I-75 to exit 138 (Martin Luther King, Jr. Blvd.), drive 5 miles west to downtown Fort Myers to Jackson St. Turn left and go one block to Peck St.

Photo courtesy of SW Florida Museum of History.

Lake Buena Vista, FL

Walt Disney World Railroad

Theme park with train ride
36" gauge

ADDRESS: PO Box 10000 Lake Buena Vista, FL 32830-1000
TELEPHONE: (407) 824-7828
WEBSITE: disneyworld.disney.go.com

DESCRIPTION: Visitors can ride the rails aboard one of four steam-powered trains as they take 20-minute journeys around the park.

NEARBY ATTRACTIONS: Walt Disney World.

Largo, FL

Largo Central Railroad
Miniature/park train

SITE ADDRESS: Largo, FL
MAILING ADDRESS: PO Box 60192
St. Petersburg, FL 33784
TELEPHONE: (727) 585-9835
E-MAIL: bcteerlin@bellsouth.net
WEBSITE: www.lcrailroad.com

DESCRIPTION: Ride through landscaped Largo Central Park, across a beautiful pond with waterfall, and through a 155-foot curved tunnel.

Photo courtesy of Florida Aerial Services Team.

Miami, FL

Gold Coast Railroad Museum
Train ride, Museum, Display, Layout
Narrow, Standard gauge

ADDRESS: 12750 SW 152 St. Miami, FL 33177
TELEPHONE: (305) 253-6300
E-MAIL: webmaster@goldcoast-railroad.org
WEBSITE: www.goldcoast-railroad.org

DESCRIPTION: The 58-acre museum houses and/or operates 15 passenger cars, 7 steam locomotives, 7 diesel locomotives, 14 freight cars, 2 cranes, 4 cabooses, and more, including the Presidential Pullman "Ferdinand Magellan" built for President Roosevelt, and used by Presidents Truman, Eisenhower, and Reagan. Also available are weekend train rides and a model train exhibition that includes a children's play area. This is the largest collection of Florida equipment in the area. The model trains include: LGB, O-27, HO, N, and Z scales; BRIO and "Thomas" play area.

SCHEDULE: Monday to Friday, 10 a.m. to 4 p.m.; Saturday and Sunday, 11 a.m. to 4 p.m.

ADMISSION/FARE: Adults, $5; children, $3; children under 3, free.

LOCOMOTIVES/ROLLING STOCK: Florida East Coast 4-6-2s nos. 153 and 113; Atlantic Coast Line-painted GP7 no.1804; US Army Hospital Car no. 89436; California Zephyr passenger train cars "Silver Crescent" and "Silver Stag."

SPECIAL EVENTS: Group tours, field trips, birthday parties, film/model shoots, corporate events, weddings, and Day Out with Thomas™.

NEARBY ATTRACTIONS: Miami Dade MetroZoo (on the same property), Coral Castle, Monkey Jungle, Florida Everglades Park, Larry & Penny Tompson Campgrounds, and restaurants and hotels within five miles.

DIRECTIONS: Florida Turnpike, Homestead Extension to SW 152 St. exit (exit no. 16), SW 152 St. westbound and follow the MetroZoo signs, enter the MetroZoo complex and look for us on the right (first turn off the Zoo Pkwy.).

Coupon available, see insert.

Palm Beach, FL
Flagler Museum
Museum

ADDRESS: Cocoanut Row and Whitehall Way, PO Box 969 Palm Beach, FL 33480
TELEPHONE: (561) 655-2833
WEBSITE: www.flaglermuseum.us

DESCRIPTION: Whitehall, a 55-room Gilded Age estate and National Historic Landmark, was the winter home of Henry M. Flagler, developer of the Florida East Coast Railway, the railroad that linked the cities on the state's east coast. Displays and exhibits focus on the contributions Flagler made to the state of Florida by building the Florida East Coast Railway and developing tourism and agriculture as the state's major industries.

SCHEDULE: Year-round: Tuesday through Saturday, 10 a.m. to 5 p.m.; Sunday, 12 to 5 p.m. Closed Thanksgiving, Christmas Day, and New Year's Day.

ADMISSION/FARE: Adults, $10; children 6-12, $3; free on Founder's Day (June 5).

LOCOMOTIVES/ROLLING STOCK: FEC Car no. 91, Henry Flagler's private railcar, built in 1886.

SPECIAL EVENTS: January to March, Flagler Museum Music Series; February and March, Whitehall Lecture Series; June 5, Founder's Day; December, holiday tours, tree lighting.

NEARBY ATTRACTIONS: Museums, zoo, Atlantic Ocean.

DIRECTIONS: I-95 to exit 70 (Okeechobee Blvd.). Travel 3 miles across Intracoastal Waterway, left on Cocoanut Row. Museum is ¾ mile on left.

Photo courtesy of Flagler Museum.

Parrish, FL

Florida Gulf Coast Railroad Museum

EDITOR'S CHOICE

Train ride, Museum
Standard gauge

ADDRESS: 12210 83rd St. E, PO Box 355 Parrish, FL
TELEPHONE: (941) 776-0906
WEBSITE: www.fgcrrm.org

DESCRIPTION: Begun in 1981, the museum has an emphasis on railroads that served Florida, and also includes a 12-mile, round-trip train ride. Exhibits display interesting and historic examples of rolling stock, artifacts, and other aspects of railroad history. Excursion trains run every weekend. Passengers can board on 83rd St. East, just behind Parrish post office. The trains are diesel powered and include open window coaches, a covered gondola, air conditioned coaches, and a lounge car.

SCHEDULE: Year-round: Saturday and Sunday, 11 a.m. and 2 p.m.

ADMISSION/FARE: Adults, $10; children 3-11, $6.

LOCOMOTIVES/ROLLING STOCK: EMD GP7 no. 1835; Alco RS3 no. 1633; GE 44-ton no. 100; passenger coach no. 2002; tavern lounge "Kentucky Club" no. 3251; Pullman MU car no. 3518; ex-UP coach; CN lounge; Pullman sleeper "Short Leaf Pine" no. 3464; more.

SPECIAL EVENTS: Several throughout the year, including Train Robbery, Civil War and WWII re-enactments, Halloween and Santa Trains. Please visit website for more information.

NEARBY ATTRACTIONS: Busch Gardens, Manatee River State Recreational Area, Roaring 20's Pizza & Pipes, J.P. Igloos Ice Rink, Ellenton Outlet Mall, Tampa Union Station (Amtrak).

DIRECTIONS: I-75 exit 299, east 5 miles to US301, south ¼ mile to 83rd St. E, left to park.

Photo courtesy of Glenn Miley.

Tampa, FL

Serengeti Express

Theme park with train ride

ADDRESS: Busch Gardens 3605 E Bougainvillea Ave. Tampa, FL 33612
TELEPHONE: (888) 800-5447
WEBSITE: www.buschgardens.com

DESCRIPTION: Passengers can see the beauty of the Serengeti Plains as they make a round-trip journey from the Nairobi train station on the Serengeti Express Railway.

SCHEDULE: Year-round, 7 days a week; for operating hours, see website.

ADMISSION/FARE: Adults, $55.95+tax; children 3-9, $45.95+tax; children 2 and younger, free. Admission includes access to all rides, shows, and most attractions.

LOCOMOTIVES/ROLLING STOCK: Propane-powered steam locomotive.

DIRECTIONS: Located in Busch Gardens Tampa Bay amusement park.

Tampa, FL

Tampa & Ybor City Street Railway Society

ADDRESS: c/o Tampa Tank 5205 Adamo Dr. Tampa, FL 33619-3251
TELEPHONE: (813) 623-2675, ext. 49

DESCRIPTION: Since 1984, the T&YCSR has been promoting the re-establishment of electric streetcar service to Tampa, as well as acting as locator, curator, and restorer of original Tampa St. car equipment, artifacts, and history, mainly from 1920 through 1946.

Winter Garden, FL

Central Florida Railroad Museum
Museum, Model train layout

ADDRESS: 101 S Boyd St. Winter Garden, FL 34787
TELEPHONE: (407) 656-0559
E-MAIL: irv_1@earthlink.net
WEBSITE: www.cfcnrhs.org

DESCRIPTION: Located in former 1913 Tavares & Gulf Railroad station, the museum emphasizes Florida railroad history.

SCHEDULE: Daily, 1 to 5 p.m.

LOCOMOTIVES/ROLLING STOCK: Clinchfield caboose no. 1073.

SPECIAL EVENTS: Occasional excursions.

NEARBY ATTRACTIONS: Winter Garden Heritage Museum, Orlando, West Orange Trail (built on ex-Orange Belt, ex-Plant System, ex-ACL line), city parks and restaurants, Citrus Tower.

DIRECTIONS: East on SR50, left on Dillard St., left on Story Rd., right on Boyd St. to museum.

Winter Garden, FL

Winter Garden Heritage Museum

Museum

ADDRESS: 1 N Main St. Winter Garden, FL 34787
TELEPHONE: (407) 656-5544
WEBSITE: www.wghf.org

DESCRIPTION: Housed in the 1918 Atlantic Coast Line Depot in downtown Winter Garden, the museum includes a large collection of local citrus labels, Native American artifacts, photographs, and railroad memorabilia dating from the days of pioneer settlement to the present in West Orange County. The museum is also a repository for the archives of the history and restoration of Lake Apopka.

SCHEDULE: Daily, 1 to 5 p.m.

LOCOMOTIVES/ROLLING STOCK: Chessie caboose no. 900296.

SPECIAL EVENTS: Craft/Crate label show.

NEARBY ATTRACTIONS: Central Florida Railroad Museum, Orlando, Lake Apopka, more.

DIRECTIONS: Florida Turnpike to Winter Garden exit. Take SR50 to Dillard St., turn north, then west on Plant St. to museum.

KEY TO SYMBOLS

Handicapped accessible	Restaurant	Arts and crafts	Association of Railway Museums
Parking	Picnic area	Memberships available	Tourist Railway Association, Inc.
Bus/RV parking	Dining car	Send S.A.S.E. for brochure	Amtrak service to nearby city
Gift, book, or museum shop	Excursions	National Register of Historic Places	VIA service to nearby city
Refreshments	Guided tours	VISA MasterCard DISCOVER AMERICAN EXPRESS Card	Credit cards accepted

GEORGIA

Albany, GA

Thronateeska Heritage Center

Museum, Display, Model train layout
Standard gauge, HO layout

ADDRESS: 100 W Roosevelt Ave. Albany, GA 31701
TELEPHONE: (229) 432-6955
E-MAIL: info@heritagecenter.org
WEBSITE: www.heritagecenter.org

DESCRIPTION: Established in 1974, Thronateeska
has a history museum located in the c.1913
Union Passenger Terminal and dedicated Albany
education. Other structures include the original 1857 freight depot and the Railway
Express Agency building, housing the Wetherbee Planetarium and Science Discovery
Center. A new transportation exhibit shed covers the railroad equipment display track.

SCHEDULE: History museum and railroad
exhibit: Thursday through Saturday, 12 to
4 p.m.; layout: most Saturdays, 12 to 4 p.m.,
and for groups by appointment.

LOCOMOTIVES/ROLLING STOCK:
There are currently 11 artifacts, 10 of
which are being restored or are
completed, including Georgia Northern
Railway locomotive no. 107, a former
Florida East Coast 4-6-2 built in 1911;
Georgia Northern combine no. 38; ACL RPO 13; SR baggage express 518, which houses an
HO scale layout; two cabooses; four boxcars, including Atlantic Coast Line no. 21271, the
last intact class 0-25 car and tank car GATX 69995.

NEARBY ATTRACTIONS: Norfolk Southern and Georgia & Florida Railway operations near
depot, with NS street running. Flint RiverQuarium and River Park, large format theater.

DIRECTIONS: Southbound: From I-75, exit to GA 300 at exit 99 (Cordele). Take 300 south to
Bus. 82 in Albany. Go west, cross the Flint River, turn right at second light. Turn right on
Roosevelt Ave. at railroad. Museum is at the end of the block. Northbound: From I-85, exit
to US82 at exit 62 in Tifton. Take US82 into Albany; follow above directions to museum.
From Columbus: Follow GA 520 to Albany. Take US82 bypass, exit at Jefferson St., and turn
right. Go south to Roosevelt Ave. and turn left. Museum is ahead three blocks.

Photo courtesy of Stephen Syfrett.

Blairsville, GA

The Misty Mountain Model Railroad

Museum, Display, Model train layout

ADDRESS: 4381 Town Creek School Rd. Blairsville, GA 30512
TELEPHONE: (706) 745-9819

DESCRIPTION: This large O gauge model railroad is also a Hi-Rail scale layout and has been featured in several publications as an outstanding model. What started out as a private hobby and layout eleven years ago has grown to a destination for 20,000 visitors.

SCHEDULE: May through December: Wednesday, Friday, and Saturday, one tour per day, starting promptly at 2 p.m.; last two weeks of December: daily.

ADMISSION/FARE: $5 donation to local charities; youth under 17, free.

LOCOMOTIVES/ROLLING STOCK: 167 train sets, mostly Lionel and M.T.H., but also others.

NEARBY ATTRACTIONS: Blue Ridge Scenic Railway in Blue Ridge, GA 30513.

DIRECTIONS: South of Blairsville for three miles on 19 & 129. Turn left on Town Creek School Rd. for three miles to 4381, the train place.

Photo courtesy of Charles Griffin.

Blue Ridge, GA

Blue Ridge Scenic Railway

Train ride

ADDRESS: 241 Depot St. Blue Ridge, GA 30513
TELEPHONE: (800) 934-1898 or (706) 632-9833
E-MAIL: brscenic@tds.net
WEBSITE: www.brscenic.com

DESCRIPTION: A 3¹/₂-hour round trip, including layover, that starts in Blue Ridge and follows the Toccoa River to McCaysville, GA/Copperhill, TN, on the old "Hook and Eye" Division of the Louisville & Nashville. The gift shop and ticket office are located in a 100-year-old depot.

SCHEDULE: Mid-March to end of December departures: Friday through Monday; June, July, and October, daily.

ADMISSION/FARE: Off-season: adults, $22; seniors, $18; children, $11. Summer: adults, $26; seniors, $22; children, $13.

LOCOMOTIVES/ROLLING STOCK: Various diesel locomotives from parent company, Georgia Northeastern Railroad. GP7 no. 2097; GP9 no. 6576; GP10s nos. 7529 and 7562; GP18s nos. 8704 and 8705; GP20s nos. 316 and 4125; SW1 no. 77, 1947; NW1 no. 81.

SPECIAL EVENTS: Memorial Day weekend, Arts in the Park; April, Adventure Race; July, Blue Grass festivals.

NEARBY ATTRACTIONS: Chattahoochee National Forest, Amicalola Falls State Park, Fort Mountain State Park, Ocoee Whitewater Center, and more.

DIRECTIONS: Ninety miles north of Atlanta and 85 miles southeast of Chattanooga, TN.

Photo courtesy of Dick Hillman.

Cordele, GA
SAM Shortline Excursion Train
Train ride

SITE ADDRESS: 105 E 9th Ave. Cordele, GA 31015
MAILING ADDRESS: PO Box 845 Cordele, GA 31010
TELEPHONE: (877) 427-2457
E-MAIL: kathy_odom@dnr.state.ga.us
WEBSITE: www.samshortline.com

DESCRIPTION: All-day, round trip excursions through the scenic countryside and historic towns of Georgia. Stops include Cordele, Georgia Veterans State Park, Leslie, Americus, Plains, and Archery. Plains is home to President Jimmy Carter.

SCHEDULE: Friday, Saturday, and Monday; two Thursdays each month. Trains leave Cordele at 9:30 a.m. Special excursions are also available.

ADMISSION/FARE: Coach (tax additional): adults, $21.95; seniors, $18.95; children, $11.95. First class (tax additional): adults, $28.95; children, $16.95.

NEARBY ATTRACTIONS: Georgia Veterans State Park, Retreat at Lake Blackshear, Habitat for Humanity's Global Village, 1892 Windsor Hotel & Spa, Plains Trading Post, 1921 Rylander Theatre, Rural Telephone Museum, Jimmy Carter's campaign museum and boyhood home.

DIRECTIONS: Please visit website for a map and directions to depot and platform locations.

See ad on page A-15.

Dawson, GA

Georgia Southwestern Railroad, Inc.

Shortline freight railroad

ADDRESS: 78 Pulpwood Rd. Dawson, GA 39842
TELEPHONE: (800) 811-1363
E-MAIL: terry.small@gswrr.com or dave.smoot@gswrr.com
WEBSITE: www.gswrr.com

DESCRIPTION: GSWR is a shortline freight railroad that maintains two FP9 diesels and four rail passenger cars for marketing and public relations purposes. Not available for private charter.

SCHEDULE: There are no regularly scheduled trips; monitor the GSWR's website for available trips.

LOCOMOTIVES/ROLLING STOCK: Two FP9 diesels nos. 6302 and 6308, ex-VIA and ex-CN; one bar/lounge/observation car no. 200; one pub car (GSWR 200); and two coach cars.

SPECIAL EVENTS: December, Santa-Holiday Express.

DIRECTIONS: The train set is generally stored at the GSWR headquarters at Dawson, GA. Approximately 55 miles south of Dawson, GA, on Hwy. GA 520, turn east onto Pulpwood Rd. Visitors must register at the office.

Duluth, GA

Southeastern Railway Museum

Train ride, Display
Standard gauge

ADDRESS: 3966 Buford Hwy., PO Box 1267 Duluth, GA 30096
TELEPHONE: (770) 476-2013
WEBSITE: www.srmduluth.org

DESCRIPTION: Visitors meet rail history "hands on" through the display of more than 90 pieces of rolling stock, including a World War II troop kitchen car, Railway Post Office car, the 1911 Pullman "Superb" used by President Harding, a modern office car, vintage steam locomotives, and restored wooden cabooses. Short on-site train rides are available aboard vintage cabooses.

SCHEDULE: April to December: Thursday through Saturday, 10 a.m. to 5 p.m.; January to March: Saturday, 10 a.m. to 5 p.m.

ADMISSION/FARE: Adults, $7; seniors 65+, $5; children 2-12, $4; children under 2, free; NRHS members (with card), buy one get one free.

LOCOMOTIVES/ROLLING STOCK: Hartwell GE 44-tonners nos. 2 and 5; Georgia Power Porter 0-6-0T no. 97; Clinchfield Railroad caboose no. 1064; Southern caboose XC7871; SCL caboose no. 01077; Atlanta & West Point 4-6-2 no. 290; Savannah & Atlanta 4-6-2 no. 750.

SPECIAL EVENTS: First April weekend, Caboose Days; last September weekend, Rail Fair.

DIRECTIONS: I-85 northwest of Atlanta to west on exit 104 (Pleasant Hill Rd.) for 3½ miles to US23 (Buford Hwy.). North ¼ mile to Peachtree Rd., turn west to museum entrance.

Helen, GA

Charlemagne's Kingdom
Museum, Display, Layout
HO scale, all German

ADDRESS: 8808 N Main St., PO Box 848 Helen, GA 30545
TELEPHONE: (706) 878-2200
WEBSITE: www.georgiamodelrailroad.com

DESCRIPTION: This Alpine model railroad features more than 300 replica buildings and thousands of figures in a two-story model of German countryside. Created by Willi and Judi Lindhorst, Charlemagne's Kingdom is the brainchild of Willi's lifelong love of trains and models. A native of Oldenburg, Germany, Willi includes moving trains, Autobahn, and balloonists. Authentic Alpine architecture, seaports, and sound effects round out this display that is fully peopled in HO scale.

SCHEDULE: Summer: daily, 10 a.m. to 7 p.m.; winter: please call.

ADMISSION/FARE: Adults, $5; seniors, $4; children over 5, $2.50.

TRAVEL TIP: *Behind the scenes tours*

A great way to experience tourist railroading is to visit the repair shop, and many railroads have begun offering special behind-the-scenes tours that take you where the hard and heavy work takes place. You'll see locomotives and cars under restoration and get a feel for the work that goes into keeping the equipment roadworthy.

Kennesaw, GA

Southern Museum of Civil War and Locomotive History

Museum

ADDRESS: 2829 Cherokee St. Kennesaw, GA 30144
TELEPHONE: (770) 427-2117
E-MAIL: groups@southernmuseum.org
WEBSITE: www.southernmuseum.org

DESCRIPTION: This museum highlights railroads during the Civil War, the Glover Locomotive Factory, and the Great Locomotive Chase. With three permanent collections and a membership in the Smithsonian Affiliations Program, the museum offers a wide range of exhibits, including a turn-of-the-century locomotive factory and a depiction of the Civil War's Great Locomotive Chase.

SCHEDULE: Monday through Saturday, 9:30 a.m. to 5 p.m.; Sunday, 12 to 5 p.m. Closed New Year's Day, Easter, Thanksgiving, and Christmas.

ADMISSION/FARE: Adults, $7.50; seniors 60+, $6.50; children 6-12, $5.50; children 5 and under, free; AAA and military discounts available with ID card.

LOCOMOTIVES/ROLLING STOCK: "The General," Western & Atlantic Railroad, Rogers Ketchum & Grosvenor, 4-4-0, no. 3.

NEARBY ATTRACTIONS: Kennesaw Mountain National Battlefield Park, Downtown Kennesaw.

DIRECTIONS: I-75 to exit 273 then 2 miles toward downtown Kennesaw.

Photo courtesy of Southern Museum of Civil War & Locomotive History.
Coupon available, see insert.

Savannah, GA

Roundhouse Railroad Museum

Museum

ADDRESS: 601 W Harris St. Savannah, GA 31401
TELEPHONE: (912) 651-6823
WEBSITE: www.chsgeorgia.org

DESCRIPTION: Savannah's Roundhouse Railroad Museum is the oldest and most complete antebellum railroad manufacturing and repair facility still standing in the US and is a National Historic Landmark. Construction of the site began in 1851, and 13 of the original structures are still standing (five contain permanent exhibits), including the roundhouse and operating turntable and the 125-foot smokestack.

SCHEDULE: Year-round, daily; self-guided tours, 9 a.m. to 5 p.m. Closed Christmas Day, Thanksgiving Day, and New Year's Day.

ADMISSION/FARE: Adults, $4; seniors, students, AAA, military, railroad employees, and children, $3.50.

LOCOMOTIVES/ROLLING STOCK: Wrightsville & Tennille 2-8-0 no. 223; Central of Georgia 0-6-0 saddle tank no. 8; Holly Hill Lumber Co. 2-4-2 no. 15; Savannah & Atlanta Railway GP35 diesel no. 2715; Davenport diesel switcher; CR&B Co. inspection car no. 2; Co G inspection cars "Columbus" and "Atlanta"; Birney Car no. 630; freight & passenger cars; two cabooses; and four motor cars.

NEARBY ATTRACTIONS: Savannah History Museum, Whistle Stop Cafe, Old Fort Jackson, and Historic Savannah.

DIRECTIONS: I-16 east to Martin Luther King, Jr. Blvd. exit. Left on Martin Luther King, Jr. Blvd., and then left on Harris St.

Stone Mountain, GA

Stone Mountain Scenic Railroad
Train ride

ADDRESS: Stone Mountain Park, PO Box 778 Stone Mountain, GA 30086
TELEPHONE: (770) 498-5600 or (770) 498-5616
WEBSITE: www.stonemountainpark.org

DESCRIPTION: A 1950s locomotive with open-air cars takes guests on a five-mile excursion around the mountain. The all-new train experience "A Look Back Down the Tracks" is a blend of narration about the chronological history of trains around Stone Mountain from the mid-1800s, when the rail line was first built at the mountain, and interesting facts about the mountain. Train-themed music and well-known sing-alongs make the ride fun for all ages.

ADMISSION/FARE: Ages 3 and up, $7 plus park admission.

SPECIAL EVENTS: Christmas train.

DIRECTIONS: Railroad Depot in Crossroads at Stone Mountain Park.

Tifton, GA

Georgia's Agrirama Living History Museum

Train ride, Museum

ADDRESS: PO Box Q Tifton, GA 31793
TELEPHONE: (800) 767-1875 or (229) 386-3344
E-MAIL: market@agrirama.com
WEBSITE: www.agrirama.com

DESCRIPTION: This site serves as Agrirama, Georgia's Museum of Agriculture and features a Historic Village. Visitors can ride the logging train into the woods. After disembarking from the railroad depot, they can walk down to the sawmill and turpentine still, see the cooper's shed and the blacksmith's shop before crossing the street to the working print shop. There is a new peanut museum on site and RV park with full hook-ups.

SCHEDULE: Museum: Tuesday through Saturday, 9 a.m. to 5 p.m.; RV park: 7 days, 24 hours.

ADMISSION/FARE: Adults, $7; seniors 55+, $6; children 5-16, $4; children 4 and under, free.

LOCOMOTIVES/ROLLING STOCK: 0-4-0 Porter no. 19, 0-4-0 Vulcan, two open wooden cars, two converted schools, two tender cars, one metal roof car.

SPECIAL EVENTS: Second Saturday in April, Folk Life & Bluegrass Festival.

DIRECTIONS: I-75 exit 63B, Tifton. 100 miles south of Macon; 63 miles north of FL border.

Waycross, GA

Okefenokee Heritage Center

Museum

ADDRESS: 1460 N Augusta Ave. Waycross, GA 31503
TELEPHONE: (912) 285-4260
E-MAIL: ohc@accessatc.net
WEBSITE: www.okeheritage.org

DESCRIPTION: History museum and art gallery. The most visible outdoor exhibit is a 1912 Baldwin steam locomotive with a 342-foot train (including a caboose), and an original train depot housing a collection of railroad memorabilia, a circa 1800s dog-trot house, a 1890 newspaper printing shop, a black heritage exhibit, and a "sacret harp" museum.

SCHEDULE: Tuesday to Saturday, 10 a.m. to 4:30 p.m.; closed on Sunday and Monday.

ADMISSION/FARE: Adults, $3; seniors and AARP members, $2; children 5-17, $2; children under 5, free.

NEARBY ATTRACTIONS: Okefenokee Swamp, Southern Forest World, and Laura Walker Park.

Coupon available, see insert.

HAWAII

Ewa Beach, HI

Hawaiian Railway Society
Train ride, Museum, Display

ADDRESS: PO Box 60369 Ewa Station
Ewa Beach, HI 96706
TELEPHONE: (808) 681-5461
E-MAIL: HawaiianRailway@aol.com
WEBSITE: www.hawaiianrailway.com

DESCRIPTION: The Hawaiian Railway operates 90-minute narrated excursions over 6½ miles of historic Oahu Railway and Land Company (OR&L) track, from the Railway Museum in Ewa to the beautiful Leeward Coast of Oahu.

SCHEDULE: Sunday, 1 and 3 p.m.; call to arrange weekday 45- and 90-minute charter trips.

ADMISSION/FARE: Adults, $10; seniors and children 2-12, $7.

LOCOMOTIVES/ROLLING STOCK: Operational: Two ex-US Navy Whitcomb 45-ton diesel-electric switchers nos. 302 and 423; ex-US Army GE 25-ton diesel-electric switcher no. 7750; more. Display: OR&L steam locomotives no. 6 (0-4-2T) and no. 12 (0-6-0); Ewa Plantation Co. no. 1 (0-4-2T+T); Waialua Agricultural Co. locomotive no. 6 (0-6-2T); more.

SPECIAL EVENTS: Halloween rides at night. Call for times and reservations.

NEARBY ATTRACTIONS: Ko'Olina Resort; Paradise Cove Luau; Hawaiian Adventure Water Park, White Plains Beach, 13 golf courses, and the new city of Kapolei are nearby.

DIRECTIONS: From Honolulu, H-1 West to the Ewa Beach exit. Drive south two miles on Fort Weaver Rd. Turn right on Renton Rd. at the Tesoro Gas Station. Drive one mile west, through Ewa, to the Railway Museum at the end of Renton Rd.

Photo courtesy of Karol J. Chordas, Sr.

Lahaina, HI

Lahaina Kaanapali & Pacific Railroad

Train ride, Dinner train

ADDRESS: 975 Limahana Pl., Ste. 203 Lahaina, HI 96761
TELEPHONE: (800) 499-2307 or (808) 667-6851 for recording
WEBSITE: www.sugarcanetrain.com

DESCRIPTION: The "Sugar Cane Train" chugs its way through Maui by bringing back memories, sounds, and experiences of turn-of-the-century sugar plantation life. The trains were used to transport sugarcane and were a popular means of transportation in the early 1900s. The train stations are designed to resemble turn-of-the-century boarding platforms and offer a delightful glimpse of Hawaii's cultural past.

SCHEDULE: Daily, 10:15 a.m. to 4:30 p.m.

ADMISSION/FARE: Day train round trip: Adults, $18.95; children 3-12, $12.95. Sunset BBQ dinner & show: Adults, $76; children 3-12, $43.

LOCOMOTIVES/ROLLING STOCK: No. 1, "Anaka," 1943 Porter 2-4-0 and no. 3, "Myrtle," 1943 Porter 2-4-0, both former Carbon Limestone Co.; no. 45, "Oahu," 1959 Plymouth diesel, former Oahu Railway; 2 non-operational displays of Oahu 5 and Oahu 86 from Oahu Railway; more.

NEARBY ATTRACTIONS: Historic town of Lahaina, Maui, and resort area of Kaanapali.

DIRECTIONS: Located near Pioneer Mill, turn off Hwy. 30 at Hinau St., turn right at Limahana St. Puukolii Station located north of Kaanapali, turn off Hwy. 30 at Puukolii Rd.

Photo courtesy of Lahaina Kaanapali Railroad.

Wahiawa, HI

Pineapple Express

Park train

ADDRESS: Dole Plantation, 64-1550 Kamehameha Hwy. Wahiawa, HI 96786
TELEPHONE: (808) 621-8408
WEBSITE: www.dole-plantation.com

DESCRIPTION: Passengers learn about the history of pineapples and agriculture in Hawaii on this two-mile, 20-minute, fully narrated train tour. Included is the fascinating story of James Dole and some of the most beautiful scenery on the North Shore.

SCHEDULE: Daily, 9 a.m. to 5 p.m.

ADMISSION/FARE: Adults, $7.50; children, $5.50.

IDAHO

Horseshoe Bend, ID
Thunder Mountain
Line Railroad

Train ride, Dinner train

ADDRESS: 120 Mill Rd., PO Box 487
Horseshoe Bend, ID 83629
TELEPHONE: (877) 432-7245
E-MAIL: cab@rgpc.com
WEBSITE: www.thundermountainline.com

DESCRIPTION: 2½-hour train rides include a passage
through a narrow canyon along Payette River. Train
rides depart from Horseshoe Bend and the mountain
community of Cascade.

SCHEDULE: Horseshoe Bend: March to December, 1:30 and 6:30 p.m.; Cascade: May to
September, 10 a.m. and 2 p.m.

ADMISSION/FARE: Adults, $24.50;
seniors, $23; children, $15; +tax.

LOCOMOTIVES/ROLLING STOCK:
EMD FP10 diesel locomotives;
Pullman passenger cars; Pullman
cars modified to a bar car and
concession car; covered and
uncovered cars.

SPECIAL EVENTS: Wild West Train Robbery, Murder Mystery Train, Wine Tasting Train, Easter
Egg Hunt Train, Pumpkin Liner, Christmas Train, Christmas Tree Cutting Train, Polar Express.

NEARBY ATTRACTIONS: River rafting, Boise National Forest, Lake Cascade, more.

DIRECTIONS: 28 miles north of Boise on Hwy. 55 to Horseshoe Bend and 70 miles north of
Boise on Hwy. 55 to Cascade.

Photo courtesy of Gerald Young.

Nampa, ID
Canyon County Historical Museum
Museum, Display, Model train layout

ADDRESS: 1200 Front St., PO Box 595 Nampa, ID 83653
TELEPHONE: (208) 467-7611
WEBSITE: www.canyoncountyhistory.com

DESCRIPTION: Built in 1903 and used as a depot until 1926, the building now houses displays of Canyon County and Union Pacific memorabilia.

SCHEDULE: Winter: Tuesday through Friday, 1 to 5 p.m.; Saturday, 11 a.m. to 3 p.m.; May 1 to October 31: Tuesday through Friday, 1 to 5 p.m.; Saturday, 10 a.m. to 3 p.m.

ADMISSION/FARE: Free. Suggested donation: adults, $2; children, $1.

LOCOMOTIVES/ROLLING STOCK: Union Pacific caboose no. 25076, can be toured; steam crane, circa 1917.

SPECIAL EVENTS: Snake River Stampede; July: Good Old Dayz, Canyon County Fair & Festival.

NEARBY ATTRACTIONS: War Hawk Air Museum, Celebration Park, Oregon Trail sites, Treasure Valley area, Old Fort Boise.

DIRECTIONS: I-84 to Garrity exit, left on Garrity Rd. to 16th Ave., left at Lakeview Park. Go over overpass, right on first street, right on 12th Ave., then two blocks to Front St.

Wallace, ID
Northern Pacific Depot Railroad Museum
Museum, Display

ADDRESS: 219 6th St., PO Box 469 Wallace, ID 83873
TELEPHONE: (208) 752-0111
E-MAIL: northernpacificdepot@cbridge.net

DESCRIPTION: Railroad artifacts housed in an elegant, chateau-style depot built at the turn of the century. Railroads have been an integral part of the mining district since 1887.

SCHEDULE: April, 10 a.m. to 3 p.m., closed Sunday; May, 9 a.m. to 5 p.m., daily; June to August, 9 a.m. to 7 p.m., daily; September, 9 a.m. to 5 p.m., daily; October, 10 a.m. to 3 p.m., closed Sunday; closed October 15 for season.

ADMISSION/FARE: Adults, $2; seniors, $1.50; children 6-16, $1; children under 6, free; family, $6.

SPECIAL EVENTS: Depot Day Festival and Car Show.

NEARBY ATTRACTIONS: Sierra Silver Mine, Wallace District Mining Museum, Oasis Bordello.

DIRECTIONS: I-90, exits 61-62, Wallace, Idaho.

ILLINOIS

Amboy, IL

Amboy Illinois Central Depot
Museum

SITE ADDRESS: 50 South East Ave. Amboy, IL 61310
MAILING ADDRESS: Amboy Depot Museum, PO Box 108 Amboy, IL 61310
TELEPHONE: (815) 857-4700

DESCRIPTION: Built in 1876, this two-story former Illinois Central division headquarters building has been completely restored as a 5,000 square-foot local history museum. It presents the history of Amboy and its relationship to the Illinois Central Railroad. Also, a country school has been brought to the museum grounds and completely restored. The IC Freight House is undergoing restoration.

SCHEDULE: Year-round: Wednesday, Thursday, and Sunday, 1 to 4 p.m.; Friday and Saturday, 10 a.m. to 4 p.m.

ADMISSION/FARE: By donation.

LOCOMOTIVES/ROLLING STOCK: Static display of USRA-design 0-8-0 switcher built for the Grand Trunk Western as no. 8376; a 1915 wooden Norfolk & Western caboose (unrestored interior).

SPECIAL EVENTS: Thursday to Sunday on the weekend prior to Labor Day weekend, Depot Days; free evening entertainment, parade, carnival, and car show.

NEARBY ATTRACTIONS: Rochelle Railroad Park, Mendota Railroad Museum, and Ronald Reagan's boyhood home in Dixon, Illinois.

DIRECTIONS: In downtown Amboy, two blocks west of US52 on Main St., at intersection of Main St. and East Ave.

Photo courtesy of Lawrence R. Hill.

Carbondale, IL

Station Carbondale
Museum

ADDRESS: 111 S Illinois Ave. Southeast corner of Main & Illinois Carbondale, IL 62901
TELEPHONE: (618) 529-8040

DESCRIPTION: Station Carbondale exhibit is located in the 1903 Old Passenger Depot. It features artifacts from local railroad history, 1950s diesel engine, and Little Reb Caboose.

SCHEDULE: Monday through Friday, 9 a.m. to 3 p.m. or by appointment.

ADMISSION/FARE: Free.

Chatham, IL

Chatham Railroad Museum
Museum

ADDRESS: 100 N State St. Chatham, IL 62629
TELEPHONE: (217) 483-7792
WEBSITE: www.chathamil.net/history/chathamrailroadstation

DESCRIPTION: The station is owned by the Village of Chatham, was restored by the Friends of the Depot in 1991, and in 1999 the Chicago & Illinois Midland Chapter of the National Railway Historical Society agreed to once again restore the station and create the museum.

SCHEDULE: Second and fourth Sundays of each month, 2 to 4 p.m., except holidays.

ADMISSION/FARE: Donations accepted.

SPECIAL EVENTS: Special events periodically during the year; contact for information.

NEARBY ATTRACTIONS: Abraham Lincoln Presidential Museum and Illinois State Capitol.

DIRECTIONS: One block east of IL Route 4 in Chatham.

Photo courtesy of Gary Shurgold.

LOCOMOTIVES/ROLLING STOCK: Milwaukee Road caboose.

SPECIAL EVENTS: First Saturday in May, Great Western Day: additional railroad-related displays.

NEARBY ATTRACTIONS: Apple River Fort, Mississippi Palisades State Park, Apple River Canyon State Park.

DIRECTIONS: Three miles east of the Great River Rd. on US Hwy. 20; turn right on Myrtle St. at the Veterans' Monument in downtown Elizabeth.

Photo courtesy of James Paglin.

Freeport, IL

Silver Creek & Stephenson Railroad

Train ride, Museum
Standard gauge

ADDRESS: US Hwy. 20, PO Box 255   Freeport, IL 61032
TELEPHONE: (815) 232-2306
E-MAIL: peggy1@mwci.net

DESCRIPTION: The turn-of-the-century depot is a tribute to an important part of our country's transportation history. On display are lanterns, locks and keys, whistles, sounders, tickets, couplers, and more, representing railroads from across the country. The 4-mile train trip travels through Illinois farmland and stands of virgin timber known as "Indian Gardens," crossing Yellow Creek on a 30-foot-high cement and stone pier bridge.

SCHEDULE: May 28 and 29, June 17 and 18, July 4, 28 to 30, September 4, 23, and 24, and October 7, 8, and 20 to 22, Train of Terror; scheduled dates: steam; tours: diesel or steam.

ADMISSION/FARE: Adults, $5; children under 12, $3; all fares for Train of Terror, $5.

LOCOMOTIVES/ROLLING STOCK: 1912, 36-ton Heisler; 1941 bay-window caboose, former Chicago, Milwaukee, St. Paul & Pacific; 1889 wooden caboose with cupola, former Hannibal & St. Joseph; 1948 caboose, former Illinois Central Gulf; covered flatcar; 14-ton Brookville switch engine; 12-ton Plymouth switch engine; UP 904493 covered flat car; and work cars.

SPECIAL EVENTS: Old time show: July 29 to 31; Train of Terror: Oct. 21 and 22, 6 to 9 p.m.

DIRECTIONS: 110 miles west of Chicago, on US20. Go 1 mile south on Walnut St.

Galesburg, IL
Galesburg Railroad Museum
Museum

ADDRESS: 211 S Seminary St., PO Box 947 Galesburg, IL 61402-0947
TELEPHONE: (309) 342-9400
E-MAIL: president@galesburgrailroadmuseum.org
WEBSITE: www.galesburgrailroadmuseum.org

DESCRIPTION: The display of artifacts and memorabilia is housed in a new building, dedicated in December, 2004. Visitors can tour a 1930 caboose, 1924 Railway Post Office/Railway Express Agency Car, and 1930 Burlington Route Hudson steam engine.

SCHEDULE: Memorial Day to Labor Day: Tuesday through Saturday, 10 a.m. to 4 p.m.; Sunday, 12 to 4 p.m.; closed Monday.

ADMISSION/FARE: Suggested donation: Adults, $4; children 8-16, $1; family, $10.

LOCOMOTIVES/ROLLING STOCK: CB&Q Hudson no. 3006; CB&Q caboose no. 13501 caboose; CB&Q 1945 Railway Post Office/Railway Express Agency combination car.

SPECIAL EVENTS: Fourth weekend of June, Galesburg Railroad Days.

NEARBY ATTRACTIONS: Discovery Depot Children's Museum, Historic Seminary St. shops.

DIRECTIONS: In downtown Galesburg north of the Amtrak depot.

Greenup, IL
Historic Greenup Depot
Museum, Display, Model train layout
HO scale

ADDRESS: 204 W Cumberland, PO Box 582 Greenup, IL 62428
TELEPHONE: (217) 923-9306
E-MAIL: historic@rr1.net
WEBSITE: www.greenupdepot.org

DESCRIPTION: Historic Greenup Depot is the preserved 1870 Vandalia Line (PRR) Depot, dedicated to the history of American railroading. It is home to the Illinois Mid-State Railroad Association.

SCHEDULE: Daily, 10 a.m. to 4 p.m.

ADMISSION/FARE: Free. Donations accepted.

SPECIAL EVENTS: See website for updates.

NEARBY ATTRACTIONS: Lincoln Log Cabin State Park, historic downtown Greenup, National Rd. covered bridge.

DIRECTIONS: Interstate 70, exit 119. Follow signs to downtown Greenup.

Photo courtesy of Walkabout, Inc.

Kankakee, IL

Kankakee Model Railroad Club and Museum
Display, Model train layout

ADDRESS: 197 S East Ave. Kankakee, IL 60901
TELEPHONE: (815) 929-9320, main or (815) 933-0527 and (815) 933-0462, reservations
WEBSITE: www.kankakeerrmuseum.us

DESCRIPTION: Display area features railroad memorabilia and a 1947 Pullman stainless steel coach. Operating layouts are comprised of three scales of model railroad trains. Stainless-steel available for parties, along with monthly Sunday Brunch with prior reservations required.

SCHEDULE: Tuesday through Sunday, 11 a.m. to 4 p.m.; Sunday, 12 to 4 p.m.

ADMISSION/FARE: Suggested donation: museum, $1; coach, $1.

LOCOMOTIVES/ROLLING STOCK: 1947 Pullman stainless-steel coach. Its original owner was Illinois Central Railroad; it spent many years leased to Santa Fe and ended up with Amtrak. Caboose now on display and a 1900-era streetcar being restored.

SPECIAL EVENTS: Last weekend in May: Kankakee County Railroad Days, crafts and shows.

NEARBY ATTRACTIONS: Kankakee River State Park and Bourbonnais, the fall practice area of the Chicago Bears football team.

DIRECTIONS: One block south of Hwy. 17 in downtown Kankakee, in historic, registered, Kankakee railroad depot.

Photo courtesy of Glenn Johnson.

Mendota, IL

Union Depot Railroad Museum

Museum, Model railroad layout

ADDRESS: 783 Main St. Mendota, IL 61342
TELEPHONE: (815) 538-3800
WEBSITE: www.mendotamuseums.org

DESCRIPTION: Housed in a fully restored portion of the 1888 depot is an HO scale model railroad layout of Mendota in the 1930s. Visitors can tour a 1923 steam locomotive, combine car, and see cafe-lounge car "Golden Trencher."

SCHEDULE: Labor Day to Memorial Day: Saturday and Sunday, 12 to 5 p.m.; Memorial Day to Labor Day: Wednesday to Sunday, 12 to 5 p.m.

ADMISSION/FARE: Adults, $2; children, $1.

LOCOMOTIVES/ROLLING STOCK: CB&Q 2-8-2 no. 4978; no. 2713 Milwaukee combine car; Southern Pacific cafe-lounge "Golden Trencher."

SPECIAL EVENTS: Railroad Days.

NEARBY ATTRACTIONS: Starved Rock State Park; near Rockford, Chicago, and Quad cities.

DIRECTIONS: Three miles west of I-39 on Route 34; 15 miles north of I-80 on Route 251.

Monticello, IL

Monticello Railway Museum

Train ride, Museum
Standard gauge
Radio frequency: 160.635

ADDRESS: 933 Iron Horse Pl., PO Box 401 Monticello, IL 61856
TELEPHONE: (877) 762-9011
WEBSITE: www.mrym.org

DESCRIPTION: An 8-mile round trip on former Illinois Central and Illinois Terminal trackage. Passengers board at Illinois Central depot at the museum or the 1899 Wabash depot in downtown Monticello. Visitors can view displays inside and outside railcars.

SCHEDULE: May to October: weekends and holidays. Museum site departures: Saturday, 11 a.m., 12:30, 2, and 3:30 p.m.; Sunday, 12:30, 2, and 3:30 p.m. Wabash depot departures: Saturday, 11:30 a.m., 1 and 2:30 p.m.; Sunday, 1 and 2:30 p.m. Others upon request.

ADMISSION/FARE: Adults, $7; seniors and children, $5. Subject to change without notice.

LOCOMOTIVES/ROLLING STOCK: 1907 Southern Railway Baldwin 2-8-0 no. 401; 1916 Mississippi Eastern Baldwin 4-6-0 no. 303; 1953 Wabash EMD F7 no. 1189; 1959 CN MLW FPA4 no. 6789; 1955 LIRR Alco RS3 no. 301; newly restored Milwaukee Road NW2 no. 1649 switcher; Illinois Central Railway Post Office car; 1942 AT&SF passenger car Pleasant Valley, newly restored Bates & Rogers 30-ton Industrial Brownhoist steam powered crane, more.

SPECIAL EVENTS: August, Throttle Times, Caboose Days; September, Railroad Days; October, Ghost Train; December, Lunch with Santa.

NEARBY ATTRACTIONS: Allerton Park, nearby Amish and Lincoln sites.

DIRECTIONS: I-72 exit 166, Market St. Turn onto Iron Horse Place at traffic light, go past Best Western to museum.

Photo courtesy of David Marshall.

Peoria, IL

Wheels O' Time Museum

Museum

ADDRESS: 11923 N Knoxville Ave., PO Box 9636 Peoria, IL 61612
TELEPHONE: (309) 243-9020
WEBSITE: www.wheelsotime.org

DESCRIPTION: Steam locomotive, combine car, caboose, switcher, three buildings displaying antique autos, fire trucks, tractors, clocks, musical devices, toys, clothing, and much more.

SCHEDULE: May to October: Wednesday to Sunday, 12 to 5 p.m.; summer holidays.

ADMISSION/FARE: Adults, $5; children, $2.50; children under 3, free.

LOCOMOTIVES/ROLLING STOCK: Rock Island Pacific no. 886; Milwaukee Road combine car; TP&W caboose.

NEARBY ATTRACTIONS: Wildlife Prairie Park, Lakeview Museum.

DIRECTIONS: On Route 40, north of Peoria, 2 miles north of the Route 6 intersection.

Coupon available, see insert.

Rochelle, IL

Rochelle Railroad Park

EDITOR'S CHOICE

Park

ADDRESS: 124 N 9th St., PO Box 331 Rochelle, IL 61068
TELEPHONE: (815) 562-7031
WEBSITE: www.rochellerailroadpark.tripod.com

DESCRIPTION: More than 80 trains pass through Rochelle each day on the UP and BNSF lines. The whole family is welcome to watch from the Hobo Jungle or Pavillion and browse the gift shop.

SCHEDULE: Railroad park: 24 hours a day, 365 days a year; gift shop: Wednesday to Sunday; closed Monday and Tuesday.

LOCOMOTIVES/ROLLING STOCK: Whitcomb industrial locomotive on display.

SPECIAL EVENTS: August 25 to 27, Lincoln Hwy. Heritage Festival; May 20 and 21, First Annual Rochelle Railroad Days.

NEARBY ATTRACTIONS: Magic Waters, Rockford, Mendoza Rail Museum, Amboy Depot, Flago Township Historical Museum.

DIRECTIONS: I-39 to Hwy. 38, west on 38 to 9th St., South on 9th St. to Railroad Park, or I-88 to 251, north on 251. Right on Washington St., left on First Ave., right on 9th St.

Rockford, IL

Trolley Car 36

Trolley ride

ADDRESS: 324 N Madison St. Rockford, IL 61107
TELEPHONE: (815) 987-8894
WEBSITE: www.rockfordparkdistrict.org

DESCRIPTION: A 45-minute trolley ride along Rockford's historic riverfront, with a ten-minute stopover at Sinnissippi Gardens and Lagoon. Meal rides available.

SCHEDULE: June to September; Thursday, Saturday, and Sunday, 12 to 4 p.m.

ADMISSION/FARE: Adults, $4; children, $3.50; children 3 and under, free.

LOCOMOTIVES/ROLLING STOCK: Trolley car no. 36.

NEARBY ATTRACTIONS: Forest City Queen Riverboat ride.

South Elgin, IL
Fox River Trolley Museum
EDITOR'S CHOICE
Train ride, Museum, Display
Standard gauge
Radio frequency: 160.905

ADDRESS: 361 S LaFox St. (IL Route 31), PO Box 315 South Elgin, IL 60177-0315
TELEPHONE: (847) 697-4676
E-MAIL: info@foxtrolley.org
WEBSITE: www.foxtrolley.org

DESCRIPTION: Passengers ride the historic 110-year-old remnant of an interurban railroad aboard Chicago-area trolleys and "L" equipment. The trip includes operation on the new ½-mile line into the Jon J. Duerr (Blackhawk) Forest Preserve.

SCHEDULE: Mother's Day to first November Sunday: Sunday and holidays, 11 a.m. to 5 p.m.; last June Saturday to Labor Day weekend: Saturday, 11 a.m. to 5 p.m.; Memorial Day, Independence Day, and Labor Day, 11 a.m. to 5 p.m.

ADMISSION/FARE: Adults, $3.50; seniors, $2; children 3-11, $2; Second ride $0.50.

LOCOMOTIVES/ROLLING STOCK: Historic Chicago interurban and "L" equipment, including CA&E no. 20, North Shore nos. 715 and 756; CTA nos. 40, 43, 4451, and L202; CRT 5001; AE&FRE no. 5 (diesel).

SPECIAL EVENTS: Mother's Day; Spring Caboose Day; Father's Day; July 4, Red, White, and Blue Day; August 19 and 20, Trolley Fest-River Fest Express; last two weekends in October, Fall Caboose Day and Pumpkin Trolley.

NEARBY ATTRACTIONS: Grand Victoria Casino, Elgin Public Museum, Batavia Depot Museum (CB&Q), Jon J. Duerr (Blackhawk) Forest Preserve, South Elgin-Peasley House; Valley Model Railroad Club (Clintonville). Historic valley towns.

DIRECTIONS: Illinois 31 south from I-90 or US20 or north from I-88. Site is 3 blocks south of State St. traffic light in South Elgin.

Photo courtesy of Jack Sowchin.

Union, IL

Illinois Railway Museum

Train ride, Dinner train, Museum, Display
Standard gauge

ADDRESS: 7000 Olson Rd. Union, IL 60180
TELEPHONE: (800) BIG-RAIL or (815) 923-4000
WEBSITE: www.irm.org

DESCRIPTION: More than 400 pieces of equipment and artifacts operate or are on display in car barns and open railyards, including steam, diesel, and electric locomotives; electric interurbans, elevated cars, and streetcars; trolley buses and motor buses, as well as passenger and freight equipment. A 9½-mile round trip over the reconstructed Elgin & Belvedere interurban right-of-way is offered, featuring steam or diesel trains and electric interurbans.

SCHEDULE: Memorial Day through Labor Day, weekdays; April through October, Sunday; May through October, Saturday.

ADMISSION/FARE: Special: Adults, $12; children and seniors, $10; fees subject to change.

LOCOMOTIVES/ROLLING STOCK: Santa Fe 4-8-4 no. 2903; Frisco 2-10-0 no. 1630; N&W 2-8-8-2 no. 2050; CB&Q EMC E5 no. 9911A; UP DDA40X no. 6930; PRR GG1 no. 4927; more.

SPECIAL EVENTS: 4th of July Trolley Pageant, Vintage Transport Day, Day Out With Thomas™.

NEARBY ATTRACTIONS: Donley's Wild West Town, McHenry County Historical Society.

DIRECTIONS: One mile east of Union off US Route 20.

Photo courtesy of B. Lanphier.
See ad on page A-38.

Union, IL

Valley View Model Railroad

Display, Model train layout

ADDRESS: 17108 Highbridge Rd. Union, IL 60180
TELEPHONE: (815) 923-4135

DESCRIPTION: Modeled after the Chicago & North Western's Northwest line, the layout has over 8 scale miles of track, 300 buildings, 350 pieces of rolling stock, 64 turnouts, 700 vehicles, 900 people, and more.

SCHEDULE: Memorial Day through Labor Day: Wednesday, Saturday, and Sunday.

ADMISSION/FARE: Adults, $5; seniors, $4; children over 5, $2.50.

DIRECTIONS: From Illinois Railway Museum, go north on Olson to Highbridge.

Photo courtesy of John Benick.
Coupon available, see insert.

Waterman, IL

Waterman & Western Railroad
Miniature train ride
15" gauge

ADDRESS: Adams & Birch in Lions Club Park, PO Box 217 Waterman, IL 60556
TELEPHONE: (815) 264-7753
WEBSITE: www.petestrain.com

DESCRIPTION: One-mile train ride around a Waterman city park.

SCHEDULE: Memorial Day to Labor Day: Sunday, 1 to 4 p.m.

ADMISSION/FARE: Adults, $1.50; children under two, free.

LOCOMOTIVES/ROLLING STOCK: $\frac{1}{3}$ scale F-3 loco, 10 passenger railbus, 4-6-4 Hudson Steam loco under restoration.

SPECIAL EVENTS: October weekends, Pumpkin Train; December, Thursday through Sunday, 5 to 9 p.m., Holiday Lights Train.

NEARBY ATTRACTIONS: Shabbona State Park Smiles.

DIRECTIONS: Two blocks south of US30 in city park in downtown Waterman.

TRAVEL TIP: *Thomas the Tank Engine*

If you have a youngster at home, Thomas the Tank Engine visits many tourist railroads and museums each year. Thomas is a great way to introduce another generation to the excitement of railroading. Check your local PBS listings for shows, and then check your favorite railroad for a visit from Thomas.

INDIANA

INDIANA

Connersville, IN

Whitewater Valley Railroad

Train ride
Standard gauge

ADDRESS: 455 Market St. Connersville, IN 47331
TELEPHONE: (765) 825-2054
WEBSITE: www.whitewatervalleyrr.org

DESCRIPTION: This line offers a 32-mile, five-hour round trip to Metamora, a restored canal town with shops and a working grist mill. A two-hour stopover gives passengers a chance to tour the town. Also offers the last operating Lima diesel.

SCHEDULE: May to October: weekends and holidays, 12:01 p.m.; May: Thursday and Friday, 10 a.m.; October: Thursday and Friday, 10 a.m.

ADMISSION/FARE: Adults, $18; children 2-12, $10; children under 2, free. One-way and group rates available.

LOCOMOTIVES/ROLLING STOCK: 1907 Baldwin 0-6-0 no. 6, former East Broad Top; 1919 Baldwin 2-6-2 no. 100; 1924 Vulcan 0-4-0T, former Southwestern Portland Cement; Lima-Hamiltons no. 25, former CUT, no. 320, former B&O, and no. 709, former Armco Steel; 1948 Alco S1 no. 9339, former Proctor & Gamble; 1946 GE 70-ton no. 8, former Muncie & Western; 1946 GE 70-ton no. 210, former Calumet & Hecla; 1954 EMD SD10 no. 532, former Milwaukee; 1943 GE 65-ton centercab no. 1, former USN; 1931 Plymouth ML 32-ton gas engine no. 2561, 1949 Baldwin S-12 no. 99, former Amhurst Ind.; 1951 Baldwin S-12 no. 346, former Patapsco and Back River; Erie Stillwell, and Rock Island coaches; 9 cabooses.

SPECIAL EVENTS: First and third Friday of each month May through October, Train-to-Dinner; first weekend in October, Metamora Canal Days; November and December, Christmas Trains; many other special events, call or write for information.

NEARBY ATTRACTIONS: Whitewater State Park, Brookville Lake, Mary Gray Bird Sanctuary.

DIRECTIONS: Corner of Fifth and Grand in downtown Connersville (Market St.).

Photo courtesy of John R. Hillman.

National New York Central Railroad Museum
Museum, Display

ADDRESS: 721 S Main St. Elkhart, IN 46515
TELEPHONE: (219) 294-3001
E-MAIL: rick1216@myvine.com
WEBSITE: http://nycrrmuseum.org

DESCRIPTION: The museum traces the history of the New York Central and its impact on Elkhart as well as the nation. Extensive hands-on exhibits bring railroading alive. Founded in 1987, the museum is a preserver of both local and national railroad heritage. Visitors enter through a 1915 passenger coach that introduces a timeline to the local railroad history beginning in 1833.

SCHEDULE: Summer hours: April to September: Tuesday to Saturday, 10 a.m. to 4 p.m.; Sunday, 12 to 4 p.m.; winter hours: October to December: Tuesday to Friday, 10 a.m. to 2 p.m.; Saturday, 10 a.m. to 4 p.m.; Sunday, 12 to 4 p.m.; January to March: Thursday and Friday, 10 a.m. to 2 p.m.; Saturday 10 a.m. to 4 p.m.; Sunday call ahead.

ADMISSION/FARE: Adults 13-61, $5; seniors 62+, $4; children 4-12, $4; children 3 and under, free. Ask about family rates.

LOCOMOTIVES/ROLLING STOCK: NYC Mohawk no. 3001; NYC E8A no. 408; PRR GG1 no. 4882; CSS&SB no. 15; six passenger cars including grill car no. 953; seven freight cars; seven cabooses; six non-revenue pieces including a 250-ton Industrial Brownhoist self-propelled crane that was used at the Selkirk, NY yard.

SPECIAL EVENTS: June, Annual Open House; October, Trackside Terror Weekends, 6 to 10 p.m.

NEARBY ATTRACTIONS: Elkhart Depot built 1901, Norfolk Southern Elkhart yard, Northern Indiana Amish Country, Midwest Museum of Art, Time Was Museum, Ruthmere 1910 House Museum, Elkhart County Historical Museum, RV/MH Museum, Old Wakarusa Railroad, and Elkhart & Western Shortline.

DIRECTIONS: Indiana Toll Rd. (I-80/90) exit 92. IN 19 to Main St. Follow to downtown Elkhart. Cross over NS mainline and immediately turn right into museum's parking lot.

Photo: Power of a Century, courtesy of Mitchell Markovitz.
Coupon available, see insert.

Forest Park, IN

Indiana Transportation Museum
Train ride, Dinner train, Museum, Display
Standard gauge

SITE ADDRESS: SR19 Forest Park, IN 46061
MAILING ADDRESS: PO Box 83 Noblesville, IN 46061
TELEPHONE: (317) 773-6000, recording or (317) 776-7887, gift shop
E-MAIL: nkp587@iquest.net
WEBSITE: www.itm.org

DESCRIPTION: Many railroad cars are on display, with an extensive locomotive and rolling stock collection. Train rides are available through rural Hamilton County.

SCHEDULE: April through October: Saturday and Sunday, 11 a.m. to 4 p.m.; closed August 13, 14, 20, and 21.

ADMISSION/FARE: Museum: adults, $3; children 3-12, $2; children under 3, free; train: varies.

LOCOMOTIVES/ROLLING STOCK: Diesels: Monon SW1, Nickel Plate GP7 no. 426, Union Pacific GP9 no. 200; Nickel Plate-painted Baldwin VO1000 no. 99; Nickel Plate-painted GE 44-tonner no. 90; Nickel Plate 2-8-2 steam locomotive no. 587; 1930 L&N diner; 8 Budd stainless-steel coaches from Santa Fe; business cars: Florida East Coast no. 90 and NKP no. 1. Cabooses: C&O no. 90876, NKP nos. 770 and 405.

SPECIAL EVENTS: August, Fair Train during Indiana State Fair; September, Atlanta New Earth Festival; December, Polar Bear Express; Friday evenings, Hamiltonian to restaurants in Cicero and Atlanta.

DIRECTIONS: Approximately 25 miles northeast of Indianapolis in Forest Park/Noblesville on SR19, just north of the intersection with SR32.

Photo courtesy of Wayne Williams.
See ad on page A-17.

French Lick, IN
French Lick, West Baden & Southern Railway
Train ride, Museum
Standard gauge

ADDRESS: 1 Monon St., PO Box 150 French Lick, IN 47432
TELEPHONE: (812) 936-2405
E-MAIL: info@indianarailwaymuseum.org
WEBSITE: www.indianarailwaymuseum.org

DESCRIPTION: Trains make a 20-mile round trip between the resort town of French Lick and Cuzco, site of Patoka Lake. The train traverses wooded Indiana limestone country and passes through a half-mile tunnel.

SCHEDULE: April through October: weekends and Memorial Day, July 4, and Labor Day, 10 a.m.; 1 and 4 p.m.; June through October: Tuesdays, 1 p.m.; November: weekends, 1 p.m.

ADMISSION/FARE: Adults 12 and up, $12; children 3-11, $6.

LOCOMOTIVES/ROLLING STOCK: 1947 Alco RS1, 1947 General Electric 80-ton switcher.

SPECIAL EVENTS: Wild West holdups are scheduled for many holiday weekends. Call or write for information.

NEARBY ATTRACTIONS: French Lick Springs Resort and Patoka Lake.

DIRECTIONS: Trains depart the old Monon Depot on Hwy. 56 in French Lick.

Photo courtesy of Alan Barnett.

Hesston, IN
Hesston Steam Museum
Train ride, Museum

SITE ADDRESS: LaPorte CR1000 N Hesston, IN
MAILING ADDRESS: 1362 E 1000 N La Porte, IN 46350
TELEPHONE: (219) 778-2260
WEBSITE: www.hesston.org

DESCRIPTION: Three railroads take visitors through deep woods and scenic Indiana countryside over 1- and 2-mile tracks. Also on display: steam saw mill, steam-powered light plant, 92-ton railroad steam crane, more.

SCHEDULE: Memorial Day weekend to Labor Day: Saturday and Sunday; September to October: Sunday; first two weekends in December. Trains depart from 12 to 5 p.m.

ADMISSION/FARE: Free except Labor Day weekend; train: adults, $5; children 3-12, $3; children 2 and under, free.

LOCOMOTIVES/ROLLING STOCK: No. 7, a 67-ton, 3-truck Shay, ex-New Mexico Lumber Co.; no. 993361 0-8-0 Orenstein and Koppel; no. 1930 12-ton 0-4-0T Koblen Danake Werke; no. 17 22-ton 2-6-0 Porter, ex-United Fruit Co.; no. 242 10-ton 2-4-2 Sandley Light Railway Works.

SPECIAL EVENTS: Memorial Day Weekend, Whistle-Stop Days; Labor Day Weekend, Annual Hesston Steam and Power Show; October, Ghost Train; December, Santa's Candy Cane Express.

NEARBY ATTRACTIONS: Lighthouse Mall, Dunes National Lakeshore, Washington Park Beach/Zoo, Blue Chip Casino, charter boat fishing, Door Prairie Auto Museum.

DIRECTIONS: South of Indiana-Michigan state line. Four miles east of State Rd. 39 north of LaPorte or south of New Buffalo to 1000 North, turn east, go for about 3 miles.

Photo courtesy of Hesston Steam Museum.

Knightstown, IN

Carthage Knightstown & Shirley Railroad
Train ride
Standard gauge
Radio frequency: 160.695

ADDRESS: 112 W Carey St. Knightstown, IN 46148
TELEPHONE: (765) 345-5561
E-MAIL: cksrrinc@netzero.net
WEBSITE: www.cksrail.com

DESCRIPTION: A 10-mile, 1¼-hour round trip from Knightstown to Carthage.

SCHEDULE: May to October: weekends, 11 a.m., 1 and 3 p.m.; Friday, 11 a.m.

ADMISSION/FARE: Adults, $7; children 3-11, $5; children under 3, free; group rates available.

LOCOMOTIVES/ROLLING STOCK: GE 44-ton no. 215; GE 44-ton no. 468; miscellaneous coaches and cabooses.

DIRECTIONS: 30 miles east of Indianapolis on US40; three miles south of I-70 on SR 109.

Photo courtesy of CKS Railroad.

Linden Railroad Museum
Museum, Display, Model train layout
HO, O, and N scale

ADDRESS: 520 N Main St., PO Box 154 Linden, IN 47955
TELEPHONE: (800) 866-3973 or (765) 339-7245
E-MAIL: weaver@tctc.com
WEBSITE: www.tctc.com/~weaver/depot.htm

DESCRIPTION: The Linden Railroad Museum displays collections of Nickel Plate Road and Monon Railroad memorabilia. Adjacent to the present-day Indianapolis-Chicago mainline of the CSX Railroad (formerly the Monon) and the abandoned Norfolk Southern Railroad (formerly the Nickel Plate), the depot was built in 1907.

SCHEDULE: May through September: Friday through Sunday, 1 to 5 p.m.

ADMISSION/FARE: Adults, $2; youth 13-17, $1; children 6-12, $0.50; children under 6, free.

LOCOMOTIVES/ROLLING STOCK: Nickel Plate caboose no. 497; Monon caboose C-283; 50' boxcar no. 1620; Monon flatcar under refurbishment; a 40-ton Plymouth diesel switch engine.

SPECIAL EVENTS: July 8, open house: free hot dogs and soft drinks. No admission charge.

NEARBY ATTRACTIONS: Museums in Crawfordsville, IN.

DIRECTIONS: Linden is 10 miles north of Crawfordsville on US231; 18 miles south of Lafayette on US231. The museum is on the north side of Linden.

Photo courtesy of Joe Weaver.
Coupon available, see insert.

KEY TO SYMBOLS

Handicapped accessible	Restaurant	Arts and crafts	Association of Railway Museums
Parking	Picnic area	Memberships available	Tourist Railway Association, Inc.
Bus/RV parking	Dining car	Send S.A.S.E. for brochure	Amtrak service to nearby city
Gift, book, or museum shop	Excursions	National Register of Historic Places	VIA service to nearby city
Refreshments	Guided tours	VISA MasterCard DISCOVER American Express Card	Credit cards accepted

Madison, IN

Jefferson County Historical Society Railroad Museum

Museum

ADDRESS: 615 W First St. Madison, IN 47250
TELEPHONE: (812) 265-2335
E-MAIL: jchs@seidata.com
WEBSITE: www.jcohs.org

DESCRIPTION: This restored 1895 Pennsylvania Railroad station is known for its 2½-story octagon waiting room topped by stained glass windows. Exhibits include history of the Madison Railroad Station, from passenger terminal to community center to freight terminal to warehouse; the Madison Railroad Incline, which was an engineering wonder in its day—over 7,000 ft. long with a 5.9% grade that took five years to build; the Reuben Wells, and other special locomotives that were built to climb the incline; a reconstructed agent's office; a restored caboose; and other local railroad memorabilia.

SCHEDULE: May 1 through October 31: Monday through Saturday, 10 a.m. to 4:30 p.m.; Sunday, 1 to 4 p.m.; November through April: weekdays only.

ADMISSION/FARE: $4; 16 and under, free.

LOCOMOTIVES/ROLLING STOCK:
1918 L&N caboose.

SPECIAL EVENTS: May 13, 14, 20, and 21, 2006, Madison in Bloom.

NEARBY ATTRACTIONS: Clifty Falls State Park, Lanier Mansion, antique shops, wineries, bed and breakfast, Ohio River.

DIRECTIONS: Hwys. 56 and 421, located in downtown historic Madison.

TRAVEL TIP: *Safety first*

It's always a good idea to practice some good basic safety around railroad tracks. Always give the trains plenty of room if you're standing close to an active track—the trains are wider than the gauge of the rails. Watch your step as you board. If you lean out of a window or open vestibule door, watch for tree limbs, and wear safety glasses, especially if there's a steam locomotive up front.

New Haven, IN

Fort Wayne Railroad Historical Society

Train ride, Museum, Display
Standard gauge

SITE ADDRESS: 15808 Edgerton Rd. New Haven, IN 46855
MAILING ADDRESS: PO Box 11017 Fort Wayne, IN 46855
TELEPHONE: (260) 493-0765
E-MAIL: kelly@765.org
WEBSITE: www.765.org

DESCRIPTION: The society is home to the recently rebuilt Nickel Plate steam locomotive 765. Visitors can tour the facility, talk to the people who maintain and operate this historic rail equipment, sit in the engineer's seat of this 400-ton iron horse, and get a conductor's eye view from a 100-year-old caboose. The society offers an Engineer for an Hour program on a diesel locomotive. Several times each year, the society has operating days with railroad equipment in action and rides aboard a vintage caboose.

SCHEDULE: Self-guided tours: Saturday, 9 a.m. to 4 p.m. Check website for operation days on site excursions being planned with 765 for 2006.

ADMISSION/FARE: Museum/self-guided tour, free; train ride, $3 to $4.

LOCOMOTIVES/ROLLING STOCK: Nickel Plate Road 2-8-4 steam locomotive no. 765; Lake Erie & Fort Wayne 0-6-0 no. 1; NKP wooden caboose no. 141; Wabash wooden caboose no. 2543; N&W wrecker no. 540019; 44-ton Davenport diesel no. 1231; NKP wooden boxcar no. 83047; NKP bay window caboose no. 451.

SPECIAL EVENTS: Annual open house with operating equipment; December, Caboose Ride with Santa; Engineer for an Hour program.

NEARBY ATTRACTIONS: Little River Railroad, Coldwater, MI; Monticello Railroad Museum, Monticello, IN; Indiana Transportation Museum, Nobelsville, IN.

DIRECTIONS: From New Haven take Lincoln Hwy./Dawkins Rd. east to Ryan Rd., then left to Edgerton Rd. Turn right, and the society is 1.5 miles on the right.

North Judson, IN

Hoosier Valley Railroad Museum

Train ride, Museum, Display
Standard gauge

ADDRESS: 507 Mulberry St., PO Box 75 North Judson, IN 46366
TELEPHONE: (574) 896-3950 depot or (574) 946-6499 secretary
E-MAIL: hvrm@yahoo.com
WEBSITE: http://hvrm.railfan.net

DESCRIPTION: Established in 1988; the collection consists of 30 pieces of rolling stock, including the former Chesapeake & Ohio 2-8-4 steam locomotive no. 2789 and various types of restored railroad signals. Short caboose rides also available.

SCHEDULE: Museum: year-round, Saturday, 8 a.m. to 5 p.m.; caboose rides/motor car rides/guest engineer program: May through September. Schedule subject to change; check website for updated information.

ADMISSION/FARE: No admission fee. Donations welcome.

LOCOMOTIVES/ROLLING STOCK: C&O 2-8-4 no. 2789; Erie Alco S1 switcher no. 310; EL caboose no. C345; 1952 GE 95-ton switcher no. 11; NKP caboose no. 471; 1941 Whitcomb 44-ton switcher no. 27; 1945 Orton locomotive crane; Pullman WWII troop/exhibit car; 30 pieces rolling stock.

NEARBY ATTRACTIONS: Tippecanoe River State Park, Bass Lake State Beach, Kersting's Cycle Center & Museum, Grand Central Station Restaurant—downtown North Judson.

DIRECTIONS: Seventy miles southeast of downtown Chicago, Indiana 10 and 39.

Santa Claus, IN

Freedom Train

Train ride
25" gauge

ADDRESS: 425 E Christmas Blvd., PO Box 179 Santa Claus, IN 47579
TELEPHONE: (812) 937-4401 or (877) 463-2645
E-MAIL: fun@holidayworld.com
WEBSITE: www.holidayworld.com

DESCRIPTION: Amusement park with live steam train ride.

SCHEDULE: Current daily operating hours and admission fees are posted on the website.

LOCOMOTIVES/ROLLING STOCK: Manufactured by George Koch and Sons, 1946.

NEARBY ATTRACTIONS: Lake Rudolph Resort, Lincoln State Park, and Lincoln Berghood National Park.

DIRECTIONS: Ten minutes south of I-64 exit 63/Hwy. 162 south.

Photo courtesy of Karen Hurst.

Terre Haute, IN
Wabash Valley Railroaders Museum
Museum, Display

ADDRESS: 1316 Plum St., PO Box 10291 Terre Haute, IN 47801
TELEPHONE: (812) 238-9958
E-MAIL: fosterwc@joink.com
WEBSITE: www.haleytower.org

DESCRIPTION: Two interlocking towers with operating machines, a depot, and viewing platform adjacent to CSXT mainlines. Haley Tower was one of the last manned interlocking towers in the Midwest. It has since been moved to its current location. Later, Spring Hill Tower was purchased by the society and also moved to the site.

SCHEDULE: May through October: Saturday, Sunday, and some holidays, 11 a.m. to 3 p.m.

ADMISSION/FARE: Free admission, donations welcomed.

BUILDINGS: C&EI Haley tower; Milwaukee Road Spring Hill tower; Vandalia Railroad Depot.

NEARBY ATTRACTIONS: Indiana State University; Swope Art Gallery; Vigo County Historical Museum; various restaurants and lodging within one to two miles.

DIRECTIONS: US41 to Eighth Ave. East to 13th St. (just before railroad tracks). Left to Plum St. Look for Spring Hill and Haley tower.

Photo courtesy of John Fuller.

IOWA

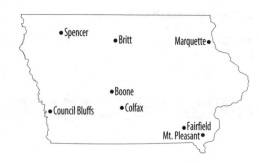

Boone, IA

Boone & Scenic Valley Railroad

*Train ride, Dinner train,
Museum, Display
Standard gauge
Radio frequency: 160.53000*

ADDRESS: 225 Tenth St., PO Box 603 Boone, IA 50036
TELEPHONE: (515) 432-4249
E-MAIL: bandsvrr@tdsi.net
WEBSITE: www.scenic-valleyrr.com

DESCRIPTION: Passengers can enjoy a 1¾-hour ride (2½-hour dinner and dessert trains) over two great bridges through the Des Moines River Valley on the former Fort Dodge, Des Moines & Southern. The railroad was begun in 1893 for the purpose of transporting coal. Visitors can further enjoy the history of railroading at the railroad's museum.

SCHEDULE: May: Saturday, 1:30 p.m.; Memorial Day to October 31: daily and weekends, 1:30 and 4 p.m.; April to second December Saturday and June to October: Friday; dinner train: Memorial Day to end of October: Saturday, 5:30 p.m.; dessert train: weekends.

ADMISSION/FARE: Adults, $14; children 3-12, $5; dinner train, $50; dessert train, $25.

LOCOMOTIVES/ROLLING STOCK:
Steam: Chinese-built 2-8-2 no. JS8419. Diesel: Alco S2 no. 1098; 80-ton GE center cab no. 2254; NW2 no. 1003; FP9 no. 6540; Alco RS1 no. 205; more. Coaches: Erie Lackawanna nos. 3238, 9101, 3213, 3207, 3218; Rock Island no. 2584.

SPECIAL EVENTS: Last weekend in July, Civil War re-enactment; weekend after Labor Day, Pufferbilley Days; September, Day Out With Thomas™.

NEARBY ATTRACTIONS: Ledges State Park, Mamie Doud Eisenhower birthplace, Iowa Arboretum, Don William County Park, Boone Speedway, Kate Shelley Memorial High Bridge, and Seven Oaks recreation area.

DIRECTIONS: Take Hwy. 30 west from I-35 at Ames to stop sign at south end of Boone, turn right. Go to 11th St. Turn west and go six blocks.

Photo courtesy of Fenner Stevenson.
See ad on page A-21.

Fairfield, IA
Rail Merchants International
Showroom

ADDRESS: 700 W Grimes, PO Box 2019 Fairfield, IA 52556
TELEPHONE: (641) 472-2020
E-MAIL: caboose@lisco.com
WEBSITE: www.railmerchants.net

DESCRIPTION: Various pieces of rolling stock and railroadiana are on display and for sale. The organization specializes in saving cabooses, private rail cars, and track inspection cars.

ADMISSION/FARE: Free.

LOCOMOTIVES/ROLLING STOCK: Various; usually at least 25 pieces of equipment.

SPECIAL EVENTS: Art and other exhibits throughout the year. Please call for details.

NEARBY ATTRACTIONS: Old Thresher's, Mt. Pleasant (20 miles), 3-ft ga. steam, standard ga. trolleys, exhibits, stage shows, stationary steam thresher demonstrations, auctions, and flea markets. Mississippi railroad bridge 50 miles away in Burlington.

DIRECTIONS: On US Hwy. 3, Fairfield, Iowa. Sixty miles south of Iowa City & I-80. At m.p. 256 on the CB&Q (BNSF) Chicago-Denver mainline (California Zephyr).

Marquette, IA
Depot Museum & Information Center

SITE ADDRESS: 216 Edgar St. Marquette, IA 52158
MAILING ADDRESS: PO Box 274-PH Marquette, IA 52158
TELEPHONE: (563) 873-1200

DESCRIPTION: Depot museum, gift shop, and information center housed in a renovated Milwaukee Road depot. Museum displays railroad artifacts and history of Milwaukee Road.

SCHEDULE: May to October: daily, 10 a.m. to 4 p.m.

SPECIAL EVENTS: September 16, Railroad Days.

DIRECTIONS: Hwy. 18 Wisconsin/Iowa Bridge.

Photo courtesy of Denise Schneider.

Mt. Pleasant, IA

Midwest Central Railroad

Train ride, Museum
3' gauge

SITE ADDRESS: 6101 Francis Ave. Des Moines, IA 50322
MAILING ADDRESS: PO Box 102 Mt. Pleasant, IA 52641
TELEPHONE: (319) 385-2912

DESCRIPTION: A one-mile steam train ride encircles the grounds of the Midwest Old Threshers grounds, with two trains and three section cars.

SCHEDULE: August 31 through September 4 in conjunction with the Old Threshers Reunion; October 14, 20, 21, 27 and 28, Ghost Train; December 1 through 3, North Pole Express.

ADMISSION/FARE: Round trip during Reunion: adults, $2; children, $1. Prices vary for Ghost Train and Christmas Train.

LOCOMOTIVES/ROLLING STOCK: 1891 Baldwin 2-6-0 no. 6 from the Surrey, Sussex & Southhampton Railway; 1923 Lima three-truck Shay no. 9 from the West Side Lumber Co.; 1951 Henschel 0-4-0T no. 16; 1935 Vulcan gas-mechanical switcher; three vintage speeders; five wooden coaches; wooden caboose; White Pass & Yukon steel caboose no. 903; 1880 Bellevue and Cascade caboose no. 055.

SPECIAL EVENTS: October, Ghost Train; December, North Pole Express.

NEARBY ATTRACTIONS: Old Threshers Heritage Museum, James VanAllen House, Harlan-Lincoln House, Dover Museum, and Lewelling House.

DIRECTIONS: Five blocks south of Hwy. 34 on Walnut St.

Photo courtesy of Paul Knowles.

TRAVEL TIP: *Take your camera!*

It's traditional to get a snapshot of you and your family with the locomotive hauling your train. Don't be shy about asking the locomotive crew or the conductor to pose. They're especially good subjects in their uniforms.

Spencer, IA

Northwest Iowa Railway Historical Society

Train ride, Dinner train
Standard gauge

ADDRESS: 1702 Grand Plaza Dr. Spencer, IA 51301
TELEPHONE: (866) 621-9600
E-MAIL: mjohn@ncn.net

DESCRIPTION: Passengers can take a nostalgic trip through the lakes, marshes, and prairies of the beautiful Iowa Great Lakes Region. Weekend excursions on the former Rock Island lines include a round trip. Passengers may board at Orleans, Spirit Lake, or Lake Park and are returned to their departure point. Dinner train operates on Saturday evening, and the Picnic on the Rails train operates at mid-day Sunday. This family-oriented activity is aboard 1940s vintage passenger cars that originally were built for long distance service.

ADMISSION/FARE: Rides: adults, $15; children 3-12, $11; dinner train: adults, $45; seniors, $40; children, $30; Sunday Picnic on the Rails: adults, $25; children 3-12, $20.

LOCOMOTIVES/ROLLING STOCK: Former Chesapeake & Ohio SD18; five CP coaches, one converted to a power car, one converted to a diner car; one ex-UP CA-8 caboose.

NEARBY ATTRACTIONS: Iowa Great Lakes, West Okoboji (major resort area in NW Iowa).

Coupon available, see insert.

KEY TO SYMBOLS

Handicapped accessible	**Restaurant**	**Arts and crafts**	**Association of Railway Museums**
Parking	**Picnic area**	**Memberships available**	**Tourist Railway Association, Inc.**
Bus/RV parking	**Dining car**	**Send S.A.S.E. for brochure**	**Amtrak service to nearby city**
Gift, book, or museum shop	**Excursions**	**National Register of Historic Places**	**VIA service to nearby city**
Refreshments	**Guided tours**		**Credit cards accepted**

KANSAS

Abilene, KS

Abilene & Smoky Valley Railroad

Train ride, Dinner train
Standard gauge

Abilene•   Baldwin City•

•Kingman

Scammon•

ADDRESS: 200 S Fifth Abilene, KS 67410
TELEPHONE: (888) 426-6687 or (888) 426-6689
WEBSITE: www.asvrr.org

DESCRIPTION: A 1½-hour, 10-mile round trip goes through the Smoky Hill River Valley from historic Abilene to Enterprise, Kansas. The track crosses the river on a high span steel bridge. The diesel-powered excursion train includes a restored 1902 wood Katy passenger car converted to a dining car, two open air gondola cars with canopy tops, and a caboose.

SCHEDULE: Memorial Day to Labor Day: Tuesday through Sunday; May, September through October: weekends; dinner train specials; call or write for more information.

ADMISSION/FARE: Persons 12 and up, $10; children 3-11, $6. Dinner train prices vary. All prices subject to change without notice.

LOCOMOTIVES/ROLLING STOCK: 1945 Alco S1; 1945 GE 44-ton; 1945 Whitcomb 45-ton side-rod; more.

SPECIAL EVENTS: Easter Bunny Train; Saturday of first full weekend in October, Abilene-Chisholm Trail Day; Santa Claus Train; call or write for details.

NEARBY ATTRACTIONS: Eisenhower Center, Dickinson County Heritage Center, C. W. Parker Carousel, Greyhound Hall of Fame, Great Plains Theater Festival, and Great Plains Theater.

DIRECTIONS: Located in Old Abilene. I-70 exit 275, south 2 miles on K-15 (Buckeye St.). Located in historic 1887 Rock Island Depot.

Baldwin City, KS

Midland Railway

Train ride
Standard gauge
Radio frequency: 160.380 and 161.400

SITE ADDRESS: 1515 W High St. Baldwin City, KS 66006
MAILING ADDRESS: PO Box 5 Baldwin City, KS 66006-0005
TELEPHONE: (800) 651-0388 info or (785) 594-6982 depot
E-MAIL: jashaw@birch.net
WEBSITE: www.midland-ry.org

DESCRIPTION: The Midland Railway operates excursion trains on a line originally constructed in 1867. The 21-mile round trip goes from Baldwin City to Ottawa Junction, KS, via Norwood, across two 200-foot trestles, and through a working rock quarry.

SCHEDULE: Baldwin City to Norwood: Memorial Day to October: Thursday, 10:30 a.m.; weekends and holidays, 11 a.m.; Baldwin City to Ottawa Junction: 1 to 3:30 p.m.

ADMISSION/FARE: Adults, $10; children under 4, free; Norwood: children 4-12, $5; OttawaJunction: children 4-12, $7; all-day fare for all ages and destinations, $25; discount for groups; charters available.

LOCOMOTIVES/ROLLING STOCK: CB&Q NW2 524; Katy R53m 142; Rock Island E6 630; Rock Island E8 652; and NYC RS3 8255.

SPECIAL EVENTS: Easter Bunny trains, Rail Fans Weekend, Maple Leaf Festival, Mystery Trains, Halloween Trains, Santa Trains. Call or see website for information on special events.

DIRECTIONS: Baldwin City is about 30 miles southwest of the Kansas City metropolitan area on US Hwy. 56. They operate out of the historic 1906 former AT&SF depot located about 7 blocks west of downtown Baldwin City.

Photo courtesy of E. N. Griffin.

TRAVEL TIP: *Streamliners*

You'll find many types of diesel locomotives on today's tourist and museum railroads, but among the most popular are streamlined units from the 1940s and 1950s. Built in an age when styling was king, these sleek and colorful locomotives are a pleasure to see in motion.

Kingman, KS

The Santa Fe Depot Foundation

Museum

ADDRESS: 201 E Sherman Kingman, KS 67068-1906
TELEPHONE: (620) 532-2142
E-MAIL: thedepot@websurf.net

DESCRIPTION: The foundation has a railroad museum and Cannonball Welcome Center. The museum features railroad memorabilia from items found within the depot to items that have been donated and loaned. There is also a display of HO gauge model trains. The brick former Santa Fe depot dates from 1910-1911.

SCHEDULE: Year-round, 8:30 to 11:30 a.m.; other times by appointment.

ADMISSION/FARE: Donations welcome.

SPECIAL EVENTS: Occasional excursions.

NEARBY ATTRACTIONS: Kingman Co. Museum, Kingman State Lake, Cheney Reservoir, Cosmosphere, Exploration Place.

DIRECTIONS: One block east of Main St. on Sherman; four blocks south of US Hwy. 54/400 on Spruce St. to Sherman.

Scammon, KS

Heart of the Heartlands

Train ride, Museum, Display
Standard gauge

ADDRESS: 6697 NW 20th St., PO Box 211 Scammon, KS
TELEPHONE: (620) 396-8594 or (417) 624-4799
E-MAIL: noffenbacker@gbronline.com
WEBSITE: http://www.geocities.com/htrainclub

DESCRIPTION: The Webb Family Railroad Heritage Education Center reflects the heritage of the Katy, Missouri Pacific, Santa Fe, Kansas City Southern and Frisco railroads in southeastern Kansas, and showcases a wealth of hand-carved scale railroad models. A static display is housed in a restored 1940s MP depot. In addition, the group hosts numerous train rides and motor car trips throughout the year.

SCHEDULE: Hours vary with the season. Available for walk-through at any time. Call or check website for tours.

ADMISSION/FARE: Museum and grounds: free. See website for train ride information.

LOCOMOTIVES/ROLLING STOCK: Southeastern Kansas (formerly Southern Pacific) caboose no. 1716; MKT caboose no. 103; ATSF caboose no. 999810; Santa Fe refrigerator car no. 36110; Missouri Pacific insulated boxcar no. 780699; Great Plains (formerly Boston & Maine) 1956 Budd RDCs nos. 9201, 9202, and 9203 (belong to Watco, Inc.); more.

SPECIAL EVENTS: Dinner trains are held a couple of times a year. Check website for details.

NEARBY ATTRACTIONS: Big Brutus Mining Museum, West Mineral, KS, is located just four miles west of our depot on Hwy. 102. Among other things, it houses "Big Brutus," the second largest electric mining shovel in the world at 16 stories tall and 11 million tons.

DIRECTIONS: Travel 9 miles west of Hwy. 69 on Hwy. 102 and then $^3/_{10}$ mile south on NW 20th St.; or travel 7 miles south of Hwy. 400 on Hwy. 7, then 2 miles west on Hwy. 102, and $^3/_{10}$ mile south on NW 20th St.

Photo courtesy of Linda Shomin.

Wichita, KS
Great Plains Transportation Museum
Museum
Standard gauge

ADDRESS: 700 E Douglas Ave. Wichita, KS 67202
TELEPHONE: (316) 263-0944
WEBSITE: www.gptm.us

DESCRIPTION: Museum with outdoor displays of locomotives, cabooses, and cars; indoor displays of artifacts and memorabilia.

SCHEDULE: Year-round: Saturday, 9 a.m. to 4 p.m.; April to October: also Sunday, 1 to 4 p.m.

ADMISSION/FARE: Adults, $4; children 3-12, $3; children 2 and under, free.

LOCOMOTIVES/ROLLING STOCK: ATSF 4-8-4 no. 3768; ATSF FP45 no. 93; BN NW2 no. 421; Whitcomb GM-2; Plymouth industrial locomotive; Frisco caboose 876; Central Kansas Railway caboose 1959; CB&Q caboose 13519; ATSF coach, baggage caboose 2312; MoPac caboose 13495; UP caboose no. 24538; ATSF baggage car 190006.

NEARBY ATTRACTIONS: In the heart of historic Old Town.

DIRECTIONS: Across from Wichita Union Station.

Photo courtesy of J. Harvey Koehn.

KENTUCKY

Bardstown, KY

My Old Kentucky Dinner Train

Dinner train

ADDRESS: 602 N 3rd St. Bardstown, KY 40004
TELEPHONE: (866) 801-DINE [3463]
E-MAIL: info@rjcorman.com
WEBSITE: www.kydinnertrain.com

DESCRIPTION: Passengers can enjoy fine dining on a 2½-hour excursion through Kentucky countryside aboard 1940s dining cars.

SCHEDULE: Year-round: lunch and dinner excursions, Tuesday through Sunday, on a demand basis.

ADMISSION/FARE: Lunch, $49.95; dinner, $69.95; Murder Mystery excursions, $87.95.

LOCOMOTIVES/ROLLING STOCK: 1950s FP7A diesels.

SPECIAL EVENTS: Murder Mystery excursions are scheduled throughout the year.

NEARBY ATTRACTIONS: My Old Kentucky Home, Civil War Museum, Makers Mark Distillery, Jim Beam Distillery, Old Talbott Tavern, and Stephen Foster the Musical.

DIRECTIONS: In Bardstown, 40 miles south of Louisville, 60 miles west of Lexington.

Photo courtesy of My Old Kentucky Dinner Train.

Covington, KY

Railway Museum of Greater Cincinnati

Museum
Standard gauge

ADDRESS: 315 W Southern Ave., PO Box 15065 Covington, KY 41015
TELEPHONE: (859) 491-7245
E-MAIL: questions@cincirailmuseum.org
WEBSITE: www.cincirailmuseum.org

DESCRIPTION: An organization with volunteers who work to preserve the historic railway equipment of the region. The outdoor railyard features a permanent collection of over 50 cars and locomotives.

SCHEDULE: Wednesday and Saturday, 10 a.m. to 4 p.m; May to October: fourth Sunday, 12:30 to 4:30 p.m.; closed holidays.

ADMISSION/FARE: Adults, $4; children, $2.

LOCOMOTIVES/ROLLING STOCK: PRR "Blue Ribbon Fleet" streamliner, Pullman heavyweight night train, miscellaneous passenger and freight cars, and diesel locomotives.

NEARBY ATTRACTIONS: Cincinnati Reds baseball, Bengals football, Paramount Kings Island amusement park, Museum Center at Union Terminal, Art Museum, Taft Museum, river cruises, Covington Landing and Newport Levee family entertainment districts, Behringer-Crawford Museum. "Turtle Creek" and "Whitewater Valley" tourist railways less than 1 hour drive.

DIRECTIONS: From I-275 in Kentucky, exit KY17 and go North about 1 mile. Turn right onto Latonia Ave. Turn left onto Southern Ave., ends at museum gate.

Photo courtesy of Railway Museum of Greater Cincinnati, by Tim Hyde.

New Haven, KY
Kentucky Railway Museum

Train ride, Dinner train, Museum, Display, Layout
HO, S, N, and G scale

ADDRESS: 136 S Main St., PO Box 240 New Haven, KY 40051
TELEPHONE: (800) 272-0152
E-MAIL: kyrail@bardstoun.com
WEBSITE: www.kyrail.org

DESCRIPTION: Visitors can recapture the romance of the local passenger train when it was small-town America's link to the world. A 22-mile train excursion through the scenic and historic Rolling Fork River Valley is available aboard a restored passenger train.

SCHEDULE: Museum: year-round; January and February: closed Sunday and Monday; Train excursions: April through December.

ADMISSION/FARE: Adults, $15; children 2-12, $10; children under 2, free; cab rides, $30; Steam weekends: adults, $17; children 2-12, $10; children under 2, free; cab rides, $35.

LOCOMOTIVES/ROLLING STOCK: L&N 4-6-2 no. 152; Monon BL-2 no. 32; Santa Fe CF7 no. 2546; C&O 2-8-4 no. 2716; L&N business car no. 363; L&N 2554; L&N 2572; SAL 821; MKT 884; TC 8038 (diner); other locomotives and rolling stock on display.

SPECIAL EVENTS: Easter, Murder Mysteries, Dining Car trips, Halloween, Christmas, and "Day out with Thomas™."

NEARBY ATTRACTIONS: My Old Kentucky Home State Park, Historic Bardstown, Mammoth Cave National Park, Lincoln birthplace (national historic site), Lincoln boyhood home, Maker's Mark Distillery (national landmark), and Bernheim Forest.

DIRECTIONS: Three-and-one-half miles east of I-65 at exit 105 (Boston exit); 12 miles south of Bluegrass Pkwy. at exit 21 (New Haven exit).

Photo courtesy of Elmer Kappell.

Paducah, KY
Paducah Railroad Museum
Museum

SITE ADDRESS: 2nd and Washington Sts. Paducah, KY
MAILING ADDRESS: PO Box 1194 Paducah, KY 42002-1194
TELEPHONE: (270) 442-4032
E-MAIL: bobj31@comcast.net
WEBSITE: www.paducahrr.org

DESCRIPTION: Museum contains displays of railroad artifacts including CTC and signal equipment, lantern, photos, maps, tools, track equipment, and all types of railroad memorabilia, speeders, and an N gauge layout.

SCHEDULE: Friday, 1 to 4 p.m.; Saturday, 10 a.m. to 4 p.m.; other times by appointment.

ADMISSION/FARE: Free; contributions are appreciated.

NEARBY ATTRACTIONS: Static display of Illinois Central 2-8-2 no. 1518, with baggage-mail combine and transfer caboose; River Heritage Museum; William Clark History Museum; and Four Rivers Performing Arts Center.

DIRECTIONS: Located at 2nd and Washington St. on the I-24 downtown loop. Get off I-24 at the US68 or US60 exits. Follow green I-24 Downtown Loop signs. Railroad museum signs at 3rd & Washington, northbound, and 4th & Washington, southbound.

Paris, KY

Kentucky Central Railway
Museum

SITE ADDRESS: 134 E 10th St. Paris, KY
MAILING ADDRESS: 1749 Bahama Rd. Lexington, KY 40509
TELEPHONE: (859) 293-0807
E-MAIL: wesleyross@alltel.net

DESCRIPTION: Railroad museum located in the former Kentucky Central and Louisville & Nashville Railroad Depot.

SCHEDULE: Most Saturdays, 10 a.m. to 4 p.m.

ADMISSION/FARE: Donations appreciated.

NEARBY ATTRACTIONS: Kentucky Horse Park, Blue Licks Battlefield State Resort Park, Bluegrass Horse Farms.

DIRECTIONS: Located in downtown Paris, Kentucky.

Photo courtesy of Wesley F. Ross.

Stearns, KY

Big South Fork Scenic Railway
Train ride
Standard gauge

ADDRESS: 100 Henderson St., PO Box 368 Stearns, KY 42647-0368
TELEPHONE: (800) 462-5664 or (606) 376-5330
E-MAIL: info@bsfry.com
WEBSITE: www.bsfsry.com

DESCRIPTION: The railway offers 3-hour and $\frac{1}{2}$-hour trips through Big South Fork National River and Recreation Area on the former Kentucky & Tennessee Railway. Departures include layover at restored mining camp of Blue Heron. Ticket fares include admission to the McCreary County Museum. The train follows mountain streams, passes through a tunnel and over a bridge as it descends over 600 feet in 5 miles to the floor of the river valley.

SCHEDULE: April: Thursday and Friday, 11 a.m.; Saturday, 11 a.m. and 2:30 p.m. May to September: Wednesday through Friday, 11 a.m.; Saturday and Sunday, 11 a.m. and 2:30 p.m. October: Tuesday through Friday, 11 a.m.; Saturday and Sunday, 11 a.m. and 2:30 p.m. November: First 2 Saturdays, 11 a.m. and 2:30 p.m.

ADMISSION/FARE: Adults, $15; seniors, $14; children, $7.50; group rates available.

LOCOMOTIVES/ROLLING STOCK: Alco diesel switchers nos. 101 and 105; enclosed and open excursion cars; caboose; 1944 Alco 0-6-0 under restoration.

SPECIAL EVENTS: Last three Fridays and Saturdays of October, Halloween trains depart at 7:30 p.m.; first three Saturdays of December, Santa Trains depart at 11 a.m. and 2 p.m.

NEARBY ATTRACTIONS: Big South Fork National River and Recreation Area, Cumberland Falls State Park, Burnside Island State Park, Lake Cumberland, Daniel Boone National Forest, and Mill Springs Battlefield.

DIRECTIONS: Located one mile west of Hwy. 27 on SR92 in downtown Stearns.

Photo courtesy of Big South Fork Scenic Railway.

Versailles, KY

Bluegrass Railroad Museum

Train ride, Museum

ADDRESS: 175 Beasley Rd. Woodford County Park, PO Box 27 Versailles, KY 40383
TELEPHONE: (800) 755-2476 or (859) 873-2476
WEBSITE: www.bgrm.org

DESCRIPTION: This volunteer organization is dedicated to the preservation of railroad history and the restoration of railroad artifacts. All revenues generated from passenger fares and donations are used for museum restoration projects and railroad operation. The museum offers a 3-mile train ride through the heart of the Bluegrass region of Kentucky. There are also static displays at the museum site.

SCHEDULE: May through October: Saturday and Sunday, 1:30 to 3:30 p.m.

ADMISSION/FARE: Adults, $9; seniors, $8; children, $7.

LOCOMOTIVES/ROLLING STOCK: Alco MRS1 no. 2086; GE 44-tonner no. 001; GP8 no. 7738; GP9 no. 675.

SPECIAL EVENTS: Civil War Encampment, Halloween Ghost Train, Santa Claus Train. Call or see website for dates.

NEARBY ATTRACTIONS: Nostalgia station, former L&N Depot, houses model train collection; Depot St. and Douglas Ave., Versailles.

DIRECTIONS: On US62 two miles west of the courthouse at the Woodford County Park.

Photo courtesy of Charles H. Bogart.

LOUISIANA

DeQuincy, LA

DeQuincy Railroad Museum

EDITOR'S CHOICE

Museum, Display

ADDRESS: PO Box 997
DeQuincy, LA 70633
TELEPHONE: (337) 786-2823 or
(337) 786-7113

• Jackson

• DeQuincy

• Long Leaf

DESCRIPTION: In 1895, DeQuincy was at the intersection of two major railroads. Its turn-of-the-century beginnings have been preserved, including the Kansas City Southern railroad depot, which houses the railroad museum. Displays include a vintage caboose, passenger coach, and a host of railroad artifacts. A play train is available for rental.

SCHEDULE: Monday through Friday, 9 a.m. to 4 p.m.; weekends, 12 to 4 p.m.

ADMISSION/FARE: Museum: free, donations appreciated; train rental: $30.

LOCOMOTIVES/ROLLING STOCK: 0-6-0 no. 124 (Alco, 1913); Pullman car no. 4472 (built 1947); MP caboose no. 13487 (built 1929).

SPECIAL EVENTS: Second weekend in April, Louisiana Railroad Days Festival.

NEARBY ATTRACTIONS: Sam Jones State Park, 20 miles; horse racing, 10 miles; Gulf fishing, 40 miles; two large casinos, 20 miles; hunting, all over; the New L'Auberge du Lac Hotel & Casino in Lake Charles.

DIRECTIONS: On Hwy. 27, about 30 miles north of Lake Charles. On Hwy. 12, about 50 miles from Beaumont, TX.

TRAVEL TIP: *Bring a picnic*

Many tourist railroads take passengers to places of beauty where they can get off the train, walk around, and relax. Many of these spots are inaccessible by car. And many operations offer picnic grounds. Be sure to ask about this when planning your next visit.

Jackson, LA

Old Hickory Railroad
Train ride
36" Narrow gauge

ADDRESS: 3406 College St., PO Box 297 Jackson, LA 70748
TELEPHONE: (225) 634-7397
E-MAIL: harv707@aol.com
WEBSITE: www.louisianasteamtrain.com

DESCRIPTION: The Old Hickory is operated by the Republic of West Florida Historical Association and commemorates the Clinton and Port Hudson Railroad, which began operations in the area in the 1830s.

SCHEDULE: Mid-March to mid-November: Saturday and Sunday, 3 p.m.

ADMISSION/FARE: Adults, $7; seniors 62+, $5; children under 12, $3; group rates and special charters available.

LOCOMOTIVES/ROLLING STOCK: Crown 4-4-0 steam locomotive; two open coaches.

SPECIAL EVENTS: Battle of Jackson Crossroads Civil War re-enactment, Jackson Antiques festival, Halloween night ride, Cruising in the Country Antique Car Show. Call for dates.

NEARBY ATTRACTIONS: Greater Baton Rouge Model Railroaders Association clubhouse and layouts located on site (call for hours of operation). Centenary State Historic Site, Feliciana Cellars Winery, Republic of West Florida Museum, Audubon State Historic Site, Port Hudson State Historic Site, and Rosedown Historic Site.

DIRECTIONS: Located two blocks north of Hwy. 10 on College St.

Photo courtesy of Andrew Martin.

KEY TO SYMBOLS

Handicapped accessible	Restaurant	Arts and crafts	Association of Railway Museums
Parking	Picnic area	Memberships available	Tourist Railway Association, Inc.
Bus/RV parking	Dining car	Send S.A.S.E. for brochure	Amtrak service to nearby city
Gift, book, or museum shop	Excursions	National Register of Historic Places	VIA service to nearby city
Refreshments	Guided tours	VISA MasterCard DISCOVER American Express Card	Credit cards accepted

Long Leaf, LA

Southern Forest Heritage Museum

Museum, Display
Standard gauge

ADDRESS: PO Box 101 Long Leaf, LA 71448-0101
TELEPHONE: (318) 748-8404
E-MAIL: longleaf@centurytel.net
WEBSITE: www.forestheritagemuseum.org

DESCRIPTION: Guided tours are available to see a historic sawmill complex encompassing 57 acres of industrial structures, steam engines, and steam logging equipment, including three early 20th-century locomotives, Clyde skidder, and two McGiffert loaders. The commissary offers exhibits, gift shop, and large screen theater. Motor car rides are ¾ mile long and run on the original Red River & Gulf railroad track.

SCHEDULE: Year-round: 9 a.m. to 4 p.m., except Easter, Thanksgiving, and Christmas. Last tour 3:30 p.m.

LOCOMOTIVES/ROLLING STOCK: Red River & Gulf 4-6-0 no. 106; Meridian Lumber Co. 2-6-0 no. 202; Crowell Long Leaf Lumber Co. 4-6-0 no. 400. Steam logging equipment: McGiffert loaders no. 1229 and no. 1230, Clyde Iron Works; 4-line skidder no. 321, Clyde Iron Works.

SPECIAL EVENTS: Biannual machine shop day, demonstration of working early 20th-century machine shop equipment.

NEARBY ATTRACTIONS: Alexander State Forest (camping), 11 miles; restaurants, 3 miles.

DIRECTIONS: From I-49 take exit 66 and travel west on SR112 to Forest Hill; follow signs 3.3 miles south on SR497. The site is halfway between Forest Hill and Glenmora on SR497.

Photo courtesy of Cena Mayo.
Coupon available, see insert.

TRAVEL TIP: *History lesson*

A visit to a tourist railroad or museum is an opportunity for an instant history lesson. Railroading is a great way to explore the development of the country and changes in technology as well as geography. If you take your kids along, make an outing into an educational adventure.

MAINE

Alna

MAINE

Alna, ME

Wiscasset Waterville & Farmington Railway

Train ride, Museum, Display
2' gauge

ADDRESS: 97 Cross Rd., PO Box 242 Alna, ME 04535-0242
TELEPHONE: (207) 882-4193
E-MAIL: webmaster@wwfry.org
WEBSITE: www.wwfry.org

DESCRIPTION: The restored WW&F Railway is on its original roadbed and uses some original equipment. The trains are pulled by a 1904 Vulcan steam engine and a 1960 Plymouth diesel on round trips almost four miles long. There is a museum, car shop, and gift shop.

SCHEDULE: Year-round, Saturday; Memorial Day through Labor Day weekends, Sunday; Memorial Day and Labor Day. All hours are 9 a.m. to 5 p.m.

ADMISSION/FARE: Museum: free; all train rides: adults, $5; children, $3.

LOCOMOTIVES/ROLLING STOCK: WW&F no. 9, ex-SR&RL no. 6 (Portland Co., 1891); WW&F no. 10 (Vulcan, 1904); Brookville no. 51; Plymouth no. 52; flatcar no. 118; boxcar no. 309; caboose no. 320; excursion car no. 103, W&Q coach no. 3 1894.

SPECIAL EVENTS: April 28 to 30 and October 13 to 16, track laying and work sessions; August 12 and 13, annual picnic; October 21 and 22, Halloween Trains; December 16, Victorian theme Christmas.

NEARBY ATTRACTIONS: Boothbay Railway Museum; Maine Eastern Railroad, Rockland.

DIRECTIONS: From south and west: I-95 to Brunswick, north on Route 1 to Wiscasset, north on Route 218 4.5 miles, left on Cross Rd. From east: south on Route 1 to Newcastle, right on Sheepscot Rd., follow signs.

Photo courtesy of Steve Hussar.

Bangor, ME
Cole Land Transportation Museum
Museum

ADDRESS: 405 Perry Rd. Bangor, ME 04401
TELEPHONE: (207) 990-3600
E-MAIL: mail@colemuseum.org
WEBSITE: www.colemuseum.org

DESCRIPTION: The museum houses 200 antique land transportation vehicles and 2,000 photographs of life in early Maine communities, enlarged, displayed, and captioned. It is home to the Maine State WWII Memorial, Military Order of the Purple Heart Memorial, and the Vietnam Veterans Memorial.

SCHEDULE: May 1 to November 11: daily, 9 a.m. to 5 p.m.

ADMISSION/FARE: Adults, $6; seniors, $4; children under 19, free.

DIRECTIONS: From I-95, take exit 182A, then follow the signs to war memorials.

Biddeford, ME
Great Northern Narrow Gauge Railroad
Train ride, Museum, Display
2' gauge

ADDRESS: Iron Trail Rd., PO Box 661 Biddeford, ME 04005-0661
TELEPHONE: (207) 967-4882

DESCRIPTION: This railroad offers a 1-mile ride through forests with picnic area and waterfront stops.

SCHEDULE: July 4 to Columbus Day: weekends and holidays, 11 a.m. to 4 p.m. (weather permitting). Call to confirm.

ADMISSION/FARE: $4.00 per seat. Fare is good for multiple rides as seating permits.

LOCOMOTIVES/ROLLING STOCK: Plymouth 15-tonner; Brookville 11-tonner; Fairmont MT-14; Great Northern caboose X 256, standard gauge.

SPECIAL EVENTS: Some daily operations in summer; call for information.

NEARBY ATTRACTIONS: Seashore Trolley Museum, Fun Town Amusement Park, Old Orchard Beach Amusements, ocean beaches, historic area, greater Portland activities.

DIRECTIONS: I-95 to Biddeford exit. Follow signs to US Route One, go south ¾ mile, watch for Shay Locomotive (on left) at entrance.

Photo courtesy of Ralph Day.

Kennebunkport, ME

Seashore Trolley Museum

Train ride, Museum, Display
Standard gauge

ADDRESS: 195 Log Cabin Rd. Kennebunkport, ME 04046
TELEPHONE: (207) 967-2800
E-MAIL: carshop@gwi.net
WEBSITE: www.trolleymuseum.org

DESCRIPTION: The museum offers a 25-minute, 3½ mile streetcar ride. There are 54 streetcars on display in three carbarns and a restoration shop. Passengers can ride by rail through the Maine countryside aboard a restored early 1900s electric streetcar, and witness the sights and sounds of a bygone era in American transportation history.

SCHEDULE: First Saturday in May to Memorial Day and Columbus Day to last Sunday in October, weekends; Memorial Day to Columbus Day, daily, 10 a.m. to 5 p.m.

ADMISSION/FARE: Adults, $7.50; seniors, $5.50; children 6-16, $5; children 5 and under, free.

LOCOMOTIVES/ROLLING STOCK: Restored streetcars, interurbans, rapid transit, trackless trolleys, and buses. "The National Collection of American Streetcars."

SPECIAL EVENTS: May, Mother's Day; June, Father's Day; July, Trolley Parade; August, Trolley Birthday Celebration; September/ October, Pumpkin Patch Trolley.

NEARBY ATTRACTIONS: Historic downtown Kennebunkport shopping area and beaches.

DIRECTIONS: Maine Turnpike (I-95) to Kennebunkport exit (exit 25). Left onto Route 35 to downtown Kennebunk. Left on Route One (Main St.), north for 2.8 miles. Right at traffic light onto Log Cabin Rd. Museum is 1.7 miles down the road, on the left.

Coupon available, see insert.

Oakfield, ME

Oakfield Railroad Museum

Display

ADDRESS: Station St., PO Box 62 Oakfield, ME 04763
TELEPHONE: (207) 757-8575
E-MAIL: oakfield.rr.museum@ainop.com
WEBSITE: www.ainop.com/users/oakfield.rr/

DESCRIPTION: Exhibits in restored Oakfield Station include: hundreds of photographs dating to the beginning of the Bangor & Aroostook Railroad in 1891. There are also vintage signs and advertising pieces, signal lanterns, original railroad maps, telegraph equipment, newspapers chronicling the area's history, restored mail cars, and a caboose.

SCHEDULE: Memorial to Labor Day: Saturday and Sunday, 1 to 4 p.m.; or by appointment.

ADMISSION/FARE: Donations appreciated.

LOCOMOTIVES/ROLLING STOCK: Bangor & Aroostook caboose C-66.

DIRECTIONS: I-95 exit 60, turn right for 1 mile, turn left at hardware store, cross bridge, turn right at end of street.

Phillips, ME

Sandy River and Rangeley Lakes Railroad

Train ride, Museum, Display
2' gauge

ADDRESS: 128 Bridge St., PO Box B Phillips, ME 04966
TELEPHONE: (207) 778-3621
E-MAIL: awb@ime.net
WEBSITE: www.srrl-rr.org

DESCRIPTION: Passengers can ride along the original roadbed of the SR&RL Railroad in 1884 Laconia Coach no. 18, powered by a replica of SR&RL no. 4. Visitors can tour the 8-stall roundhouse and see the ongoing restoration of original SR&RL equipment.

SCHEDULE: June 4 and 18; July 2, 3, 15, 16; August 6, 18, 19, 20; September 3, 4, 16, 17, 30; October 1, 7, and 8.

ADMISSION/FARE: Train: $4; children under 13, free.

LOCOMOTIVES/ROLLING STOCK: SR&RL no. 4 (replica); coaches nos. 17 and 18; cabooses nos. 556 and 559 (a replica of no. 556); flangers nos. 503 and 505; boxcars nos. 86, 59, 155, 73, and 121; tool car no. 562; flatcar; handcars; Brookville and Plymouth industrial locomotives; MEC coach no. 170; Concord & Montreal coach no. 77.

SPECIAL EVENTS: August 18, 19, and 20, Phillips Old Home Days.

NEARBY ATTRACTIONS: Stanley Museum, Nordica Homestead, Logging Museum in Rangeley, Small Falls, and Mount Blue State Park.

DIRECTIONS: Eighteen miles north of Farmington on SR4. Cross the bridge in downtown Phillips and up the hill (Bridge St.) ½ mile.

Photo courtesy of Bob Troup.
Coupon available, see insert.

Portland, ME

Maine Narrow Gauge Railroad & Museum
Train ride
2' gauge

ADDRESS: 58 Fore St. Portland, ME 04101
TELEPHONE: (207) 828-0814
E-MAIL: mngrr@maine.rr.com
WEBSITE: www.mngrr.org

DESCRIPTION: A 3-mile round trip travels along the shore of scenic Casco Bay and the Portland waterfront in authentic Maine narrow gauge cars. The train museum has historic cars, displays, railroad artifacts, and a unique gift shop.

SCHEDULE: Museum: daily, 10 a.m. to 4 p.m.; trains: mid-February to mid-May: weekends; mid-May to mid-October: daily, 11 a.m. to 4 p.m.; mid-October to Thanksgiving: weekends; Thanksgiving to Christmas: weekends, 4 to 7 p.m.; "Santa Fest Event," trains run along lighted tracks with holiday decorations.

ADMISSION/FARE: Adults, $8; seniors, $7; children 3-12, $5; children 2 and under, free.

LOCOMOTIVES/ROLLING STOCK: Brighton & Harrison steam locomotives nos. 7 and 8; Monson steam locomotives nos. 3 and 4; Edaville diesel no. 1; coaches from former Edaville collection.

SPECIAL EVENTS: Memorial Day, July 4th, Labor Day, and Columbus Day weekends: steam engines; September 10, SteamFest; November 25 through December 23, Santa Fest.

NEARBY ATTRACTIONS: Portland's "Old Port" shopping and dining, Portland observatory.

DIRECTIONS: Old Portland Co. site Hwy. 295 to exit 7, Franklin St., left on Fore St.

Photo courtesy of Art Hussey.

Richmond, ME

New England Railroad

Train ride, Dinner train
Standard gauge

ADDRESS: 17 Church St. Richmond, ME 04357
TELEPHONE: (603) 294-4367
WEBSITE: http://newenglandrailroad.com

DESCRIPTION: Passengers can relax with full ADA accessibility and glass-domed roofs that allow for panoramic views. There are bi-level dome entertainment and dining cars with mezzanine overlooking a lower-level piano bar. The domed dining level car seats up to 76 in four-top configuration and has a food service area.

LOCOMOTIVES/ROLLING STOCK: DMU, dining car, parlor car, coaches.

SPECIAL EVENTS: Vacation packages to Montreal, New Hampshire, and Vermont.

DIRECTIONS: 95 north to Portland, ME.

Coupon available, see insert.

KEY TO SYMBOLS

Handicapped accessible	Restaurant	Arts and crafts	Association of Railway Museums
Parking	Picnic area	Memberships available	Tourist Railway Association, Inc.
Bus/RV parking	Dining car	Send S.A.S.E. for brochure	Amtrak service to nearby city
Gift, book, or museum shop	Excursions	National Register of Historic Places	VIA service to nearby city
Refreshments	Guided tours	VISA MasterCard DISCOVER AMERICAN EXPRESS Card	Credit cards accepted

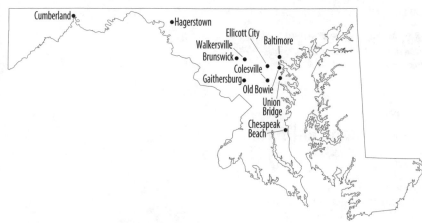

MARYLAND

Baltimore, MD
Baltimore & Ohio Railroad Museum
Museum

EDITOR'S CHOICE

ADDRESS: 901 W Pratt St. Baltimore, MD 21223
TELEPHONE: (410) 752-2490
WEBSITE: www.borail.org

DESCRIPTION: The museum is home to one of the oldest, most comprehensive collections of railroad artifacts in the Western Hemisphere, including a roster of 19th and 20th century railroad equipment. The 40-acre historic site is regarded as the birthplace of American railroading and includes the 1851 Mt. Clare Station, the 1884 Baldwin Roundhouse, and the first mile of railroad track in America.

SCHEDULE: Open daily, except for major holidays. Call for hours or visit website.

ADMISSION/FARE: Adults, $14; seniors 60+, $10; children 2-12, $8; children under 2, free.

LOCOMOTIVES/ROLLING STOCK: More than 150 locomotives and other pieces of rolling stock, ranging from replicas of the first locomotives, to the present.

NEARBY ATTRACTIONS: Camden Yards, Raven's Stadium, Babe Ruth Museum, Inner Harbor.

DIRECTIONS: Take I-95 to 395 to Martin Luther King, Jr. Blvd. Follow signs to the museum.

Coupon available, see insert.

Baltimore, MD

Baltimore Streetcar Museum
Streetcar ride, Museum
5' 4¹/₂" gauge

ADDRESS: 1901 Falls Rd., PO Box 4881 Baltimore, MD 21211
TELEPHONE: (410) 547-0264
WEBSITE: www.baltimoremd.com/streetcar/

DESCRIPTION: Visitors can relive rail transit in the city of Baltimore from 1859 to 1963 through a 16-car collection. Cars operate over 1¹/₄-mile, round-trip trackage. The visitor's center contains displays, a museum store, and the Trolley Theatre (a streetcar mockup and video presentation).

SCHEDULE: June 1 through October 31: weekends; November 1 through May 31: Sunday, 12 to 5 p.m.

ADMISSION/FARE: Adults, $6; seniors and children 4-11, $3; family, $24.

LOCOMOTIVES/ROLLING STOCK: No. 417, circa 1888 single-truck closed car; no. 3715, 1913 double-track crane; no. 554, 1896 single-truck summer car; no. 1050, 1898 single-truck closed car; no. 264, 1900 double-truck convertible car, all Brownell Car Co.; no. 1164, 1902 double-truck summer car; no. 3828, 1902 double-truck closed car; no. 4533, 1904 single-truck closed car; and no. 6119, 1930 Peter Witt car, all J.G. Brill Co.; no. 7303, 1936 St. Louis Car Co. PCC car; no. 7407, 1944 Pullman-Standard PCC car; more.

SPECIAL EVENTS: Mother's, Father's, and Grandparents' Days; Museum Birthday; December, Tinsel Trolley; more. Call, write, or check website for more information.

NEARBY ATTRACTIONS: B&O Railroad Museum.

DIRECTIONS: One block west on Lafayette Ave. to Falls Rd.

Photo courtesy of Andrew S. Blumberg.
Coupon available, see insert.

Brunswick, MD
Brunswick Museum
Museum, Display, Model train layout
HO scale

ADDRESS: 40 W Potomac St. Brunswick, MD 21716
TELEPHONE: (301) 834-7100
WEBSITE: www.brrm.net

DESCRIPTION: Brunswick yards handled all B&O passenger and freight on the east-west main line. There are 863 feet of track in an interactive HO layout that traces the route from Washington, D.C., to Brunswick. Railroad artifacts include historic photographs, tools, signals, equipment, and uniforms; exhibitions of life circa 1900 in a railroad town; more.

SCHEDULE: Year-round: Saturday, 10 a.m. to 5 p.m.; Sunday, 1 to 5 p.m.; April through September: additional Thursday and Friday, 10 a.m. to 2 p.m.

ADMISSION/FARE: Adults, $5; seniors, $4; youth 6-12, $2.50; children 3-5, $1.25; babies, free.

SPECIAL EVENTS: First full weekend in April (unless Easter, then following weekend), Railroad Heritage Weekend; first full weekend in October, Railroad Days; weekend after Thanksgiving, Victorian Christmas.

NEARBY ATTRACTIONS: Harper's Ferry Toy Train Museum, Walkersville Southern Railroad, River and Trail Outfitters, Potomac and Shenandoah expeditions and ski tours.

DIRECTIONS: From Washington, D.C.: I-270 north to US340 west to Brunswick. From Baltimore: I-70 west to I-340 west to Brunswick. From Leesburg: US15 north to US340 west.

Coupon available, see insert.

Chesapeake Beach, MD
Chesapeake Beach Railway Museum
Museum, Historic railway station building

ADDRESS: 4155 Mears Ave., PO Box 1227 Chesapeake Beach, MD 20732
TELEPHONE: (410) 257-3892
WEBSITE: www.cbrm.org

DESCRIPTION: The Chesapeake Beach Railway brought people from Washington, D.C., to the resorts of Chesapeake Beach and North Beach from 1900 until 1935. The museum exhibits photographs and artifacts of the railroad and resort.

SCHEDULE: April, May, September, and October: weekends, 1 to 4 p.m.; May 1 to September 30: weekdays, 1 to 4 p.m.; June, July, and August: weekends, 11 a.m. to 5 p.m.

ADMISSION/FARE: Free.

TS: Fourth Sunday in September, Gaithersburg Olde Towne Day.

ACTIONS: Restaurants, antique shops in Olde Towne Gaithersburg, and
re Museum featuring 1941 Diamond T fire truck.

Maryland Route 355 (Frederick Ave.) to S Summit Ave.; north on S Summit
B&O (now CSX) passenger station and freight house.

of Gerald A. Hott.

MD

wn Roundhouse Museum

S Burhans Blvd. Hagerstown, MD 21741-2858
01) 739-4665
roundhouse.org

DESCRIPTION: The museum houses
memories of the Western Maryland
Railway Complex, artifacts, photos, and
displays. There are model trains available
for kids to run, model train layouts on
display, and a gift shop.

SCHEDULE: Year-round: Friday through
Sunday, 1 to 5 p.m.; closed December 24
and 25, January 1, and Easter.

E: Adults, $3.50; children under 13, $.50.

OLLING STOCK: Western Maryland Railway Baldwin VO1000 diesel
wn & Frederick trolley no. 168.

: Spring, Railroad Heritage Days; summer and fall, excursions; December
y, Trains of Christmas.

TIONS: Antietam National Battlefield, Hagerstown City Park, Hager House,
Arts, C&O Canal, and Fort Frederick.

to exit 2, then US11 north to museum; I-70 to exit 32; US40 west to
useum.

rystal Sprecher.

LOCOMOTIVES/ROLLING STOCK:
The CBR chair car "Dolores" is
undergoing restoration.

SPECIAL EVENTS: First April Saturday/rain
day second Saturday, Right of Way Hike;
second Thursday evenings of June
through September, Bay Breeze Summer
Concerts; mid-June through mid-August,
summer children's programs, Thursday,
10 a.m.; Spring and Fall Family Fun Days,
dates to be announced; first Sunday of December, Holiday Open House.

NEARBY ATTRACTIONS: Chesapeake Beach Water Park, Bayfront Park, Breezy Point Beach.

DIRECTIONS: From Washington's Capital Beltway: I-95 to Route 4 south. From Baltimore
Beltway: I-695 to Route 301 south to Route 4 south. Left on Route 260, right on Route 261.

Coupon available, see insert.

Colesville, MD

National Capital Trolley Museum

EDITOR'S CHOICE

Streetcar ride, Museum
Standard gauge

ADDRESS: 1313 Bonifant Rd. Colesville, MD 20905-5955
TELEPHONE: (301) 384-6088
WEBSITE: www.dctrolley.org

DESCRIPTION: Visitors can see streetcar communities and visit the computer-based
exhibit, From Streetcars to Light Rail. There is also a 1¾-mile, 20-minute round trip
available in Northwest Branch Park on cars selected from the museum's collections.
The National Capital Streetcar Museum was founded in 1959. The collections consist
of 17 streetcars; many are operated on a one-mile demonstration railway. There is also
an O-scale model layout representing a Washington streetscape from the 1930s, a film
program, and traditional exhibits of street railway artifacts and photographs.

SCHEDULE: January 2 to November 30: weekends, 12 to 5 p.m.; June 15 to August 15:
Thursday and Friday, 11 a.m. to 3 p.m.; October 1 to November 15 and March 15 to
May 15: Thursday and Friday, 10 a.m. to 2 p.m.; December: weekends, 5 to 9 p.m.

ADMISSION/FARE: Full fare, $3; reduced fare
for people 2-17 and 65+, $2; under 2, free.

LOCOMOTIVES/ROLLING STOCK: TARS 678;
Washington streetcars; Toronto PCC no. 4603;
European trams.

SPECIAL EVENTS: April 16, Cavalcade of Street
Cars; May 29, Homefront Street Cars;
September 4, Trolleymen at Work; October 15,
Fall Open House; December, Holly Trolleyfest.

NEARBY ATTRACTIONS: Brookside Gardens, Sandy Spring Museum, Montgomery County Historical Society, and nation's capital.

DIRECTIONS: On Bonifant Rd. between Layhill Rd. (Route 182) and New Hampshire Ave. (Route 650), north of Wheaton.

Photo courtesy of Larry Velte.
Coupon available, see insert.

Cumberland, MD

Western Maryland Scenic Railroad

Dinner train, Museum
Standard gauge
Radio frequency: 161.550

ADDRESS: 13 Canal St. Cumberland, MD 21502
TELEPHONE: (800) TRAIN-50 or (301) 759-4400
E-MAIL: wmsrinfo@wmsr.com
WEBSITE: www.wmsr.com

DESCRIPTION: From May to mid-December, trips are available aboard a train powered by a restored 1916 Baldwin steam engine and vintage diesel locomotives that travel the scenic mountains of western Maryland. This 32-mile round trip runs between Cumberland's restored Western Maryland Railway station and the 1891 Cumberland & Pennsylvania depot in Frostburg.

SCHEDULE: May through mid-December.

ADMISSION/FARE: Standard: adults, $23; seniors, $21; children 12 and under, $12; children under 2 or not occupying a seat, free; first class Saturday and some Sundays, includes lunch: adults, $43; seniors, $41; children, $26; children without lunch, $10.

LOCOMOTIVES/ROLLING STOCK: "Western Maryland 734," an ex-LS&I 2-8-0; GP30s 501 and 502.

SPECIAL EVENTS: Many throughout the year. Call, write, or see website for information.

NEARBY ATTRACTIONS: CanalFest/RailFest, Thrasher Carriage Museum, Canal Place, Allegany Highland Bike Trail, C&O Canal, many lakes and rivers.

DIRECTIONS: Take I-68, exit 43C to Harrison St. to the station.

Photo courtesy of Ed Mullan.

Ellicott City, MD

Ellicott City B&O Railroad Station

Museum, Model train layout
HO scale

ADDRESS: 2711 Maryland Ave. Ellicott City, MD 21043
TELEPHONE: (410) 461-1944
WEBSITE: www.ecbo.org

DESCRIPTION: Dubbed the "oldest railroad station in A[m]... Museum houses a 40' layout of the first 13 miles of the...

SCHEDULE: Friday and Monday, 11 a.m. to 4 p.m.; Satur... 12 to 5 p.m.; closed Mondays after Labor Day. Call for h...

ADMISSION/FARE: A... children 3-12, $3; ch...

LOCOMOTIVES/ROl... caboose, speeder ...

SPECIAL EVENTS: S...

DIRECTIONS: Corn... historic Ellicott Cit...

Gaithersburg, MD

Gaithersburg Community Mus[eum]

Museum

SITE ADDRESS: 9 S Summit Ave. Gaithersburg, MD...
MAILING ADDRESS: 506 S Frederick Ave. Gaithersb...
TELEPHONE: (301) 258-6160 or (301) 926-9125
WEBSITE: www.gaithersburgmd.gov/museum

DI...
lo...
w...
in...
ra...

S...
t...

A...

LOCOMOTIVES/ROLLING STOCK: Buffalo Creek &... troops kitchen car, Western Maryland Railway M... kitchen car); Baltimore & Ohio wagontop bay w...

SPECIAL EVE...

NEARBY ATT...
G.W.G.V.F.D. F...

DIRECTIONS:...
three blocks...

Photo courtesy...

Hagerstown,...

Hagerst[own]

Museum

ADDRESS: 30[0]...
TELEPHONE: (...
WEBSITE: ww...

ADMISSION/FA...

LOCOMOTIVES...
no. 132; Hagers...

SPECIAL EVENT...
through Februa...

NEARBY ATTRA...
Museum of Fin[e]...

DIRECTIONS: I-8... US11, south to...

Photo courtesy of...

Hagerstown, MD

The Train Room

Museum, Display, Model train layout
O scale

ADDRESS: 360 S Burhans Blvd. Hagerstown, MD 21740
TELEPHONE: (301) 745-6681
WEBSITE: www.the-train-room.com

DESCRIPTION: The museum houses a large O scale model railroad display. There is a collection of rare and unusual items from Lionel and Marx. Much of the collection is pre-WWII.

SCHEDULE: Year-round: Monday and Friday, 9 a.m. to 8 p.m.; Tuesday, Thursday, and Saturday, 9 a.m. to 6 p.m.; Sunday, 12 to 6 p.m.

ADMISSION/FARE: Adults, $4; children 3-12, $0.50; children under 3, free with adult.

NEARBY ATTRACTIONS: Hagerstown Roundhouse Museum, New Hagerstown Railroad Museum, the City Park and Arts Museum, Prime Outlets, and Valley Mall.

DIRECTIONS: Close to I-81 and I-70 interchange; check website.

Photo courtesy of Charles Mozingo.

Old Bowie, MD

Bowie Railroad Station Museum

Museum

SITE ADDRESS: Chestnut Ave. & 11th St. Old Bowie, MD 20715
MAILING ADDRESS: 12207 Tulip Grove Dr. Bowie, MD 20715
TELEPHONE: (301) 809-3089
E-MAIL: museumevents@cityofbowie.org
WEBSITE: www.cityofbowie.org/comserv/museums.htm

DESCRIPTION: A restored Pennsylvania Railroad 1910 depot with interlocking tower, caboose, and model trains. Collections illustrate local rail history, 1870 to today, alongside Amtrak/MARC corridor.

SCHEDULE: Wednesday through Sunday, 12 to 4 p.m.

ADMISSION/FARE: Free.

LOCOMOTIVES/ROLLING STOCK: N&W caboose no. 518303, built 1922.

SPECIAL EVENTS: Last April Sunday, Spring Fling; last September Sunday, Fall Fest; last November Sunday, Train Spotting; first December Sunday, Old Bowie Family Holiday Festival.

NEARBY ATTRACTIONS: Belair Mansion and Stable Museums, Radio and TV Museum, Six Flags, Bowie Baysoxs/Prince George's Stadium.

DIRECTIONS: US50 E/W to Maryland Route 197 for Bowie. Route 564 to Old Bowie. Route 564 becomes 11th St. The museum is at 11th and Chestnut on the south side.

Photo courtesy of City of Bowie Museums.
See ad on page A-36.

Union Bridge, MD

Western Maryland Railway Historical Society, Inc.
Museum, Model train layout

SITE ADDRESS: 41 N Main St. Union Bridge, MD 21791
MAILING ADDRESS: PO Box 395 Union Bridge, MD 21791
TELEPHONE: (410) 775-0150
WEBSITE: http://westernmarylandrhs.com

DESCRIPTION: A former Western Maryland office building and the adjoining passenger depot form a museum complex that houses an extensive collection of artifacts and memorabilia. Holdings include a photo archive, archival material directly from the Western Maryland Railway, an extensive railroaders' library featuring historical and technical publications about the WM and other roads in the region, and a model train layout.

SCHEDULE: Year-round, except Easter, New Year's Day, and Christmas when on Sunday: Sunday, 1 to 4 p.m.; Wednesday, 9 a.m. to 12 p.m. and 1 to 3 p.m.; and by appointment.

ADMISSION/FARE: None. Donations appreciated.

NEARBY ATTRACTIONS: Gettysburg National Battlefield, Monocacy National Battlefield, Antietam National Battlefield, Pen Mar Park, and Frederick Keys Baseball Park.

DIRECTIONS: Museum is on Maryland Route 75, Main St. in Union Bridge, Maryland. It is easy to reach from I-70, I-270, I-795, US15, MD 26, MD 97, and MD 140.

Photo courtesy of Western Maryland Railway Historical Society, Inc.

Walkersville, MD

Walkersville Southern Railroad
Train ride, Dinner train, Museum, Display, Model train layout
Standard gauge
Radio frequency: 160.650

SITE ADDRESS: 34 W Pennsylvania Ave., PO Box 651 Walkersville, MD 21793-0651
MAILING ADDRESS: 8832 N Westland Dr. Gaithersburg, MD 20877-1206
TELEPHONE: (877) 363-WSRR
E-MAIL: president@wsrr.org
WEBSITE: www.wsrr.org

DESCRIPTION: The Walkersville Southern Railroad takes passengers on an 8-mile, 70-minute round trip that goes through the woods and rural farm country north of Frederick, Maryland.

SCHEDULE: May through October: Saturday, departures at 11 a.m., 1 and 3 p.m.; May, June, September, and October: Sunday, departures at 11 a.m. and 1 p.m.

ADMISSION/FARE: Adults, $8; seniors 55 and over, $7; children 3-12, $4; children under 3, free for regular excursions. Special rates for some trains.

LOCOMOTIVES/ROLLING STOCK: EMD model 40 no. 101, Davenport 0-4-0 no. 2, converted flatcar no. 11, coaches nos. 7045 & 7128 (former LIRR P54D cars), former Wabash caboose no. 2827, former PRR N5 cabin car no. 477532.

SPECIAL EVENTS: Saturday evening Mystery Dinner Trains, Midweek Teddy Bear Picnic, Father's and Mother's Day Specials, 4th of July Fireworks Special, Track Car Days, Nature Trains, Jesse James Day, Circus Day, Haunted Rail & Trail. Available for private charters; if interested, call for details.

NEARBY ATTRACTIONS: Fountain Rock Nature Center and Heritage Farm Park, in Walkersville and Catoctin Mountain Zoological Park in Thurmont, Maryland.

DIRECTIONS: Two miles east on Biggs Ford Rd., off US15, 3 miles north of Frederick, Maryland. Located 50 miles west of Baltimore and 50 miles northwest of Washington, D.C.

Photo courtesy of Paul J. Bergdolt.

MASSACHUSETTS

Beverly, MA
Walker Transportation Collection, Beverly Historical Society & Museum
Museum

ADDRESS: 117 Cabot St. Beverly, MA 01915
TELEPHONE: (978) 922-1186
E-MAIL: info@beverlyhistory.org
WEBSITE: www.walkertrans.org

DESCRIPTION: A repository of photos, slides, maps, documents, artifacts, and models relating to most modes of transportation in Massachusetts/Eastern New England.

SCHEDULE: Year-round, except for week between Christmas and New Year's: Wednesday, 7 to 10 p.m., or by appointment.

ADMISSION/FARE: Donations requested; annual supporter, $25.

NEARBY ATTRACTIONS: Historic Salem, Massachusetts, and renowned Peabody-Essex Museum. John Hale Farm and historic Balch House are located in Beverly.

DIRECTIONS: US Route 1A, North; WTC at Beverly Historical Society & Museum in Beverly, housed in historic John Cabot house.

Carver, MA
Edaville U.S.A.
Train ride
Narrow gauge

ADDRESS: 7 Eda Ave. Carver, MA 02330
TELEPHONE: (877) EDAVILL or (508) 866-8190
E-MAIL: swentworth@edaville.com
WEBSITE: www.edaville.com

DESCRIPTION: This is a family fun park with a 2-mile train ride through a 1300-acre cranberry plantation. There are 11 amusement rides, indoor play area, National Cranberry Festival, Holiday Festival of Lights, many summer special events, and fishing (seasonal).

SCHEDULE: See website for events and dates of operation.

ADMISSION/FARE: See website.

LOCOMOTIVES/ROLLING STOCK:
1949 GE diesel, 1951 Whitcomb diesel; coaches and combine.

SPECIAL EVENTS: October, National Cranberry Festival; Festival of Lights. Please call or visit our website for exact dates.

NEARBY ATTRACTIONS: Plymouth Plantation, Cape Cod, Myles Standish State Forest.

DIRECTIONS: 495 to exit 2, follow Route 58 3½ miles.

Chatham, MA
Chatham Railroad Museum
Museum, Model train display

SITE ADDRESS: 153 Depot Rd. Chatham, MA 02633
MAILING ADDRESS: Town of Chatham/Railroad Museum 549 Main St. Chatham, MA 02633
TELEPHONE: (508) 945-5199
WEBSITE: www.chathamrailroadmuseum.com

DESCRIPTION: This restored country depot is on its original site. Exhibits include hundreds of railroad artifacts from the Chatham Railroad Company and other US railroads, including a restored caboose, Western Union instruments, HO replica of original yard, and O scale locomotive models.

SCHEDULE: June 15 through September 18: Tuesday through Saturday, 10 a.m. to 4 p.m.

ADMISSION/FARE: Donations accepted.

LOCOMOTIVES/ROLLING STOCK: Restored NYC wood-sided caboose no. 18452.

NEARBY ATTRACTIONS: Cape Cod beaches, fishing, boating, shopping, trips to Nantucket and Martha's Vineyard, and Cape Cod Baseball League games.

DIRECTIONS: US6 to exit 11, then Route 137 to Route 28. Turn left, and follow Route 28 to Chatham rotary. Exit rotary for Orleans. Depot St. is the first street on the left.

Photo courtesy of Larry Larned.

Fall River, MA

Old Colony & Fall River Railroad Museum, Inc.

Museum
Standard gauge

SITE ADDRESS: 2 Water St. at Battleship Cove Fall River, MA 02720
MAILING ADDRESS: PO Box 3455 Fall River, MA 02722
TELEPHONE: (508) 674-9340
E-MAIL: railroadjc@aol.com
WEBSITE: www.ocandfrrailroadmuseum.com

DESCRIPTION: The museum, located in railroad cars that include a renovated Pennsylvania Railroad coach, features artifacts of the New Haven, Penn Central, Conrail, Amtrak, and other New England railroads.

SCHEDULE: May 1 to July 1 and September to mid-October: Saturday, 12 to 4 p.m.; Sunday, 10 a.m. to 2 p.m.; July 1 to early September: Friday to Sunday, 12 to 5 p.m. Please call or visit website for exact dates.

ADMISSION/FARE: Adults, $2.50; seniors, $2; children 5-12, $1.50; children under 5, free. Group rates available.

LOCOMOTIVES/ROLLING STOCK: Pennsylvania P-70 coach, New Haven 40-foot boxcar no. 33401, New Haven RDC no. 42, New York Central caboose no. 21052.

SPECIAL EVENTS: Third weekend in January, Annual Railroad Show; mid-August, Fall River Celebrates America waterfront festival; late October, Haunted Railroad Museum.

NEARBY ATTRACTIONS: Battleship Cove (six warships on display), Marine Museum at Fall River, Heritage State Park, and Fall River Carousel.

DIRECTIONS: The museum is located in a railroad yard at the corner of Central and Water Streets, across from the entrance to Battleship Cove.

Photo courtesy of Jack Darmody.
Coupon available, see insert.

TRAVEL TIP: *Cab rides*

Many railroads offer the chance to ride the in the cab, the compartment where the engine crew rides. Here you'll get to see the engineer work the throttle and the brakes. If it's a steam engine you can watch the fireman manipulate the oil firing or shovel coal. Either way, you'll get a great view and be the envy of all your friends.

Hyannis, MA

Cape Cod Central Railroad

Train ride, Dinner train

ADDRESS: 252 Main St., PO Box 537 Hyannis, MA 02601
TELEPHONE: (508) 771-3800
E-MAIL: sales@capetrain.com
WEBSITE: http://capetrain.com/

DESCRIPTION: Passengers can take a two-hour scenic excursion and luncheon train from Hyannis to Cape Cod Canal. Three-hour elegant dinner trains are also available. Sights include: cranberry bogs, salt marshes, sand dunes, kettle ponds, and Cape Cod Bay.

SCHEDULE: Scenic trains: May to October; Dinner train: April to December.

ADMISSION/FARE: Adults, $15; seniors 62+, $13; children 3-11, $11; dinner train: $59.

LOCOMOTIVES/ROLLING STOCK: RS3m no. 1201; 2 GP7s; 3 ex-LIRR coaches; 2 ex-CN/VIA coaches converted to table cars for dinner train; ex-Illinois Central parlor-lounge car built in 1917, used on dinner trains.

NEARBY ATTRACTIONS: Boat lines, beaches, and many other area attractions.

DIRECTIONS: Take Route 6 to exit 7. Go left off the exit and follow for approximately 2 miles to Route 28. Cross Route 28 and continue straight to the end of the road. At Main St. turn right. The depot is on the right at the corner of Main and Center Sts.

KEY TO SYMBOLS

♿ Handicapped accessible	🍴 Restaurant	🎨 Arts and crafts	**arm** Association of Railway Museums
P Parking	⛽ Picnic area	**M** Memberships available	**TRAIN** Tourist Railway Association, Inc.
P Bus/RV parking	Dining car	✉ Send S.A.S.E. for brochure	**AMTRAK** Amtrak service to nearby city
🎁 Gift, book, or museum shop	Excursions	**NRHP** National Register of Historic Places	**VIA** VIA service to nearby city
☕ Refreshments	**TOUR** Guided tours	VISA MasterCard DISCOVER AMERICAN EXPRESS Card	Credit cards accepted

Lenox, MA

Berkshire Scenic Railway

Train ride, Museum, Display, Model railroad layout

ADDRESS: 10 Willow Creek Rd., PO Box 2195 Lenox, MA 01240
TELEPHONE: (413) 637-2210
E-MAIL: pieter.lips@berkshireScenicRailroad.org
WEBSITE: www.berkshirescenicrailroad.org

DESCRIPTION: Twenty-mile, round trip excursion between Lenox and Stockbridge, Massachusetts, along the Housatonic River. The museum is located in the restored Lenox Station. Restored New York, New Haven & Hartford NE-5 caboose; Fairmont speeder and track gang train; displays about Berkshire railroading history; railroad videos; exhibit of photos and artifacts about Gilded-Age Berkshire "Cottages" in restored coach.

SCHEDULE: Memorial Day to October: weekends and holidays; depart 10 a.m. and 2:15 p.m.

ADMISSION/FARE: Adults, $12; seniors, $12; children 4-14, $9.

LOCOMOTIVES/ROLLING STOCK: Ex-Conrail EMD SW8 8619; ex-Maine Central Alco S1 0954; Housatonic RR RS 3(M) 9935; ex-DL&W coaches (7) Pullman Standard 70-foot 310, 328, 329, 341, 453, 3204, 3224 & 4301

NEARBY ATTRACTIONS: Tanglewood (summer home of the Boston Symphony Orchestra), Jacob's Pillow, Hancock Shaker Village, Berkshire Theatre Festival, Norman Rockwell Museum, Red Lion Inn, Blantyre.

DIRECTIONS: US7/20 to Housatonic St., travel east 1.5 miles.

Photo courtesy of Tom Delasco.

Lowell, MA

Lowell National Historical Park

ADDRESS: 67 Kirk St. Lowell, MA 01852
TELEPHONE: (978) 970-5000
WEBSITE: www.nps.gov/lowe

DESCRIPTION: The park encompasses a canal system, restored mill buildings, two circa 1901 open-air trolleys, one circa 1919 closed car, a combine/tool car, and a locomotive.

SCHEDULE: Year-round, seven days except Thanksgiving, Christmas, and New Year's Day.

ADMISSION/FARE: Park admission: free; some exhibits and tours, free.

LOCOMOTIVES/ROLLING STOCK: Boston & Maine combine/toolcar no. M3031, Boston & Maine 0-6-0 no. 410 (Manchester, 1911).

SPECIAL EVENTS: Last full weekend in July, Lowell Folk Festival.

NEARBY ATTRACTIONS: National Streetcar Museum of Lowell, New England Quilt Museum, American Textile History Museum, Brush Art Gallery, Revolving Museum, more.

DIRECTIONS: Interstate 495 to Lowell Connector to Thorndike Street. Follow signs to Lowell National Historical Park.

Shelburne Falls, MA
Shelburne Falls Trolley Museum
Train ride, Museum, Display, Model railroad layout

ADDRESS: 14 Depot St., PO Box 272 Shelburne Falls, MA 01370
TELEPHONE: (413) 625-9443
EMAIL: trolley@sftm.org
WEBSITE: www.sftm.org

DESCRIPTION: Museum with 15-minute trolley ride and interpretive talk by motorman/conductor; locomotive, caboose, handcar, trolley, and railroad displays.

SCHEDULE: May to November: weekends and holidays, 11 a.m. to 5 p.m.; July and August: also Monday and Wednesday, 1 to 5 p.m.

ADMISSION/FARE: Adults, $2.50; children 6-12, $1.25; children under 6, free.

LOCOMOTIVES/ROLLING STOCK: 1896 Wason trolley car no. 10.

DIRECTIONS: Route 91 or Route 2 to Greenfield. Go west on Route 2 approximately eight miles to Shelburne Falls. Follow the signs to the Buckland side of Shelburne Falls. Take Depot St. to the railyard next to the tracks.

Photo courtesy of David C. Bartlett.

Wenham, MA

Wenham Museum

Museum, Model train layout

ADDRESS: 132 Main St. Wenham, MA 01984
TELEPHONE: (978) 468-2377
EMAIL: info@wenhammuseum.org
WEBSITE: www.wenhammuseum.org

DESCRIPTION: The model and toy train room features 6 operating layouts in G, O, HO, N, and Z gauges. Railroad artifacts, memorabilia, and antique toy trains are also on display. Highlights include large scale models by Wilbur Frey, such as the 8-ft long model of the Union Pacific "Big Boy," and a 1934 Lionel standard gauge work train headed by the famed 400E locomotive. Model train and railroad experts are available to answer questions, discuss scenery building and layout construction, and offer advice to railroad hobbyists.

SCHEDULE: Tuesday to Sunday, 10 a.m. to 4 p.m.; closed Mondays and major holidays.

ADMISSION/FARE: Adults, $5; seniors 65+, $4; children 2-16, $3.

SPECIAL EVENTS: First weekend in January, Annual Railroad Hobby Show.

NEARBY ATTRACTIONS: Wenham Tea House and shops, numerous historical sites and museums in region. Beautiful beaches, scenic drives, quaint towns.

DIRECTIONS: Route 128 north to exit 20A (Route 1A north). Follow Route 1A north for 2.3 miles. The museum is on the right next to Town Hall.

KEY TO SYMBOLS

♿ Handicapped accessible	🍴 Restaurant	🎨 Arts and crafts	**arm** Association of Railway Museums
🅿 Parking	🏕 Picnic area	Ⓜ Memberships available	**TRAIN** Tourist Railway Association, Inc.
🅿 Bus/RV parking	Dining car	✉ Send S.A.S.E. for brochure	Amtrak service to nearby city
🎁 Gift, book, or museum shop	Excursions	National Register **NRHP** of Historic Places	VIA service to nearby city
☕ Refreshments	**TOUR** Guided tours	VISA MasterCard DISCOVER AMERICAN EXPRESS	Credit cards accepted

MICHIGAN

Old Road Dinner Train (Adrian & Blissfield Rail Road)
Train ride, Dinner train
Standard gauge

ADDRESS: 301 E Adrian St. Blissfield, MI
TELEPHONE: (888) GO-RAIL-1
WEBSITE: www.murdermysterytrain.com

DESCRIPTION: The railroad offers a variety of 12- to 14-mile round trips over the historic "Old Road" of the former Lake Shore & Michigan Southern. This is a 2- to 3-hour round trip featuring traditional dining car service including a five-course dinner. The murder mystery dinner train is a 2½- to 3-hour fine dining and entertaining experience accompanied by a troupe of actors performing a comical, interactive murder mystery.

SCHEDULE: Year-round dinner trains, charters, and excursions; see website for information.

ADMISSION/FARE: Dinner train: $69.95 per person; excursion train: adults, $10; seniors, $9; children 3-12, $6. Reservations recommended.

LOCOMOTIVES/ROLLING STOCK: Two GP9s, dining cars from Union Pacific, Canadian National, Southern Pacific, and Kansas City Southern.

SPECIAL EVENTS: Two to three weeks prior to Easter, Bunny Trains; December, Santa Train.

NEARBY ATTRACTIONS: Many antique and specialty shops in Blissfield.

DIRECTIONS: US23 to US223 west to Blissfield, MI. Depot on north side of Adrian St. (US223), 20 minutes north of Toledo, OH.

Photo courtesy of Paul Allan & Phil Russo.

Bridgeport, MI

Junction Valley Railroad
Miniature train, Display
14¹⁄₈" gauge

ADDRESS: 7065 Dixie Hwy. Bridgeport, MI 48722
TELEPHONE: (989) 777-7480
WEBSITE: www.jvrailroad.com

DESCRIPTION: The 2-mile ride travels down into a valley, around a lake, over 22 bridges and trestles, and through a 100-foot tunnel. Visitors can see a 10-stall roundhouse with turntable, 5-track switchyard, and railroad and hobby shops.

SCHEDULE: Train rides: summer: weekdays and Saturday, 10 a.m. to 6 p.m.; Sunday, 1 to 5 p.m.; September through October: weekends, 1 to 5 p.m.

ADMISSION/FARE: Adults, $5.50; seniors, $5; children, $4.50.

LOCOMOTIVES/ROLLING STOCK: Nine scale diesel engines and 74 freight hauling passenger cars all built to ¼ scale.

SPECIAL EVENTS: Weekends in June, July, and August, Railroad Days Train; October, Halloween train ride.

NEARBY ATTRACTIONS: Frankenmuth has the world's largest Christmas store.

DIRECTIONS: Exit 144 off I-75, 2 miles south on Dixie Hwy. 5 miles west of Frankemuth.

Photo courtesy of Lillian Stenger.
Coupon available, see insert.

Capac, MI

Capac Community Museum
Museum, Display, Model train layout

ADDRESS: 401 E Kempf Ct. Capac, MI 48014
TELEPHONE: (810) 395-2859

DESCRIPTION: The 1912 Grand Trunk Depot Museum has railroad and other historical artifacts from around the area. It also has the Kempf Model City and a Grand Trunk Western caboose.

SCHEDULE: First June Sunday to last Sunday in September: 1 to 4 p.m., or by special appointment for individuals or groups.

ADMISSION/FARE: Donations.

LOCOMOTIVES/ROLLING STOCK: GTW caboose no. 78899, C&O speeder.

SPECIAL EVENTS: Last Saturday of October, a fundraising dinner with area history program.

NEARBY ATTRACTIONS: Motels in Imlay City; campground on Beech Grove Rd. in Emmett; ½ hour away from Port Huron, MI, and Canada.

DIRECTIONS: Just ¼ mile east of the Village of Capac off Capac Rd. on the south side of Downey Rd. (M-21).

Photo courtesy of Kempf Model City.

Charlotte, MI

Charlotte Southern/Old Road Dinner Train
Dinner train
Standard gauge

SITE ADDRESS: 451 N Cochrane St. Charlotte, MI 48813
MAILING ADDRESS: PO Box 95 Blissfield, MI 49228
TELEPHONE: (888) 726-8277
WEBSITE: www.murdermysterytrain.com

DESCRIPTION: This working, common-carrier freight and passenger railroad offers 2½-hour round trips from downtown Charlotte over a former New York Central line. The Old Road Dinner Train features traditional dining-car service, including an elegant five-course dinner, cash bar, and murder mystery.

SCHEDULE: Saturdays, year-round.

ADMISSION/FARE: $57.95 per person for five-course dinner and mystery show.

LOCOMOTIVES/ROLLING STOCK: GE 44-ton locomotive and ex-CN dining cars.

SPECIAL EVENTS: Easter Bunny Trains and Santa Trains.

NEARBY ATTRACTIONS: Michigan State Historical Museum in Lansing.

DIRECTIONS: Located in Charlotte, MI, near the intersection of I-69 and Lansing Rd.

Clinton, MI
Southern Michigan Railroad Society
Train ride, Museum
Standard gauge

ADDRESS: 320 S Division, PO Box K Clinton, MI 49236
TELEPHONE: (517) 456-7677
WEBSITE: www.southernmichiganrailroad.org

DESCRIPTION: The organization is dedicated to building an operating museum railroad using the first branch rail lines into Michigan—the Palmyra and Jacksonburgh—and preserving its historical railroad era (1838-1982). They aim to promote the awareness of railroading through activities, including a train ride that travels from Clinton to Tecumseh.

SCHEDULE: May through September: Saturday, 11 a.m. and 2 p.m. departures from Clinton, and 12:30 p.m. departure from Tecumseh. Call for additional dates and times.

ADMISSION/FARE: May to September: adults, $8; seniors, $7; youth 2-12, $5; fall color tours: adults, $15; seniors, $10; youth 2-12, $8. Fees subject to change.

LOCOMOTIVES/ROLLING STOCK: Regular passenger service–1943 GE 44-ton diesel no. 75; 1926 Chicago South Shore & South Bend commuter car no. 1, NYC gondola no. 726456, 1952 NYC bay window caboose no. 21692. Other–1960 GM GMDH-3 prototype, 1938 Plymouth no. 1, more.

SPECIAL EVENTS: Special events have included holiday events, Crazy Hat Weekend, Clinton Fall Festival and River Raisin Color Tours, Pow Wow Firecracker Express, and more.

NEARBY ATTRACTIONS: Downtown shopping and eating; park facilities.

DIRECTIONS: Clinton: US12 to Clinton, south three blocks on Division St.; or M-52 south from Chelsea and I-94 to US12 east. Tecumseh: M-50 to Tecumseh. Corner of Evans and M-50.

Photo courtesy of Cynthia L. Given.

Coldwater, MI
Little River Railroad

Train ride, Dinner train
Standard gauge

SITE ADDRESS: Coldwater Train Depot West Park Ave. Coldwater, MI
MAILING ADDRESS: 13187 SR 120 Middlebury, IN 46540
TELEPHONE: (260) 316-0529
E-MAIL: customerservice@littleriverrailroad.com
WEBSITE: www.littleriverrailroad.com

DESCRIPTION: This not-for-profit organization restores and operates historic railroad equipment. Round trip, steam-powered rides leave from both Coldwater and Quincy, travel through the countryside, and last approximately 1½ hours.

SCHEDULE: Memorial Day weekend through October with Christmas Runs in December. Times vary; check website for details.

ADMISSION/FARE: Adults, $16; children, $9; family (2 adults and 2 or more children), $50. Annual pass: $50 per person or $100 per family.

LOCOMOTIVES/ROLLING STOCK: 4-6-2 no. 110 (Baldwin, 1911); 0-4-0T no. 1 (Vulcan, 1908).

SPECIAL EVENTS: See website or call for special events.

NEARBY ATTRACTIONS: Capri Drive-in, Tibbelts Open House, Sauk Trail Trading Post.

DIRECTIONS: I-69 to exit 13. West on US12. South on Division St. Call for more details.

KEY TO SYMBOLS

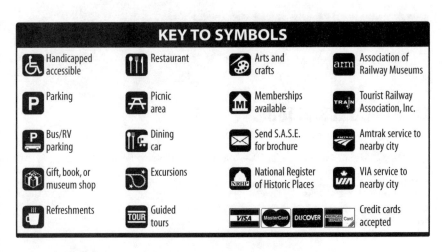

Handicapped accessible	Restaurant	Arts and crafts	Association of Railway Museums
Parking	Picnic area	Memberships available	Tourist Railway Association, Inc.
Bus/RV parking	Dining car	Send S.A.S.E. for brochure	Amtrak service to nearby city
Gift, book, or museum shop	Excursions	National Register of Historic Places	VIA service to nearby city
Refreshments	Guided tours		Credit cards accepted

Coopersville, MI

Coopersville & Marne Railway

Train ride

ADDRESS: 311 Danforth St. Coopersville, MI 49404
TELEPHONE: (616) 997-7000
E-MAIL: jerryricard@comcast.net
WEBSITE: www.coopersvilleandmarne.org

DESCRIPTION: The 1950s-era diesel locomotive pulls cars dating from the 1920s and '30s for a 14-mile, 1-hour-long excursion through the countryside. The train travels through family-owned farmlands, crosses an open-deck girder bridge, four creeks, and a bridge.

SCHEDULE: May to October: Wednesday and Saturday, 11 a.m. and 1 p.m.; March, April, November, and December: Saturday only; January and February: closed.

ADMISSION/FARE: Regular fare: adults, $10; seniors, $9; children 2-12, $6; children under 2, free. Fares slightly higher for Bunny Train, Great Train Robbery, Pumpkin Train, and Santa Train.

LOCOMOTIVES/ROLLING STOCK: Grand Trunk Western SW9 no. 7014; GE center-cab no. 3049; GTW caboose no. 1159; ex-CN car no. 7003; ex-Lackawanna car nos. 7001 and 7002; dining car no. 7010; ex-C&O 250-ton Brownhoist Crane no. 101003.

SPECIAL EVENTS: April 1, 8, and 15, Bunny Train; May 29, Vet's Free Troop Train; June 18, History Train; July 8, 15, and 23, Great Train Robbery; October 7, 14, 21, and 28, Pumpkin Train; November 25 and December 1, 8, 15, and 22, Santa Train.

NEARBY ATTRACTIONS: Coopersville Farm Museum, Coopersville Area Historical and Railroad Museum, Hoffmaster State Park, Holland State Park, Michigan Adventure Amusement Park, Lake Express Ferry.

DIRECTIONS: Interstate 96, exit 16 or 19. Drive north after exiting I-96 and follow signs.

Photo courtesy of Jerry Ricard.

Corunna, MI

Lake Central Rail Tours

Train ride

SITE ADDRESSES: 128 Westmore St., 500 S Washington St., 506 W Broadway, and 127 W Cass St. Corunna, MI 48817
MAILING ADDRESS: PO Box 221 Corunna, MI 48817
TELEPHONE: (810) 638-7248
E-MAIL: ra1508vh@cs.com
WEBSITE: www.lcrt.homestead.com

DESCRIPTION: Passenger train excursions across the state of Michigan operate over the rails of the Tuscola & Saginaw Bay Railway.

ADMISSION/FARE: Tickets must be purchased in advance. Call (866) 608-0746.

SPECIAL EVENTS: Dinner trains, day long excursions, fall color excursions, steam excursions, and the "Santa Express."

Dearborn, MI
Henry Ford Museum and Greenfield Village Railroad
Train ride, Museum
Standard gauge

ADDRESS: 20900 Oakwood Blvd. Dearborn, MI 48124
TELEPHONE: (800) 835-5237 or (313) 271-1620
WEBSITE: www.hfmgv.org

DESCRIPTION: A 2½-mile, 35-minute narrated circuit of the world-famous Greenfield Village in open-air passenger cars. The Henry Ford Museum contains an extensive transportation collection. Greenfield Village offers a re-creation of the Detroit, Toledo & Milwaukee roundhouse and a six-stall repair facility from 1884. Visitors can get an up-close look at repairs taking place on the trains of Greenfield Village.

SCHEDULE: April 15 through October 31: daily, 9:30 a.m. to 5 p.m.; July 9 through August 20: also Saturday until 9 p.m.; November 1 to December 31: Friday through Sunday, 9:30 a.m. to 5 p.m.; open New Year's Day; closed Thanksgiving and Christmas Day.

ADMISSION/FARE: Members, free; adults, $20; seniors 62+, $19; youth 5-12, $14; children under 5, free. Call to confirm.

LOCOMOTIVES/ROLLING STOCK: Ford Motor Co. 4-4-0 no. 1; Calumet & Hecla Mining 0-6-4T no. 3; Michigan Alkali Co. 0-6-0 no. 8; Chesapeake & Ohio 2-6-6-6 no. 1601; 4-4-2 (Alco, 1902); 4-4-0 (Rogers, 1858); 1893 DeWitt Clinton replica; Bessemer & Lake Erie 2-8-0 no. 154.

DIRECTIONS: ½ mile south of US12 between Southfield and Oakwood Blvd./freeway M39.

Photo courtesy of E.J. Gulash.

Durand, MI

Michigan Railroad History Museum, Durand Union Station

Museum, Display, Model train layout

ADDRESS: 200 Railroad St. Durand, MI 48429
TELEPHONE: (989) 288-3561
WEBSITE: www.durandstation.org

DESCRIPTION: This 100-year-old museum was the second busiest depot in Michigan during the "Golden Era of Railroads." The village was built around the railroads in the late 1870s. The depot museum offers an educational and entertaining source of Michigan's rich railroad history. Included in the collection are ledgers, technical railroad information, union materials, and other documents pertaining to railroading in Michigan.

SCHEDULE: Tuesday through Sunday, 1 to 5 p.m.; closed Mondays.

ADMISSION/FARE: Admission free, donations appreciated.

SPECIAL EVENTS: First weekend after Mother's Day, Railroad Days,.

NEARBY ATTRACTIONS: 20 minutes to Steam Railroading Institute in Owosso, MI.

DIRECTIONS: Exit 118 from I-69. Follow green signs.

Photo courtesy of Durand Union Station, Inc.

Fairview, MI

Michigan AuSable Valley Railroad

Train ride

ADDRESS: 230 S Abbe Rd. Fairview, MI 48621
TELEPHONE: (989) 848-2229 or (989) 848-2225
WEBSITE: www.michiganausablevalleyrailroad.com

DESCRIPTION: Visitors can take a 1½-mile ride on a ¼ scale passenger train that runs through Huron National Forest. The tour passes through a wooden tunnel and over two wooden trestles to view AuSable Valley.

SCHEDULE: Memorial Day weekend through Labor Day: weekends and holidays only, 10 a.m. to 5 p.m.; first two weekends in October: fall color.

ADMISSION/FARE: $4; children under 2, free.

Flint, MI
Huckleberry Railroad
Train ride
3' Narrow gauge

ADDRESS: 6140 Bray Rd. Flint, MI 48506
TELEPHONE: (800) 648-PARK or (810) 736-7100
E-MAIL: parkswebteam@gcparks.org
WEBSITE: www.geneseecountyparks.org

DESCRIPTION: The Huckleberry Railroad has 8 historic coaches, 2 open cars, 4 excursion cars, and 1 replica combination car to take passengers on an 8-mile, 35-minute train ride.

SCHEDULE: Summer: May to August; fall: October; winter: November (day after Thanksgiving) to December 30; closed Christmas Day and New Year's Eve; Monday night drive through only.

ADMISSION/FARE: Weekday rates: adults, $11; seniors 60+, $10; children 3-12, $8.50; children 2 and under, free; weekend rates: adults, $13; seniors 60+, $12; children 3-12, $9.50; children 2 and under, free.

LOCOMOTIVES/ROLLING STOCK: Baldwin 4-6-0 no. 2, Baldwin 2-8-2 no. 464, GE 50-ton diesel-electric no. 7, caboose, 8 historic coaches, 2 open cars (gondolas), 4 excursion cars, 1 replica combination baggage passenger.

SPECIAL EVENTS: Weekend events throughout summer; August, Railfans weekend; Halloween trains; Christmas trains.

NEARBY ATTRACTIONS: Stepping Stone Falls, outlet shopping, and Genesee Belle Paddlewheel Riverboat specialty cruises.

DIRECTIONS: Just north of Flint, Michigan. I-475 off either I-75 or I-69 to exit 11, follow signs to railroad and Crossroads Village.

Photo courtesy of Marty Knox.
See ad on page A-33.

Flushing, MI

Flushing Area Historical Society & Cultural Center
Museum

ADDRESS: 431 W Main St. Flushing, MI 48433
TELEPHONE: (810) 487-0814
WEBSITE: www.flushinghistorical.org

DESCRIPTION: The collection includes artifacts from the area's past, including permanent displays of railroad items. Other displays change periodically. The Flushing Depot was built in 1888 and provided passenger service until 1971. Afterward, it became a restaurant and was later donated in 1997 to the Flushing Area Historical Society to restore to its former appearance and become a museum.

SCHEDULE: April through December: Sunday, 1 to 4 p.m.; closed all holiday weekends; open to groups by appointment.

ADMISSION/FARE: Free.

DIRECTIONS: Take I-75 to exit 122 (Pierson Rd.) and go west approximately 5 miles. Pierson Rd. becomes Main St. in Flushing.

Grand Haven, MI

Tri-Cities Historical Museum
Museum

SITE ADDRESS: 1 N Harbor Grand Haven, MI 49417
MAILING ADDRESS: 200 Washington Ave. Grand Haven, MI 49417
TELEPHONE: (616) 842-0700
E-MAIL: tcmuseum@grandhaven.com
WEBSITE: www.tri-citiesmuseum.org

DESCRIPTION: An 1871 depot of the Grand Trunk Western has exhibits on railroading, shipping, and the US Coast Guard. Also on display is a large collection of ship models.

SCHEDULE: Monday to Friday, 9:30 a.m. to 7:30 p.m.; Saturday and Sunday, 12:30 to 7:30 p.m.

ADMISSION/FARE: Public is admitted at no charge; donations are welcome.

LOCOMOTIVES/ROLLING STOCK: The Pere Marquette 2-8-4 no. 1223 was built in 1941 by the Lima Locomotive Works. Also included are a tender and two cabooses.

Copper Country Railroad Heritage Center/ Lake Linden & Torch Lake Railroad
Train ride, Museum, Display, Model railroad layout

ADDRESS: Houghton County Historical Society 5500 M26 Lake Linden, MI 49945
TELEPHONE: (906) 296-4121
E-MAIL: info@houghtonhistory.com
WEBSITE: www.houghtonhistory.com

DESCRIPTION: The ⅓-mile-long line includes a 102-foot wooden trestle and an interpretative program on the C&H Copper Mill, which the restored no. 3 steam locomotive once served. HO layout of the Copper Range Railroad in 1920 and other displays in restored 1880s Mineral Range Depot (ex-DSS&A/Soo Line).

SCHEDULE: Train rides and tours: Monday to Saturday, 10 a.m. to 4 p.m.; HO layout: Saturday and Sunday; other days by appointment.

ADMISSION/FARE: Train ride and museum: adults, $8; seniors 65+, $6; children under 12, $4.

LOCOMOTIVES/ROLLING STOCK: 1915 H.K. Porter 36"-gauge 0-4-0T steam loco (operational on weekends only), former Calumet & Helca; 1968 36" gauge Plymouth gas/hydraulic switcher, former OLIN Badger no. 592 (operates on weekdays); Soo Line caboose no. 261; C&H snowplow/flanger no. 2; various other 36"-gauge equipment.

SPECIAL EVENTS: First August weekend, Railroad Days, weekend before Memorial Day, "Tractors, Trains & More," Halloween Train, Santa Train.

NEARBY ATTRACTIONS: Lake Linden Village campground (hook-ups, swimming beach, boat launch), Quincy Mine Hoist, McClain and Port Wilkens State Parks, Keweenaw National Historical Park, 40 miles by boat to Isle Royale National Park.

DIRECTIONS: Take US41 or M-26 to Houghton, cross Portage Lift Bridge to M-26 (right), 10 miles on southwest side of Lake Linden.

Photo courtesy of Rick Taylor.

Manistee, MI

SS City of Milwaukee—National Historic Landmark
Museum

SITE ADDRESS: 51 9th St. Manistee, MN
MAILING ADDRESS: 111 Arthur St. Manistee, MN 49660
TELEPHONE: (231) 398-0328
E-MAIL: sscitymilw@aol.com
WEBSITE: www.carferry.com

DESCRIPTION: The S.S. *City of Milwaukee* is the last surviving traditional Great Lakes railroad car ferry. For more than a century, these vessels carried passengers and freight trains across the Great Lakes. Built in 1931, the *City of Milwaukee* served the Grand Trunk Western and Ann Arbor railroads and now serves as a National Historic Landmark museum. The car deck houses five Ann Arbor boxcars that serve as gift shop, theater, and exhibit spaces.

SCHEDULE: Guided tours, onboard bed and breakfast, special events, and private parties are available. Schedule varies; check website.

ADMISSION/FARE: Adults, $6; children 6-12, $4; children under 6, free.

DIRECTIONS: On US31, ½ mile north of downtown Manistee.

Mount Clemens, MI

Michigan Transit Museum
Train ride, Museum
Standard gauge

SITE ADDRESS: 200 Grand Ave. Mount Clemens, MI
MAILING ADDRESS: PO Box 12 Mount Clemens, MI 48046
TELEPHONE: (586) 463-1863 or (586) 286-9336, special events
WEBSITE: www.mtmrail.com

DESCRIPTION: 1920s interurban and rapid transit cars go 45 minutes round trip on the trackage of the Selfridge Air National Guard Base. Optional stop at Selfridge Military Air Museum.

SCHEDULE: Train: June through October, Sunday, 1, 2, 3, and 4 p.m.; depot museum: year-round, weekends, 1 to 4 p.m.

ADMISSION/FARE: 2005 rates: June to September: adults, $7; children 4-12, $3; October/Fall: adults, $10; children 4-12, $5; 2006 subject to change.

TOURIST TRAINS 2006
GUEST COUPONS
Arranged alphabetically by attraction name

AC&J Scenic Line Railway

$0.50 discount from any fare
up to a max of 6.

Valid February 2006 through January 2007

American Association of Railroaders

American Freedom Train full color
20"x24" poster from 1976 ($35 value);
mailed in a protective tube for $1.

Valid February 2006 through January 2007

Arkansas & Missouri Railroad

Coach seating: buy one get one free
(not in October).

Valid February 2006 through January 2007

Baltimore & Ohio Railroad Museum

Buy one adult admission, get one free.
Offer valid for one free admission. May
not be combined with any other offer or
discount. Not valid during special events.

Valid February 2006 through January 2007

Baltimore Streetcar Museum

Buy one admission, get equal
price admission free.
Limit four persons per coupon.

Valid February 2006 through January 2007

Bear Creek Park Train

Present this coupon and receive
50% off one to six tickets.
Not valid during special events.

Valid February 2006 through January 2007

Bellefonte Historical Railroad Society

$10 adult, $5 children tickets
(up to four persons).

Valid February 2006 through January 2007

Brunswick Museum

Buy one admission, get second one free
(any age category).

Valid February 2006 through January 2007

Camp Five

$2 off adult ticket.

Valid February 2006 through January 2007

Campo Railroad Museum
and San Diego & Arizona Railway

Adult admission, $12 (regular, $15).

Valid February 2006 through January 2007

Casey Jones Museum & Train Store

10% off museum admission.

Valid February 2006 through January 2007

Catskill Mountain Railroad

With coupon regular adult fare $12,
admit one child free.

Valid February 2006 through January 2007

American Association of Railroaders
St. Louis, MO
Tourist Trains 2006
Guest Coupon

AC&J Scenic Line Railway
Jefferson, OH
Tourist Trains 2006
Guest Coupon

Baltimore & Ohio Railroad Museum
Baltimore, MD
Tourist Trains 2006
Guest Coupon

Arkansas & Missouri Railroad
Springdale, AR
Tourist Trains 2006
Guest Coupon

Bear Creek Park Train
Surrey, BC
Tourist Trains 2006
Guest Coupon

Baltimore Streetcar Museum
Baltimore, MD
Tourist Trains 2006
Guest Coupon

Brunswick Museum
Brunswick, MD
Tourist Trains 2006
Guest Coupon

Bellefonte Historical Railroad Society
Bellefonte, PA
Tourist Trains 2006
Guest Coupon

Campo Railroad Museum
Campo, CA
Tourist Trains 2006
Guest Coupon

Camp Five
Laona, WI
Tourist Trains 2006
Guest Coupon

Catskill Mountain Railroad
Mt. Pleasant, NY
Tourist Trains 2006
Guest Coupon

Casey Jones Museum & Train Store
Jackson, TN
Tourist Trains 2006
Guest Coupon

TOURIST TRAINS 2006
GUEST COUPONS
Arranged alphabetically by attraction name

Chesapeake Beach Railway Museum

Free admission.

Valid February 2006 through January 2007

Choo Choo Barn, Traintown USA

Buy one adult admission, get one free.

Valid February 2006 through January 2007

Coe Rail Excursion Train

Buy one fare ($10),
get one fare at $1/2$ off.

Valid February 2006 through January 2007

Collis P. Huntington Railroad Society, Inc.

Adult, $103.50 (regular $115).
Child, $80 (regular $88).

Valid February 2006 through January 2007

Connecticut Eastern Railroad Museum

$1 off admission with coupon.

Valid February 2006 through January 2007

Crooked River Dinner Train

$10 off per adult on Murder Mystery.
$8 off per adult on Sunday Supper.

Valid February 2006 through January 2007

Danbury Railway Museum

Buy one adult admission, get one free.
Not valid on event days.

Valid February 2006 through January 2007

Delaware & Ulster Railride

Buy one ticket, get one free.

Valid February 2006 through January 2007

Dennison Railroad Depot Museum

Buy one admission, get one free.

Valid February 2006 through January 2007

East Broad Top Railroad

Adult, $9.50 (regular $10).
Child, $6.50 (regular $7).

Valid February 2006 through January 2007

Forney Museum of Transportation

Buy one adult admission, get one free.

Valid February 2006 through January 2007

Gold Coast Railroad Museum

Buy one adult admission, get one free.

Valid February 2006 through January 2007

Choo Choo Barn, Traintown USA	**Chesapeake Beach Railway Museum**
Strasburg, PA	Chesapeake Beach, MD
Tourist Trains 2006	**Tourist Trains 2006**
Guest Coupon	Guest Coupon
Collis P. Huntington Railroad Society, Inc.	**Coe Rail Excursion Train**
Huntington, WV	Walled Lake, MI
Tourist Trains 2006	**Tourist Trains 2006**
Guest Coupon	Guest Coupon
Crooked River Dinner Train	**Connecticut Eastern Railroad Museum**
Redmond, OR	Willimantic, CT
Tourist Trains 2006	**Tourist Trains 2006**
Guest Coupon	Guest Coupon
Delaware & Ulster Railride	**Danbury Railway Museum**
Arkville, NY	Danbury, CT
Tourist Trains 2006	**Tourist Trains 2006**
Guest Coupon	Guest Coupon
East Broad Top Railroad	**Dennison Railroad Depot Museum**
Rockhill Furnace, PA	Dennison, OH
Tourist Trains 2006	**Tourist Trains 2006**
Guest Coupon	Guest Coupon
Gold Coast Railroad Museum	**Forney Museum of Transportation**
Miami, FL	Denver, CO
Tourist Trains 2006	**Tourist Trains 2006**
Guest Coupon	Guest Coupon

TOURIST TRAINS 2006
GUEST COUPONS
Arranged alphabetically by attraction name

Halton County Radial Railway Museum

Buy one, get one of equal value free.

Valid February 2006 through January 2007

Hartmann Model Railroad Ltd.

Adult, $5 (regular $6).
Senior, $4 (regular $5).
Child, $3 (regular $4).

Valid February 2006 through January 2007

Hocking Valley Scenic Railway

Good for $2 off one ticket only.
Cannot be used in conjunction with other
discounts or special pricing.

Valid February 2006 through January 2007

Horseshoe Curve National Historic Landmark

Buy one adult admission, get one free.

Valid February 2006 through January 2007

Iron Mountain Iron Mine

$1 off on guided tour.
Limit four people per coupon.

Valid February 2006 through January 2007

Irvine Park Railroad

Buy one admission,
get equal price admission free.
Limit six persons per coupon.

Valid February 2006 through January 2007

Junction Valley Railroad

Buy one admission,
get equal price admission free.

Valid February 2006 through January 2007

Kruger Street Toy and Train Museum

Present this coupon for $1 off regular
admission for each member of your party,
and 10% off all gift shop purchases.
Cannot be combined with other offers.

Valid February 2006 through January 2007

Lake Shore Railway Museum

10% discount on purchase of $5
or more at the museum gift shop.

Valid March 2006 through February 2007

Linden Railroad Museum

Buy one adult admission, get one free.

Valid February 2006 through January 2007

Mad River & NKP Railroad Museum

Get $1 off admission. Limit four people.

Valid February 2006 through January 2007

Medina Railroad Museum

$1 off regular admission.

Valid February 2006 through January 2007

Hartmann Model Railroad Ltd.	**Halton County Radial Railway Museum**
Intervale, NH	Milton, ON
Tourist Trains 2006	**Tourist Trains 2006**
Guest Coupon	Guest Coupon
Horseshoe Curve National Historic Landmark	**Hocking Valley Scenic Railway**
Altoona, PA	Nelsonville, OH
Tourist Trains 2006	**Tourist Trains 2006**
Guest Coupon	Guest Coupon
Irvine Park Railroad	**Iron Mountain Iron Mine**
Orange, CA	Iron Mountain, MI
Tourist Trains 2006	**Tourist Trains 2006**
Guest Coupon	Guest Coupon
Kruger Street Toy and Train Museum	**Junction Valley Railroad**
Wheeling, WV	Bridgeport, MI
Tourist Trains 2006	**Tourist Trains 2006**
Guest Coupon	Guest Coupon
Linden Railroad Museum	**Lake Shore Railway Museum**
Linden, IN	North East, PA
Tourist Trains 2006	**Tourist Trains 2006**
Guest Coupon	Guest Coupon
Medina Railroad Museum	**Mad River & NKP Railroad Museum**
Medina, NY	Bellevue, OH
Tourist Trains 2006	**Tourist Trains 2006**
Guest Coupon	Guest Coupon

TOURIST TRAINS 2006
GUEST COUPONS
Arranged alphabetically by attraction name

Michigan Star Clipper Dinner Train

AAA discount or $5 off per person.

Valid February 2006 through January 2007

Michigan Transit Museum

$0.50 off regular adult or children's train ride fare.

Valid February 2006 through January 2007

Mid-Continent Railway Historical Society

Buy one, get one free of equal or lesser value.

Valid May 6 through September 4, 2006

Millbrae Train Museum

Buy one adult admission, get one free.

Valid February 2006 through January 2007

Mining Museum & Rollo Jamison Museum

10% off admission tickets.

Valid February 2006 through January 2007

Minnesota Transportation Museum/ Jackson St. Roundhouse

Present this coupon for $1 off adult or child fare.

Valid February 2006 through January 2007

Model Railroad Club, Inc.

Buy one adult admission, get one free. Limit one per visit.

Valid February 2006 through January 2007

National Capital Trolley Museum

Buy one admission, get one free. Limit one coupon per person.

Valid February 2006 through January 2007

National New York Central Railroad Museum

Buy one adult admission and get one admission of equal value or less free.

Valid February 2006 through January 2007

Naugatuck Railroad/ Railroad Museum of New England

$1 off any adult or child ticket with coupon.

Valid February 2006 through January 2007

New England Railroad

Buy one vacation package, receive 10% discount.

Valid February 2006 through January 2007

New Hope & Ivyland Railroad

$1 off each adult and $0.50 off each child (2-11). Coupon valid only on hourly excursion trains. Not valid during special events.

Valid February 2006 through January 2007

Michigan Transit Museum
Mt. Clemens, MI
Tourist Trains 2006
Guest Coupon

Michigan Star Clipper Dinner Train
Walled Lake, MI
Tourist Trains 2006
Guest Coupon

Millbrae Train Museum
Millbrae, CA
Tourist Trains 2006
Guest Coupon

Mid-Continent Railway Historical Society
North Freedom, WI
Tourist Trains 2006
Guest Coupon

**Minnesota Transportation Museum/
Jackson St. Roundhouse**
St. Paul, MN
Tourist Trains 2006
Guest Coupon

Mining Museum & Rollo Jamison Museum
Platteville, WI
Tourist Trains 2006
Guest Coupon

National Capital Trolley Museum
Colesville, MD
Tourist Trains 2006
Guest Coupon

Model Railroad Club, Inc.
Union, NJ
Tourist Trains 2006
Guest Coupon

Naugatuck Railroad/ Railroad Museum of New England
Thomaston, CT
Tourist Trains 2006
Guest Coupon

National New York Central Railroad Museum
Elkhart, IN
Tourist Trains 2006
Guest Coupon

New Hope & Ivyland Railroad
New Hope, PA
Tourist Trains 2006
Guest Coupon

New England Railroad
Richmond, ME
Tourist Trains 2006
Guest Coupon

TOURIST TRAINS 2006
GUEST COUPONS
Arranged alphabetically by attraction name

New York Museum of Transportation

Buy one adult admission, get one free.

Valid February 2006 through January 2007

North Carolina Transportation Museum at Historic Spencer Shops

$1 off train ride;
not valid during special events.

Valid February 2006 through January 2007

Northwest Iowa Railway Historical Society

Buy one adult admission, get one free.

Valid February 2006 through January 2007

Northwest Ohio Railroad Preservation, Inc.

Buy one admission,
get equal price admission free.
Limit one person per coupon.

Valid February 2006 through January 2007

Oil Creek Railway Historical Society, Inc.

Buy one adult ticket, get second ticket free.

Valid February 2006 through January 2007

Okefenokee Heritage Center

$1 off regular admission.

Valid February 2006 through January 2007

Old Colony & Fall River Railroad Museum, Inc.

Buy one adult admission, get ½ off second.

Valid February 2006 through January 2007

Old Depot Railroad Museum

10% off.

Valid February 2006 through January 2007

Orange Empire Railway Museum

$1 off each adult ticket.
Not available on special events.
Not available with other discounts.

Valid February 2006 through January 2007

Orr Family Farm and Railroad, LLC

Buy one, get one free.

Valid February 2006 through January 2007

Osceola & St. Croix Valley Railway

Present this coupon for $2 off
any adult fare or $5 off family fare.
Good on regular schedule only.

Valid February 2006 through January 2007

Patee House Museum

One adult admission free with
one paid admission.

Valid February 2006 through January 2007

North Carolina Transportation Museum at
Historic Spencer Shops
Spencer, NC
Tourist Trains 2006
Guest Coupon

New York Museum of Transportation
West Henrietta, NY
Tourist Trains 2006
Guest Coupon

Northwest Ohio Railroad Preservation, Inc.
Findlay, OH
Tourist Trains 2006
Guest Coupon

Northwest Iowa Railway Historical Society
Spencer, IA
Tourist Trains 2006
Guest Coupon

Okefenokee Heritage Center
Waycross, GA
Tourist Trains 2006
Guest Coupon

Oil Creek Railway Historical Society, Inc.
Titusville, PA
Tourist Trains 2006
Guest Coupon

Old Depot Railroad Museum
Dassel, MN
Tourist Trains 2006
Guest Coupon

Old Colony & Fall River Railroad Museum, Inc.
Fall River, MA
Tourist Trains 2006
Guest Coupon

Orr Family Farm and Railroad, LLC
Oklahoma City, OK
Tourist Trains 2006
Guest Coupon

Orange Empire Railway Museum
Perris, CA
Tourist Trains 2006
Guest Coupon

Patee House Museum
St. Joseph, MO
Tourist Trains 2006
Guest Coupon

Osceola & St. Croix Valley Railway
Osceola, WI
Tourist Trains 2006
Guest Coupon

TOURIST TRAINS 2006
GUEST COUPONS
Arranged alphabetically by attraction name

Pennsylvania Trolley Museum

Buy one admission,
get one admission of equal price for free.

Valid February 2006 through January 2007

Pike's Peak
Historical Street Railway

Adult, $2 (regular $3).
Child, $1 (regular $1.50).

Valid February 2006 through January 2007

Railroad & Heritage Museum

Buy one adult admission, get one free.

Valid February 2006 through January 2007

Railroad Historical Center

50% discount with coupon.

Valid February 2006 through January 2007

Railroaders Memorial Museum

Buy one adult admission, get one free.

Valid February 2006 through January 2007

Revelstoke Railway Museum

20% discount on admission with
presentation of this coupon.

Valid February 2006 through January 2007

Riverside &
Great Northern Railway

Buy one admission, get equal price
admission free. Limit one person per coupon.

Valid Memorial Day through Labor Day

Rockhill Trolley Museum

Buy one admission, get one free.

Valid February 2006 through January 2007

Sacramento RiverTrain

50% off one adult ticket,
or free children's ticket.

Valid February 2006 through January 2007

San Diego
Model Railroad Museum

Buy one adult admission, one adult free.

Valid February 2006 through January 2007

Sandy River and
Rangeley Lakes Railroad

Buy one adult train ride, get one free.

Valid February 2006 through January 2007

Seashore Trolley Museum

Adult $6.50 (regular $7.50).
Limit one per person per coupon.

Valid February 2006 through January 2007

Pike's Peak Historical Street Railway	**Pennsylvania Trolley Museum**
Colorado Springs, CO	Washington, PA
Tourist Trains 2006	**Tourist Trains 2006**
Guest Coupon	Guest Coupon
Railroad Historical Center	**Railroad & Heritage Museum**
Greenwood, SC	Temple, TX
Tourist Trains 2006	**Tourist Trains 2006**
Guest Coupon	Guest Coupon
Revelstoke Railway Museum	**Railroaders Memorial Museum**
Revelstoke, BC	Altoona, PA
Tourist Trains 2006	**Tourist Trains 2006**
Guest Coupon	Guest Coupon
Rockhill Trolley Museum	**Riverside & Great Northern Railway**
Rockhill Furnace, PA	Wisconsin Dells, WI
Tourist Trains 2006	**Tourist Trains 2006**
Guest Coupon	Guest Coupon
San Diego Model Railroad Museum	**Sacramento RiverTrain**
San Diego, CA	Woodland, CA
Tourist Trains 2006	**Tourist Trains 2006**
Guest Coupon	Guest Coupon
Seashore Trolley Museum	**Sandy River and Rangeley Lakes Railroad**
Kennebunkport, ME	.Phillips, ME
Tourist Trains 2006	**Tourist Trains 2006**
Guest Coupon	Guest Coupon

TOURIST TRAINS 2006
GUEST COUPONS
Arranged alphabetically by attraction name

Shore Line Trolley Museum

$0.50 off each fare.
Maximum discount $3.

Valid February 2006 through January 2007

Sierra Madre Express

Early booking discount available.

Valid February 2006 through January 2007

Sierra Railroad Dinner Train

Present coupon for choice of:
complementary premium seating,
bottle of Silkwood wine, or children's ticket.

Valid through 2006 except October weekends

The SoNo Switch Tower Museum

10% discount in gift shop.

Valid February 2006 through January 2007

The South Carolina Railroad Museum, Inc.

10% off on gift shop purchases.

Valid February 2006 through January 2007

Southern Forest Heritage Museum

Adult, $5.
Senior, $5.
Child, $2.50.

Valid February 2006 through January 2007

Southern Museum of Civil War and Locomotive History

$2 off adult admission,
$1 off child admission,
up to six admissions.

Valid February 2006 through January 2007

Tahquamenon Falls & Toonerville Trolley/Wilderness Ride

10% off any tour.
Good for up to six passengers per coupon.
Not valid with any other discount offer.

Valid February 2006 through January 2007

Thomas T. Taber Museum of the Lycoming County Historical Society

One free admission with
one paid admission of equal value.

Valid February 2006 through January 2007

Three Rivers Rambler

$2 off regular ticket price.

Valid February 2006 through January 2007

Trails & Rails Museum

Buy one adult admission, get one free.

Valid February 2006 through January 2007

Trainland, U.S.A.

Buy one admission,
get equal price admission free.

Valid February 2006 through January 2007

Sierra Madre Express
Tucson, AZ
Tourist Trains 2006
Guest Coupon

Shore Line Trolley Museum
East Haven, CT
Tourist Trains 2006
Guest Coupon

The SoNo Switch Tower Museum
South Norwalk, CT
Tourist Trains 2006
Guest Coupon

Sierra Railroad Dinner Train
Oakdale, CA
Tourist Trains 2006
Guest Coupon

Southern Forest Heritage Museum
Long Leaf, LA
Tourist Trains 2006
Guest Coupon

The South Carolina Railroad Museum, Inc.
Winnsboro, SC
Tourist Trains 2006
Guest Coupon

Tahquamenon Falls & Toonerville Trolley/ Wilderness Ride
Newberry, MI
Tourist Trains 2006
Guest Coupon

Southern Museum of Civil War and Locomotive History
Kennesaw, GA
Tourist Trains 2006
Guest Coupon

Three Rivers Rambler
Knoxville, TN
Tourist Trains 2006
Guest Coupon

Thomas T. Taber Museum of the
Lycoming County Historical Society
Williamsport, PA
Tourist Trains 2006
Guest Coupon

Trainland, U.S.A.
Colfax, IA
Tourist Trains 2006
Guest Coupon

Trails & Rails Museum
Kearney, NE
Tourist Trains 2006
Guest Coupon

TOURIST TRAINS 2006
GUEST COUPONS
Arranged alphabetically by attraction name

Train-O-Rama

$1 off per person per coupon
(limit six people).

Valid February 2006 through January 2007

Trolley Museum of New York

$1 discount for each family member.

Valid February 2006 through January 2007

Valley View Model Railroad

$1 off all adult admissions.
$0.50 off all child admissions.

Valid February 2006 through January 2007

Wabash Frisco & Pacific Steam Railway

Regular fare $3 each;
with coupon fare is $2 each.
Limit six with coupon.

Valid February 2006 through January 2007

Walt Disney's Carolwood Barn & Museum

Free admission/free parking.

Valid February 2006 through January 2007

Wanamaker, Kempton & Southern Railroad

One child free with each paying adult
(special events excluded).

Valid February 2006 through January 2007

West Chester Railroad/ 4 States Railway Service Inc.

10% discount with coupon.

Valid February 2006 through January 2007

West Coast Railway Heritage Park

Buy one admission,
get another of equal value free.

Valid February 2006 through January 2007

Wheels O' Time Museum

$1 off.

Valid February 2006 through January 2007

Wilmington & Western Railroad

Buy one adult admission, get one free.

Valid February 2006 through January 2007

Wilmington Railroad Museum

With coupon $1 off admission.
Limit two persons per coupon.

Valid February 2006 through January 2007

Yuma Valley Railway

This coupon good for $1 off regular
admission prices.

Valid February 2006 through January 2007

Trolley Museum of New York
Kingston, NY
Tourist Trains 2006
Guest Coupon

Train-O-Rama
Marblehead, OH
Tourist Trains 2006
Guest Coupon

Wabash Frisco & Pacific Steam Railway
Glencoe, MO
Tourist Trains 2006
Guest Coupon

Valley View Model Railroad
Union, IL
Tourist Trains 2006
Guest Coupon

Wanamaker, Kempton & Southern Railroad
Kempton, PA
Tourist Trains 2006
Guest Coupon

Walt Disney's Carolwood Barn & Museum
Thousand Oaks, CA
Tourist Trains 2006
Guest Coupon

West Coast Railway Heritage Park
Squamish, BC
Tourist Trains 2006
Guest Coupon

West Chester Railroad/4 States Railway Service Inc.
West Chester, PA
Tourist Trains 2006
Guest Coupon

Wilmington & Western Railroad
Wilmington, DE
Tourist Trains 2006
Guest Coupon

Wheels O' Time Museum
Peoria, IL
Tourist Trains 2006
Guest Coupon

Yuma Valley Railway
Yuma, AZ
Tourist Trains 2006
Guest Coupon

Wilmington Railroad Museum
Wilmington, NC
Tourist Trains 2006
Guest Coupon

LOCOMOTIVES/ROLLING STOCK: US Army Alco S1 no. 1807; Baldwin-Lima-Hamilton RST4C no. 4040; South Shore interurban no. 11; Chicago Rapid Transit ("L" cars) nos. 4442, 4450; Detroit Street Railway PCC no. 268; Toronto PCC no. 4601; GTW caboose no. 77058; numerous freight and work equipment.

SPECIAL EVENTS: October, fall color tours on train; Polar Express Train, call for information.

DIRECTIONS: Train ride: from Mount Clemens take Gratiot north one mile to Joy Blvd., turn right, go ¼ mile to Joy Park (back of park). Depot: ¾ mile west of downtown Mount Clemens on Cass Ave., between Gratiot and Groesbeck Aves.

Photo courtesy of Timothy D. Backhurst.

Newberry, MI

Tahquamenon Falls Tours and Toonerville Trolley/ Wilderness Train Ride
Train ride
24" gauge

ADDRESS: Soo Junction (CR381) 5883 CR441 Newberry, MI 49868
TELEPHONE: (888) 778-7246 or (906) 876-2311
E-MAIL: soojunction@portup.com
WEBSITE: www.exploringthenorth.com/toonerville/trolley.html

DESCRIPTION: Visitors can take the train and boat tour to Taquamenon Falls or the Wilderness Train Ride. The attraction is 50 miles from the Mackinac Bridge. Tour 1 is a 6½-hour train and riverboat tour to Tahquamenon Falls. Tour 2 is a 1¾-hour wilderness train ride.

SCHEDULE: June 15 to June 30: Riverboat tour, Monday to Thursday; wilderness train ride, Friday and Saturday; July 1 to August 24: riverboat tour, Monday to Saturday; wilderness train ride, Tuesday to Saturday; August 25 to October 6: riverboat tours, Wednesday to Saturday. Call for schedule.

ADMISSION/FARE: 6½-hour falls trip: adults, $31.50; children 6-15, $15; 5 and under, free; 1¾-hour train ride: adults, $12.50; children 6-15, $6.25; 5 and under, free.

LOCOMOTIVES/ROLLING STOCK: Two 1964 Plymouth 5-ton diesels, 11 passenger cars.

SPECIAL EVENTS: July to September, Fridays are family days, tour to the falls only: children 12 and under, free.

NEARBY ATTRACTIONS: Twenty minutes from Newberry, Michigan; motels; restaurants; camping. One hour from many major attractions.

DIRECTIONS: Two miles off Hwy. M-28 at Soo Junction. One hour from Mackinac Bridge: travel seven miles north on I-75, exit at Hwy. M-123 (Newberry). Turn left at the top of the exit ramp, travel 37 miles to blinking light at M-28. Turn left (west) onto M-28, travel 12 miles, turn right at large yellow sign at Soo Junction (CR381), then two miles into parking lot. Twenty minutes from Newberry: travel south on M-123 to blinking light for M-28. Turn left (east), travel 12 miles on M-28 to Soo Junction (CR381). Turn left (north) at large yellow sign. Travel two miles to parking lot.

Coupon available, see insert.

Owosso, MI

Steam Railroading Institute

Train ride, Museum, Model train layout
Standard gauge

ADDRESS: 405 S Washington St. Owosso, MI 48867
TELEPHONE: (989) 725-9464
E-MAIL: info@mstrp.com
WEBSITE: www.mstrp.com

DESCRIPTION: The institute has steam railroad equipment displayed in an interactive, educational format. Classroom programs explain railroading's impact on our economy and culture. Weekend train rides and charter train rides are available by appointment.

SCHEDULE: Summer: daily, 10 a.m. to 5 p.m.; winter: Friday to Sunday, 10 a.m. to 4 p.m.; group tours by appointment.

ADMISSION/FARE: $5 each; children 4 and under, free; additional charge for train rides.

LOCOMOTIVES/ROLLING STOCK: Pere Marquette 2-8-4 no. 1225; Flagg Coal Co. 0-4-0T no. 75; Mississippian 2-8-0 no. 76; Pullman Sleeper C&O no. 2624; tool car, ex-C&O troop sleeper no. 1701; two museum display cars, ex-Amtrak passenger nos. 1610 and 1614; classroom car, ex-Amtrak baggage no. 1316; auxiliary tank car, ex-Rock Island tender no. 5000; two Ann Arbor Railroad boxcars, nos. 1314 and 4633; Pere Marquette caboose no. A909; wooden boxcar PM no. 88305; two GTW "idler" flatcars nos. 54263 and 54262; operating turntable. PM 1225 was featured in the *Polar Express* motion picture.

SPECIAL EVENTS: Groups and organizations can "rent" the facility or equipment for special outings; private trains and caboose rides available; also the real Polar Express.

NEARBY ATTRACTIONS: Huckleberry Railroad, Durand Union Station, and Curwood Castle.

DIRECTIONS: Take I-69 to M-52 or M-71. Follow map route north to Owosso.

Photo courtesy of John Field.

Thomas Edison Depot Museum
Museum, Model train layout
G scale

SITE ADDRESS: 510 Edison Pkwy. Port Huron, MI 48060
MAILING ADDRESS: 1115 Sixth St. Port Huron, MI 48060
TELEPHONE: (810) 982-0891 x16
E-MAIL: depot@phmuseum.org or tjgaffney@phmuseum.org
WEBSITE: www.phmuseum.org

DESCRIPTION: Dedicated to Thomas Edison's boyhood in Port Huron, displays are set in the 1858 CD&CGT Jct. Railroad Depot he worked out of as a news butcher. Displays include an 1870s-era combine from the Grand Trunk Railroad, with a re-creation of Edison's train-borne laboratory and printing press.

SCHEDULE: Memorial to Labor Day: 7 days; rest of year: Thursday to Monday, 11 a.m. to 5 p.m.

ADMISSION/FARE: Adults, $5; students and seniors, $3; children under 6, free; passport to all four museum sites (includes Fort Gratiot Lighthouse): adults, $10; students and seniors, $5.

LOCOMOTIVES/ROLLING STOCK: C&GT no. 1842.

SPECIAL EVENTS: Thomas Edison's birthday, celebration of the invention of the electric light, Railroad Days.

NEARBY ATTRACTIONS: Port Huron Museum, Huron Lightship Museum, USCG cutter Bramble Museum, Capal Community Historical Museum, and CN St. Clair River Tunnel.

DIRECTIONS: I-94 or I-69 to Hancock St. exit. Right and go five blocks to Gratiot Ave. (M-25). Turn right, travel until it ends in the Thomas Edison Inn parking lot. Museum is to the left.

Photo courtesy of Port Huron Museum.

KEY TO SYMBOLS

Handicapped accessible	Restaurant	Arts and crafts	Association of Railway Museums
Parking	Picnic area	Memberships available	Tourist Railway Association, Inc.
Bus/RV parking	Dining car	Send S.A.S.E. for brochure	Amtrak service to nearby city
Gift, book, or museum shop	Excursions	National Register of Historic Places	VIA service to nearby city
Refreshments	Guided tours		Credit cards accepted

Royal Oak, MI

Bluewater Michigan Chapter NRHS

Train ride

ADDRESS: 300 E Fourth St., PO Box 296 Royal Oak, MI 48068-0296
TELEPHONE: (800) 594-5162 or (248) 541-1000
WEBSITE: www.bluewaternrhs.com

DESCRIPTION: This chapter of the National Railway Historical Society operates excursions in Michigan using its own equipment and fleet of historic passenger cars, and offers railroad-themed package tours. Please call or write to be added to the mailing list and to receive more information.

LOCOMOTIVES/ROLLING STOCK: Grand Trunk Western dining car "Silver Lake" 899; Seaboard observation car 6604; Southern coaches 829 and 832; RF&P coach 857; Canadian Natrional coaches 5226 and 5228; NYC baggage/sleeper "Haverstraw Bay" 9486.

Photo courtesy of Chris Jacks/Bluewater Michigan Chapter NRHS.
See ad inside back cover.

Royal Oak and Southgate, MI

Great Lakes Live Steamers

Train ride
7½" and 1½ scale

SITE ADDRESSES: Star Park 13 Mile Rd. in Royal Oak, and Kiwanis Park, Corner of Trenton Rd. and Leory St. in Southgate
MAILING ADDRESS: c/o Jim Slimp 14096 Pearl St. Southgate, MI

DESCRIPTION: The Great Lakes Live Steamers run miniature electric, gas, and live steam trains.

SCHEDULE: Star Park: first full weekend each month, 12 to 4 p.m.; Kiwanis Park: third weekend each month, 12 to 4 p.m.

ADMISSION/FARE: No charge, donations welcome.

SPECIAL EVENTS: Third Saturday in October, 6 to 8 p.m., Halloween Run at Southgate.

NEARBY ATTRACTIONS: Greenfield Village in Dearborn, MI.

Photo courtesy of Jim Slimp.

Saginaw Railway Museum
Museum, Display, Model train layout
HO scale

ADDRESS: 900 Maple, PO Box 20454 Saginaw, MI 48602-0454
TELEPHONE: (989) 790-7994
WEBSITE: www.rypn.org/SVRHS

DESCRIPTION: Restored 1907 Pere Marquette Railway depot houses artifacts, GP9 and RS1 locomotives GE 25-ton, 3 cabooses, a "combine" coach, boxcars, 1898 "Armstrong" interlocking tower, and an HO model train layout.

SCHEDULE: First Saturday each month, model train display; April to November: second and fourth Sunday; tours, year-round.

ADMISSION/FARE: General admission $2; family rate $5; children under 8, free.

LOCOMOTIVES/ROLLING STOCK: GTW GP9 4428; Rutland RS1 401; GE 25 Ton; CSX cabooses 900977, 903577, 900342; boxcars.

NEARBY ATTRACTIONS: Children's zoo, state recreation area, Frankenmuth Bavarian Village, 15" gauge 2-mile train ride, Huckleberry Narrow Gauge Railway and Crossroads Village.

DIRECTIONS: I-75 exit 149A (Holland Ave. M46 West), go to first stoplight past bridge (Michigan Ave.), turn left (south), go to museum sign beyond railroad tracks, turn right.

Photo courtesy of Herb McCullagh.

KEY TO SYMBOLS

Handicapped accessible	Restaurant	Arts and crafts	Association of Railway Museums
Parking	Picnic area	Memberships available	Tourist Railway Association, Inc.
Bus/RV parking	Dining car	Send S.A.S.E. for brochure	Amtrak service to nearby city
Gift, book, or museum shop	Excursions	National Register of Historic Places	VIA service to nearby city
Refreshments	Guided tours	VISA MasterCard DISCOVER AMERICAN EXPRESS Card	Credit cards accepted

Traverse City, MI
Spirit of Traverse City
Miniature train ride

SITE ADDRESS: Clinch Park Zoo 161 E Grandview Pkwy. (at Cass St.) Traverse City, MI 49684
MAILING ADDRESS: Clinch Park Zoo Railway 625 Woodmere Ave. Traverse City, MI 49686
TELEPHONE: (231) 922-4910
E-MAIL: lvaughn@ci.traverse-city.mi.us
WEBSITE: www.ci.traverse-city.mi.us/services/train.htm

DESCRIPTION: A ¼-scale, 4-4-2 steam locomotive pulls open-air cars through the Clinch Park Zoo, marina, and beach.

SCHEDULE: May 27 to September 4 and September 9, 10, 16, and 17: daily, 10:30 a.m. to 4 p.m.

ADMISSION/FARE: Adults, $1.50; children 4-12, $1; children under 4, free.

LOCOMOTIVES/ROLLING STOCK: ¼-scale, 4-4-2 Atlantic, oil-fired steam locomotive, 3 open-air passenger cars.

SPECIAL EVENTS: Sunday June 4: Family Fun Day, reduced rates for zoo and train.

NEARBY ATTRACTIONS: Clinch Park Zoo, Grand Traverse Heritage Center, and Great Lakes Children's Museum.

DIRECTIONS: On US31, M-37, M-72 (Grandview Pkwy.) at Cass St. in downtown Traverse City.

Photo courtesy of Lauren Vaughn.

Vulcan, MI
Iron Mountain Iron Mine
Museum
24" gauge

SITE ADDRESS: US-2 Vulcan, MI 49892
MAILING ADDRESS: PO Box 177 Iron Mountain, MI 49801
TELEPHONE: (906) 563-8077
WEBSITE: www.ironmountainironmine.com

DESCRIPTION: Designated as a Michigan Historical Site, the Iron Mountain Iron Mine offers guided underground tours by mine train. Visitors travel 2,600 feet into the mine to see mining demonstrations and the history of iron mining in Michigan's Upper Peninsula. Mining equipment dating from the 1870s is shown and explained.

SCHEDULE: June 1 through October 15: daily, 9 a.m. to 5 p.m.

ADMISSION/FARE: Adults, $8.50; children 6-12, $7; under 6, free; group rates available.

LOCOMOTIVES/ROLLING STOCK: Electric locomotive and five cars.

DIRECTIONS: Nine miles east of Iron Mountain on US2.

Photo courtesy of Dennis Carollo.
Coupon available, see insert.

Walled Lake, MI
Coe Rail Excursion Train
Train ride
Standard gauge

ADDRESS: 840 N Pontiac Trail Walled Lake, MI 48390
TELEPHONE: (248) 960-9440
E-MAIL: info@michiganstarclipper.com
WEBSITE: www.michiganstarclipper.com

DESCRIPTION: Vintage diesel engines pull 1917-era Lackawana coaches, a 1947 Milwaukee Road tap car, several 1920 baggage cars, and 1947 bay window cabooses. Located at the Michigan Star Clipper Dinner Train site in Metro Detroit. Family-oriented one-hour rides offered Sundays, April to October, rain or shine. Tickets are sold in an 1887 train depot. Patron food is allowed on board, but no outside beverages are allowed. There is a snack bar in lounge car, and gift items available in the depot. Private day charters are welcomed mid-week for school field trips and incoming bus tours.

SCHEDULE: April through October: Sunday.

ADMISSION/FARE: $10 per person, all ages.

SPECIAL EVENTS: Easter Express, Hobo Halloween, Santa Express.

DIRECTIONS: I-96 to exit 162, Novi Rd., west on Maple Rd., north on Pontiac Trail, 100 yards, cross tracks, and turn right into parking lot.

Coupon available, see insert.

Walled Lake, MI

Michigan Star Clipper Dinner Train

Dinner train
Standard gauge

ADDRESS: 840 N Pontiac Trail Walled Lake, MI 48390
TELEPHONE: (248) 960-9440
E-MAIL: info@michiganstarclipper.com
WEBSITE: www.michiganstarclipper.com

DESCRIPTION: A five-course dinner is prepared from scratch on board the train. The three-hour ride offers four dining cars and a variety of entertainment, including Murder Mysteries, Jazz, Broadway shows, and "Motown," with various entertainers like the Fabulous Motown Four. Full bar service. Reservations and dress code are required. Also available: two-hour luncheons, private charter, overnight train with B&B service, group requests, and more.

SCHEDULE: Tuesday, Wednesday, Thursday, and Saturday, 7 to 10 p.m.; Friday, 7:30 to 10:30 p.m.; Saturday, optional overnight B&B train; Sunday, 5 to 8 p.m.; schedule includes most holidays. Other nights upon group request. Boarding begins one hour prior to departure. Private charter is also available.

ADMISSION/FARE: Dinners are $79 per person.

LOCOMOTIVES/ROLLING STOCK: GR-10 no. 52; EL/NJT nos. 4315 and 4317; Milw/PVTC/CRLE no. 165; C&EI no. 85258; caboose no. 60; ATSF/Amtrak no. 9604; PRR nos. 9604, 9605, and 9606; more.

SPECIAL EVENTS: Many murder mysteries, special theme events. New! Motown show with original Motown stars, including the Fabulous Motown Four. Departures every night except Monday.

NEARBY ATTRACTIONS: Henry Ford Museum, Greenfield Village, Detroit/Windsor casinos.

DIRECTIONS: I-96 to exit 162, north on Novi Rd., west on Maple Rd., north on Pontiac Trail, 100 yards, cross tracks, turn right into parking lot.

Coupon available, see insert.

MINNESOTA

Callaway, MN

Maplelag Resort
Resort lodging

•Callaway

Chisolm•

Two Harbors
Duluth

Shoreview
Dassel   • •Stillwater
Minneapolis • •St. Paul

Excelsior

•Currie

ADDRESS: 30501 Maplelag Rd.
Callaway, MN 56521-9643
TELEPHONE: (800) 654-7711 or
(218) 375-4466
E-MAIL: maplelag@tvutel.com
WEBSITE: www.maplelag.com

DESCRIPTION: This cross-country ski
resort has five cabooses on site and a
large depot sign collection. The
switchyard houses two cabooses: the
Great Northern X-85 and the Milwaukee Road 02118.

SCHEDULE: Labor Day to Memorial Day; Summer, Concordia College language villages.

ADMISSION/FARE: No charge to visit; fee to stay in the various Maplelag lodging setups.

LOCOMOTIVES/ROLLING STOCK: Great Northern caboose x85, Milwaukee caboose 2118,
Milwaukee caboose 2119, Soo Line extended cupola caboose 170, NP high cupola
caboose (built at Brainerd shops in 1950). Also a display of over 200 depot or station signs.

NEARBY ATTRACTIONS: Voted the number one cross country ski resort in North America.

DIRECTIONS: 20 miles north of Detroit Lakes, MN; One hour from Fargo-Moorhead.

Chisholm, MN

Ironworld Discovery Center
Train ride

ADDRESS: Hwy. 169 W Chisholm, MN 55719
TELEPHONE: (800) 372-6437 or (218) 254-7959
E-MAIL: marketing@ironworld.com
WEBSITE: www.ironworld.com

DESCRIPTION: Preserving Minnesota's mining and immigration history, the center offers
a trolley ride with spectacular mine views, the Iron Range Research Center, museum and
outdoor exhibits, and cultural arts programs. The Mesabi Railway transports visitors by
trolley from the main park to the Glen location. The 2½-mile round trip runs along the
edge of the Glen mine.

SCHEDULE: May through September.

ADMISSION/FARE: Rates vary.

LOCOMOTIVES/ROLLING STOCK: Two 16-ton electric trolleys, the Glen and Mesaba, both 1928 W-2 class Melbournes.

SPECIAL EVENTS: Call for calendar.

NEARBY ATTRACTIONS: For information, contact the Iron Trail Convention and Visitor's Bureau at (800) 777-8497.

DIRECTIONS: Hwy. 169 west in Chisholm, Minnesota.

Photo courtesy of Ironwold Image.

Currie, MN

End-O-Line Railroad Park & Museum
Museum, Display, Model train layout
3 1/2" gauge and HO scale

ADDRESS: 440 N Mill St. Currie, MN 56123
TELEPHONE: (507) 763-3708 or (507) 763-3113 off-season
WEBSITE: www.endoline.com

DESCRIPTION: End-O-Line Railroad Park is a working railroad yard that includes a 1901 manually operated turntable, a rebuilt engine house on its original foundation, an original four-room depot, a water tower, an 1899 section foreman's house, a Grand Trunk Western caboose, and two steam locomotives.

SCHEDULE: Memorial Day to Labor Day: Monday through Friday, 10 a.m. to 12 p.m. and 1 to 5 p.m.; Saturday and Sunday, 1 to 5 p.m. No tours are given after 4 p.m., daily.

ADMISSION/FARE: Adults, $3; students 7-12, $2; household, $10.

LOCOMOTIVES/ROLLING STOCK: 4-6-0 steam locomotive no. 102, 1875 2-6-0 Baldwin steam locomotive no. 13, GTW caboose no. 77046, diesel switcher.

NEARBY ATTRACTIONS: Lake Shetek State Park, Pipestone National Monument, and Laura Ingalls Wilder Museum.

DIRECTIONS: From US Hwy. 59 turn east on State Hwy. 30 (4 miles). In Currie, turn north on CR38 (Mill St.) for 1 mile. The park is on the east side of the road.

Dassel, MN

Old Depot Railroad Museum
Museum, Display, Model train layout
HO scale

ADDRESS: 651 W Hwy. 12, PO Box 99 Dassel, MN 55325
TELEPHONE: (320) 275-3876 or (320) 275-3629
WEBSITE: www.theolddepot.com

DESCRIPTION: A former Great Northern depot displays lanterns, telegraph equipment, semaphores, and other signals; section crew cars, a hand pump car, and a velocipede; tools and oil cans; depot and crossing signs; buttons, badges, service pins, and caps; a large date-nail collection; and many baggage carts. Also included are children's toy trains, an HO scale model railroad, and railroad advertising items. Children can play on a static ½-scale train. Authentic recorded sounds of steam locomotives and the clicking of the telegraph key create the realistic feel of an old, small-town depot.

SCHEDULE: Memorial Day through October 1: daily, 10 a.m. to 4:30 p.m.

ADMISSION/FARE: Adults, $2.50; children under 12, $1; babies, free.

LOCOMOTIVES/ROLLING STOCK: Caboose, two boxcars, and section gang speeder.

SPECIAL EVENTS: Labor Day, Red Rooster Day.

NEARBY ATTRACTIONS: Historical Society Museum, many lakes, restaurants.

DIRECTIONS: 50 miles west of Minneapolis on US Hwy. 12; 14 miles north of Hutchinson on State Hwy. 15.

Coupon available, see insert.

TRAVEL TIP: *Rail and raft*

Several tourist railroads offer the option now of riding the train in one direction and then rafting back down an adjacent river.

This is a good way to include a train ride on a summertime vacation when you want to both ride the rails and hit the water.

Duluth, MN

Lake Superior & Mississippi Railroad

Train ride
Standard gauge
Radio frequency: AAR#18 160.380

ADDRESS: 506 W Michigan St. Duluth, MN 55816
TELEPHONE: (218) 624-7549
E-MAIL: info@lsmrr.org
WEBSITE: www.lsmrr.org

DESCRIPTION: A 90-minute, 12-mile train ride in antique coaches alongside the St. Louis River.

SCHEDULE: July 4, Labor Day, and June 10 to October 8, weekends.

ADMISSION/FARE: Adults, $9; children, $7; children 3 and under, free. Rates subject to change.

LOCOMOTIVES/ROLLING STOCK: GE center-cab no. 46, Pullman chair car no. 85, Pullman chair car no. 29, flat car no. 100R.

NEARBY ATTRACTIONS: Duluth Zoo; locations of railroad interest in Duluth and Superior.

DIRECTIONS: Exit I-35 west on Grand Ave. ½ mile to site. Departure is from Fremont and Grand Ave. Signed from Grand Ave.

Photo courtesy of Dave Schauer.

Duluth, MN

Lake Superior Railroad Museum

Train ride, Dinner train, Museum, Display, Model train layout

ADDRESS: 506 W Michigan St. Duluth, MN 55816
TELEPHONE: (218) 733-7590
E-MAIL: museum@lsrm.org
WEBSITE: www.lsrm.org

DESCRIPTION: A diverse collection of railroad artifacts, including the Great Northern's famous "William Crooks" locomotive and cars of 1861; Duluth, Missabe & Iron Range 2-8-8-4 no. 227, displayed with revolving drive wheels and recorded sound; and an 1887 steam rotary snowplow in addition to other steam, diesel, and electric engines. There is also a Railway Post Office car, a dining-car China exhibit, freight cars, work equipment, an operating electric single-truck streetcar, and much railroadiana.

SCHEDULE: Museum: year-round; train/trolley: Memorial Day weekend through Labor Day weekend. Hours: Memorial Day through mid-October: 9:30 a.m. to 6 p.m.; mid-October through Memorial Day: Monday through Saturday, 10 a.m. to 5 p.m.; Sunday, 1 to 5 p.m.

ADMISSION/FARE: Combination tickets (museum and train), $8 to $21.

LOCOMOTIVES/ROLLING STOCK: There are over 100 pieces of rolling stock on display, mostly indoors, including very rare and unique items dating back to railroading's earliest days. Includes: Northern Pacific 0-4-0 no. 1 "Minnetonka;" Soo Line FP7 no. 2500A; and Missabe Road 2-8-8-4 no. 227.

SPECIAL EVENTS: Thomas the Tank Engine Weekends.

NEARBY ATTRACTIONS: Downtown Duluth, Canal Park, Duluth waterfront, and Bayfront Park.

DIRECTIONS: I-35 exit downtown Duluth/Michigan St.

Photo courtesy of Bruce Ojard Photography.

Duluth, MN

North Shore Scenic Railroad
Train ride, Dinner train, Museum, Display, Model train layout

ADDRESS: 506 W Michigan St. Duluth, MN 55802
TELEPHONE: (800) 423-1273 or (218) 722-1273
E-MAIL: nssr@cpinternet.com
WEBSITE: www.lsrm.org

DESCRIPTION: Formerly the Duluth Missabe & Iron Range Railway's Lake Front Line, this railroad's 26 miles of track run between the depot in downtown Duluth, along the Lake Superior waterfront, and through the residential areas and scenic woodlands of northeastern Minnesota to the Two Harbors Depot adjacent to DM&IR's active taconite yard and ship-loading facility. The line offers 1¹/₂-, 2¹/₂-, and 6-hour round trips departing from Duluth.

SCHEDULE: To Lester River: Memorial to Labor Day, Sunday to Thursday, 12:30 and 3 p.m.; Friday and Saturday, 10 a.m., 12:30, and 3 p.m. Pizza train: Wednesday to Saturday, 6:30 p.m. Two Harbors: Friday and Saturday, 10:30 a.m. Reduced schedule Labor Day to mid-October.

ADMISSION/FARE: Lester River: adults, $11; children, $5. Pizza train: adults, $18; children, $12. Two Harbors: adults, $20; children, $10.

LOCOMOTIVES/ROLLING STOCK: Missabe Road SD18 no. 192; Great Northern NW5 no. 192; Soo FP7 no. 2500A; Soo GP30 no. 700; Missabe and GN coaches; more.

SPECIAL EVENTS: Steam excursions, dinner trains, murder mystery train, beer tasting train, and Railfan weekend (second weekend in September).

NEARBY ATTRACTIONS: "William A. Irvin" (retired ore boat) Vista Fleet.

DIRECTIONS: Located in downtown Duluth in the St. Louis County Heritage & Arts Center.

Photo courtesy of Tim Schandel.

Excelsior, MN

Minnesota Streetcar Museum, Excelsior Streetcar Line

Train ride, Museum
Standard gauge

SITE ADDRESS: Water St. between 3rd and George Sts. Excelsior, MN
MAILING ADDRESS: PO Box 14467 University Station Minneapolis, MN 55414-0467
TELEPHONE: (952) 922-1096
WEBSITE: www.trolleyride.org

DESCRIPTION: A one-mile, 15-minute trip on the former Minneapolis & St. Louis right-of-way takes passengers through historic Excelsior, including a tour of the Excelsior Carbarn. Streetcars serve the Excelsior Farmer's Market. Excelsior was the western outpost of the Twin City Rapid Transit Company's 523-mile system, the last lines of which were abandoned in 1954. The Excelsior line, featuring high-speed suburban cars, was abandoned in 1932.

SCHEDULE: May 6 to September 10: Thursday, 3 to 6 p.m.; Saturday, 10 a.m. to 4 p.m.; Sunday and holidays, 1 to 4 p.m.; September 16 to October 29: Thursday, 3 to 6 p.m.

ADMISSION/FARE: Adults, $1.50; children under 3, free. Chartered streetcars, $65 for ½ hour.

LOCOMOTIVES/ROLLING STOCK: No. 78, 1893 Duluth St. Railway (LaClede Car Co.); no. 1239, 1907 Twin City Rapid Transit Company (TCRT 31st St. Shops); No. 10, 1912 Mesaba Electric Railway (Niles Car Co.), unrestored; No. 10, 1913 Winona Railway, Power, & Light (St. Louis Car Co.), under restoration.

SPECIAL EVENTS: Halloween Ghost Trolley.

NEARBY ATTRACTIONS: Steamboat Minnehaha, Excelsior-Lake Minnetonka museum.

DIRECTIONS: Hwy. 7 west from Minneapolis; right on CR19, right on Water St.; or follow signs. Board between Lyman Park and First Class Car Care (between 3rd and George Sts.).

Photo courtesy of The Minnesota Streetcar Museum Collection.

Minneapolis, MN

Minnesota Streetcar Museum, Como-Harriet Streetcar Line

EDITOR'S CHOICE

Train ride, Museum
Standard gauge

SITE ADDRESS: 2330 W 42nd St. Minneapolis, MN
MAILING ADDRESS: PO Box 14467 University Station Minneapolis, MN 55414-0467
TELEPHONE: (952) 922-1096
WEBSITE: www.trolleyride.org

DESCRIPTION: A two-mile, 15-minute round trip on a restored portion of the former Twin City Rapid Transit Company's historic Como-Harriet route. Streetcars operate over a scenic line through a wooded area between Lakes Harriet and Calhoun. This is the last operating portion of the 523-mile Twin City Lines system, abandoned in 1954. The Linden Hills Station, a re-creation of the 1900 depot located at the site, houses historical displays about electric railways in Minnesota.

SCHEDULE: May 29 to September 10: weekends and holidays, 12:30 p.m. to dusk; Monday through Friday, 6:30 p.m. to dusk; May 6 to 14 and September 16 to October 1: weekends, 12:30 p.m. to dusk; October 7 to November 26: weekends, 12:30 to 5 p.m.

ADMISSION/FARE: $2; children under 3, free. Chartered streetcars, $65 per half hour.

LOCOMOTIVES/ROLLING STOCK: No. 265, 1915 Duluth St. Railway (TCRT Snelling Shops, St. Paul); no. 322, 1946 Twin City Lines PCC (St. Louis Car Co.); no. 1300, 1908 Twin City Lines (Snelling Shops).

SPECIAL EVENTS: Halloween Ghost Trolley.

NEARBY ATTRACTIONS: Lake Harriet Park.

DIRECTIONS: I-35W, 46th St. west to Lake Harriet Pkwy., then to west shore at Linden Hills Station. Metro Transit routes 6 and 28.

Photo courtesy of Louis Hoffman.

Minneapolis, MN

Minnesota Transportation Museum,
Minnehaha Depot

Museum, Display

SITE ADDRESS: 4926 Minnehaha Ave. Minneapolis, MN
MAILING ADDRESS: 193 E Pennsylvania Ave. St. Paul, MN 55101
TELEPHONE: (651) 228-0263
WEBSITE: www.mtmuseum.org

DESCRIPTION: Built in 1875, the Minnehaha Depot replaced an even smaller Milwaukee Road depot on the same site. Milwaukee Road agents quickly nicknamed the depot the "Princess" because of its intricate architectural details. In the depot's early years, Minneapolis residents flocked to Minnehaha Park via train to enjoy summer weekends.

SCHEDULE: Memorial Day weekend through Labor Day weekend: Sundays and holidays, 12:30 to 4:30 p.m.; other times by advance reservation.

ADMISSION/FARE: Donations appreciated; Group tours outside scheduled hours, $25.

NEARBY ATTRACTIONS: Fort Snelling State Park, Historic Fort Snelling, Mall of America.

DIRECTIONS: In Minnehaha Falls Park just off State Hwy. 55 (Hiawatha Ave.). Metro transit routes 27 and 55 (Hiawatha light rail line).

Photo courtesy of Eric Mortensen, Minnesota Historical Society.

Minneapolis, MN

Friends of the 261

Train ride

SITE ADDRESS: 401 Harrison St. NE Minneapolis, MN
MAILING ADDRESS: 4322 Lakepoint Ct. Shoreview, MN 55126
TELEPHONE: (651) 765-9812
WEBSITE: www.261.com

DESCRIPTION: Friends of the 261 operates a day-long, steam-powered excursion over various Class 1 and regional railroads. In 1993, Milwaukee Road 4-8-4 no. 261 became the 9th US locomotive of that wheel arrangement to be returned to service after years of retirement. The restoration was completed by a group of people who are both lovers of steam and three generations of one family.

SCHEDULE: Varies with trip. Call or write for information.

ADMISSION/FARE: Varies. Reservations recommended.

LOCOMOTIVES/ROLLING STOCK: No. 261, a 1944 Alco 4-8-4, former Milwaukee Road class S3, leased to Friends of the 261 by the National Railroad Museum in Green Bay, WI.

Photo courtesy of Victor Hand.

St. Paul, MN

Minnesota Transportation Museum/
Jackson Street Roundhouse

EDITOR'S CHOICE

Museum
Radio frequency: 161.355

ADDRESS: 193 E Pennsylvania Ave. St. Paul, MN 55101
TELEPHONE: (651) 228-0263
WEBSITE: www.mtmuseum.org

DESCRIPTION: The roundhouse at Jackson St. and Pennsylvania Ave. was built by the Great Northern Railroad in 1907 to service steam passenger locomotives. It was part of the Jackson Street shop complex, founded just after the Civil War. The turntable has been restored, and the roundhouse is open to visitors all year long. Children of all ages can enjoy train rides on Saturday.

SCHEDULE: Wednesday, 10 a.m. to 4 p.m.; Saturday, 10 a.m. to 5 p.m. or by appointment.

ADMISSION/FARE: $5 per person; $2 for additional train ride.

LOCOMOTIVES/ROLLING STOCK: Northern Pacific steam locomotives 328, 2153, and 2156; Dan Patch Lines gas-electric 100; Burlington doodlebug 9735; GN parlor-observation Twin Ports; more.

SPECIAL EVENTS: Steamin' Along, Halloween Haunt, Santa Express, and more.

NEARBY ATTRACTIONS: Hill House Museum, Science Museum, Downtown St. Paul, more.

DIRECTIONS: Take the Pennsylvania Ave. exit off I-35 E Go west two blocks to 193 Pennsylvania Ave. E Parking in front lot.

Photo courtesy of Jackson Street Roundhouse.
Coupon available, see insert.

St. Paul, MN

Twin City Model Railroad Museum
Museum, Model train layout
O scale, 2 rail

ADDRESS: 1021 Bandana Blvd. E, Ste. 222 St. Paul, MN 55108
TELEPHONE: (651) 647-9628
E-MAIL: tcmrm@tcmrm.org
WEBSITE: www.tcmrm.org

DESCRIPTION: An operating 3,000-square-foot O scale model of Minneapolis, St. Paul, and the Mississippi River from the 1930s to the 1950s. Also on display: railroad art, maps, and photographs.

SCHEDULE: Year-round; please visit website for specific times.

ADMISSION/FARE: General admission, $3; children under 5, free.

LOCOMOTIVES/ROLLING STOCK: Grand Trunk Western 0-8-0 no. 8327.

SPECIAL EVENTS: Visit the website for up-to-date schedule of events.

NEARBY ATTRACTIONS: Como Park and Zoo, Minnesota State Fair grounds, Amtrak Depot, and Jackson Street Roundhouse.

DIRECTIONS: In Bandana Square, on north side of Energy Park Dr., between Lexington and Snelling Aves., 1 mile north of I-94.

Photo courtesy of Larry Vanden Plas.

KEY TO SYMBOLS

Handicapped accessible	Restaurant	Arts and crafts	Association of Railway Museums
Parking	Picnic area	Memberships available	Tourist Railway Association, Inc.
Bus/RV parking	Dining car	Send S.A.S.E. for brochure	Amtrak service to nearby city
Gift, book, or museum shop	Excursions	National Register of Historic Places	VIA service to nearby city
Refreshments	Guided tours	VISA MasterCard DISCOVER AMERICAN EXPRESS Card	Credit cards accepted

Stillwater, MN

Minnesota Zephyr Limited

Dinner train
Standard gauge

ADDRESS: 601 N Main, PO Box 573 Stillwater, MN 55082
TELEPHONE: (800) 992-6100 or (612) 430-3000
E-MAIL: minnzephyr@aol.com

DESCRIPTION: The Minnesota Zephyr offers the opportunity to experience railroad dining of decades gone by. This 3½ hour journey boards in the historic city of Stillwater and travels through St. Croix River Valley. The Stillwater Depot Logging and Railroad Museum displays the history of Stillwater through relics, displays, and photographs.

SCHEDULE: Updated schedule on website.

LOCOMOTIVES/ROLLING STOCK: FP9 no. 788 and F7 no. 787; dining cars.

NEARBY ATTRACTIONS: Historic Stillwater, Minnesota, and the Twin Cities.

DIRECTIONS: Follow Hwy. 36 east from the Twin Cities to Stillwater.

Two Harbors, MN

Lake County History & Railroad Museum

Museum

ADDRESS: 520 S Ave. , PO Box 128 Two Harbors, MN 55616
TELEPHONE: (218) 834-4898
E-MAIL: lakehist@lakenet.com
WEBSITE: www.lakecountyhistoricalsociety.com

DESCRIPTION: Railroad exhibits include two steam locomotives.

SCHEDULE: May 1 through October 31: Monday through Saturday, 9 a.m. to 5 p.m.; Sunday, 10 a.m. to 3 p.m.

ADMISSION/FARE: Adults, $2; children 9-17, $1.

LOCOMOTIVES/ROLLING STOCK: 1882 Baldwin no. 3; Missabe 2-8-8-4 no.229.

NEARBY ATTRACTIONS: Two Harbors Lighthouse Museum.

DIRECTIONS: From Hwy. 61 turn right onto Waterfront Drive; go seven blocks to the depot.

MISSISSIPPI

Vaughan, MS

Casey Jones Museum
Museum

ADDRESS: 10901 Vaughan Rd. #1 Vaughan, MS 39179
TELEPHONE: (662) 673-9864

DESCRIPTION: Casey Jones Railroad Museum State Park is located near the site of Casey Jones's famous train wreck. The museum contains railroad memorabilia and photos, as well as parts of the trains that were in the accident.

•Vaughn

SCHEDULE: Year-round, Monday to Friday, 8 a.m. to 4 p.m.; Wednesday and Saturday, 8 a.m. to noon.

ADMISSION/FARE: Adults and seniors, $1; under 12, $0.50.

LOCOMOTIVES/ROLLING STOCK: 1923 steam engine no. 841.

NEARBY ATTRACTIONS: Holmes County State Park, 15 miles north of museum.

DIRECTIONS: One mile east of I-55, exit 133 Vaughan, MS.

KEY TO SYMBOLS

Handicapped accessible	Restaurant	Arts and crafts	Association of Railway Museums
Parking	Picnic area	Memberships available	Tourist Railway Association, Inc.
Bus/RV parking	Dining car	Send S.A.S.E. for brochure	Amtrak service to nearby city
Gift, book, or museum shop	Excursions	National Register of Historic Places	VIA service to nearby city
Refreshments	Guided tours	VISA MasterCard DISCOVER American Express Card	Credit cards accepted

MISSOURI

Belton, MO

Belton, Grandview & Kansas City Railroad Company

Train ride, Dinner train
Standard gauge

Map of Missouri showing: St. Joseph, Marceline, Kansas City, Webster Groves, Independence, Kirkwood, St. Louis, Belton, Glencoe, Jackson, Springfield, Branson

ADDRESS: 502 Walnut
Belton, MO 64012-2516
TELEPHONE: (816) 331-0630
E-MAIL: bgkcinfo@aol.com
WEBSITE: www.orgsites.com/mo/beltonrailroad

DESCRIPTION: This 6-mile round trip is aboard a NYC coach that was used in the movie *Biloxi Blues*. The train is pulled by a B&O GP9. Static displays include two steam engines and numerous other rolling stock.

SCHEDULE: May through October: weekends, 2 p.m. Charter trips available.

ADMISSION/FARE: Persons 11 and over, $7; persons 3-10, $6; persons under 3, free.

LOCOMOTIVES/ROLLING STOCK: B&O GP9 no. 102; Frisco 1918 Baldwin 2-10-0 no. 1632, a Russian Decapod; Okmulgee no. 5 Alco 2-8-0; KCS observation lounge; ATSF instruction car, Wabash heavyweight and baggage car, NYC no. 4365 1920 coach, MoPac 1972 wide vision caboose, UP 1928 wood CA-1 caboose.

SPECIAL EVENTS: Ice cream train, Fridays, 7 p.m.; second Saturday in June to September, Hot Dog Train; third Saturday in June to September, Bar-B-Que Train ($20, reservations suggested); October, Pumpkin Patch Express; Halloween weekend, Children's Halloween trains. Specialty and discount days.

NEARBY ATTRACTIONS: President Truman's farm home, Kansas City, Missouri, Westport entertainment area, KC Royals baseball, and several switching yards.

DIRECTIONS: From 435 and Hwy. 71, take US71 south to Route Y. Follow Route Y through traffic light to Commercial St., turn right and go 4 blocks. Yards and depot are on the left.

Photo courtesy of Belton, Grandview & Kansas City Railroad.

Branson, MO

Branson Scenic Railway

Train ride, Dinner train
Standard gauge

EDITOR'S CHOICE

ADDRESS: 206 E Main St., PO Box 924 Branson, MO 65615
TELEPHONE: (417) 334-6110
WEBSITE: www.bransontrain.com

DESCRIPTION: This railway operates a 40-mile, 1¾-hour round trip through the Ozark foothills over the former Missouri Pacific White River Route, now operated by the Missouri & North Arkansas Railroad. Most trips take passengers south into Arkansas, across Lake Taneycomo and two high trestles, and through two tunnels. The original 1906 Branson depot houses the ticket office, waiting room, gift shop and business offices.

SCHEDULE: Excursions: March through mid-December: 9 and 11:30 a.m., 2 and 4:30 p.m.; seasonal: 4:30 p.m.; dinner train: April through December: Saturday, 5 p.m.

ADMISSION/FARE: Call (800) 2TRAIN2 for fares.

LOCOMOTIVES/ROLLING STOCK: F9PH no. 98; GP30M no. 99; 1949 Budd coach "Silver Eagle;" 1951 Budd buffet-lounge "Silver Lake;" 1947 Budd dome-lounge "Silver Island;" 1956 Budd diner "Silver Chef;" 1952 Budd lounge-observation "Silver Garden;" 1952 Budd dome-observation "Silver Terrace;" 1939 Budd lounge-observation from Atlantic Coast Line's "Champion;" more.

SPECIAL EVENTS: Downtown see Plumb Nellie Days and Fiddler's Contest.

NEARBY ATTRACTIONS: Theme park, historic downtown, restaurants, flea market, crafts festivals, lake, campgrounds, and lodging.

DIRECTIONS: Downtown Branson, ¾ mile east of US65.

TRAVEL TIP: *Take a guide*

Before you board your train ride, stop by the gift shop to see if the railroad offers a guide book. Some railroads offer a guide that tells you about the railroad mile-by-mile. This is a handy tool to help you understand more of what you get to see, and it makes a great souvenir.

Glencoe, MO
Wabash Frisco & Pacific Steam Railway
Miniature train ride
12" gauge

SITE ADDRESS: 199 Grand Ave. Wildwood Glencoe, MO
MAILING ADDRESS: 1569 Ville Angela Ln. Hazelwood, MO 63042-1630
TELEPHONE: (636) 587-3538
WEBSITE: www.wfprr.com

DESCRIPTION: The "Uncommon Carrier" offers a 2-mile, 30-minute round trip over a former Missouri Pacific right-of-way along the Meramec River and over three bridges. Formed in 1939, the WF&P Railway organization was started by a group of enthusiasts who acquired a 12-inch-gauge steam locomotive. The railway grew to four steam locomotives, one mile of track, and regulated timetables.

SCHEDULE: May through October: Sunday, 11:15 a.m. to 4:15 p.m.

ADMISSION/FARE: $3; children under 3, free. No reservations.

LOCOMOTIVES/ROLLING STOCK: There are 10 steam locomotives: no. 171 (1907) 4-4-0 (coal), no. 180 (1922) 4-4-0 (oil), no. 102 (1983) 2-6-2 (oil), no. 300 (1958) 4-6-0 (coal), no. 400 (1925) 4-6-2 (oil), no. 401 (1925) 4-6-2 (coal), no. 403 (1955) 4-6-2 (oil), no. 534 (1955) 4-6-4 (oil), no. 535 (1959) 4-6-4 (coal), no. 928 (2005) 4-8-2 (oil). 4 diesel replicas: no. 13 (2002) GP-9 (gasoline), no. 704 (1982) FM (gas), no. 802 (1982) SW-11, and no. 5205 (1991) Alco FA-1. There are 47 cars, a roundhouse, carbarn, three turntables, and a wye.

NEARBY ATTRACTIONS: The new Al Foster Hiking & Biking Trail, Mainlines of Union Pacific and/or Burlington Northern Santa Fe, Museum of Transportation, Route 66 State Park, and the new track of the St. Louis Live Steamers.

DIRECTIONS: 3.5 miles north of Eureka, exit 264 of I-44. Make two right turns at Hwy. 109 and Old State Rd. Four blocks to WF&P station. 25 miles west of downtown St. Louis.

Photo courtesy of James N. Strain.
Coupon available, see insert.

Independence, MO

Chicago & Alton Railroad Depot

Museum

ADDRESS: 318 W Pacific St. Independence, MO 64050
TELEPHONE: (816) 358-1919
WEBSITE: www.pagehost.com/rrstuff/candaone.htm

DESCRIPTION: Built in 1879, the restored, two-story Chicago & Alton Railroad Depot has two floors with seven rooms, including station master's residence. Each room is furnished in the period circa 1879. There are two original restored Railway Express baggage carts with camel-back top trunks, old railroad tools and equipment, and many other items used at that time.

SCHEDULE: April to October: Monday and Thursday to Saturday, 9:30 a.m. to 4:30 p.m.; Sunday, 12:30 to 4:30 p.m.

ADMISSION/FARE: Donations requested.

NEARBY ATTRACTIONS: National Frontier Trails Center, Missouri Pacific "Truman" Depot, Truman Home, Jesse James Jail, Bingham-Waggoner Estate, and Vaile 1800s Victorian Home.

DIRECTIONS: Located three blocks south of Independence Square, go south on Main St. to Pacific St. and west to the parking lot, which is next to the National Frontier Trails Center.

Jackson, MO

St. Louis Iron Mountain & Southern Railway

Train ride, Dinner train
Standard gauge
Radio frequency: 160.845

ADDRESS: 252 E Jackson Blvd., PO Box 244 Jackson, MO 63755
TELEPHONE: (800) 455-RAIL or (573) 243-1688
WEBSITE: www.rosecity.net/trains

DESCRIPTION: This is a not-for-profit organization; volunteers welcome.

ADMISSION/FARE: Adults, $16; children, $9; special events, call for prices.

LOCOMOTIVES/ROLLING STOCK: Former Pennsylvania Railroad E8 no. 5898.

DIRECTIONS: I-55 exit 99, 4 miles west to Jackson on Hwy. 61. Station at Hwy. 61/25&72.

Kansas City Northern Railroad
Miniature train ride
16" gauge

ADDRESS: Line Creek Park Waukomis Dr. & NW 60th St. Kansas City, MO 64118
TELEPHONE: (816) 734-0203
E-MAIL: wohrnell@sbcglobal.net

DESCRIPTION: Run by the Kansas City Parks and Recreation Department Volunteers in the Parks. 100% of fares and donations go toward railroad maintenance and improvements.

SCHEDULE: May 1 through September 30: weekends and holidays; Saturday, 10 a.m. to 6 p.m.; Sunday and holidays, 12 to 6 p.m. Charters are available by appointment.

ADMISSION/FARE: $0.50 for everyone.

LOCOMOTIVES/ROLLING STOCK: Three 16" replicas of F7s; one handicapped car. Color schemes are the Union Pacific, Kansas City Southern, and Missouri Pacific Eagle.

NEARBY ATTRACTIONS: Kansas City's many railroad yards, Union Station and train museum, Worlds of Fun Amusement Park, Kansas City Royals baseball, and Chiefs football.

DIRECTIONS: Go north on I-29, cross the Missouri River, exit 3A to Waukomis Dr. Go north on Waukomis Dr. to NW 60th St. Turn left.

Photo courtesy of Don Gregory.

KEY TO SYMBOLS

Handicapped accessible	Restaurant	Arts and crafts	Association of Railway Museums
Parking	Picnic area	Memberships available	Tourist Railway Association, Inc.
Bus/RV parking	Dining car	Send S.A.S.E. for brochure	Amtrak service to nearby city
Gift, book, or museum shop	Excursions	National Register of Historic Places	VIA service to nearby city
Refreshments	Guided tours	VISA MasterCard DISCOVER AMERICAN EXPRESS Card	Credit cards accepted

Kirkwood, MO

Friends of Landmark Kirkwood Station (F.O.L.K.S.)

Train ride, Dinner train, Display

ADDRESS: 110 W Argonne Rd., PO Box 221122 Kirkwood, MO 63122
TELEPHONE: (314) 752-3148

DESCRIPTION: F.O.L.K.S. supports the Kirkwood Amtrak station by providing passenger amenities. The station, built in 1893, is listed in the National Register of Historic Places. The exhibits are provided by the Museum of Transportation and the American Association of Railroaders, Inc.

SCHEDULE: Daily, 7:45 to 8:30 a.m.; 12:30 to 3:30 p.m.; and 7:45 to 8:15 p.m.

ADMISSION/FARE: Station, free. Fares for excursions vary according to destination and activity.

SPECIAL EVENTS: Saturday and Sunday afternoons, train watchers gather; monthly, sightseeing and dinner excursions on Amtrak; May, Kirkwood Jct. Festival; Kirkwood Station Celebration.

NEARBY ATTRACTIONS: Museum of Transportation; Route 66 State Park; WF&P Railway.

DIRECTIONS: In downtown Kirkwood at Kirkwood (Lindbergh) Blvd.

Photo courtesy of Richard A. Eichhorst.

Marceline, MO

Walt Disney Hometown Museum

Museum

SITE ADDRESS: 120 E Santa Fe St. Marceline, MO 64658
MAILING ADDRESS: 207 N Main St. Marceline, MO 64658
TELEPHONE: (660) 376-3343 or (660) 376-2332
E-MAIL: toonfest@shighway.com

DESCRIPTION: Exhibits on the life of Walt Disney are displayed in the Marceline Depot on original Santa Fe rails. On display: railroad memorabilia, Walt Disney's life, and his interest in railroads.

SCHEDULE: Tuesday through Friday, 11 a.m. to 4 p.m.; Saturday, 10 a.m. to 4 p.m.; Sunday, 1 to 4 p.m.

ADMISSION/FARE: Adults, $5; children 6-10, $2.50; children under 6, free.

SPECIAL EVENTS: 3rd weekend in September, Cartoon Festival.

NEARBY ATTRACTIONS: Walt Disney's Farm Property open to public with the exception of the house, which is private property.

DIRECTIONS: On 120 E Santa Fe, west of RR tracks, 1 block west of Hwy. 5 in Marceline.

Photo courtesy of Walt Disney's Hometown Marceline, Missouri.

Springfield, MO
Railroad Historical Museum, Inc.
Museum, Display

SITE ADDRESS: Grant Beach Park, 1400 N Grant Ave. Springfield, MO
MAILING ADDRESS: 3661 S Fort Springfield, MO 65807
TELEPHONE: (417) 882-9106

DESCRIPTION: Steam locomotive, rolling stock, artifacts, and memorabilia in a city park.

SCHEDULE: April to November: Saturday, 2 to 4 p.m., weather permitting (sunny, dry, and at least 60 degrees). Also by request.

ADMISSION/FARE: Free. Donations accepted.

LOCOMOTIVES/ROLLING STOCK: Frisco 4-8-4 no. 4524 ; BN Express car no. 976100, double-deck passenger car seating 100 on lower deck and 60 on the upper level, more.

NEARBY ATTRACTIONS: Bass Pro Shop; Dickerson Park Zoo; Grant Beach Park; Wild Animal Paradise, 12 miles east; Branson and Silver Dollar City, 40 miles south.

DIRECTIONS: I-44 to exit 77, south on Kansas Expressway, east on Division St., ¾ mile then south on Grant Ave., two blocks to 1400 N Grant, west on Lynn St. to museum entrance.

Photo courtesy of Railroad Historical Museum, Inc.

St. Joseph, MO

Patee House Museum

Museum
Standard gauge

SITE ADDRESS: 1202 Penn St. St. Joseph, MO 64501
MAILING ADDRESS: Box 1022 St. Joseph, MO 64502
TELEPHONE: (816) 232-8206
E-MAIL: patee@ponyexpress.net
WEBSITE: www.stjoseph.net/ponyexpress

DESCRIPTION: Patee House Museum was Pony Express headquarters in 1860. Now it features a steam locomotive, mail car, antique cars, trucks, fire trucks, buggies, and wagons. On the grounds is the Jesse James Home, where the outlaw was killed.

SCHEDULE: April to October: Monday to Saturday, 10 a.m. to 5 p.m.; Sunday, 1 to 5 p.m.; November to March: Saturday, 10 a.m. to 5 p.m.; Sunday 1 to 5 p.m.

ADMISSION/FARE: Adults, $4; seniors, $3.50; students 6-17, $2.50; children under 6, free with family. Carousel rides: $1.50 each or four rides for $5.

LOCOMOTIVES/ROLLING STOCK: 1892 Baldwin 4-4-0 no. 35, backdated by Burlington in 1933 to resemble Hannibal & St. Joseph locomotive no. 35.

NEARBY ATTRACTIONS: House where Jesse James was killed, Pony Express Museum, and Doll Museum.

DIRECTIONS: From Hwy. 36 take the 10th St. exit, follow 10th St. north. Turn right on Mitchell to 12th St.

Photo courtesy of Patee House Museum.
Coupon available, see insert.

KEY TO SYMBOLS

Handicapped accessible	Restaurant	Arts and crafts	Association of Railway Museums
Parking	Picnic area	Memberships available	Tourist Railway Association, Inc.
Bus/RV parking	Dining car	Send S.A.S.E. for brochure	Amtrak service to nearby city
Gift, book, or museum shop	Excursions	National Register of Historic Places	VIA service to nearby city
Refreshments	Guided tours	Credit cards accepted	

St. Louis, MO

American Association of Railroaders

Train ride, Dinner train, Excursion and rail industry tours

ADDRESS: 4351 Holy Hills Blvd. St. Louis, MO 63116
TELEPHONE: (314) 752-3148
WEBSITE: www.aar-therailroaders.org

DESCRIPTION: More than 50 rail activities are sponsored each year. These events include industry tours, one-day sightseeing excursions, dinner excursions, mystery destination adventures, and mainline Amtrak tours. Also charters for private sleepers, coaches, and observation cars for operation on Amtrak trains and regional railroads. Several train tours in Canada and at least one extended European tour are scheduled each year.

SCHEDULE: Year-round. At least three activities every month.

ADMISSION/FARE: Varies. Determined by distance, activities, and amenities.

SPECIAL EVENTS: An annual slide show the first weekend in March to review the previous year. The "Nostalgia Program" brings back historic subjects from the last 35 years. Several excursions (free for members) aboard the organization's 1958 GM PD4104 Trailways bus.

Photo courtesy of Richard A. Eichhorst.
Coupon available, see insert.

St. Louis, MO

American Railway Caboose Historical Educational Society, Inc.

Museum, Display

ADDRESS: St. Louis, MO 63116
TELEPHONE: (314) 752-3148
WEBSITE: www.arches.org

DESCRIPTION: The Caboose Museum has at least one of their 30 "cabeese" on display at any given time. Some of the cars are on loan to other rail museums. In addition to the interpretive center that is open to the public, ARCHES is an international association with members in 33 states and Canada.

SCHEDULE: April 1, May 6, June 3, July 1, August 5, September 2, and October 7.

ADMISSION/FARE: Dues start at $15.

LOCOMOTIVES/ROLLING STOCK: Cabooses from: A&S, ATSF, B&O, C&O, C&NW, CC, CGW, Essex Terminal, Frisco, IC, Manufacturers, Milwaukee, Missouri Pacific, N&W, RI, Soo, more.

SPECIAL EVENTS: Caboose Chili Cook-off, Caboose Chase excursions, Santa on Amtrak, Rail Caboose tours, one Western Caboose tour and one Eastern tour each year. Charters and special trains. Write for annual meeting.

DIRECTIONS: Varies. Write for specific date information.

Photo courtesy of Richard A. Eichhorst.

St. Louis, MO

Museum of Transportation
Museum

ADDRESS: 3015 Barrett Station Rd. St. Louis, MO 63122
TELEPHONE: (314) 965-7998
WEBSITE: www.museumoftransport.org

DESCRIPTION: One of the largest and most comprehensive collections of transportation vehicles in the world, according to the Smithsonian Institution. Over 70 locomotives, including 34 steamers.

SCHEDULE: Tuesday to Saturday, 9 a.m. to 4 p.m.; Sunday, 11 a.m. to 4 p.m.; summer: Monday to Wednesday and Friday to Saturday, 9 a.m. to 5 p.m.; Thursday, 9 a.m. to 7 p.m.; Sunday, 11 a.m. to 5 p.m.

ADMISSION/FARE: Adults, $4; seniors 65+ and children 5-12, $2; children under 5, free; group rates for 20 people or more.

LOCOMOTIVES/ROLLING STOCK: UP Big Boy no. 4006; UP Centennial no. 6944; N&W Y6a no. 2156; GM FT demonstrator no. 103; Milwaukee Road bi-polar electric no. E-2; 34 steam, 28 diesel/gas, 10 electric, one gas-turbine locomotives; 30 passenger and 55 freight cars.

SPECIAL EVENTS: Second weekend in September, Transportation Celebration: free admission and special exhibits. See website for details.

NEARBY ATTRACTIONS: St. Louis Arch, Grant's Farm, Union Station.

DIRECTIONS: I-270 to exit 8. Take Dougherty Ferry Rd. west one mile to Barrett Station Rd. (second traffic light), turn left. Museum is ½ mile on right.

St. Louis, MO

The John W. Barriger III National Railroad Library
Library

ADDRESS: St. Louis Mercantile Library, University of Missouri – St. Louis
Thomas Jefferson Library Building, One University Blvd. St. Louis, MO 63121
TELEPHONE: (314) 516-7240 or (314) 516-7247
E-MAIL: gpames@umsl.edu
WEBSITE: www.umsl.edu/barriger/

DESCRIPTION: The John W. Barriger III National Railroad Library is a special library within the St. Louis Mercantile Library. One of this country's best known and most distinguished railroad executives, John Walker Barriger III (1899-1976) was also widely recognized as a scholar of the railroad industry and its fascinating history. He avidly collected books and corporate papers, and took thousands of photographs, all of which form the core of these collections. The library includes over 45,000 volumes covering all aspects of railroading, and dating from the beginnings of railroads in the 1820s to the present day. The collections focus strongly on railway economics, finance, corporate history, management practice, regulatory history, mergers, labor relations, operations, and engineering.

SCHEDULE: Monday to Thursday, 7:30 a.m. to 10:30 p.m.; Friday, 7:30 a.m. to 5 p.m.; Saturday, 9 a.m. to 5 p.m.; Sunday, 1 to 9 p.m.; by appointment for some collections. Hours may vary during summer and intersession; please call before coming.

St. Louis, MO

Rail Cruise America
Train ride

ADDRESS: #400 St. Louis Union Station St. Louis, MO 63103
TELEPHONE: (314) 231-9500
E-MAIL: info@railcruiseamerica.com
WEBSITE: www.railcruiseamerica.com

DESCRIPTION: Rail Cruise America's eight luxury cars were designed for corporate and private travel events. Together, the modernized private cars offer a meeting space with an intimate atmosphere, exquisite cuisine, and fabulous scenery. The train is available for corporate, leisure, and social private charter travel. The eight passenger cars have been thoroughly refitted inside and out, retaining the style and charm of classic rail travel.

NEARBY ATTRACTIONS: Located in historic St. Louis Union Station. See website or call for updated details and futher information.

MISSOURI

Webster Groves

Webster Groves, MO
Big Bend Railroad Club
Model train layout

SITE ADDRESS: 8833 Big Bend Blvd. Webster Groves, MO 63119-3731
MAILING ADDRESS: 855 Windemere Ave. Des Peres, MO 63131-4531
TELEPHONE: (314) 966-5227
E-MAIL: kc0esl@juno.com
WEBSITE: www.geocities.com/bbrrclub/

DESCRIPTION: Located in a 1910 passenger depot, the Springfield & Ozark Railway is a ¼" O scale railroad modeled after an old branch line that became part of the St. Louis & San Francisco Railway in 1885.

SCHEDULE: First Tuesday of each month, 7:30 to 9 p.m., except holidays.

ADMISSION/FARE: Free. Tax-deductible donations accepted.

DIRECTIONS: I-44 to exit 280. North to Big Bend Blvd. Turn left, travel about two blocks, and cross the railroad tracks.

Photo courtesy of Ken Rimmel.

KEY TO SYMBOLS

♿ Handicapped accessible	🍴 Restaurant	🎨 Arts and crafts	arm Association of Railway Museums
P Parking	🪑 Picnic area	Ⓜ Memberships available	TRAIN Tourist Railway Association, Inc.
P Bus/RV parking	Dining car	✉ Send S.A.S.E. for brochure	Amtrak service to nearby city
Gift, book, or museum shop	Excursions	National Register of Historic Places	VIA service to nearby city
Refreshments	TOUR Guided tours	VISA MasterCard DISCOVER AMERICAN EXPRESS Card	Credit cards accepted

MONTANA

Anaconda, MT
Copper King Express
Train ride, Museum

ADDRESS: 300 W Commercial Ave.
Anaconda, MT 59711
TELEPHONE: (406) 563-7121
WEBSITE: www.copperkingexpress.com

Essex • Missoula • Lewistown • Virginia City

DESCRIPTION: The story of the Butte, Anaconda & Pacific railroad (built in 1894), the smelter, and mines is told through video monitors located in the passenger cars. The Copper King Express is a 26-mile excursion that operates through many of the area's historic points of interest and also through Durant Canyon. The world's largest smokestack can be seen from 20 miles away. There is also a museum at the former B.A. & P. General Office.

SCHEDULE: June to September: Friday and Saturday; special trains available on demand.

ADMISSION/FARE: Adults, $15; students and seniors, $19; child 5 and under, free with adult.

SPECIAL EVENTS: Coordinate with area festivals; some include: Art in the Park, An-Ri-Ra Irish Heritage Festival, Evel Knievel Days, July 4th, Smelterman's Day. Special trains available for class reunions, family reunions, weddings, corporate outings, etc.

NEARBY ATTRACTIONS: Smelter State Park, B.A. & P. Roundhouse, Berkeley Open Pit Copper Mine, World Museum of Mining, Our Lady of the Rockies, Copper King Mansion, Grant Kohrs Ranch National Park, Washoe Park and Washoe Park Fish Hatchery.

DIRECTIONS: I-90 exit 208 Anaconda. Road will turn into East Commercial Ave. after entering Anaconda. Depot is located three blocks past stoplight on Commercial Ave.

See ad on page A-22.

Essex, MT

Izaak Walton Inn

Museum, Display

EDITOR'S CHOICE

ADDRESS: 290 Izaak Walton Inn Rd. Essex, MT 59916
TELEPHONE: (406) 888-5700
WEBSITE: www.izaakwaltoninn.com

DESCRIPTION: Built in 1939, the hotel is located just west of the Continental Divide. Trains are central to the Izaak Walton experience. Each renovated caboose cabin is heated and contains a full kitchen and bath. Amtrak serves the Inn twice a day. The hotel is a railfan's haven and a great complement to a train travel vacation. The pedestrian overpass provides excellent views of a working rail yard.

SCHEDULE: Year-round, 7 a.m. to 10 p.m.

SPECIAL EVENTS: May 5 to 7, Railfan Weekend.

NEARBY ATTRACTIONS: Glacier National Park, Historic GN Line, Amtrak's Empire Builder Route.

DIRECTIONS: On southern tip of Glacier National Park off Hwy. 2 in Essex.

Photo courtesy of Richard Kern.

Lewistown, MT

Charlie Russell Chew-Choo Dinner Train

Dinner train

ADDRESS: 211 E Main Lewistown, MT 59457
TELEPHONE: (406) 538-8721
WEBSITE: www.yogoinn.com

DESCRIPTION: A 3½-hour narrated dinner train ride includes full course prime rib dinner and Western musicians. Passengers should be on the lookout for masked bandits as they ride up, with guns blazing, to rob the train.

SCHEDULE: Year-round: June through September, Saturday; some special trains.

LOCOMOTIVES/ROLLING STOCK: Five stainless-steel Budd RDC cars.

SPECIAL EVENTS: December, Polar Express children's ride: enjoy a 1½-hour visit to the "North Pole" to meet Santa while drinking hot chocolate and munching on cookies.

NEARBY ATTRACTIONS: Many within a two-hour drive.

DIRECTIONS: 2.7 miles north of Lewistown on Hwy. 191, then west 8 miles on Hwy. 426.

Photo courtesy of Cherie Neudick.

Missoula, MT

Historical Museum at Fort Missoula
Museum

ADDRESS: Building #322 Fort Missoula Missoula, MT 59804
TELEPHONE: (406) 728-3476
E-MAIL: ftmslamuseum@montana.com
WEBSITE: www.fortmissoulamuseum.org

DESCRIPTION: This County Historical Museum is on a 32-acre site with 13 historic structures depicting the history of western Montana.

SCHEDULE: Memorial to Labor Day weekend: Monday through Saturday, 10 a.m. to 5 p.m.; Sunday, 12 to 5 p.m.; Labor Day to Memorial Day weekend: Tuesday through Sunday, 12 to 5 p.m.

ADMISSION/FARE: Adults, $3; seniors, $2; students, $1; children under 6 and members of the Friends of the Historical Museum, free; Wednesdays are free.

LOCOMOTIVES/ROLLING STOCK: Anaconda Copper No. 7, a Willamette-type 3-truck geared steam locomotive; 1930 Anaconda Co. Library Car; flatcars with log loads; Slide Jammer log loader; ACM "shuttle" car to transport lumberjacks; section motor car.

SPECIAL EVENTS: April 22, Forestry Day; 4th of July Celebration; occasional operation of steam-powered sawmill; motor cars on track; model railroad; Willamette cab tours.

NEARBY ATTRACTIONS: A Carousel for Missoula, Rocky Mountain Elk Foundation, Smokejumpers Visitor's Center, Rocky Mountain Museum of Military History.

DIRECTIONS: From I-90 take Reserve St. exit south to South Ave. (traffic signal). Turn right (west) on South Ave. to left at sign for museum.

Photo courtesy of Historical Museum at Fort Missoula.

Virginia City, MT
Montana Heritage Commission
Train ride, Museum, Display
Narrow gauge

ADDRESS: 300 Wallace St., PO Box 338 Virginia City, MT 59755
TELEPHONE: (406) 843-5247
E-MAIL: julijohnson@mt.gov
WEBSITE: www.virginiacitychamber.com

DESCRIPTION: The Montana Heritage Commission manages the Alder Gulch Shortline Railroad, a 1½-mile narrow-gauge trip between Virginia City and Nevada City. A small gasoline-powered train operates weekdays. 1911 steam locomotive operates weekends.

SCHEDULE: Train rides: Memorial Day through Labor Day, 11 a.m. to 6 p.m.

ADMISSION/FARE: Steam Locomotive no. 12, $10; gas-powered no. 8, $6; children 6 and under, free. Group rates available for 15 or more people; combination tickets are available and include admission to Nevada City Museum.

LOCOMOTIVES/ROLLING STOCK:
1911 Baldwin 2-8-0 no. 12, gasoline-powered CA Bovey no. 8.

SPECIAL EVENTS: Moonlight & Steam moonlight train ride: August full moon, closest Friday night; other special events can be found on the website.

DIRECTIONS: 70 miles southeast of Butte on Hwy. 287. 85 miles northwest of West Yellowstone.

Photo courtesy of Montana Heritage Commission.

KEY TO SYMBOLS

♿ Handicapped accessible	🍴 Restaurant	🎨 Arts and crafts	arm Association of Railway Museums
P Parking	🪑 Picnic area	iMi Memberships available	TRAIN Tourist Railway Association, Inc.
P Bus/RV parking	Dining car	✉ Send S.A.S.E. for brochure	Amtrak service to nearby city
Gift, book, or museum shop	Excursions	NRHP National Register of Historic Places	VIA VIA service to nearby city
Refreshments	TOUR Guided tours	VISA MasterCard DISCOVER AMERICAN EXPRESS Card	Credit cards accepted

NEBRASKA

Fremont●
Omaha●
Kearney● ●Grand Island

Chadron, NE
Nebkota Dinner Train
Train ride, Dinner train

ADDRESS: 111 N Main Chadron, NE 69337
TELEPHONE: (308) 432-2487
E-MAIL: fitzrisp@prairieweb.com

DESCRIPTION: Dining car excursions through the scenic Pine Ridge area. Also available for private rental and special events.

SCHEDULE: April through October, Friday and Saturday evenings.

ADMISSION/FARE: $35 per seat.

Fremont, NE
Fremont & Elkhorn Valley Railroad
Train ride, Museum

ADDRESS: 1835 N Somers Ave. Fremont, NE 68025
TELEPHONE: (402) 727-0615
E-MAIL: fevr@fremontrailroad.com
WEBSITE: www.fremontrailroad.com

DESCRIPTION: Laid out in 1869, this route served as the gateway for the Chicago & North Western Railroad until the mid-1980s. The railroad offers a 16-mile, round-trip excursion train for the public using diesel locomotives. En route from Fremont to Nickerson, passengers cross the historic Indian Rd., the route of Major Stephen Long's 1820s western military expedition, and the 1840s Mormon Trail.

SCHEDULE: May through October: Saturday and Sunday, 1 p.m. departures.

ADMISSION/FARE: Vintage Coach: adults, $8; children 3-11, $6; children 2 and under, free. Luxury A/C Coach: adults, $12; children, $8.

LOCOMOTIVES/ROLLING STOCK: SW1200 no. 1219, 1925-era Pullman cars, concession car.

SPECIAL EVENTS: July, John C. Fremont Days.

NEARBY ATTRACTIONS: May Heritage Museum, city swimming pool.

DIRECTIONS: 5 blocks south on Somers Ave. from US30 Lincoln Hwy.

Grand Island, NE
Stuhr Museum of the Prairie Pioneer
Display

ADDRESS: 3133 W Hwy. 34 Grand Island, NE 68801
TELEPHONE: (308) 385-5316
E-MAIL: info@stuhrmuseum.org
WEBSITE: www.stuhrmuseum.org

DESCRIPTION: A hands-on living history tells the story of early town building. In the 1890s village, Railroad Town, townspeople dressed in period clothing go about daily life on the Plains. There is also an authentic railroad display of a 1901 steam locomotive, a 1912 caboose, and an 1871 coach at walk-in level.

SCHEDULE: May 1 to September 30: Monday to Saturday, 9 a.m. to 5 p.m.; Sunday 12 to 5 p.m.

ADMISSION/FARE: Varies by season; call or see website for more information.

LOCOMOTIVES/ROLLING STOCK: Union Pacific 2-8-0 steam locomotive no. 437; 1912 caboose; 1871 coach.

SPECIAL EVENTS: See website for special events.

NEARBY ATTRACTIONS: Crane Meadows Nature Center, Island Oasis Water Park, Mormon Island State Recreation Area.

DIRECTIONS: Corner of US Hwys. 34 and 281, or I-80 exit 312 then 4 miles north.

Photo courtesy of Stuhr Museum of the Prairie Pioneer.

Kearney, NE
Trails & Rails Museum
Museum

SITE ADDRESS: 710 W 11 St. Kearney, NE 68845
MAILING ADDRESS: PO Box 523 Kearney, NE 68848
TELEPHONE: (308) 234-3041
WEBSITE: www.bchs.us

DESCRIPTION: On site: a 2-8-0 Baldwin steam engine no. 481, Union Pacific flat car, caboose, depot, and 5 additional turn-of-the-century buildings.

SCHEDULE: Memorial to Labor Day: Monday to Saturday, 10 a.m. to 6 p.m., Sunday, 1 to 5 p.m.; Labor to Memorial Day: Monday to Friday, 1 to 5 p.m. or by appointment.

ADMISSION/FARE: Adults, $2; children 14 and under, free. Donations appreciated.

LOCOMOTIVES/ROLLING STOCK: Union Pacific 1903 Baldwin steam engine no. 481, Union Pacific flat car and caboose.

SPECIAL EVENTS: June, annual Wagons West Celebration; December, annual Christmas Tree Walk. Several other events rotate years or dates: May Day Extravaganza, Collections Day, Genealogy Open House, Easter Egg Hunt.

NEARBY ATTRACTIONS: Cody Park Railroad Museum and Golden Spike Tower and Visitor's Center, Stuhr Museum of the Prairie Pioneer, and Pioneer Village.

DIRECTIONS: Take exit 272 off I-80, head north approximately 1 mile, turn left (west) on 11th St. Drive a few blocks; the train is on the left side.

Photo courtesy of Olivia Roby.
Coupon available, see insert.

Omaha, NE
Durham Western Heritage Museum
Museum

ADDRESS: 801 S 10th St. Omaha, NE 68108
TELEPHONE: (402) 444-5071
WEBSITE: www.dwhm.org

DESCRIPTION: Beautiful 1931 Art Deco historic railroad station houses exhibits depicting the history of Omaha. Exhibits include a restored 1931 old-fashioned soda fountain, a theater, restored train cars, home replicas with period furnishings, model trains, and a rare coin collection. Named as an affiliate of the Smithsonian Institution, this museum has access to Smithsonian artifacts on a long-term loan basis.

SCHEDULE: Tuesday to Saturday, 10 a.m. to 5 p.m.; Sunday, 1 to 5 p.m.

ADMISSION/FARE: Adults, $6; seniors 62+, $5; children 3-12, $4; children 2 and under and museum members, free.

SPECIAL EVENTS: Christmas at Union Station, Ethnic Holiday Festival, and other seasonal and limited special events.

NEARBY ATTRACTIONS: Omaha, Henry Doorly Zoo, Lauritzen Gardens, Omaha Children's Museum, Joslyn Art Museum, Rosenblatt Stadium, Old Market shopping and dining.

DIRECTIONS: Located in the Old Market at 801 S 10th St.

Omaha, NE

Omaha Zoo Railroad
Train ride
30" gauge

ADDRESS: 3701 S 10th Omaha, NE 68107
TELEPHONE: (402) 733-8401
WEBSITE: www.omahazoo.com

DESCRIPTION: Passengers take a guided trip through the 1¾ miles of zoo grounds, seeing hundreds of animals (including many rare and endangered species) over the course of 20 to 30 minutes. Steam is scheduled 11 a.m. to 4 p.m.

SCHEDULE: Memorial Day through Labor Day, seven days a week; April through Memorial Day and Labor Day through October, weekends only.

ADMISSION/FARE: For train only: adults, $3; children under 12, $2; children under 3, free round trip (subject to change). Additional admission fee for zoo entrance.

LOCOMOTIVES/ROLLING STOCK: No. 119, 1968 Crown 4-4-0 narrow gauge replica of Union Pacific no. 119; Fairmont MT14 motor car; locomotives no. 395-104, 1890 Krauss 0-6-2T; passenger cars; 11 open-air coaches; caboose; ballast maintainer.

SPECIAL EVENTS: Members' Day, with free train ride to zoo members; Halloween Terror Train during zoo-sponsored Halloween party, children in costume ride free.

NEARBY ATTRACTIONS: Omaha Royals baseball, Children's Museum, Western Heritage Museum, Lauritzen Gardens, Rails West Museum.

DIRECTIONS: I-80 and 10th St.

Photo courtesy of Aaron Zorko.

NEVADA

Virginia City
Carson City
East Ely
Boulder City

Boulder City, NV

Nevada State Railroad Museum/Boulder City

Train ride
Standard gauge

ADDRESS: 600 Yucca St. Boulder City, NV 89006
TELEPHONE: (702) 486-5933
E-MAIL: gcorbin@govmail.state.nv.us
WEBSITE: www.NevadaCulture.org

DESCRIPTION: Situated within the former Union Pacific rail yards in Boulder City, the NSRM operates the excursion train on a 4-mile portion of the historic Boulder Branch Line that was built in 1931. Refurbished, air-conditioned Pullman coaches date back to 1911. The 7-mile, 45-minute round-trip offers views of Mojave Desert plant life, El Dorado Valley, river, and McCullough Mountain Ranges.

SCHEDULE: Call for current schedule of dates and times.

ADMISSION/FARE: Adults, $8; seniors, $7; children 11 and under, $4.

LOCOMOTIVES/ROLLING STOCK: Union Pacific GP30 no. 844 and NW2 no. 1000 are used on excursions. On display are a 1953 Fairbanks-Morse H12-44 no. 1855; Union Pacific 2-8-0 steam locomotive no. 264; Pacific Lumber Co. 2-8-2 no. 35; Southern Pacific Harriman-type coaches nos. 1182, 1240, and 1208; former Union Pacific Harriman-type coach no. 904379; former Union Pacific streamline dining car no. 4813; and many other examples of early to mid-1900s coaches, cars, and equipment.

SPECIAL EVENTS: First weekend in December, Santa Train event, $2.

NEARBY ATTRACTIONS: Hoover Dam, Lake Mead National Recreation Area, Boulder City.

DIRECTIONS: 22 miles southeast of Las Vegas on Hwy. 93/95.

Photo courtesy of Bob Freedman.

Carson City, NV

Nevada State Railroad Museum/Carson City

Museum
Standard and narrow gauge

ADDRESS: 2180 S Carson St. Carson City, NV 89701
TELEPHONE: (775) 687-6953
WEBSITE: http://dmla.clan.lib.nv.us/docs/museums/

DESCRIPTION: Included in the collection of over 65 pieces of railroad equipment are seven steam locomotives with restored coaches and freight cars. The bulk of the equipment is from the Virginia & Truckee Railroad. Museum offers operation of historic railroad equipment, handcar rides, lectures, an annual railroad history symposium, changing exhibits, and more. Steam train or motorcar rides are available on the museum's one-mile loop track.

SCHEDULE: Daily, 8:30 a.m. to 4:30 p.m.; closed Thanksgiving, Christmas, and New Year's.

ADMISSION/FARE: Adults, $4; seniors, $3; children under 18, free. Prices are subject to change.

LOCOMOTIVES/ROLLING STOCK: No. 25, 1905 Baldwin 4-6-0; no. 18, "Dayton," 1873 Central Pacific 4-4-0; no. 22, "Inyo," 1875 Baldwin 4-4-0; no. 1, "Glenbrook," 1875 Baldwin narrow gauge 2-6-0; no. 8, 1888 Cooke 4-4-0; no. 1, "Joe Douglass," 1882 Porter narrow gauge 0-4-2. Coaches nos. 3, 4, 8, 11, 12, 17, and 18; express/mail nos. 14 and 21; caboose-coaches nos. 9, 10, and 15; 11 freight cars; more.

SPECIAL EVENTS: Annual railroad history symposium, free monthly programs, special holiday trains, off-site outreach programs, train crew training opportunities. New interactive children's program—Whistlin' Billy.

NEARBY ATTRACTIONS: Nevada State Museum, Lake Tahoe, Virginia & Truckee Railroad Co.

DIRECTIONS: At intersection of US395/US50 and Fairview Dr. in South Carson City.

Photo courtesy of Peter Barton, Nevada State Railroad Museum.

TRAVEL TIP: *Steam locomotives*

Once numbering in the thousands when they were in regular use, only about 150 steam locomotives are still active in the United States on tourist and museum railroads.

Union Pacific Railroad's No. 844 is the only main line steam locomotive that has never been retired. It still pulls occasional public trips on the UP system.

East Ely, NV

Nevada Northern Railway Museum

Train ride, Dinner train, Museum, Display
Standard gauge
Radio frequency: 161.370

ADDRESS: 1100 Ave. A, PO Box 150040 East Ely, NV 89315
TELEPHONE: (775) 289-2085
E-MAIL: nnry@mwpower.net
WEBSITE: www.nnry.com

DESCRIPTION: The East Ely Shops and Yard National Historic District is home to the Nevada Northern locomotive and railcar collection. The Keystone steam excursion lasts two hours and travels the historic Robison Canyon Mining District. The Adverse diesel excursion climbs a 1½ percent grade on the old high line to McGill.

SCHEDULE: Excursion trains: May 13 to Sept. 30, daily; late April, May, and October, weekends; November and December, holiday trains. Check website for times.

ADMISSION/FARE: Adults, $22; children 4-12, $15. Museum admission: adults, $4; children 4-12, $2.

LOCOMOTIVES/ROLLING STOCK: Nevada Northern Ry. 4-6-0 no. 40; NN Ry. 2-8-0 no. 93; NN Ry. 2-8-0 no. 81; Kennecott VO1000 no. 801; 1907 steam rotary snowplow and steam powered 100-ton wrecking crane, six passenger cars, 60 freight cars.

SPECIAL EVENTS: Locomotive rental program (both steam and diesel); February, Steam Spectacular; June through September, Wine Trains; Fourth of July BBQ & Fireworks Train; Steptoe Valley Flyer Heritage Train; Father's Day Weekend, Long Steel Rails; September 29, Centennial Celebration; more. Check website.

NEARBY ATTRACTIONS: Great Basin National Park, Cave Lake State Park, Ward Charcoal Ovens, Ely Outdoor Mural Tour.

DIRECTIONS: Ely is located at US50 and US93 in east central Nevada.

Photo courtesy of Nevada Northern Railway Museum.
See ad on page A-1.

Virginia City, NV

Virginia & Truckee Railroad

Train ride
Standard gauge

ADDRESS: Washington and F Sts., PO Box 467 Virginia City, NV 89440
TELEPHONE: (775) 847-0380

DESCRIPTION: This 5-mile round trip from Virginia City to Gold Hill runs through the heart of the historic Comstock mining region. A knowledgeable conductor gives a running commentary on the 127-year-old railroad and the area.

SCHEDULE: May 28 through October 31, daily; April and May, weekends only.

ADMISSION/FARE: Adults, $7; children 5-12, $3.50; children under 5, free.

LOCOMOTIVES/ROLLING STOCK: no. 29, a 1916 Baldwin 2-8-0 from the Longview Portland & Northern; no. 8, a 1907 Baldwin 2-6-2 from the Hobart Southern; 1888 Northwestern Pacific combine and coach; former Tonopah & Tidewater coach; former Northern Pacific caboose; former Southern Pacific 1919 0-6-0 no. 30.

SPECIAL EVENTS: Party and Night train, once a month during the season.

NEARBY ATTRACTIONS: Historic Virginia City, mines, mansions, shops.

DIRECTIONS: 21 miles from Reno, 17 miles from Carson City.

Photo courtesy of Virginia & Truckee RR.

KEY TO SYMBOLS

Handicapped accessible	Restaurant	Arts and crafts	Association of Railway Museums
Parking	Picnic area	Memberships available	Tourist Railway Association, Inc.
Bus/RV parking	Dining car	Send S.A.S.E. for brochure	Amtrak service to nearby city
Gift, book, or museum shop	Excursions	National Register of Historic Places	VIA service to nearby city
Refreshments	Guided tours	VISA MasterCard DISCOVER AMERICAN EXPRESS Card	Credit cards accepted

NEW HAMPSHIRE

Andover, NH
Andover Historical Society
Depot museum

ADDRESS: 105 Depot St., PO Box 167 Andover, NH 03216
WEBSITE: www.andoverhistory.org

DESCRIPTION: The 1874 railroad depot museum has an authentically furnished stationmaster's office, railroad artifacts, Rutland caboose, early post office, and general store. It is also the home site and gravesite of 19th-century magician Richard Potter.

SCHEDULE: Memorial Day to Columbus Day: Saturday, 10 a.m. to 3 p.m.; Sunday, 1 to 3 p.m.

ADMISSION/FARE: Donations accepted.

LOCOMOTIVES/ROLLING STOCK: Rutland caboose.

SPECIAL EVENTS: First August Sunday, annual 19th Century Fair: Flea market, auction, entertainment, food, drinks, crafts, and railroad handcar rides.

DIRECTIONS: Potter Place, corner of Routes 4 and 11, 10 miles on Route 11 from I-89, 20 miles on Route 4 from I-93.

Photo courtesy of Mary Hiller.

Ashland, NH
Ashland Railroad Station Museum
Museum

SITE ADDRESS: 69 Depot St. Ashland, NH 03217-0175
MAILING ADDRESS: PO Box 175 Ashland, NH 03217-0175
TELEPHONE: (603) 968-3902
E-MAIL: ashlandrrstation@yahoo.com
WEBSITE: www.ashlandnh.org

DESCRIPTION: The museum was originally built as a station circa 1869 by the Boston, Concord & Montreal Railroad and served as the gateway for passengers to Ashland and the Squam Lakes. The local scenic railroad occasionally stops here during excursions.

SCHEDULE: July, August: Saturday, 1 to 4 p.m.

ADMISSION/FARE: Suggested donation for adults, $12; children 12 and under, free.

NEARBY ATTRACTIONS: Lakes Regional White Mountains, Hobo Railroad, and Winnipesaukee Scenic Railroad.

DIRECTIONS: On Route 132 about a half mile south of junction with Route 3.

Photo courtesy of Ann Hodsdon.

Bretton Woods, NH
Mount Washington Cog Railway
Train ride

ADDRESS: Base Rd. Bretton Woods, NH
TELEPHONE: (603) 278-8805
E-MAIL: info@thecog.com
WEBSITE: www.thecog.com

DESCRIPTION: The world's first mountain-climbing cog railway since 1869, Mount Washington Cog Railway has all coal-fired steam engines and 1870s Victorian replica coaches. The three-hour round trip travels 3¼ miles.

SCHEDULE: May through December: daily, 9 a.m. to 4 p.m.

ADMISSION/FARE: Adults, $49; children, $35; $9 off regular price on second ticket if first or last train of the day.

LOCOMOTIVES/ROLLING STOCK: Seven operational 0-2-2-0 cog steam locomotives, 1870-style replica coaches.

SPECIAL EVENTS: July, Family Days; October, Rail Fan Day.

NEARBY ATTRACTIONS: Located in the White Mountain National Forest, Mount Washington's highest peak in the Northeast.

DIRECTIONS: Route 302 Bretton Woods, New Hampshire.

Gorham, NH
Gorham Historical Society
Museum, Display
HO scale

ADDRESS: 25 Railroad St. Gorham, NH 03581
TELEPHONE: (603) 466-5570

DESCRIPTION: The 1907 museum displays rail, local, and area items, including a model railroad in a 1929 boxcar, 1911 steam locomotive, and 1949 F-7 diesel locomotive, ex-B&M.

ADMISSION/FARE: Donation.

LOCOMOTIVES/ROLLING STOCK: 1911 steam locomotive ex-Eastern Gas & Fuel, 1949 ex-B&M F-7 diesel, 1923 boxcars, N5C ex-Conrail Caboose.

NEARBY ATTRACTIONS: Close to Conway Scenic Railroad, COG RX., HOBO RR.

DIRECTIONS: Just off Routes 2 & 16 downtown Gorham, NH.

Intervale, NH
Hartmann Model Railroad, Ltd.
Museum
G to Z scales

ADDRESS: Route 302 & 16, PO Box 165 Intervale, NH 03845
TELEPHONE: (603) 356-9922
E-MAIL: info@hartmannrr.com
WEBSITE: www.hartmannrr.com

Hartmann Model Railroad™
RAILROAD MUSEUM
HOBBY SHOP   CAFE   CRAFTS

DESCRIPTION: Operating layouts from G to Z scales, including a replica of Crawford Notch, New Hampshire, in the mid-1950s to early 1960s. Other layouts have trains winding through tunnels, over bridges, and past miniature stations and buildings, as well as a Thomas the Tank Engine™. Also on display are 5,000 American and European model locomotives and coaches. The outdoor railroad has six- to eight-minute train rides on 12" narrow gauge trains (weather permitting).

SCHEDULE: Year-round: daily, 10 a.m. to 5 p.m. Closed Easter, Mother's Day, Thanksgiving, and Christmas.

ADMISSION/FARE: Adults, $6; seniors, $5; children 5-12, $4; group rates available.

SPECIAL EVENTS: Early December, Santa is Coming; free classes: how to build a layout.

NEARBY ATTRACTIONS: Storyland, 2 miles north; Conway Scenic Railroad, 4 miles south.

DIRECTIONS: 4 miles north of North Conway in the White Mountains, on Routes 302 & 16.

Coupon available, see insert.

Lincoln, NH

Hobo Railroad
Train ride
Standard gauge

ADDRESS: 64 Railroad St., PO Box 9 Lincoln, NH 03251
TELEPHONE: (603) 745-2135
E-MAIL: ride@hoborr.com
WEBSITE: www.hoborr.com

DESCRIPTION: A train excursion goes along the Pemigewasset River and lasts 1 hour, 20 minutes in a natural woodsy setting. The unique specialty offered on most trains is the Hobo Picnic Lunch.

SCHEDULE: Memorial Day to mid-June: weekends, 11 a.m. and 1 p.m.; late June to Labor Day: daily, 11 a.m., 1 and 3 p.m.; Labor Day to mid-October: daily, 11 a.m. and 1 p.m.; mid-October to December: select weekends.

ADMISSION/FARE: Adults, $10; children, $9; Hobo Picnic Lunch, $8.

LOCOMOTIVES/ROLLING STOCK: Alco S-3 no. 1186, former Boston & Maine; Alco S-1 no. 959, former Maine Central; Alco S-1 no. 958, former Maine Central. Coaches: former DL&W open-window cars and Boston & Maine Budd RDC coaches (non-powered).

SPECIAL EVENTS: See website for new events and Christmas season train specials.

NEARBY ATTRACTIONS: Clark's Trading Post, Franconia Notch State Park, Loon Mountain, Whale's Tale Water Park, Flume Gorge, Lost River Gorge.

DIRECTIONS: Exit 32 from I-93, Main St., across from McDonald's at 64 Railroad St.

Photo courtesy of Alan Thomas.

Lincoln, NH

White Mountain Central Railroad

Train ride, Museum, Display
Standard gauge

ADDRESS: Route 3 Lincoln, NH
TELEPHONE: (603) 745-8913
E-MAIL: info@clarkstradingpost.com
WEBSITE: www.clarkstradingpost.com

DESCRIPTION: Passengers can ride a steam train for 30 minutes through the White Mountains. The train departs from a beautiful depot at Clark's Trading Post, travels over a 1904 covered bridge, and climbs a 2 percent grade through Wolfman's Territory. The ticket includes a trained bear show, museum, bumper boats, Merlin's Mansion, climbing tower, and much more.

SCHEDULE: July and August, daily; June and September through mid-October, weekends.

ADMISSION/FARE: Age 6 and up, $12; children 3-5, $3; children under 3, free. Group discounts are available. Price and schedule subject to change without notice.

LOCOMOTIVES/ROLLING STOCK: Former International Shoe Co. 2-truck Heisler no. 4; former Beebe River Railroad 2-truck Climax no. 6; former East Branch & Lincoln 2-4-2 Baldwin no. 5; 0-4-0T Porter no. 1; 1898 B&M caboose no. 104082; 1943 GE 65-ton locomotive; boxcars, flatcars, and log trucks.

SPECIAL EVENTS: September 16 and 17, Railroad Days.

NEARBY ATTRACTIONS: Hobo Railroad, Cog Railway, Conway Scenic Railroad, White Mountain National Forest.

DIRECTIONS: On Route 3, 1 mile north of North Woodstock; located at Clark's Trading Post.

TRAVEL TIP: *Go first class*

A few tourist railroads offer the chance to charter a private or first-class car. These cars are often plush, and are former business cars once used by railroad executives. They'll give you an entirely different perspective on your trip—and you can say you rode like one of the Robber Barons of old!

Meredith, NH

Winnipesaukee Scenic Railroad

Train ride
Standard gauge

SITE ADDRESS: 154 Main St. Meredith, NH 03253
MAILING ADDRESS: PO Box 9 Lincoln, NH 03251
TELEPHONE: (603) 745-2135
E-MAIL: ride@hoborr.com
WEBSITE: www.hoborr.com

DESCRIPTION: Scenic train rides, lunch trips, and lakeside dinner trains travel along the shores of Lake Winnipesaukee. Features include ice cream parlor car, party caboose, and private charters. One- and two-hour rides are also available.

SCHEDULE: Memorial Day to late June, weekends; late June to Labor Day, daily; after Labor Day, weekends, fall foliage.

ADMISSION/FARE: Adults, $11; children, $9; Hobo Picnic Lunches, $8.

LOCOMOTIVES/ROLLING STOCK: Alco S-1 no. 1008, former Portland Terminal; EMD GP-7 no. 302, former Rock Island; GE 44-ton no. 2, former US government. Coaches: former DL&W open-window cars and Boston & Maine Budd RDCs (non-powered).

SPECIAL EVENTS: Caboose rides, fall foliage tours, and fireworks specials.

NEARBY ATTRACTIONS: Lake Winnipesaukee, Mt. Washington cruises, Funspot, Weirs Beach.

DIRECTIONS: I-93 to exit 23, Route 104 east to Route 3; Route 3 north for ¼ mile, left on Mill St.

Photo courtesy of Alan Thomas.

North Conway, NH

Conway Scenic Railroad

Standard gauge
Radio frequency: 161.250

ADDRESS: 38 Norcross Cir., PO Box 1947 North Conway, NH 03860
TELEPHONE: (800) 232-5251 or (603) 356-5251
E-MAIL: info@conwayscenic.com
WEBSITE: www.conwayscenic.com

DESCRIPTION: Nostalgic round-trip train rides are powered by steam or early diesel and last for varying durations. Valley Train goes to Conway/Bartlett, Notch Train travels to Crawford Depot/Fabyan. Features include museum, gift shop, roundhouse, and operating turntable. Dining and First Class services are available.

SCHEDULE: Valley Train: May 15 to October 22, daily; mid-April to mid-May, November, and December, weekends; Notch Train: June 20 to September 3, Tuesday to Thursday and Saturday; September 12 to October 15, daily.

ADMISSION/FARE: Fares vary. Adult fares range from $12 to $60; child fares from $8.50; ages 3 and under, free in Coach on Valley Train. See website for details.

LOCOMOTIVES/ROLLING STOCK: Grand Trunk Railway 0-6-0 no. 7470; Maine East Central GP7 no. 573; Boston & Maine F7 no. 4266; nos. 6505/6516, ex-Canadian National Railways/VIA FP9s; more.

SPECIAL EVENTS: Bunny Express, Easter Lily Express, Mother's/Father's Day, Junior Railroader's Day, Day Out with Thomas™, 32nd Birthday Celebration, 32nd Annual Railfan's Weekend, Pumpkin Patch Run, Armed Forces Appreciation Day, The Holiday Santa Claus Express, and Polar Express™.

NEARBY ATTRACTIONS: Storyland, Mount Washington Auto Road, and Settler's Green Outlet Shopping.

DIRECTIONS: Route 16/US302 and Norcross Circle in the heart of North Conway Village. The depot faces Schouler Park.

North Woodstock, NH

Cafe Lafayette Dinner Train
Dinner train
Standard gauge

ADDRESS: PO Box 8 North Woodstock, NH 03262
TELEPHONE: (800) 699-3501 or (603) 745-3500
WEBSITE: www.cafelafayette.com or www.nhdinnertrain.com

DESCRIPTION: A leisurely, two-hour evening train ride spent criss-crossing the picturesque Pemigewasset River. As dinner is served on this 20-mile round trip, period music keeps time with the rail's rhythmic rumbling. After dinner, with the compartment lights down low, riders can view a dramatic New England sunset outside the windows.

SCHEDULE: Late May to last October Sunday; call for details.

ADMISSION/FARE: Adults, $65; children 6-11, $45; no children under 6.

LOCOMOTIVES/ROLLING STOCK: 1923 Pennsylvania Railroad caboose no. 10069; 1924 Pullman dining car no. 221, former NYC; 1953 Army kitchen car; 1954 CN cafe coach no. 3207; 1952 Pullman dome car, former MoPac/Illinois Central no. 2211; 1946 Pullman sleeper, former CNR/VIA no. 323.

NEARBY ATTRACTIONS: Heart of the White Mountain National Forest, Franconia Notch State Park, White Mountain Central Railway, Cog Railway, Mount Washington, Hobo Railroad, Winnipesaukee Scenic Railroad.

DIRECTIONS: Take I-93 to exit 32; on Route 112, midway between Lincoln, New Hampshire, and North Woodstock.

Photo courtesy of Chet Burak.

Sandown, NH
Sandown Historical Society & Museum
Museum, Display

ADDRESS: 1 Depot Rd., PO Box 300 Sandown, NH 03873
TELEPHONE: (603) 887-4520
E-MAIL: history@sandownNH.com
WEBSITE: www.sandown.us/historical%20society/museum_main.htm

DESCRIPTION: Since its founding in 1978, the Society has been preserving historical artifacts and information about the town of Sandown and the Worcester, Nashu, and Portland division of the B&M Railroad. They restored the Old Sandown RR Depot, complete with the stationmaster's room containing telegraph, old ringer telephone, and separate ticket windows for men and women. The men's waiting room features a big round stove and waiting bench.

SCHEDULE: May to October, the Historical Society meets the third Wednesday at the no. 1 Flanger Car. This old 1909 Maine Central car is now a luxurious parlor car.

ADMISSION/FARE: No admission fees; donations accepted.

LOCOMOTIVES/ROLLING STOCK: "Put Put," Velocipede; "road" equipped 2-man hand car; two Flanger cars.

SPECIAL EVENTS: Second weekend in August, "Old Home Day."

Photo courtesy of Mr. Paul Densen.

Wilton Scenic Railroad
Train ride, Dinner train

ADDRESS: 148 Main St. Wilton, NH 03086-0419
TELEPHONE: (603) 654-7245
E-MAIL: info@wiltonscenicrr.com
WEBSITE: www.wiltonscenicrr.com

DESCRIPTION: As New England's newest tourist rail line, the Wilton Scenic Railroad offers 2- to 3-hour scenic excursions. Passengers can relax in the comfort of their seats as they wind through the woods, past ledges, along scenic Zephyr Lake and over the trestles. They can also take in the serene views of the most climbed mountain in the world, Mt. Monadnock. Box lunches are available on this 28-mile round trip on Budd Liners from Wilton to Greenfield, New Hampshire.

SCHEDULE: May through November. See website for further details.

ADMISSION/FARE: Adults, $14; youth, $10; children 5 and under, $4.

LOCOMOTIVES/ROLLING STOCK: Budd RDC 1 WSRX 15, Budd RDC 3 WSRX30.

NEARBY ATTRACTIONS: Greenfield State Park, Cathedral in the Pines.

DIRECTIONS: See website for directions.

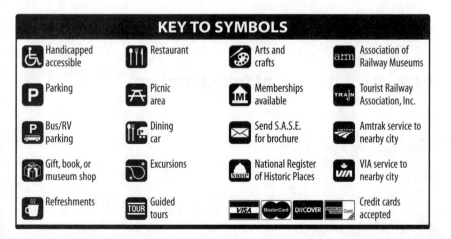

KEY TO SYMBOLS

Handicapped accessible	Restaurant	Arts and crafts	Association of Railway Museums
Parking	Picnic area	Memberships available	Tourist Railway Association, Inc.
Bus/RV parking	Dining car	Send S.A.S.E. for brochure	Amtrak service to nearby city
Gift, book, or museum shop	Excursions	National Register of Historic Places	VIA service to nearby city
Refreshments	Guided tours	Credit cards accepted	

NEW JERSEY

Cape May, NJ

Cape May Seashore Lines
Train ride
Standard gauge

SITE ADDRESS: Cape May, NJ
MAILING ADDRESS: PO Box 152 Tuckahoe, NJ 08250
TELEPHONE: (609) 884-5300
WEBSITE: www.cmslrr.com

DESCRIPTION: Regional/tourist railroad in Cape May County operates passenger Budd RDCs. For most recent schedule, fare, locomotives and rolling stock, and special events, please call, write, or check website.

LOCOMOTIVES/ROLLING STOCK: Eight Budd RDC1s, former Pennsylvania-Reading Seashore Lines; two RDC9s, former Boston & Maine; Alco/EMD RS2, former PRR; EMD GP9, former PRR; three P-RSL P70 coaches, former PRR; two P-RSL P70 coaches, former P-RSL.; CNJ GP7 1523.

NEARBY ATTRACTIONS: Victorian Cape May City, Wildwood Beaches, Boardwalk and Amusement Piers, Cape May Lighthouse, Cap May-Lewes Ferry, Cape May County Park and Zoo, historic Cold Spring Village, Mid-Atlantic Center for the Arts, and Middle Township Performing Arts Center.

DIRECTIONS: 4-H Fairgrounds Station: off South Dennisville Rd., Middle Township. Cape May Court House: Route 615/ Mechanic St. Smith Court House: Elementary School 2 off Pacific Ave. in Cape May Court House (flag stop). Cold Spring: Route 9, Cold Spring. Cape May City–Lafayette St., Cape May.

Photo courtesy of Lion Photography.

Farmingdale, NJ

New Jersey Museum of Transportation
Train ride, Display
36" gauge

ADDRESS: PO Box 622 Farmingdale, NJ 07727
TELEPHONE: (732) 938-5524
E-MAIL: crawsat@juno.com
WEBSITE: www.njmt.org

DESCRIPTION: This is one of the oldest continuously operated steam preservation railroads in the U.S., established 1952. Also on site: museum and restoration shops.

SCHEDULE: Weekends, March to December, 12 to 4:30 p.m. Daily, July to August, 12 to 4:30 p.m.

ADMISSION/FARE: $3 and up per person.

SPECIAL EVENTS: Palm Sunday and Easter weekends, Easter Express; Sunday after Labor Day, Railroader's Day; late October, Haunted Halloween Express; four weekends after Thanksgiving, Christmas Express.

NEARBY ATTRACTIONS: Historic Allaire Village, Jersey Shore beach attractions.

DIRECTIONS: Route 524 at Allaire State Park. Garden State Pkwy. exit 98, I-195 exit 31.

Photo courtesy of Gary S. Crawford.

Flemington, NJ

Black River & Western Railroad

EDITOR'S CHOICE

Train ride, Museum

SITE ADDRESS: Stangle Rd. Flemington, NJ
MAILING ADDRESS: PO Box 200 Ringoes, NJ 08551
TELEPHONE: (908) 782-6622
E-MAIL: psgrinfo@brwrr.com
WEBSITE: www.brwrr.com

DESCRIPTION: A steam/diesel excursion through the rolling hills of Hunterdon Country. The 1-hour, 10-minute ride travels between Flemington and Ringoes.

SCHEDULE: March to December: weekends, departing Flemington Station 11:30 a.m., 1, 2:30, and 4 p.m.; January to March, Jack Frost trains: Saturday only; one ticket ride all day to Three Bridges, NJ.

ADMISSION/FARE: Adults, $10; children 3-12, $5; children under 3, free. Groups/private charters available, call Marian (908) 797-7300.

LOCOMOTIVES/ROLLING STOCK: 1937 Alco 2-8-0 no. 60; 1950 EMD GP7 no. 780; 1956 EMD GP9 no. 752; GP7s nos. 752 and 780; GP9s nos. 1848 and 1849; SW1200s nos. 8142 and 8159; NW1200 no. 820; nos. 320-323 commuter cars, former Central of New Jersey; more.

SPECIAL EVENTS: Easter Bunny Express, Great Train Robbery, Columbus Day, Halloween Haunted Train, Santa Express, Jack Frost. Please visit the website for special event details.

NEARBY ATTRACTIONS: Northlandz, New Hope Ivyland Railroad.

DIRECTIONS: Route 202 to Flemington Circle, 12W through second circle, after railroad tracks turn right on Stangle Rd., station is on right.

Photo courtesy of Elizabeth Griswold.

Phillipsburg, NJ

Phillipsburg Railroad Historians

Train ride, Museum
9⁷/₁₆ gauge

ADDRESS: 292 Chambers St. Phillipsburg, NJ 08865
TELEPHONE: (908) 859-1277 or (610) 826-2580
E-MAIL: prrh@angelfire.com
WEBSITE: www.prrh.org

DESCRIPTION: The train ride is aboard a historic Centerville & Southwestern miniature train. The museum houses equipment, displays, and a gift shop. There are also circus displays and motorcar rides.

SCHEDULE: Seasonal train operation. Museum: May 1 to October 1, Sunday, 10 a.m. to 4 p.m.; please call for hours of operation.

ADMISSION/FARE: Donations accepted.

LOCOMOTIVES/ROLLING STOCK: Ingersoll-Rand GE 45-tonner; L&HR cabooses; CNJ caboose no. 91197; lowside gondola; L&HR flanger; Centerville & Southwestern, two locomotives and 31 cars.

SPECIAL EVENTS: Open House with train rides first Sunday in May, second Sunday in July, and second Sunday in September. Please call to confirm.

NEARBY ATTRACTIONS: NYS&W Steam Train Ride, Union Station display.

DIRECTIONS: US22, exit at S Main St. Museum entrance is across from Joe's Steak Shop. Use driveway next to Noto/Wyncoop Funeral Home. Drive around to rear.

Photo courtesy of Paul M. Carpenito.

Tuckahoe, NJ
South Jersey Railroad Museum
Museum, Model train layout
O, S, Standard, HO, N, and LGB scale

ADDRESS: 1721 Mt. Pleasant Rd. Tuckahoe, NJ 08250
TELEPHONE: (609) 628-2850
WEBSITE: www.sjrails.org

DESCRIPTION: Six operating layouts, special exhibits, and railroad artifacts. New layouts include children's O Lamont & Postwar/Modern S gauge. LGB under construction. Members bring and run their trains.

SCHEDULE: Year-round: Wednesday and Saturday, 11 a.m. to 4 p.m.; second August weekend and third December weekend, train shows; December, 11 a.m. to 4 p.m.

ADMISSION/FARE: Free; donations accepted.

LOCOMOTIVES/ROLLING STOCK: Over 100 assorted locomotives and rolling stock.

SPECIAL EVENTS: Holiday exhibits, visits from Easter Bunny and Santa.

NEARBY ATTRACTIONS: Penna-Reading Sea Shore Line Tuckahoe Junction Station.

DIRECTIONS: Off Route 50 in Tuckahoe. Call or write for directions.

Union, NJ
Model Railroad Club, Inc.
Model train layout
HO and N scale

ADDRESS: 295 Jefferson Ave., PO Box 1146 Union, NJ 07083-1146
TELEPHONE: (908) 964-8808
WEBSITE: www.tmrci.com

DESCRIPTION: 40' x 40' HO scale and 20' x 27' N scale operating layouts.

SCHEDULE: Saturday, 1 to 4 p.m.

ADMISSION/FARE: Adults, $5; children 12 and under, $3; seniors 60+, $4.

DIRECTIONS: NJ Route 22 east, off Jefferson Ave.

Photo courtesy of Robert Salfi. Coupon available, see insert.

Whippany, NJ

Whippany Railway Museum

Museum
Standard gauge
Radio frequency: 160.230 (Morristown & Erie Railway)

ADDRESS: 1 Railroad Plaza Route 10 West and Whippany Rd. Whippany, NJ 07981-0016
TELEPHONE: (973) 887-8177
E-MAIL: paultup@optonline.net
WEBSITE: www.whippanyrailwaymuseum.org

DESCRIPTION: Headquartered in the restored 1904 freight house of the Morristown & Erie, the museum displays an outstanding collection of railroad artifacts and memorabilia, an operating model train layout, and ocean liner memorabilia. The railroad yard is complete with the elegant Whippany passenger depot, coal yard, wooden water tank, and historic rail equipment. The train ride is a 10-mile round-trip excursion that lasts for 45 minutes.

SCHEDULE: April through October, Sunday, 12 to 4 p.m.

ADMISSION/FARE: Museum: adults, $1; children under 12, $0.50. Special event train ride: adults, $12; children under 12, $8.

LOCOMOTIVES/ROLLING STOCK: Morris County Central no. 4039, an 0-6-0 built for the US Army by ALCO in 1942 and now listed on the National Register of Historic Places; NYS&W no. 150, a 20-ton Whitcomb industrial locomotive; Morristown & Erie railbus no. 10, built in 1918; PRR N5C Cabin Car No. 477823, and more.

SPECIAL EVENTS: April 8, 9, and 15, 2006, Easter Bunny Express; October 1, 2006, Pumpkin Festival; December 2, 3, 9, 10, and 16, 2006, Santa Claus Special. Please call or visit the website for additional rides during the summer months.

NEARBY ATTRACTIONS: Morris Museum, General Washington's Headquarters; Jockey Hollow National Historic Site.

DIRECTIONS: At the intersection of Route 10 West and Whippany Rd. in Morris County, NJ.

Photo courtesy of Steve Hepler.

NEW MEXICO

Alamogordo, NM

Toy Train Depot Foundation

Train ride, Museum, Display, Model train layout G to Z scales

ADDRESS: 1991 N White Sands Blvd. Alamogordo, NM 88310
TELEPHONE: (888) 207-3564 or (505) 437-2855
E-MAIL: railfanewmexico@hotmail.com
WEBSITE: toytraindepot.homestead.com

- Chama
- Santa Fe
- Clovis
- Alamogordo

DESCRIPTION: Remember when every village park or drive-in movie theater had a park train ride? The Toy Train Depot Foundation is saving as many of these unique rides as possible, especially those from the Miniature Train Company. 20-minute, two-mile train rides are available on one of three G-16s, an S-16, or a 12" Addison Train. Visitors can also become acquainted with the railroad history of Alamogordo, the Cloud Climbing route, and current Union Pacific rail traffic on the Golden State Route (Tucumcari Cutoff).

SCHEDULE: Year-round, Wednesday through Sunday, 12 to 4:30 p.m.

ADMISSION/FARE: Train ride: adults, $4; children under 13, $3. Museum tour: $3.

LOCOMOTIVES/ROLLING STOCK: Three G-16s, an S-16, and a 12" Addison Train.

NEARBY ATTRACTIONS: White Sands National Monument, International Space Hall of Fame, Trinity Site.

DIRECTIONS: North end of Alameda Park is on N White Sands Blvd. in Alamogordo.

Photo courtesy of John Koval.

Chama, NM

Cumbres & Toltec Scenic Railroad

Train ride

SITE ADDRESS: 500 S Terrace Ave. US285 Antonito, CO and Chama, NM 87520
MAILING ADDRESS: PO Box 789 Chama, NM 87520
TELEPHONE: (888) CUMBRES or (505) 756-2151
E-MAIL: info@cumbresandtoltec.com
WEBSITE: www.cumbresandtoltec.com

DESCRIPTION: The Cumbres & Toltec Scenic Railroad is the finest remaining example of the original Denver & Rio Grande narrow gauge railroad, built in the 1880s to reach the mines at Silverton. Unspoiled scenery awaits travelers through the San Juan Mountains. The train passes over high bridges and through tunnels, alongside ghostly rock formations and restored company towns.

SCHEDULE: Call or check website for schedule and fares.

LOCOMOTIVES/ROLLING STOCK: Locomotives: Denver & Rio Grande Western K27 no. 463, built by Baldwin in 1903; D&RGW K36 locomotives nos. 483, 484, 487, 488, and 489, built by Baldwin in 1925; and D&RGW K37 497, built by Baldwin in 1890 as a standard gauge locomotive and converted to narrow gauge 1930. Rolling stock: passenger cars constructed in the 1970s and 1980s, over 140 pieces of ex-D&RGW equipment from 1880 to 1968.

SPECIAL EVENTS: May 26, Opening Day; others to be announced later.

NEARBY ATTRACTIONS: Antonito: Great Sand Dunes National Monument, Taos, Santa Fe, Royal Gorge. Chama: Santa Fe, Durango (D&SNGRR), Mesa Verde.

Clovis, NM
Clovis Depot Model Train Museum
Museum, Display, Model train layout
All scales

ADDRESS: 221 W First St. Clovis, NM 88101
TELEPHONE: (888) 762-0064
E-MAIL: philipw@3lefties.com
WEBSITE: www.clovisdepot.com

DESCRIPTION: The museum displays railroad history in Clovis, NM, as well as Australia, Great Britain, and the rest of the southwestern United States. Layouts depict the history of toy trains in the US and Great Britain. The depot has been restored to its condition in the 1950-1960 era and has displays of historic documents and pictures. Artifacts of railroad significance are continuously being added to the collection.

SCHEDULE: Wednesday to Sunday, 12 to 5 p.m. May be closed in February and September; call first. Closed New Year's Day, Easter, Thanksgiving, and Christmas Day.

ADMISSION/FARE: Adults, $5; children 5-15 and seniors 65+, $3; under 5, free; family $15.00.

LOCOMOTIVES/ROLLING STOCK: Fairmont Railway Speeder.

NEARBY ATTRACTIONS: Blackwater Draw pre-historic site and museum, Norman Petty Recording Studio, Clovis Zoo.

DIRECTIONS: Two blocks west of Main St. on US Hwy. 60/84.

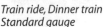

Photo courtesy of Phil Williams.

Santa Fe, NM

Santa Fe Southern Railway

Train ride, Dinner train
Standard gauge

ADDRESS: 410 S Guadalupe Santa Fe, NM 87501
TELEPHONE: (888) 989-8600 or (505) 989-8600
E-MAIL: depot@sfsr.com
WEBSITE: www.santafesouthernrailway.com

DESCRIPTION: The Santa Fe Southern offers 2¹/₂-hour and 4¹/₂-hour excursions with freight movement. Scenic trains run year-round. May through October, visitors can enjoy highball trains on Friday and barbecue dinner trains on Saturday.

SCHEDULE: Gift shop/ticket office: Monday through Saturday, 9 a.m. to 5 p.m.; Sunday, 11 a.m. to 5 p.m.

ADMISSION/FARE: Adults, $28 to $55; seniors 60+, discount.

LOCOMOTIVES/ROLLING STOCK: GP 7s nos. 92 and 93; New Jersey Cental coach no. 1158; Santa Fe Pleasure Dome "Plaza Lam;" New Jersey Central coach no. 1195; New Jersey Central combine no. 300.

SPECIAL EVENTS: February 14, Valentine's Dinner; Easter Bunny Train; Fourth of July barbecue and fireworks; Fiesta barbecue; Halloween Ghost Story Train; post-Thanksgiving barbecue; December 15 through 24, Santa Claus and caroling trains; December 31, New Year's Eve dinner.

NEARBY ATTRACTIONS: Santa Fe downtown, art galleries, museums, fine clothing, restaurants, within walking distance of depot.

DIRECTIONS: I-25 at St. Francis to Cerrillos, turn right to Guadalupe, turn left, depot on left behind Tomasita's Restaurant.

Photo courtesy of Mark Rounds.

Map of New York

- N. Tonawanda
- Medina
- Rush
- West Henrietta
- Geneva
- Marcellus
- Central Square
- Utica
- North Creek
- Arcade
- Dunkirk
- Angelica
- Salamanca
- Cooperstown
- Norwich
- Arkville
- Phoenicia
- Roscoe
- Maybrook
- Kingston
- Chester
- Hyde Park
- Mt. Pleasant
- Greenport
- Riverhead
- New York

NEW YORK

Angelica, NY

Pittsburg Shawmut & Northern Railroad Company Historical Society Museum
Museum, Display

ADDRESS: Allegany County Fairgrounds, PO Box 222 Angelica, NY 14709

DESCRIPTION: This is the historical society site and museum exhibit for the Pittsburg, Shawmut & Northern Railroad.

SCHEDULE: Open the first full weekend of June and during the Allegany County Fair in July. The exhibit can be seen at other times only by appointment. Winter months not advisable.

ADMISSION/FARE: First weekend of June, Shawmut Day: free; July: Allegany County Fair admission prices; no admission charge for visits by appointment.

LOCOMOTIVES/ROLLING STOCK: Home-built steam engine no. 88; passenger coach no. 278, formerly no. 104 built in the late 1880s and used on the Shawmut Railroad; private car, "Clara," no. 99, built by Pullman Company in 1883 and purchased by the Shawmut Railroad in 1905; bobber caboose no. 175, built in the Shawmut Shops in Angelica in 1912 using DL&W Railroad plans; duplicate railroad station of the Shawmut that was used in Farmer's Valley, Pennsylvania.

SPECIAL EVENTS: First full weekend in June, Shawmut Days; third week in July, Monday through Saturday, Allegany County Fair.

NEARBY ATTRACTIONS: Historic Angelica, New York; Six-S Golf Course; Swain Resort; International Ceramics Museum, Alfred, New York; Letchworth State Park; Genesee Valley Greenway and many other attractions.

DIRECTIONS: Exit 31, Interstate 86, Allegany County Angelica exit. Follow the signs to the Allegany County Fairgrounds.

Photo courtesy of John M. Muchler.

Arcade, NY

Arcade & Attica Railroad

Train ride, Display, Model train layout

ADDRESS: 278 Main St. Arcade, NY 14009
TELEPHONE: (585) 496-9877 or (585) 492-3100
E-MAIL: LLK@anarr.com
WEBSITE: anarr.com

DESCRIPTION: Two-hour scenic train ride aboard an early 1900s engine and coaches. The A&A was chartered in 1917 to keep a railroad between Arcade and Attica when the Buffalo, Attica, & Arcade went bankrupt. Today, the railroad continues to haul freight along the 15-mile right-of-way, in addition to the 7½-mile passenger excursions.

SCHEDULE: May to December, hours vary.

ADMISSION/FARE: Adults, $12; seniors, $10; children 3-11, $7; under 3, free on a lap.

LOCOMOTIVES/ROLLING STOCK: A 1945 GE 65-ton diesel locomotive no. 112; 1915 and 1917 DL&W coaches. Also on site: no. 18, a 1920 Alco 2-8-0 steam locomotive; and no. 14, a 1920 American 4-6-0 steam locomotive.

SPECIAL EVENTS: Civil War Days, children's trains, Murder Mystery dinner trains, Halloween Haunted House, Santa rides.

NEARBY ATTRACTIONS: Letchworth State Park, Beaver Meadows Nature Sanctuary, Niagara Falls, Salamanca Rail Museum, and Allegany State Park.

DIRECTIONS: In the village of Arcade, 3 miles east of Route 16 or ½ mile west of Route 98.

Photo courtesy of Peter Swanson.

Arkville, NY

Delaware & Ulster Railride

Train ride, Museum
Standard gauge

SITE ADDRESS: 43510 St. Route 28 Arkville, NY 12406
MAILING ADDRESS: PO Box 310 Stamford, NY 12167
TELEPHONE: (800) 225-4132 or (845) 586-DURR
E-MAIL: fun@durr.org
WEBSITE: www.durr.org

DESCRIPTION: Operating on the route of the historic Ulster & Delaware Railroad, these 19 miles of rail offer a 1- or 1¾-hour trip through the scenic Catskill Mountains.

SCHEDULE: Memorial Day weekend through October, weekends; July and August, Wednesday through Friday.

ADMISSION/FARE: $6 to $11.

LOCOMOTIVES/ROLLING STOCK: D&H RS36 no. 5017; no. 5106 1953 Alco S-4, former Chesapeake & Ohio; no. 1012 1954 Alco S-4, former Ford Motor Co.; M-405, a 1928 J.G. Brill Co. diesel-electric rail car that belonged to New York Central; two slat cars with benches, former PRR; two boxcars, former NYC; 44-ton locomotive, former Western Maryland.

SPECIAL EVENTS: Train Robberies, Tractor Pulls, Twilight Runs, Fall Foliage, Halloween Train, A Day Out with Thomas™, Santa Train.

DIRECTIONS: Route 28, in Arkville, 45 miles west of New York State Thruway.

Photo courtesy of Aaron Keller.
Coupon available, see insert.

Brooklyn, NY

New York Transit Museum

Train ride, Museum

ADDRESS: 130 Livingston St., 9th Floor, Box E Brooklyn, NY 11201
TELEPHONE: (718) 243-8601
WEBSITE: www.mta.info/mta/museum

DESCRIPTION: Housed in a historic subway station, the New York Transit Museum collects, preserves, exhibits, and interprets the history, sociology, and technology of public transportation in the region.

SCHEDULE: Brooklyn: Tuesday to Friday, 10 a.m. to 4 p.m.; weekends 12 to 5 p.m. Grand Central: weekdays, 8 a.m. to 8 p.m.; Saturday and Sunday, 10 a.m. to 6 p.m. Closed holidays.

ADMISSION/FARE: Brooklyn: adults, $5; seniors and children 3-17, $3; Manhattan: free.

LOCOMOTIVES/ROLLING STOCK:
Brooklyn: 20 vintage railcars, including elevated and subway cars from 1878 to the late 1960s. Money Car G, on display, is New York's oldest existing elevated rail car.

NEARBY ATTRACTIONS: Five minutes from Manhattan by subway.

DIRECTIONS: A, C, or F train to Jay St.–Borough Hall; or 3, 4, 5, M, N, or R trains to Borough Hall. Other trains and buses also come close.

Central Square, NY
Central Square Railroad Museum
Museum, Display
Standard gauge

SITE ADDRESS: Railroad St. Central Square, NY
MAILING ADDRESS: PO Box 229 Marcellus, NY 13108-0229
TELEPHONE: (315) 676-7582
E-MAIL: cnynrhs@aol.com
WEBSITE: www.rrhistorical-2.com/cnynrhs/

DESCRIPTION: The station museum has various rail equipment on display outside, including two speeders (one an original O&W RR model 40-B) and two steam locomotives, a brill car, a circus car (with circus displays and a circus layout), and a 25-ton diesel locomotive.

SCHEDULE: Sunday, 12 to 5 p.m. and other times by appointment.

ADMISSION/FARE: Free, donations accepted.

LOCOMOTIVES/ROLLING STOCK: ALCO 0-4-0 no. 53; 0-4-0 no. 7; Brill car no. M39; 25-ton diesel General Electric 1941; CN Fairmont; Speeder 1-O&W Model B Speeder; 80' Circus Car with displays.

NEARBY ATTRACTIONS: St. Lawrence Seaway, Thousand Islands, Adirondack Park.

DIRECTIONS: Museum is off US11 on Railroad Ave. in Central Square, NY.

Chester, NY

The Chester Historical Society

Museum

ADDRESS: 1915 Erie Railroad Station 14 Winkler Pl. Chester, NY 10918
TELEPHONE: (845) 469-2591
E-MAIL: chester_historical@mac.com
WEBSITE: homepage.mac.com/chester_historical

DESCRIPTION: Housed in a restored 1915 Erie Railroad Station is a collection of items (photos, manuscripts, books, artifacts, documents, news clippings, etc.) relating to greater Chester community's history. The rail line was built in 1834 from Piermont on the Hudson to Dunkirk on Lake Erie to aid Jeremiah Pierson (a mine and mill owner and operator) in distributing his products.

SCHEDULE: May through October: Saturday, 9 a.m. to 1 p.m. Other hours by appointment.

ADMISSION/FARE: Donations appreciated.

SPECIAL EVENTS: January, annual meeting and program; June, fund raising yard sale; September, Penny Social; December, Holiday Tree Lighting.

NEARBY ATTRACTIONS: Orange County Heritage Trail on the former Erie main line. Downtown Chester: restaurants, shops. Twenty miles west of USMA at West Point.

DIRECTIONS: New York State Thruway exit 16. Take Route 17 west 10 miles, exit 126 Chester, right at end of ramp. From Route 17 eastbound, exit 126, left at end of ramp, then straight at light onto Academy Ave. Left on Main St., right at firehouse and continue on Main St. through downtown Chester. The station is on the left.

Photo courtesy of Norma Stoddard and Clif Patrick.

Cooperstown & Charlotte Valley Railroad/ Leatherstocking Railway Historical Society

Train ride, Dinner train, Museum, Display, Model train layout
Standard gauge
Radio frequency: 151.67

SITE ADDRESS: 136 East Main SR166 Cooperstown, NY
MAILING ADDRESS: PO Box 681 Oneonta, NY 13820
TELEPHONE: (607) 432-2429
E-MAIL: lrhs@lrhs.com
WEBSITE: www.lrhs.com

DESCRIPTION: A 16-mile round trip runs between Milford and Cooperstown, and an 8-mile, 1-hour trip goes between Cooperstown and Cooperstown Dreams Park Baseball Camp. Explore artifacts in a restored 1869 Milford Depot, including an operating Lionel display.

SCHEDULE: May to October, daytime and some evening excursions. Call, write, or see website for days of operation and departure times.

ADMISSION/FARE: Adults, $10; seniors 62+, $9; children 4-12, $8; children under 4, free.

LOCOMOTIVES/ROLLING STOCK: S4 no. 3051 and S7 no. 3052; FL9's nos. 2028 and 2010, both undergoing restorations.

SPECIAL EVENTS: Easter Bunny Express, Railfan Days, Halloween Express, Santa Express, Christmas Lights trains, plus more specials.

NEARBY ATTRACTIONS: National Baseball Hall of Fame, Farmer's Museum, Fenimore Art Museum, Glimmerglass State Park, National Soccer Hall of Fame, Cooperstown Brewery.

DIRECTIONS: I-88, exit 17, north on Route 28 for 10 miles to Milford. East on Route 166 one block. Cooperstown facility is at the village's Blue Trolley parking lot off NYS Route 28.

Photo courtesy of Wendy S. York.

Dunkirk, NY

Alco Brooks Railroad Display

Museum, Display
Standard gauge

SITE ADDRESS: Chautauqua County Fairgrounds, 1089 Central Ave. Dunkirk, NY
MAILING ADDRESS: Historical Society of Dunkirk, 513 Washington Ave. Dunkirk, NY 14048
TELEPHONE: (716) 366-3797
E-MAIL: davrr@netsync.net

DESCRIPTION: Located at the Chautauqua County Fairgrounds since 1987, the display features: an original Alco-Brooks steam locomotive, a wood-sided boxcar housing displays of Chautauqua County commerce and railroads, gift shop, restored wooden caboose, Nickel Plate work car, Erie Railroad concrete telephone booth, New York Central harp switch stand, Pennsylvania Railroad cast-iron crossing sign, DAV&P land line marker, and an operating crossing flasher.

SCHEDULE: June 1 to August 31: Saturday, 1 to 3 p.m., weather permitting; by appointment.

ADMISSION/FARE: Donations appreciated.

LOCOMOTIVES/ROLLING STOCK: 1916 Alco-Brooks 0-6-0 no. 444, former Boston & Maine; 1907 Delaware & Hudson wood-sided boxcar no. 22020; 1905 New York Central wood caboose no. 19224.

SPECIAL EVENTS: May 19-21, antique auto flea market; June 18, Strawberry Festival; July 24-30, Chautauqua County Fair.

NEARBY ATTRACTIONS: Dunkirk Historical Museum, Dunkirk Lighthouse, and Chautauqua Institution.

DIRECTIONS: I-90, exit 59, to Chautauqua County Fairgrounds.

TRAVEL TIP: *Bring safety goggles, wear smart shoes*

Ready to go? When riding a tourist train, it's a great idea to bring along a pair of safety glasses so you can ride the open Dutch door. Smart shoes are a must, too—wear sturdy, closed-toe shoes, and watch your step!

Geneva, NY
Finger Lakes Railway
Train ride, Dinner train

ADDRESS: 68 Border City Rd., PO Box 1099 Geneva, NY 14456
TELEPHONE: (315) 781-1234
E-MAIL: events@backbohne.com
WEBSITE: www.fingerlakesscenicrailway.com

DESCRIPTION: Operation began in 1995 with the purchase of 118 miles from Conrail, formerly the Geneva Cluster. The main track from Syracuse to Canandaigua was formerly the New York Central Auburn Road and dates back to 1835. Other portions of the line were once the Lehigh Valley (Geneva to Kendaia) and the Pennsylvania Railroad (Penn Yan to Watkins Glen). The Railroad owns 10 locomotives and moves over 16,000 freight cars annually.

SCHEDULE: Please check website for an updated schedule and current rates.

NEARBY ATTRACTIONS: Wine tasting excursions, boating, and fast ferry to Canada. Refer to local tourism offices for New York.

DIRECTIONS: Exit 42 NYS Thruway, 8 miles south on Route 14 to Geneva.

Greenport, NY
Peconic County Miniature Railroad
Miniature train ride
16" gauge

ADDRESS: PO Box 631 Greenport, NY 11944
TELEPHONE: (631) 477-2433
E-MAIL: pcmrr@msn.com

DESCRIPTION: This two-lap, 12-minute ride travels through a forest, alongside a pond, and over a bridge.

SCHEDULE: Memorial Day to Halloween: Sundays and holidays, 1 to 4 p.m.

ADMISSION/FARE: Donations appreciated.

LOCOMOTIVES/ROLLING STOCK: Three miniature Train Company G-16 trains.

NEARBY ATTRACTIONS: Railroad Museum of Long Island at Greenport and Riverhead.

DIRECTIONS: Route 25 to Greenport; left at traffic light (3rd St.); left on Webb St. to end.

Photo courtesy of F.A. Field.

Greenport, NY

Railroad Museum of Long Island, Greenport

Museum, Display, Model train layout

ADDRESS: 440 4th St., PO Box 726 Greenport, NY 11944
TELEPHONE: (631) 477-0439
E-MAIL: info@rmli.org (general) or secretaryRMLI@aol.com (specific)
WEBSITE: www.rmli.org

DESCRIPTION: Located in a historic 1890 LIRR freight station. Displays include photos, artifacts, HO gauge layout of Greenport terminal, operating tower (Bliss), outside "Jaws" snowplow, and 1927 LIRR wooden caboose. The Museum is chartered by the New York State Education Department, and is dedicated to historical artifacts pertaining to the growth of Long Island and its communities and industries.

SCHEDULE: Memorial Day weekend through Columbus Day weekend: weekends and holidays. Also, first weekend in December (Santa visit).

ADMISSION/FARE: Adults, $3; children 5-12, $1.50; under 5, free. Good at Riverhead site.

LOCOMOTIVES/ROLLING STOCK: LIRR Russell snowplow no. 83, "Jaws"; LIRR wood caboose no. 14.

SPECIAL EVENTS: Weekend prior to Labor Day, Rail Fest; first December weekend, Santa Visit.

NEARBY ATTRACTIONS: East End Seaport Museum, Historic Museums of Southold, Vineyards (over 20), charter fishing.

DIRECTIONS: From New York Route 25 in Greenport, go south two blocks on 4th St. to the museum, located at the tracks.

Photo courtesy of Railroad Museum of Long Island.

DIRECTIONS: Interstate 90 to exit 48A. Fifteen miles north on NY 77 and NY 63 to Medina, one block west of Main St. at the railroad tracks.

Coupon available, see insert.
See ad on page A-9.

Mt. Pleasant, NY

Catskill Mountain Railroad

Train ride
Standard gauge

SITE ADDRESS: Route 28 Mt. Pleasant, NY
MAILING ADDRESS: PO Box 46 Shokan, NY 12481
TELEPHONE: (845) 688-7400
E-MAIL: spiegler@netstep.com
WEBSITE: www.catskillmtrailroad.com

DESCRIPTION: The railroad offers a six-mile round trip on the Esopus Creek Shuttle and a 14-mile round trip on the Scenic Train through the Catskill Mountains with fisits to Phoenicia and the Empire State Railway Museum.

SCHEDULE: Esopus: May 27 to September 4, weekends and holidays, 11 a.m. to 5 p.m. Scenic: May 27 to October 29, weekends and holidays; 11:30 a.m., 1:30, and 3:30 p.m.

ADMISSION/FARE: Esopus Creek Shuttle: adults, one way $5, round trip $8; children 4-11, y ride $5; children under 4, free. Scenic Train: adults, $12; children 4-11, $8; under 4, free.

LOCOMOTIVES/ROLLING STOCK: No. 1, "The Duck," 1942 Davenport 38-ton diesel-chanical, former US Air Force; no. 2, "The Goat," H.K. Porter 50-ton diesel-electric, mer US Navy; 1922 Lackawanna coach; no. 2361, 1952 Alco RS-1, former Wisconsin tral (Soo Line).

SPECIAL EVENTS: There is no better way to experience the spectacular colors in the skills than with a ride on the Scenic Train's Leaf Peeper Special.

NEARBY ATTRACTIONS: World's largest kaleidoscope, tubing the Esopus Creek, museums, ts activities, restaurants, lodging, campgrounds, state parks, and scenic sites.

DIRECTIONS: New York State Thruway, exit 19 (Kingston). Travel west 22 miles on Route 28 e railroad depot in Mt. Pleasant.

courtesy of John Prestopino.
on available, see insert.

Hyde Park, NY

Hudson Valley Railroad Society/Railroad Station

Museum, Model train layout
HO and N gauge

SITE ADDRESS: 34 River Rd. Hyde Park, NY 12538
MAILING ADDRESS: PO Box 135 Hyde Park, NY 1253
TELEPHONE: (845) 229-2338
E-MAIL: revaul@aol.com
WEBSITE: www.hydeparkstation.com or hvrrs.org

DESCRIPTION: Operating displays and layouts that relate to the history of the Roosevelt and Vanderbilt connection are housed in a restoration of a 1914 railroad station by a railroad club.

SCHEDULE: Year-round: Monday, 7 to 10 p.m.; mid-June to mid-September: weekends, 11 a.m. to 5 p.m.; Memorial Day and July 4.

ADMISSION/FARE: Free; donations welcome.

NEARBY ATTRACTIONS: Franklin Delano Roosevelt home and library, Vanderbilt mansion, Old Rhinebeck Aerodome, bicycle tours, hiking trails, golf course, river tours, and Mills Norrie State Park.

DIRECTIONS: West on W Market St. from US9 (historic signs posted on US9) to bottom of hill. The station is in Town Park on right.

Photo courtesy of Larry Laliberte.

Kingston, NY

Trolley Museum of New York

EDITOR'S CHOICE

Museum, Trolley ride

ADDRESS: 89 E Strand Kingston, NY 12401
TELEPHONE: (845) 331-3399
E-MAIL: info@tmny.org
WEBSITE: www.tmny.org

DESCRIPTION: Established in 1955, the museum was moved to its present location in 1983, becoming part of the Kingston Heritage Area. A 2.5-mile, 40-minute round trip takes passengers from the foot of Broadway to Kingston Point, with stops at the museum in both directions. A gas-powered railcar operates on private right-of-way and in-street trackage along Rondout Creek to the Hudson River over part of the former Ulster & Delaware Railroad main line. An exhibit hall features trolley exhibits and a theater.

SCHEDULE: Memorial weekend to Columbus Day: 12 to 5 p.m.; last ride: 4:10; charters available.

ADMISSION/FARE: Adults, $4; seniors and children, $3.

LOCOMOTIVES/ROLLING STOCK: 11 trolleys; eight rapid transit cars; Whitcomb diesel-electric; Brill model 55 interurban.

SPECIAL EVENTS: Mother's Day (moms ride free); Father's Day (dads ride free); first weekend of December, Santa Days.

NEARBY ATTRACTIONS: Catskill Mountain Railroad, Empire State Railroad Museum, Hudson River Maritime Museum, Senate House, Catskill Mountains, Kingston Heritage Area Visitors Center, and Hudson River Cruises.

DIRECTIONS: Located in the historic Rondout Waterfront area of Downtown Kingston. For directions, see the map on their webpage or call Kingston Tourism at (800) 331-1518.

Photo courtesy of Evan Jennings.
Coupon available, see insert.

Marcellus, NY

Martisco Station Museum
Museum

ADDRESS: Martisco Rd., PO Box 229 Marcellus, NY 13108
TELEPHONE: (315) 673-1749

DESCRIPTION: A restored former New York Central rail station houses items pertaining to local railroads on two floors. The brick structure was constructed in 1870 in the Victorian style. The first story replicates a small town railroad station and the second floor contains many railroad exhibits.

SCHEDULE: Memorial Day Weekend through October 15: Sunday, 2 to 5 p.m.

ADMISSION/FARE: Donations accepted.

DIRECTIONS: Route 174, between Camillus and Marcellus.

Photo courtesy of Edwin Past.

Maybrook, NY

Maybrook Railroad Historical Society Museum
Display

ADDRESS: 101 Main St. (rear of library), PO Box 105 Maybrook, NY 12543
TELEPHONE: (845) 427-2591
E-MAIL: petzok@frontiernet.net

DESCRIPTION: The museum offers rail photographs and memorabilia.

SCHEDULE: April to October: weeken 1 to 4 p.m.; also by appointment.

ADMISSION/FARE: Free.

LOCOMOTIVES/ROLLING STOCK: Caboose no. C512.

NEARBY ATTRACTIONS: Museum Village in Monroe, New York; O&W Railroad Histo Society archives in Middletown; Erie depot and hiking trail in Chester, New York.

DIRECTIONS: I-84 to exit 5, two miles south on Route 208. At the rear of Maybrool

---

Medina, NY

Medina Railroad Museum
Train ride, Museum

ADDRESS: 530 West Ave., PO Box 136 Medina, NY 14103
TELEPHONE: (585) 798-6106
E-MAIL: office@railroadmuseum.net
WEBSITE: www.railroadmuseum.net

DESCRIPTION: One of the largest fr museums in New York has an abur collection of railroad artifacts and and a huge HO scale layout. The m offers seasonal 34-mile round-trip the scenic Erie Canal Heritage Cor 1947 Budd passenger coaches be Road Railroad Alco diesel.

SCHEDULE: Year-round: Tuesday 11 a.m. to 5 p.m.

ADMISSION/FARE: Adults, $5; seniors, $4; children 3-15, $3.

SPECIAL EVENTS: October weekends, fall foliage excursions; December, S

NEARBY ATTRACTIONS: Six Flags Darien Lake, Niagara Falls, and Rocheste

New York, NY
Station at Citigroup Center
Display, Model train layout
O, S, and HO scale

SITE ADDRESS: 153 E 53rd St. (atrium) New York, NY 10022
MAILING ADDRESS: Dunham Studios, PO Box 117 Pottersville, NY 12860
TELEPHONE: (212) 559-5350
E-MAIL: clarke@dunhamstudios.com
WEBSITE: www.dunhamstudios.com

DESCRIPTION: Holiday exhibit sponsored by Citigroup and Boston Properties.

SCHEDULE: Thanksgiving to New Year's: Monday to Saturday, 10 a.m. to 6 p.m.; Sunday, 12 to 5 p.m.

ADMISSION/FARE: Free.

NEARBY ATTRACTIONS: Grand Central Terminal.

DIRECTIONS: 53rd & Lexington Ave., NYC. Served by E, F, & 6 trains.

Photo courtesy of Clarke Dunham/Dunham Studios.

North Creek, NY
North Creek Railway Depot Museum
Museum, Model train layout

ADDRESS: 5 Railroad Pl., PO Box 156 North Creek, NY 12853
TELEPHONE: (518) 251-5842
E-MAIL: northcreekraildepot@frontier.net
WEBSITE: www.northcreekraildepot.org

DESCRIPTION: Railway Museum and Owens House Gallery.

SCHEDULE: Museum hours: Tuesday through Saturday, 12 p.m. to 4 p.m., Sunday through Monday, 12 p.m. to 2 p.m. Gallery hours: Tuesday through Saturday, 11 a.m. to 4 p.m.

ADMISSION/FARE: No charge.

NEARBY ATTRACTIONS: Upper Hudson River Railroad Tourist Train.

North Creek, NY

Upper Hudson River Railroad

Train ride, Museum

ADDRESS: 3 Railroad Pl. Box 424 North Creek, NY 12853
TELEPHONE: (518) 251-5334
WEBSITE: www.UpperHudsonRiverRR.com

DESCRIPTION: Scenic trains run seasonally and offer a view of the Adirondack Mountains and the Hudson River. The Upper Hudson River has several rail coaches to choose from, all of which have been restored in an effort to preserve the important historic era.

SCHEDULE: May 28 to 30, Memorial Day weekend, 1 p.m.; June 4 to 12, 18, and 19, 1 p.m.; Mother's Day: mothers free; Father's Day: fathers free; June 25 to September 4, Monday to Saturday, 10 a.m. and 1 p.m; Sunday 1 p.m.; September 7 to October 7, daily, 10 a.m. and 1 p.m.

ADMISSION/FARE: Adults, $15; seniors 60+, $14; children 3-11, $10.

LOCOMOTIVES/ROLLING STOCK: Alco RS-36 no. 5019, Alco S-1 no. 5.

SPECIAL EVENTS: July and August: Payroll Robbery train, Tuesday and Friday, 1 p.m.; Fun with Mike, Wednesday, 10 a.m. and 1 p.m.; Tunes Trains: Thursday, 4:30; August 6: Race the Train Runners, ride train to Riparius and race back to North Creek; proceeds go to Johnsburg Dollars for Scholars; October 8 and 9, 10 a.m., 1, 4 p.m.; October 29 and 30, 10 a.m.: costumes welcome, treats, and pumpkins for all the kids, 1 p.m.; Haunted Payroll robbery; December 17, 28, and 29: Winter Holiday trains with stories and refreshments.

NEARBY ATTRACTIONS: North Creek Depot Museum.

North Tonawanda, NY

Niagara Frontier Railroad Museum

Museum

SITE ADDRESS: 111 Oliver St. N Tonawanda, NY 14120
MAILING ADDRESS: Niagara Frontier Chapter, NRHS, PO Box 136 Hamburg, NY 14075-0136
TELEPHONE: (716) 694-9588
WEBSITE: www.nfcnrhs.com

DESCRIPTION: Railroad station with displays and industrial locos and two cabooses (Erie and New York Central). Special tours by appointment. Housed in the historic Erie Railroad Freight Depot (originally built in 1922), the museum contains various railroad artifacts which celebrate the rich heritage of railroading in the Niagara Frontier Region.

SCHEDULE: Tuesday and Saturday, 10 a.m. to 3 p.m. By appointment, (716) 692-6265.

LOCOMOTIVES/ROLLING STOCK: 50-ton center cab CLC industrial, 35-ton Plymouth industrial, Erie and NYC caboose.

Bullthistle Model Railroad Society and Museum

Museum, Model train layout
Multiple gauges

ADDRESS: 33 Rexford St. NY SR23 Norwich, NY 13815
TELEPHONE: (607) 334-4166
E-MAIL: eled@frontiernet.net

DESCRIPTION: Museum has display of the O&W Railroad Heritage of Norwich, NY. Operating exhibits include N, HO, 027, O, and S gauge layouts. Static displays show a wide range of toy and model railroad equipment.

SCHEDULE: Saturday and Sunday, 1 to 4 p.m.; business meeting 3rd Wednesday; toy train meeting Sunday after Thanksgiving.

ADMISSION/FARE: Donations accepted.

SPECIAL EVENTS: June, Railroad Day; Sunday after Thanksgiving, toy train meeting.

NEARBY ATTRACTIONS: Northeast Classic Car Museum.

DIRECTIONS: Museum on NY Route 23, East of Junction of NY 12 & NY 23.

Photo courtesy of Eric Robb.

Old Forge, Utica, Thendara, Saranac Lake, Lake Placid, NY

Adirondack Scenic Railroad

Train ride, Dinner train
Standard gauge

ADDRESS: PO Box 84 Thendara, NY 13472
TELEPHONE: (315) 369-6290, (315) 724-0700, or (518) 891-3238
WEBSITE: www.adirondackrr.com

DESCRIPTION: The Adirondack Scenic Railroad offers three separate rides: Utica to Old Forge (50 miles); Old Forge (Thendara) round-trip local (10 miles); Lake Placid to Saranac Lake (10 miles).

SCHEDULE: Spring, summer, and fall, schedules and admission vary. Refer to brochure or website for more information.

LOCOMOTIVES/ROLLING STOCK: Twenty-seven passenger cars (cafe, open air, baggage, coaches, of mostly Canadian origin–CNR or CPR). Locomotives: two F7s, one F10, one RS3, one C420, one C424, and one SW1.

NEARBY ATTRACTIONS: Scenic Adirondack Park (six million acres), Adirondack Mountains (peaks over 5,000 feet), lakes, rivers, fishing, canoeing, restaurants.

Phoenicia, NY

Empire State Railway Museum

Display, Model train layout

ADDRESS: 70 Lower High St., PO Box 455 Phoenicia, NY 12464
TELEPHONE: (845) 688-7501
WEBSITE: www.esrm.com

DESCRIPTION: The restored museum, located in the former 1899 Ulster & Delaware Railroad Station, publishes the *Telegraph Dispatch*, and serves as terminal for the Catskill Mountain Railroads scenic rail ride. Volunteers work to bring alive the history of the Catskill Mountain Railroads.

SCHEDULE: Memorial to Columbus Day: weekends and holidays, 11 a.m. to 4 p.m.

ADMISSION/FARE: Museum (suggested donation): adults, $3; seniors and students, $2; children under 12, $1; families, $5. With scenic round-trip CHRR rail tickets sold separately here: adults, $12; children 4-12, $8; children under 4, free.

LOCOMOTIVES/ROLLING STOCK: No. 23, a 1910 Alco 2-8-0 that once belonged to the Lake Superior & Ishpeming, under restoration; 1920 D&H dining car "Lion Gardner;" 1926 CV autocarrier; 1920 B&M railway post office car.

SPECIAL EVENTS: Photo exhibit, lectures, slide shows, Santa Claus Special.

NEARBY ATTRACTIONS: Catskill Mountain Railroad, kayaking, tubing, hiking, campgrounds, state parks, and restaurants.

DIRECTIONS: New York State Thruway, exit 19 (Kingston). Route 28 west 23 miles (3 miles or first right turn past Mt. Pleasant Station) on to Lower High St.

Riverhead, NY

Railroad Museum of Long Island, Riverhead

Museum, Display
Standard gauge and 16"

SITE ADDRESS: 416 Griffing Ave. Riverhead, NY 11944
MAILING ADDRESS: PO Box 726 Greenport, NY 11944
TELEPHONE: (631) 727-7920
E-MAIL: info@rmli.org (general) or secretaryrmli@aol.com (direct answer)
WEBSITE: www.rmli.org

DESCRIPTION: The museum displays three steam locomotives, eight rail cars, two speeders, conducts a miniature (16" gauge) 1964-65 World's Fair train ride around the site, and has a gift shop. The Riverhead restoration site is located at the junction of the North and South forks of Long Island, in a former lumber yard opposite the Riverhead Long Island Rail Road station.

SCHEDULE: Year-round: Saturday, 10 a.m. to 4 p.m.; Memorial Day to Columbus weekend: weekends and holidays, 10 a.m. to 4 p.m.

ADMISSION/FARE: Adults, $3; children 5-12, $1.50; children under 5, free. Good at Greenport site same day.

LOCOMOTIVES/ROLLING STOCK: Locomotives: LIRR G5s no. 39 (under restoration); LIRR RS3 no. 1556; Defiance Coal Co. 0-4-0 no. 1. Railroad cars: LIRR T62, double-deck passenger car no. 200, the world's first all-aluminum car; LIRR caboose no. C-68; LIRR motor RPO no. 4209; LIRR baggage no. 7727; LIRR combine no. 1391; LIRR baggage-mail no. 7737; steam to diesel ceremonial passenger cars; Reading track car (speeder) ca. 1920; B&O track car.

SPECIAL EVENTS: Weekend before Labor Day, Railfest.

NEARBY ATTRACTIONS: Hallockville Museum Farm, aquarium, wineries.

DIRECTIONS: Long Island Expressway (I-495) exit 72 eastbound, go four miles east on New York Route 25 to Griffing Ave., turn north, go three blocks to museum at tracks.

Photo courtesy of Railroad Museum of Long Island.

Roscoe, NY

Roscoe O&W Railway Museum

Museum

ADDRESS: Historic Depot St., 7 Railroad Ave., PO Box 305 Roscoe, NY 12776
TELEPHONE: (607) 498-5500
E-MAIL: wilsip@wpe.com or oandw@intergate.com
WEBSITE: www.nyow.org/museum.html

DESCRIPTION: This museum was established in 1984 under the charter of the Ontario & Western Railway Historical Society in a former Erie Railroad caboose. The museum complex consists of an Erie Hack restored O&W caboose, watchman's shanties, the O&W station motif building, and Beaverkill Trout Car Museum. The museum contains displays of O&W memorabilia and other railroadiana, as well as local history displays that show the impact of the O&W on community life.

SCHEDULE: Memorial weekend to Columbus Day: Saturday and Sunday, 11 a.m. to 3 p.m.

ADMISSION/FARE: Donations welcomed.

SPECIAL EVENTS: July 8, The O&W Penny Social; July 15 and 16, 10 a.m. to 4 p.m., 22nd Annual O&W Railway Festival; September 16, Annual Dinner.

Rush, NY

Rochester & Genesee Valley Railroad Museum **EDITOR'S CHOICE**

Train ride, Museum, Display
Standard gauge

SITE ADDRESS: 282 Rush-Scottsville Rd. Rush, NY 14626
MAILING ADDRESS: PO Box 23326 Rochester, NY 14692
TELEPHONE: (585) 533-1431
WEBSITE: www.rgvrrm.org

DESCRIPTION: The museum, housed in a restored 1909 Erie Railroad station, displays railroad artifacts from western New York. A number of railroad cars and diesel locomotives are open for display on outdoor tracks. Tours and track car rides are available.

SCHEDULE: May to October: Sunday, 11 am. to 5 p.m.; July to August: Saturday, 11 a.m. to 5 p.m.; other times by appointment.

ADMISSION/FARE: Adults, $6; seniors, $5; children 3-15, $4.

LOCOMOTIVES/ROLLING STOCK: 1946 GE 80-ton diesel, former Eastman Kodak; 1953 Alco RS-3, former Lehigh Valley; 1953 Alco S4, former Nickel Plate; 1941 GE 45-tonner, former Rochester Gas & Electric; Fairbanks-Morse H12-44, former US Army; caboose, former Erie C254; caboose, former Penn Central 18526.

SPECIAL EVENTS: Mid-August, Diesel Days.

NEARBY ATTRACTIONS: Strong Museum, George Eastman House, Genesee Country Museum, and New York Museum of Transportation.

DIRECTIONS: The depot is located on Route 251, 1 mile west of E River Rd.

Photo courtesy of Christopher R. Hauf.

Salamanca, NY
Salamanca Rail Museum
Museum

ADDRESS: 170 Main St. Salamanca, NY 14779
TELEPHONE: (716) 945-3133
E-MAIL: salarail@localnet.com

DESCRIPTION: Fully restored BR&P depot and freight house. Artifacts and photos tell the history of railroads in western New York and Pennsylvania. The museum grounds offer the permanent display of a boxcar, crew camp car, and two cabooses.

SCHEDULE: April to December: Monday to Saturday, 10 a.m. to 5 p.m.; Sunday, 12 to 5 p.m.; closed Mondays in April and October to December.

LOCOMOTIVES/ROLLING STOCK: B&O caboose; P&WV caboose; Erie crane crew car; Conrail boxcar; Jordan spreader; DL&W electric commuter coach.

NEARBY ATTRACTIONS: Allegany State Park, Seneca Iroquois National Museum, Holiday Valley Summer-Winter Resort, Chautauqua Institution, casino, and antique mall.

DIRECTIONS: Downtown Salamanca on New York Route 17/US I-86, Route 219.

Utica, NY

Utica & Mohawk Valley Chapter, NRHS

Display

SITE ADDRESS: Union Station 321 Main St. Utica, NY 13501
MAILING ADDRESS: PO Box 257 Whitesboro, NY 13492
TELEPHONE: (315) 787-8199

DESCRIPTION: There are archives and a display at the 1914 Union Station (Adirondack Scenic Railroad and Amtrak), with a Children's Museum next door. A brochure with the history of the station and self-guided tour of the "Williamsburg of Railroading" is available with SASE.

SCHEDULE: Union Station is open daily, 24 hours each day. Archives open by appointment. For Children's Museum hours, call (315) 724-6129.

ADMISSION/FARE: Free, except for Children's Museum interior exhibits.

LOCOMOTIVES/ROLLING STOCK: New York Central Alco-built 0-6-0 6721; Adirondack Railway Alco RSC2 no 25; Santa Fe Budd-built dining car no. 1479; Pennsylvania Railroad Altoona Shops-built cabin car 477594.

SPECIAL EVENTS: Check website for full listing.

NEARBY ATTRACTIONS: Adirondack Scenic, CSX, MA&N, and NYS&W Railroads; Erie Canal Village (2' gauge train with Davenport 0-4-0 side tanker); Munson-Williams-Proctor Arts Institute; Saranac Brewery; Fort Stanwix National Monument; Adirondack Park; and Cooperstown.

DIRECTIONS: One mile south of New York Thruway (I-90), exit 31 (Utica); follow signs for downtown Utica and Rail/Bus Station.

Photo courtesy of Doug Preston.
See ad on inside back cover.

TRAVEL TIP: *Caboose rides*

Who hasn't wanted to go for a ride in a little red caboose? Many tourist railroads and museums offer that opportunity, either on regularly scheduled trains or during special events. Some lines even offer the chance to rent a caboose for exclusive use during a trip. Check the offerings at the lines you'd like to visit; you might just get your chance.

New York Museum of Transportation

Train ride, Museum, Model train layout
Standard gauge
Radio frequency: 160.440

ADDRESS: 6393 E River Rd., PO Box 136 West Henrietta, NY 14586
TELEPHONE: (585) 533-1113
E-MAIL: info@nytmuseum.org
WEBSITE: www.nymtmuseum.org

DESCRIPTION: The site includes trolleys, rail and road vehicles, artifacts and exhibits, an 11' x 21' operating HO model railroad, and a video/photo gallery. A 2-mile track car ride connects with Rochester & Genesee Valley Railroad Museum, departing every half hour.

SCHEDULE: Museum: year-round, Sunday, 11 a.m. to 5 p.m. July 4 to Labor Day, also open on Saturdays. Weekday group visits by appointment. Track car ride operates May through October, weather permitting.

ADMISSION/FARE: Adults, $6; seniors, $5; students 3-15, $4. Includes entry to NYMT, Rochester & Genesee Valley Railroad Museum, and ride. Lower rates November through April.

LOCOMOTIVES/ROLLING STOCK: Rochester & Eastern interurban car no. 157; North Texas Traction interurban car no. 409; P&W cars nos. 161 and 168; Elmira, Corning & Waverly no. 107; Philadelphia snow sweeper no. C-130; Rochester Railway no. 437; Batavia St. Railway no. 33; Alco 0-4-0 no. 47; Genesee & Wyoming caboose no. 8; Rochester Railway no. 1402; more.

SPECIAL EVENTS: June, Caboose Day; July, Casey Jones Day; August, Diesel Days.

NEARBY ATTRACTIONS: Finger Lakes Region, Niagara Falls, Arcade & Attica Railroad, and Genesee Country Museum.

DIRECTIONS: I-90, exit 46, south three miles on I-390, exit 11. Route 251 west 1½ miles, right on E River Rd., one mile to museum entrance.

Photo courtesy of Charles Lowe.
Coupon available, see insert.

NORTH CAROLINA

Blowing Rock, NC

Tweetsie Railroad

Train ride, Museum
36" gauge

SITE ADDRESS: Hwy. 321 N Blowing Rock, NC 28605
MAILING ADDRESS: 300 Tweetsie Railroad Ln. Blowing Rock, NC 28605
TELEPHONE: (828) 264-9061
E-MAIL: info@tweetsie.com
WEBSITE: www.tweetsie.com

DESCRIPTION: Wild West theme park with ride on historic coal-fired narrow gauge locomotives. Admission includes amusement rides, live shows, deer park zoo, and many other attractions.

SCHEDULE: May 5 to 22: Friday to Sunday; May 26 to August 27: daily; August 31 to October 29: Friday to Sunday and Labor Day, 9 a.m. to 6 p.m.

ADMISSION/FARE: Adults, $27; children ages 3-12, $19.

LOCOMOTIVES/ROLLING STOCK: East Tennessee & Western North Carolina 4-6-0, built in 1917, and White Pass & Yukon 2-8-2 no. 190, built in 1943.

SPECIAL EVENTS: Early June, Day Out With Thomas™; late summer, Railfan Weekend; October, Ghost Train Halloween Festival; more special events and details on website.

NEARBY ATTRACTIONS: Located in a popular resort and vacation area, with many nearby scenic attractions, state and national parks, and the Blue Ridge Pkwy.

DIRECTIONS: Hwy. 321 between Boone and Blowing Rock.

See ad on page A-25.

TRAVEL TIP: *Thomas the Tank Engine*

If you have a youngster at home, Thomas the Tank Engine visits many tourist railroads and museums each year. Thomas is a great way to introduce another generation to the excitement of railroading. Check your local PBS listings for shows, and then check your favorite railroad for a visit from Thomas.

Bonsal, NC

New Hope Valley Railway

Train ride, Museum
Standard gauge
Radio frequency: 160.425

SITE ADDRESS: 5121 Daisey St. Bonsal, NC 27562
MAILING ADDRESS: PO Box 40 New Hill, NC 27562
TELEPHONE: (919) 362-5416
EMAIL: info@nhvry.org
WEBSITE: www.nhvry.org

DESCRIPTION: Nine miles of historic, century-old railroad through the quiet woodlands of Chatham and Wake Counties.

SCHEDULE: May to November, first Sunday each month; first two December weekends. Trains run: 11 a.m., 12:15, 1:30, 2:45, and 4 p.m.

ADMISSION/FARE: Adults, $8; children, $6.

LOCOMOTIVES/ROLLING STOCK: 0-4-0 T no. 17; GE 45-ton no. 67; Whitcomb 45-ton no. 70; GE 80-ton no. 71; BLH 80-ton no. 75; GE 80-ton no. 1686; caboose no. 335; caboose no. 5228; caboose no. 308; GE 65-ton no. 399; GE 25-ton no. 10; assorted other cars and equipment.

SPECIAL EVENTS: October 28, evening, Halloween Train; Saturday and Sunday on the first two weekends in December, Santa Claus Trains.

NEARBY ATTRACTIONS: Jordan Lake State Park.

DIRECTIONS: Just off old US1, exit 89 on current US1, nine miles south of downtown Apex, NC. See website for specific directions from your area.

Photo courtesy of Timothy Telkamp.

Bryson City, NC

Great Smoky Mountains Railroad

Train ride, Dinner train
Standard gauge

ADDRESS: 225 GH Everett St., PO Box 1490 Bryson City, NC 28713
TELEPHONE: (800) 872-4681 or (828) 586-8811
EMAIL: info@gsmr.com
WEBSITE: www.gsmr.com

DESCRIPTION: Departures from quaint Dillsboro and Bryson City's historic depot, travel through scenic mountains. Whitewater rafting packages, gourmet dinner, and mystery theater trains.

SCHEDULE: Year-round; call or write for schedule and reservations.

ADMISSION/FARE: Starting at: adults, $28; children under 13, $14. Rates vary seasonally. Club car upgrade available.

LOCOMOTIVES/ROLLING STOCK: Former US Army 2-8-0 No. 1702; EMD GP7s nos. 711 and 777; and GP9s nos. 1751 and 1755.

SPECIAL EVENTS: Day out with Thomas™, Railfest, Little Engine That Could™, Fall leaf viewing trains, and Polar Express™.

NEARBY ATTRACTIONS: Great Smoky Mountains National Park, Biltmore Estate, Cherokee Indian Reservation, and whitewater rafting.

DIRECTIONS: From Asheville, I-40 west to exit 27 to US74 west. Exit 81 for Dillsboro, or exit 67 for Bryson City. From Atlanta, 85 to 441 North.

Bryson City, NC

Smoky Mountain Trains

Museum, Model train layout
O and S scale

ADDRESS: 100 Greenlee St., PO Box 2390 Bryson City, NC 28713
TELEPHONE: (866) 914-5200
WEBSITE: www.smokymountaintrains.com

DESCRIPTION: The collection of over 7,000 Lionel locomotives and cars dates back to 1918. There is also a 24' x 45' layout with over 450 locomotives and cars.

SCHEDULE: Monday to Saturday, 8:30 a.m. to 5:30 p.m.; closed Sunday, Thanksgiving, Christmas, and New Year's Day.

ADMISSION/FARE: Adults, $8; under 12, $5; under 3, free; discounts available.

NEARBY ATTRACTIONS: Great Smoky Mountains Railroad (scenic rides), Cherokee Indian Reservation, and Great Smoky Mountains National Park.

DIRECTIONS: From North Carolina State Hwy. 74, take exit 67 into downtown Bryson City. Next to the Great Smoky Mountains RR depot.

Photo courtesy of Ron Roman.

Charlotte Trolley, Inc.

Train ride, Museum
Standard gauge

ADDRESS: 2104 South Blvd. Charlotte, NC 28203
TELEPHONE: (704) 375-0850
WEBSITE: www.charlottetrolley.org

DESCRIPTION: Vintage trolley service through the center of Charlotte. Also available are educational programs, museum, and gift shop. Charlotte Trolley Car 85 is Charlotte's only original electric trolley car still in operation. The vintage trolley is preserved for educational purposes, neighborhood improvement, and economic development. In conjunction with restoring vintage electric streetcars, CTI has developed a museum devoted to the history of streetcars in the South.

SCHEDULE: Daily trolley service. Museum: Monday through Saturday, 9:30 a.m. to 5 p.m.; Sunday, 11 a.m. to 4:30 p.m.

ADMISSION/FARE: $1 each way; seniors and disabled, $0.50 each way; children 3 and under, free; all-day passes, $3.

LOCOMOTIVES/ROLLING STOCK: Car no. 85, 4-axle, 35-foot, double-ended, built by original operator, Southern Public Utilities Co.; 3 Gomaco 4-axle, double-ended "replica" trolleys.

NEARBY ATTRACTIONS: Restaurants, shops, galleries, tea house, antiques, convention center, Charlotte's cultural district.

DIRECTIONS: South 1 mile from town on South Blvd. at Atherton Mill.

Photo courtesy of Jim Lockman-Click.

National Railroad Museum and Hall of Fame

Museum

ADDRESS: 23 Hamlet Ave., PO Box 1583 Hamlet, NC 28345
TELEPHONE: (910) 582-2383
WEBSITE: www.nationalrrmuseum.tripod.com

DESCRIPTION: The museum aims to re-create the time when railroads were the main source of long-distance travel and passenger train service was at its zenith. The museum preserves railroad history and promotes that history in modern-day railroading with exhibits that include photographs and maps, displays, a model railroad layout, four pieces of rolling stock, and a gift shop.

Spencer, NC

North Carolina Transportation Museum at Historic Spencer Shops

Train ride, Museum

ADDRESS: 411 S Salisbury Ave., PO Box 165 Spencer, NC 28159
TELEPHONE: (877) NCTM-FUN or (704) 636-2889
E-MAIL: nctransportation@bellsouth.net
WEBSITE: www.nctrans.org

DESCRIPTION: A museum in Southern Railway's largest steam locomotive repair shop with 13 buildings dating back to the early 1900s. Site includes the largest preserved roundhouse in North America, with 37 stalls. Also offers a 25-minute narrated train tour of the site behind steam or diesel power; automobile museum; displays on aviation.

SCHEDULE: April to October: Monday to Saturday, 9 a.m. to 5 p.m.; Sunday, 1 to 5 p.m.; November to March: Tuesday to Saturday, 10 a.m. to 4 p.m.; Sunday 1 to 4 p.m.; closed New Year's Day, Veteran's Day, Thanksgiving Day, and Christmas holiday.

ADMISSION/FARE: Museum: free; train rides: adults, $5; children and seniors 60+, $4. Rates may vary for special events.

LOCOMOTIVES/ROLLING STOCK: Operating diesels: Southern Railway E8 no. 6900; SR FP7 no. 6133; Norfolk & Western GP9 no. 620; SR GP30 no. 2601. Operating steam: Graham County Railroad Shay no. 1925. Roundhouse features 25-30 locomotives, passenger cars, and freight cars on static display including Atlantic Coast Line E3 no. 501.

SPECIAL EVENTS: Easter weekend and weekend prior, Easter Bunny Express; first weekend in May, Rail Days; first two weekends in October, A Day Out with Thomas™; Halloween weekend, Haunted Roundhouse Tours; three weekends prior to Christmas, Santa Train.

NEARBY ATTRACTIONS: Dan Nicolas Park, Rowan Museum, Salisbury depot, various Civil War sites, and restaurants within two miles.

DIRECTIONS: I-85 to exit 79/Spencer (use exit 81 during construction). Follow brown museum signs to site.

Photo courtesy of North Carolina Transportation Museum.
Coupon available, see insert.

Wilmington, NC

Wilmington Railroad Museum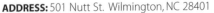

Museum, Display, Model train layout
HO and Lionel scales

ADDRESS: 501 Nutt St. Wilmington, NC 28401
TELEPHONE: (910) 763-2634
WEBSITE: www.wilmingtonrailroadmuseum.org

DESCRIPTION: The museum is housed in the 1900 ACL freight office building. Visitors may interact with an extensive artifact collection, model train layouts, children's play area, 1910 Baldwin steam locomotive, hobo display in a boxcar, and red caboose.

SCHEDULE: March 15 to October 14: Monday to Saturday, 10 a.m. to 5 p.m.; Sunday, 1 to 5 p.m. October 15 to March 14: Monday to Saturday, 10 a.m. to 4 p.m. Closed Thanksgiving, Christmas Eve, Christmas Day, New Year's Day, and Easter Sunday.

ADMISSION/FARE: Adults, $4.50; seniors 60+, $4; children 2-12, $2.50; members and children under 2, free; group rates available.

LOCOMOTIVES/ROLLING STOCK: Atlantic Coast line 4-6-0 steam locomotive no. 250; Seaboard Coast Line caboose no. 01036 as ACL no. 01983; 1963 RF&P boxcar no. 2379.

SPECIAL EVENTS: April, Azalea Festival; October, Model Railroad Show, Riverfest.

NEARBY ATTRACTIONS: Battleship U.S.S. North Carolina, Fort Fisher State Historical Site, beaches, and North Carolina Aquarium.

DIRECTIONS: I-40 east to Route 17 south to Water St. Turn right, 4 blocks to Red Cross St.

Photo courtesy of Herman Moeller.
Coupon available, see insert.

KEY TO SYMBOLS

♿ Handicapped accessible	🍴 Restaurant	🎨 Arts and crafts	arm Association of Railway Museums
P Parking	🪑 Picnic area	IMI Memberships available	TRAIN Tourist Railway Association, Inc.
P Bus/RV parking	Dining car	✉ Send S.A.S.E. for brochure	Amtrak service to nearby city
Gift, book, or museum shop	Excursions	NRHP National Register of Historic Places	VIA VIA service to nearby city
Refreshments	TOUR Guided tours	VISA MasterCard DISCOVER AMERICAN EXPRESS Card	Credit cards accepted

NORTH DAKOTA

Mandan, ND
Fort Lincoln Trolley
Trolley ride

North Dakota state map showing Minot, Mandan, and West Fargo.

ADDRESS: 29 Captain Leach Dr. Mandan, ND 58554
TELEPHONE: (701) 663-9018

DESCRIPTION: Trolley service runs 4.5 miles between Mandan and Ft. Lincoln State Park. The rolling stock includes a restored American Car Co. streetcar and an eight-bench open car.

SCHEDULE: Memorial Day through Labor Day: daily departures at 1, 2, 3, 4, and 5 p.m.

ADMISSION/FARE: Round trip fare, $5; children under 5, free.

LOCOMOTIVES/ROLLING STOCK: American Car Co. 32 passenger semi-convertible wood body trolley car.

NEARBY ATTRACTIONS: Fort Lincoln State Park, Lewis and Clark Riverboats, and Mandan Railroad Museum.

DIRECTIONS: I-94 to Hwy. 1806 to 3rd St. SE; east on 3rd St. SE about five blocks.

Photo courtesy of James Beck.

KEY TO SYMBOLS

♿ Handicapped accessible	🍴 Restaurant	🎨 Arts and crafts	arm Association of Railway Museums
P Parking	🪑 Picnic area	MI Memberships available	TRAIN Tourist Railway Association, Inc.
P Bus/RV parking	Dining car	✉ Send S.A.S.E. for brochure	AMTRAK Amtrak service to nearby city
Gift, book, or museum shop	Excursions	NRHP National Register of Historic Places	VIA VIA service to nearby city
Refreshments	TOUR Guided tours	VISA MasterCard DISCOVER AMERICAN EXPRESS Card	Credit cards accepted

Minot, ND

Magic City Express
Miniature/park train

ADDRESS: 129 Burdick Expressway E Minot, ND 58702
TELEPHONE: (701) 838-2205
E-MAIL: sassy@min.midco.net

DESCRIPTION: Old-time miniature train ride through the park and past the zoo.

SCHEDULE: May to August: Daily, 1 to 5 p.m., weather permitting.

ADMISSION/FARE: Adults, $2.50; 5 and under, free.

DIRECTIONS: Located in Roosevelt Park across from the swimming pool.

Minot, ND

Old Soo Depot Transportation Museum & Western History Research Center
Museum

SITE ADDRESS: 15 North Main Minot, ND 58701
MAILING ADDRESS: PO Box 2148 Minot, ND 58702
TELEPHONE: (701) 852-2234

DESCRIPTION: A museum and research center in a completely restored 1912 Soo Line Depot. The focuses is on transportation history of the American West, including GN, NP, Soo, Milwaukee Road, and Amtrak.

SCHEDULE: Open year-round.

ADMISSION/FARE: Donations accepted.

LOCOMOTIVES/ROLLING STOCK: Burlington Northern Santa Fe, Canadian Pacific, and Amtrak trains frequently operate beside or across from the building.

SPECIAL EVENTS: December, CP Holiday.

NEARBY ATTRACTIONS: Taube Art Museum, Railroad Museum of Minot, Charlie's Main Street Cafe, 10 North Main, and Dragon Delight.

DIRECTIONS: North end of Main St. in downtown Minot, along the main line of the Canadian Pacific and Burlington Northern Santa Fe Railroads.

Photo courtesy of Dennis Lutz, M.D.

Minot, ND

Railroad Museum of Minot

Museum

ADDRESS: 19 1st St. NE, PO Box 74 Minot, ND 58703
TELEPHONE: (701) 852-7091

DESCRIPTION: Photographs and memorabilia show the progression of the railroad.

SCHEDULE: Monday, Wednesday, and Friday, 10 a.m. to 12 p.m. and 1 to 4 p.m.

West Fargo, ND

Bonanzaville U.S.A.

Museum

SITE ADDRESS: 1351 Main Ave. W West Fargo, ND 58078
MAILING ADDRESS: PO Box 719 West Fargo, ND 58078
TELEPHONE: (701) 282-2822
E-MAIL: info@bonanzaville.com
WEBSITE: www.bonanzaville.com

DESCRIPTION: The museum includes two vintage train depots, 1883 Northern Pacific steam locomotive no. 684, among the last of the 4-4-0 steam engines left; a 1930s Pullman car, a caboose, and a 100-year-old velocipede.

SCHEDULE: Memorial to Labor Day: Monday through Saturday, 9 a.m. to 5 p.m.; Sunday, 12 to 5 p.m.

ADMISSION/FARE: Adults, $7; youth, $4.

LOCOMOTIVES/ROLLING STOCK: Northern Pacific steam locomotive no. 684; 1930s Pullman car; caboose; snowplow; velocipede.

SPECIAL EVENTS: July, Cart and Buggy Fest; August, Pioneer Days.

NEARBY ATTRACTIONS: Red River Zoo, Fargo Air Museum, and Heritage Center.

DIRECTIONS: I-94 in Fargo; located in West Fargo.

Photo courtesy of R. A. Young.

OHIO

Marblehead
Sandusky Elyria   Jefferson
Conneaut
Bedford
Bellevue
Findlay   Peninsula
Marion   Orrville
Dover
Dennison
Nelsonville
Cincinnati

Bellevue, OH

Mad River & NKP Railroad Museum

Museum

EDITOR'S CHOICE

SITE ADDRESS: 253 Southwest St.
Bellevue, OH 44811-1377
MAILING ADDRESS: 233 York St.
Bellevue, OH 44811-1377
TELEPHONE: (419) 483-2222
E-MAIL: madriver@onebellevue.com
WEBSITE: www.madrivermuseum.org

DESCRIPTION: The museum opened in 1976 to commemorate one of the earliest railroads that ran through Bellevue in 1839—the Mad River & Lake Erie Railroad. Henry Flagler, who built the Florida East Coast Railroad, once lived on the property where the museum is now located. The private collection of Ted & Sarah Church of Erie, PA is displayed in former troop sleepers 9210, 9211, and 9212, which were used by the US Army during World War II.

SCHEDULE: Memorial Day to Labor Day: daily, 12 to 4 p.m.; May, September, and October: weekends only.

ADMISSION/FARE: Adults 13+, $7; seniors, $6; children 4-12, $5; children under 4, free. Prices are subject to change.

LOCOMOTIVES/ROLLING STOCK: Nickel Plate Road Alco RSD12 no. 329; NKP EMD GP30 no. 900; Milwaukee Road FM H1244 no. 740; Wabash F7 diesel no. 671; PRR Railway Post Office car; NKP dynamometer car; three NKP cabooses; N&W caboose; troop sleeper car; refrigerator cars; four passenger cars, including the first dome car built; and various other cars and equipment.

SPECIAL EVENTS: Limited number of bus/rail tours throughout the year. Call for information. Guided tours, if scheduled in advance.

NEARBY ATTRACTIONS: Cedar Point Amusement Park, Sorrowful Mother Shrine, Seneca Caverns, Historic Lyme Village.

DIRECTIONS: Two blocks south of downtown. Follow the green signs.

Photo courtesy of George Leader.
Coupon available, see insert.

Cincinnati, OH

Cincinnati Railroad Club

Museum

ADDRESS: 1301 Western Ave., PO Box 14157 Cincinnati, OH 45250
TELEPHONE: (513) 651-7245
WEBSITE: www.cincinnatirrclub.org

DESCRIPTION: Located in a former Cincinnati Union Terminal (CUT) control tower. There are a few museum items.

SCHEDULE: Saturday, 10 a.m. to 5 p.m.

ADMISSION/FARE: Free; donations accepted.

NEARBY ATTRACTIONS: Bengals football, Cincinnati Reds baseball, zoo, Newport Aquarium, Kings Island Amusement Park.

DIRECTIONS: Take I-75 to exits 2A, 1H, or 1F; at Ezzard Charles Dr.

Photo courtesy of Dale W. Brown.

Conneaut, OH

Conneaut Railroad Museum

Museum

ADDRESS: 342 Depot St., PO Box 643 Conneaut, OH 44030
TELEPHONE: (440) 599-7878

DESCRIPTION: Displays of railroad memorabilia and an HO scale model railroad.

SCHEDULE: Memorial Day through Labor Day: daily, 12 to 5 p.m.

ADMISSION/FARE: Donations appreciated.

LOCOMOTIVES/ROLLING STOCK: Nickel Plate Road 2-8-4 No. 755. A 90-ton hopper car and a wooden caboose, both former Bessemer & Lake Erie.

NEARBY ATTRACTIONS: Lake Erie.

DIRECTIONS: In the old New York Central station at Depot and Mill Sts., north of US20 and I-90. Blue-and-white locomotive signs point the way to the museum.

Dennison, OH

Dennison Railroad Depot Museum
Museum, Model train layout

ADDRESS: 400 Center St., PO Box 11 Dennison, OH 44621
TELEPHONE: (740) 922-6776
E-MAIL: depot@tusco.net
WEBSITE: www.dennisondepot.org

DESCRIPTION: The museum, restaurant, and gift shop are housed in a restored 1873 Pennsylvania Railroad depot. There are train rides from May through December: all-day excursions, murder mysteries, fall foliage trips, Halloween rides, holiday trips, and Train Festival 2006.

SCHEDULE: Year-round, Tuesday to Saturday, 11 a.m. to 5 p.m.; Sunday, 11 a.m. to 3 p.m. Tours by appointment.

ADMISSION/FARE: Museum: adults, $3; seniors, $2.50; students, $1.75. Train rides: $7 to $100.

LOCOMOTIVES/ROLLING STOCK: See www.ohiocentralrr.com for rolling stock. On display: 1940s Thermos Bottle Vulcan engine; caboose; freight cars; Chesapeake & Ohio 2-8-4 steam locomotive no. 2700.

SPECIAL EVENTS: Third week of May, Railroad festival.

NEARBY ATTRACTIONS: Amish Country, Roscoe Village, Zoar and Schoennbrunn (Ohio Historical Society sites), Warthers Train Carvings, and Football Hall of Fame.

DIRECTIONS: Located halfway between Columbus, Ohio, and Pittsburgh, Pennsylvania, 18 miles east of I-77 and 36 miles north of I-70. At the junction of Routes 250, 36, and 800.

Photo courtesy of James J. Celuch.
Coupon available, see insert.

Dover, OH

Warther Carvings
Museum

ADDRESS: 331 Karl Ave. Dover, OH 44622
TELEPHONE: (330) 343-7513
E-MAIL: info@warthers.com
WEBSITE: www.warthers.com

DESCRIPTION: Carvings of ivory, ebony, and walnut depict the evolution of the steam engine. Ernest "Mooney" Warther felt that the steam engine was one of the most wonderful inventions of all time. His works of art depict the evolution of the steam engine in 64 carvings that are mechanically accurate and carved to a scale of $1/2$" to the foot.

SCHEDULE: Daily, 9 a.m. to 5 p.m. Closed Christmas, New Year's, Easter, and Thanksgiving.

ADMISSION/FARE: Adults, $9; students 6-17, $5.

NEARBY ATTRACTIONS: Gateway to Ohio's Amish Country.

DIRECTIONS: I-77 exit no. 83, east on Route 211, ¼ mile.

Photo courtesy of Warther Carvings.

Findlay, OH
Northwest Ohio Railroad Preservation, Inc.
Train ride, Museum, Model train layout
Standard and 15" gauge, HO scale

ADDRESS: 11600 CR99 Findlay, OH 45840-9601
TELEPHONE: (419) 423-2995
WEBSITE: www.nworrp.org

DESCRIPTION: This 1-mile ride is aboard the ¼ scale live steam Engine 901, a 2-6-2 prairie-style locomotive, with open-seat coaches. No. 901 was designed and built in the 1940s by the Israelite House of David, Benton Harbor, MI. Tours of a B&O caboose are available; HO model train layout and railroad gift shop inside museum building.

SCHEDULE: April to December, weekends; check website or call for dates and times.

ADMISSION/FARE: Train rides: $1 per passenger; additional charge for some special events.

LOCOMOTIVES/ROLLING STOCK: Static display of standard gauge B&O caboose C2157, Plymouth switcher, and wood boxcar. In 15" gauge Engine no. 901, four passenger coaches, diesel Engine no. 101, tank car, and coal car.

SPECIAL EVENTS: March 26, Flag City Train Show; September 9 and 10, Tracks to the Past; October, Pumpkin Train, Train of Terror & Haunted Engine House; December, North Pole Exp.

NEARBY ATTRACTIONS: Deshler (crossroads of CSX) and Fostoria (major arteries of CSX and NS) and Lima (last Berkshire no. 779 at Allen County Museum, Lincoln Park).

DIRECTIONS: NE corner of I-75, exit #161 and CR99 at the north end of Findlay.

Coupon available, see insert.

Jefferson, OH

AC&J Scenic Line Railway
Train ride
Standard gauge

ADDRESS: E Jefferson St., PO Box 517 Jefferson, OH 44047-0517
TELEPHONE: (440) 576-6346
E-MAIL: info@acjrscenic.net
WEBSITE: www.acjrscenic.net

DESCRIPTION: A 1-hour, 12-mile round trip over the last remaining portion of the New York Central's Ashtabula-to-Pittsburgh "High Grade" passenger line. Vintage passenger cars are pulled by a first generation diesel. An educational adventure for the whole family.

SCHEDULE: June 17 to October 29: Saturday and Sunday, departures at 1 and 3 p.m.; September after Labor Day weekend: Sunday only; no reservations.

ADMISSION/FARE: Adults, $9; seniors 60+, $8; children 3-12, $6; children under 3, free when not occupying a seat.

LOCOMOTIVES/ROLLING STOCK: Nickel Plate Road Alco S2 no. 107; Erie Alco S2 no. 518; NKP caboose no. 425; Erie coach no. 1022; Long Island coaches nos. 7133 and 7136; Erie Lackawanna baggage cars nos. 200 and 201.

SPECIAL EVENTS: July: Civil War Train Raid (variable dates, reservations suggested), departures Saturday, 1, 3, & 5 p.m.; Sunday, 1 & 3 p.m.; December 2 and 9: Santa on the train, departures 11 a.m., 1 & 3 p.m. Paid reservations required.

NEARBY ATTRACTIONS: Adjacent Jefferson Depot Village, Victorian Perambulator Museum, Geneva-on-the-Lake, and covered bridges.

DIRECTIONS: I-90 east/west exit Ohio 11 south, to Ohio 46 and south to Jefferson, left at second light onto E Jefferson St., two blocks to tracks. Or north on Route 11, exit 307 west to Jefferson, right on 46 to second light, right to tracks.

Coupon available, see insert.

Jefferson, OH

Jefferson Depot, Inc.
Museum

ADDRESS: 147 E Jefferson St., PO Box 22 Jefferson, OH 44047
TELEPHONE: (440) 576-0496 or (440) 858-2261
WEBSITE: http://members.tripod.com/jeffersonhome

DESCRIPTION: A restored 1872 Lake Shore & Michigan Southern Railroad station/museum features an 1838 one-room schoolhouse, 1845 post office, 1848 church, 1888 Victorian house, 1918 PRR caboose, circuit-rider barn, and more. Train rides are next door.

SCHEDULE: June through September: Sunday, 1 to 4 p.m. Group tours by appointment. Buses welcome.

ADMISSION/FARE: Suggested donation: Adults, $3 or more; children, free.

SPECIAL EVENTS: Third June weekend, Strawberry Festival and Craft Bazaar; third July weekend, Early America re-enactments.

NEARBY ATTRACTIONS: Tour 19th century AG&J Scenic Train Rides next door, Jefferson Depot Village, campgrounds, and Pymatuning State Park.

DIRECTIONS: From I-90, south on I-11 to SR46 south to E Jefferson St. From I-11, north to SR307 west to SR46 north, to E Jefferson St.

Marblehead, OH

Train-O-Rama

Display, Model train layout
All gauges

ADDRESS: 6732 E Harbor Rd. Route 163 East Marblehead, OH 43440
TELEPHONE: (419) 734-5856
E-MAIL: mail@trainorama.com
WEBSITE: www.trainorama.com

DESCRIPTION: Train-O-Rama is Ohio's largest operating multi-gauge train layout. It is also a gift/hobby store.

SCHEDULE: Year-round: Monday to Saturday, 11 a.m. to 5 p.m. (in summer, 10 a.m. to 5 p.m.); Sunday, 1 to 5 p.m.

ADMISSION/FARE: Adults, $5; seniors, $4; children 4-11, $3.

NEARBY ATTRACTIONS: Mad River RR Museum in Bellevue, OH.

DIRECTIONS: Route 2 to Route 269 north to Route 163 east (E Harbor Rd.).

Coupon available, see insert.

Marion, OH

Marion Union Station Association

Museum, Display, Model train layout

ADDRESS: 532 W Center St. Marion, OH 43302-3533
TELEPHONE: (740) 383-3768
E-MAIL: unionstation@marion.net

DESCRIPTION: The station is a museum and model railroader club with a fully-restored tower. With more than 100 trains passing Union Station every day, the museum also showcases an impressive collection of memorabilia.

SCHEDULE: Monday through Friday, 10 a.m. to 2 p.m.; Saturday and Sunday, after church. The model railroad club is open Sundays only, to 5 p.m.

ADMISSION/FARE: Donations appreciated.

LOCOMOTIVES/ROLLING STOCK: Erie/EL caboose no. C-306; 3-ton Plymouth model TLC; interlocking tower.

SPECIAL EVENTS: First Sunday in October, chicken barbecue; First Saturday in December, model train/hobby show.

NEARBY ATTRACTIONS: President Harding's homes and memorial, two Veterans' Parks, and the Popcorn Museum.

DIRECTIONS: Route 309 on west side of Marion (between railroad tracks). Go through town, heading west on Center St.

Photo courtesy of Matt Miller.

Nelsonville, OH

Hocking Valley Scenic Railway

Train ride, Museum, Display
Standard gauge

SITE ADDRESS: Intersection of US Route 33 and Hocking Pkwy. (Fulton St.), behind the Rocky Boots Outlet Nelsonville, OH 45764
MAILING ADDRESS: PO Box 427 Nelsonville, OH 45764
TELEPHONE: (800) 967-7834 or (614) 470-1300
WEBSITE: www.hvsry.org

DESCRIPTION: Indoor and outdoor museum offers 14- and 22-mile diesel-powered round trips aboard vintage equipment. The route between Nelsonville and Logan was once a part of the original Hocking Valley Railway's Athens Branch. It was eventually merged into the Chesapeake & Ohio Railway in 1930. Since 1985, the HVSR has offered scenic rides.

SCHEDULE: Memorial Day weekend to first November weekend: 12 and 2:30 p.m.; last November weekend, first three weeks of December: Santa specials, 11 a.m. and 2 p.m.

ADMISSION/FARE: Logan 22-mile round trip: adults, $14; students, $11; children3-12, $9. Haydenville 14-mile round trip: adults, $10; students, $8; children3-12, $7. Santa Train: adults, $14; students, $12; children 3-12, $10.

LOCOMOTIVES/ROLLING STOCK: GE 45-ton industrial 7318; EMD GP7 5833; Baldwin-Lima-Hamilton RS4TC 4005; 65-ton Whitcomb 8122; three RI commuter cars, "City of Logan," "City of Nelsonville," and "Village of Haydenville"; B&O combine "City of Athens"; two open air cars; more.

SPECIAL EVENTS: Saturday of Labor Day weekend, Easter egg hunt, all-caboose train with a photo run; Saturday before Easter, Easter train special; June and September, two Train Robbery specials; November to December, Santa specials; call or check website for more.

NEARBY ATTRACTIONS: Rock Boot Factory Outlet, Victorian Square, Stuart's Opera House, and Famous Dew Hotel.

DIRECTIONS: I-70 or I-270, exit US33 (Lancaster) south to Nelsonville, right at second light.

Photo courtesy of Dwight Jones.
Coupon available, see insert.

Orrville, OH
Orrville Railroad Heritage Society
Train ride, Museum, Display

ADDRESS: 145 Depot St., PO Box 11 Orrville, OH 44667
TELEPHONE: (330) 683-2426
WEBSITE: www.orrvillerailroad.com

DESCRIPTION: Located at the junction of two former Pennsylvania Railroad lines, 50- to 120-mile excursions run on the Wheeling & Lake Erie Railway, the Ohio Central Railroad System, and other railroads with Amtrak specials. Some excursions powered by steam. Approximately 10 pieces of rolling stock have been restored by volunteers. The ORHS also owns the interlocking tower that controlled the junction.

SCHEDULE: Depot: May to October: Saturday, 10 a.m. to 4 p.m. Trips vary; send for information. Ticket office: March 1 to November 30: Monday, Tuesday, Thursday, and Friday, 12 to 4 p.m. or by appointment.

ADMISSION/FARE: Depot tours: no charge; mainline trips: fares vary per trip.

LOCOMOTIVES/ROLLING STOCK: Ex-New Haven GP9; Pennsylvania Railroad N5C caboose; five Budd passenger coaches; ex-Amtrak baggage car; privately owned caboose and passenger cars; switch block tower.

SPECIAL EVENTS: 2nd June weekend, Depot Days; weekend after Thanksgiving, Open House.

NEARBY ATTRACTIONS: Amish Country, Rubbermaid store, Smucker Jam and Jelly store.

DIRECTIONS: Twelve miles south of I-76; 3 miles north of Route 30, on Route 57.

Photo courtesy of Robert Cutting.

Peninsula, OH
Cuyahoga Valley Scenic Railroad
Train ride

EDITOR'S CHOICE

ADDRESS: 1664 Main St., PO Box 158 Peninsula, OH 44264
TELEPHONE: (800) 468-4070 x3034 or (330) 657-1915
WEBSITE: www.cvsr.com

DESCRIPTION: The Scenic Limited is a 1³/₄-hour round-trip excursion to the historic village of Peninsula, through Cuyahoga Valley National Park. Our longer (6½-hour round-trip) excursions go through the park to downtown Akron. Spend the day at Hale Farm and Village or Stan Hywet Hall and Gardens, or visit Quaker Square or the National Inventors Hall of Fame. New Excursions to Canton now available.

SCHEDULE: Akron: June to August and October, weekends and Thursdays, 10 a.m.; Scenic Limited: June to December, weekends; June to August and October, also Wednesday to Friday; train departs at 10:15 a.m. and 1 p.m.

ADMISSION/FARE: Fares vary by excursion and event.

LOCOMOTIVES/ROLLING STOCK: FPA4 nos. 14, 15, 800, 6767; 44-ton switcher no. 21; C420 no. 365; RS18 road/switcher no. 1822; more.

SPECIAL EVENTS: Wine Tasting Train; monthly, Murder Mystery Train; Thomas the Tank Engine™; November and December, Polar Express™.

NEARBY ATTRACTIONS: Hale Farm and Village, Cuyahoga Valley National Park, Village of Peninsula, Pro Football Hall of Fame, Rock and Roll Hall of Fame, Stan Hywet Hall & Gardens, and Akron Zoo.

DIRECTIONS: Depots are located in Independence, Peninsula, Akron, and Canton, OH. Specific directions will be provided at time of reservations.

Photo courtesy of Larry Blanchard.

Sandusky, OH

Cedar Point & Lake Erie Railroad

Train ride

ADDRESS: 1 Cedar Point Dr. Sandusky, OH 44870
TELEPHONE: (419) 627-2350
E-MAIL: BEdwards@cedarpoint.com
WEBSITE: www.cedarpoint.com

DESCRIPTION: The Cedar Point and Lake Erie (CP&LE) railroad is a 15-minute train ride that covers a 2-mile trip around the Frontiertown section of Cedar Point Amusement Park.

SCHEDULE: Please see website for operating schedule and admission costs.

LOCOMOTIVES/ROLLING STOCK: "Myron H.," a 1922 Vulcan 0-4-0 rebuilt as 2-4-0; "Albert," a 1910 Davenport 2-6-0; "George R.," a 1942 H. K. Porter Co. 0-4-0 rebuilt as 2-4-0; "Jennie K.," a 1909 H. K. Porter Co. 0-4-0 rebuilt as a 2-4-0; "Judy K.," a Vulcan 0-4-0 rebuilt as 2-4-0.

NEARBY ATTRACTIONS: Train-O-Rama, Port Clinton, OH.

DIRECTIONS: Please see website for directions.

Photo courtesy of Dan Feicht.

Waterville, OH

Toledo, Lake Erie & Western Railway and Museum

Train ride

ADDRESS: 49 N 6th St., PO Box 168 Waterville, OH 43566-0168
TELEPHONE: (866) 63-TRAIN or (419) 878-2177
WEBSITE: www.tlew.org

DESCRIPTION: Passengers board the Blue Bird train at Waterville, OH for a 15-mile round trip on the tracks of the Toledo, Lake Erie & Western Railway and Museum, Inc., once a part of the Cloverleaf Division of the Nickel Plate Rd. The train takes 60 minutes to travel across northwest Ohio.

SCHEDULE: May 10 to October 31: Saturday, Sunday, and holidays, 1, 2:30, and 4 p.m.; June to August: Wednesday and Thursday, 10:30 a.m., 12 and 1:30 p.m.

ADMISSION/FARE: Adults, $9; seniors, $8; children 3-12, $5.50.

Wellington, OH
Lorain & West Virginia Railway
Train ride
Standard gauge
Radio frequency: 160.83

SITE ADDRESS: SR18 Wellington, OH 44090
MAILING ADDRESS: Lakeshore Railway Assoc., PO Box 1131 Elyria, OH 44036
TELEPHONE: (440) 647-6660
E-MAIL: membership@lakeshorerailway.org
WEBSITE: www.lakeshorerailway.org

DESCRIPTION: A 12-mile round trip over the only original line-haul railroad that is entirely in one county in the state of Ohio.

SCHEDULE: Mid-July through October, weekends and some weekdays.

ADMISSION/FARE: Adults, $7; children under 12, $5.

LOCOMOTIVES/ROLLING STOCK: L&WV EMD E8A No. 101; 4 commuter coaches; 2 Chessie cabooses; Orton 200-ton rail crane; boom car; and maintenance-of-way equipment.

SPECIAL EVENTS: August, Lorain County Fair week; October, Halloween Trains.

NEARBY ATTRACTIONS: Cedar Point, Spirit of 76 Museum, Lake Erie fishing, Findley State Park, and Lorain Co. Fairgrounds.

DIRECTIONS: 1 mile west of downtown Wellington on SR18.

Photo courtesy of Marc Chappo—LSRA.

KEY TO SYMBOLS

Handicapped accessible	Restaurant	Arts and crafts	Association of Railway Museums
Parking	Picnic area	Memberships available	Tourist Railway Association, Inc.
Bus/RV parking	Dining car	Send S.A.S.E. for brochure	Amtrak service to nearby city
Gift, book, or museum shop	Excursions	National Register of Historic Places	VIA service to nearby city
Refreshments	Guided tours	Credit cards accepted	

285

Worthington, OH

Ohio Railway Museum

Train ride, Museum
Standard gauge

SITE ADDRESS: 990 Proprietors Rd. Worthington, OH
MAILING ADDRESS: PO Box 777 Worthington, OH 43085
TELEPHONE: (614) 885-7345
WEBSITE: www.ohiorailwaymuseum.org

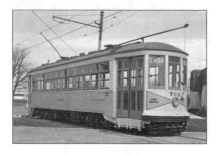

DESCRIPTION: One of the oldest railway museums in the country; currently operating a PCC car, offers a trolley ride on 1½ miles of track.

SCHEDULE: May through September: Sundays, 1 to 5 p.m. Trolley ride included in price of admission.

ADMISSION/FARE: Adults, $4; seniors and children, $3.

LOCOMOTIVES/ROLLING STOCK: N&W Pacific-type steam locomotive no. 578; OPS no. 21 interurban; passenger cars, street cars, and interurbans.

SPECIAL EVENTS: Ghost Trolley in October.

NEARBY ATTRACTIONS: Ohio Historical Museum, Polaris Amphitheatre, Columbus Zoo.

DIRECTIONS: I-71 to SR161 exit, west to Worthington.

Photo courtesy of Dave Bunge.

KEY TO SYMBOLS

♿ Handicapped accessible	🍴 Restaurant	🎨 Arts and crafts	**arm** Association of Railway Museums
P Parking	🪑 Picnic area	**IML** Memberships available	**TRAIN** Tourist Railway Association, Inc.
P Bus/RV parking	🍽 Dining car	✉ Send S.A.S.E. for brochure	**AMTRAK** Amtrak service to nearby city
🎁 Gift, book, or museum shop	Excursions	**NRHP** National Register of Historic Places	**VIA** VIA service to nearby city
☕ Refreshments	**TOUR** Guided tours	**VISA** **MasterCard** **DISCOVER** **AMERICAN EXPRESS Card**	Credit cards accepted

OKLAHOMA

Clinton, OK

Farmrail System, Inc.

Train ride

ADDRESS: 1601 West Gary Blvd.
Clinton, OK 73601
TELEPHONE: (800) 933-7345
E-MAIL: cityoflonewolf@swoi.net
WEBSITE: www.farmrail.com

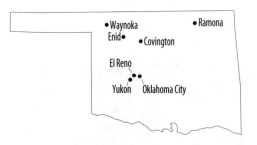

DESCRIPTION: Named the "Quartz Mountain Flyer," this is a 2-hour round trip that shows off the views and scenery surrounding the Witchita Mountains and Lake Altus-Lugert. The trip includes a brief stop in Lone Wolf. There are also Murder Mystery excursions.

SCHEDULE: Excursion departs Quartz Mountain at 10 a.m. on selected dates. Please call or visit website for dates and information.

ADMISSION/FARE: Adults, $15; children 4-12, $10. Locomotive cab rides are available on a limited basis for an additional $25 per person.

LOCOMOTIVES/ROLLING STOCK: The train is pulled by two of FarmRail's GP10 locomotives. The cars are restored 1950s-era 60-seat passenger coaches that were purchased from VIA Rail. They are painted in the FarmRail color scheme and were renumbered as FMRC 5627 and FMRC 5478. They have new heating and cooling units and the "kids' car" has a play area for children.

NEARBY ATTRACTIONS: Quartz Mountain Resort, Quartz Mountain Arts and Conference Center, Quartz Mountain State Park, Wichita Mountains Wildlife Refuge near Lawton, Lake Altus-Lugert, Old Town Museum and Carousel in Elk City, Route 66 museum in Clinton.

DIRECTIONS: Between Altus and Lone Wolf, OK. From Altus: Hwy. 283/44 north 18 miles to the Hwy. 44A junction. From Clinton: I-40 west to Foss, exit Hwy. 44. Travel south on Hwy. 44 approximately 45 miles to Hwy. 44A junction.

Covington, OK
Johnny's Trains and Garden Railroad
Museum, Model train layout

ADDRESS: Route 1, Box 113 Covington, OK 73730
TELEPHONE: (580) 336-2823

DESCRIPTION: Museum of working trains includes a 30' x 40' layout with a circus, mountains, and lakes. Two garden railroads: one measures 10' x 21' with a pond in the center; the other consists of a 100' x 50' layout with working creek and pond with goldfish as well as a business district and farm scene.

SCHEDULE: Daily, year-round, 9 a.m. to 5 p.m.

ADMISSION/FARE: Free; donations appreciated.

NEARBY ATTRACTIONS: Cherokee Strip Parade in Perry, OK (September).

DIRECTIONS: From I-35, take exit 185 west (on Hwy. 164). Continue on Hwy. 164 for 10 miles, then south on Dirt Rd. for ¼ mile.

El Reno, OK
Canadian County Historical Museum
Train ride, Depot museum, Display

ADDRESS: 300 S Grand El Reno, OK 73036
TELEPHONE: (405) 262-5121

DESCRIPTION: Historical buildings and a museum in Rock Island train depot. The 25-minute trolley ride is the only rail-based trolley in operation in the state.

SCHEDULE: Wednesday through Saturday, 10 a.m. to 5 p.m. and Sunday, 1 to 5 p.m.

ADMISSION/FARE: Museum: free. Trolley rides: adults, $3 for 4 rides; seniors and children 12 and under, $1.50 per ride.

LOCOMOTIVES/ROLLING STOCK: Rock Island caboose, coal tender.

SPECIAL EVENTS: Last Saturday in March, Railroaders Day; last Saturday in April, 89ers Day; first Saturday in May, Onion Burger Day; last weekend in September, Tombstone Tales at Fort Reno.

NEARBY ATTRACTIONS: Historic Fort Reno in El Reno, Frontier City and White Water Bay

Amusement Park in Oklahoma City, Western Heritage Museum and Cowboy Hall of Fame, Watonga Cheese Factory, and Chisholm Trail Museums in Kingfisher and Duncan.

DIRECTIONS: Approximately 30 miles west of Oklahoma City. Take I-40 west out of Oklahoma City to Hwy. 81. Take Hwy. 81 north and come into El Reno on old Route 66. On Wade St. continue west at 2-way stop sign. 3 blocks west you will see Rock Island Depot (museum) and trolley barn.

Enid, OK

Railroad Museum of Oklahoma
Train ride, Museum, Display, Layout
Lionel, N, and HO scale

SITE ADDRESS: 702 N Washington Enid, OK 73701
MAILING ADDRESS: 3805 N Lincoln Enid, OK 73703
TELEPHONE: (580) 233-3051
WEBSITE: www.rmo.org

DESCRIPTION: Housed in a 1926-27 former Santa Fe freight house, this museum is focused on preserving historically significant railroad equipment and has a large collection of railroad memorabilia. Visitors can climb aboard a 1925 steam locomotive, wander through cabooses from nine different railroads, and view 13 different types of freight cars.

SCHEDULE: Year-round: Tuesday through Friday, 1 to 4 p.m.; Saturday, 10 a.m. to 1 p.m.; Sunday, 2 to 5 p.m. Closed on major holidays.

ADMISSION/FARE: A donation of $2 per person is suggested.

LOCOMOTIVES/ROLLING STOCK: Frisco 4-8-2 no. 1519; 1937 three-dome riveted tank car; 1928 automobile boxcar; operable 1965 GE 50-ton switcher with side rods; renovated BN, NP, RI, MoP, SF, SL&SF, MK&T, SP and UP cabooses; 1920 gondola with arch-bar trucks; Amtrak lounge/diner; Long Island Commuter Coach; TTX spine car with single axle trucks.

SPECIAL EVENTS: April, Railroad Appreciation Day; May and September, two caboose excursions; September, model railroad swap meet; Christmas party.

NEARBY ATTRACTIONS: Water park, winery, Science and Discovery Center; Cherokee Strip, Midgley, and Heritage museums.

DIRECTIONS: Enid is located on Hwys. 60, 81, 64, 412. The museum is six blocks northwest of the downtown square.

Photo courtesy of Robert Chester.

Hugo, OK
Frisco Depot Museum
Depot museum

ADDRESS: 309 North B St. Hugo, OK 74743
TELEPHONE: (888) 773-3768 or (580) 326-6630

Oklahoma City, OK
Oklahoma Railway Museum
Train ride, Museum, Display, Model train layout
Standard gauge

ADDRESS: 3400 NE Grand Blvd. Oklahoma City, OK 73111-4417
TELEPHONE: (405) 424-8222
WEBSITE: www.oklahomarailwaymuseum.org

DESCRIPTION: The Oklahoma Railway Museum operates 3.4-mile round-trip train rides and a railroad museum.

SCHEDULE: Museum: Saturday, 9 a.m. to 4 p.m.; closed on holidays. Train rides: April through October: first and third Saturday of the month, 10 a.m. to 2 p.m. on the hour; third weekend in December, Christmas trains.

ADMISSION/FARE: Museum: free; train rides: adults, $8; children 3-14, $5; under 3, free.

LOCOMOTIVES/ROLLING STOCK: No. 301 45-ton GE, former US Army; Northern Pacific F9 no. 81; Rock Island RS1 no. 743; Santa Fe FP45 no. 90; OKRX caboose x-21; ATSF diner GN coach; UP open car; CNW commuter car; Rock Island "Golden State" combine no. 6015; ATSF choir car 3113; ATSF choir car 3115; various freight equipment.

SPECIAL EVENTS: Third weekend in December, Christmas trains.

NEARBY ATTRACTIONS: National Softball Hall of Fame, 45 Infantry Division Museum, National Cowboy and Western Heritage Museum, Oklahoma Firefighters Museum, Omniplex Museum, Lincoln Park, and Oklahoma City Zoo.

DIRECTIONS: Exit I-35 at NE 36th St. in Oklahoma City. Go west on NE 36th St. ½ mile to Grand Blvd. Turn south (a sign is at the intersection). The museum is two blocks south on the east side of Grand Blvd.

Photo courtesy of Drake Rice.

Oklahoma City, OK
Omniplex Science Museum
Museum, Display, Model train layout

ADDRESS: 2100 NE 52nd St. Oklahoma City, OK 73111-7198
TELEPHONE: (405) 602-OMNI
E-MAIL: mcarroll@omniplex.org
WEBSITE: www.omniplex.org

DESCRIPTION: The Toy Train Collection features the M. G. Martin Model Train Exhibit, a complete 1,000-square-foot layout with several toy trains running through a miniature town, including an industrial, agricultural, and amusement area. The layout is maintained and operated by the Toy Train Operating Society, Sooner Division. The full-size Parlor Car is a 1929 Missouri Pacific Railroad Car built by the Pullman Company and used for executive business. It has four staterooms, three bathrooms, a dining salon, observation parlor, kitchen, and an open observation platform.

SCHEDULE: Monday through Friday, 9 a.m. to 5 p.m.; Saturday, 9 a.m. to 6 p.m.; Sunday, 11 a.m. to 6 p.m.

ADMISSION/FARE: The Big Ticket (including exhibits, planetarium, and OmniDome Theater): adults 13-64, $13.50; seniors 65+ and children 3-12, $10.25. Exhibits and planetarium only: adults, $9.50; seniors and children, $8.25. OmniDome only: adults, $8.25; seniors and children, $6.75. Prices do not include tax surcharge. Children under 3, free (must be held in lap in OmniDome and Kirkpatrick Planetarium). Group rates for 15 people or more, call for reservations at (800) 532-7652 or (405) 602-3760. Wheelchairs and strollers are available at admissions on a first-come, first-served basis.

SPECIAL EVENTS: Please visit the website for a complete calendar of events.

NEARBY ATTRACTIONS: National Cowboy and Western Heritage Museum, Oklahoma City Zoo, Remington Park Horse Racing Facility, National Softball Hall of Fame, Oklahoma State Firefighters Museum, and Cinemark Tinseltown U.S.A.

DIRECTIONS: Take I-35 to NE 50th St. Next to zoo and across from Remington Park.

TRAVEL TIP: *Take a guide*

Before you board your train, stop by the gift shop to see if the railroad offers a guide book. Some railroads offer a guide that tells you about the railroad mile-by-mile. This is a handy tool to help you understand more of what you get to see, and it makes a great souvenir.

Oklahoma City, OK

Orr Family Farm & RR LLC

Train ride
24" gauge, ⅓ scale

SITE ADDRESS: 14400 S Western Ave. Oklahoma City, OK 73170
MAILING ADDRESS: Orr Family Farms RR LLC 14200 South Western Ave.
Oklahoma City, OK 73170
TELEPHONE: (405) 799-3276
E-MAIL: info@orrfamilyfarm.com
WEBSITE: www.orrfamilyfarm.com

DESCRIPTION: Their ⅓ scale Jupiter looks, sounds, and puffs like a steam engine, but has the safety of a diesel. The scale replica of the US's first transcontinental locomotive comfortably holds approximately 75 children and adults. The train includes a beautifully handcrafted oak-lined caboose. When lit up at night, the coaches look like Pullman cars.

SCHEDULE: See website or call for schedule and admission.

LOCOMOTIVES/ROLLING STOCK: ⅓ scale replica of the Central Pacific's Jupiter that met the 119 of Union Pacific May 10, 1869 on first transcontinental line. It has TV cameras, a loudspeaker system, and a sander. Also a diesel Santa Fe switch engine.

SPECIAL EVENTS: Father's Day, ½ price for fathers; June 17, toe fishing, etc.; July 1, Farm Contests; October, Pumpkin Patch; November 24, Christmas lights and animation.

NEARBY ATTRACTIONS: Oklahoma Railway museum, 3400 NE Grand Blvd., Oklahoma City.

DIRECTIONS: See website for detailed directions. Take I-35 to exit 117. Go west to Western (2 miles), then south for ½ mile.

Photo courtesy of Orr Family Farm.
Coupon available, see insert.

TRAVEL TIP: *History lesson*

A visit to a tourist railroad or museum is an opportunity for an instant history lesson. Railroading is a great way to explore the development of the country and changes in technology as well as geography. If you take your kids along, make an outing into an educational adventure.

Ramona, OK

The Train House

Model train layout

ADDRESS: 26811 N 3990 Rd. Ramona, OK
TELEPHONE: (918) 335-2360
E-MAIL: mariphiloo@aol.com

DESCRIPTION: Wagon ride through the park and HO and Lionel O scale layouts.

SCHEDULE: Daily, 10 a.m. to 5 p.m., except Monday. By reservation only.

ADMISSION/FARE: Donations appreciated.

NEARBY ATTRACTIONS: Osage State Park, Woolrock Museum, and Buffalo Beach.

DIRECTIONS: US75 to CR2700, east 2 miles to stop sign, north 1.5 blocks.

Waynoka, OK

Waynoka History Museum

Museum and historic display

ADDRESS: 202 S Cleveland, PO Box 193 Waynoka, OK 73860
TELEPHONE: (580) 824-5871
WEBSITE: www.waynoka.org

DESCRIPTION: A restored 1910 Santa Fe Depot, 1910 Harvey House, diesel locomotive static display, section foreman's house, log cabin, restaurant, and museum with air and rail displays and more.

SCHEDULE: Tuesday through Saturday, afternoons. Other times by appointment.

ADMISSION/FARE: Adults, $2; students, $1.

LOCOMOTIVES/ROLLING STOCK: Hudson Bay Railway GP10 no. 2511.

NEARBY ATTRACTIONS: 65+ trains daily on BNSF Transcon, El Charro Mexican Restaurant in Harvey House, Little Sahara State Park, Alabaster Caverns, Curtis Hill.

DIRECTIONS: 120 miles northwest of Oklahoma City. From Tulsa, west on Hwy. 412 to US281, north 12 miles on US281. 70 miles west of Enid in Northwest Oklahoma.

Photo courtesy of Sandie Olson.

Yukon, OK

Yukon's Best Railroad Museum

Museum

SITE ADDRESS: Third and Main St. Yukon, OK
MAILING ADDRESS: 410 Oak Ave. Yukon, OK 73099
TELEPHONE: (405) 354-5079

DESCRIPTION: An extensive display of railroad antiques and artifacts of the Rock Island lines and other railroads.

SCHEDULE: Year-round by chance or appointment. Call or write for information.

ADMISSION/FARE: Free.

LOCOMOTIVES/ROLLING STOCK: Rock Island Boxcar no. 5542, Union Pacific caboose no. 25865.

DIRECTIONS: On historic Route 66. Main St., across from "Yukon's Best Flour" wheat elevator.

KEY TO SYMBOLS

♿ Handicapped accessible	🍴 Restaurant	🎨 Arts and crafts	arm Association of Railway Museums
P Parking	🏕 Picnic area	📖 Memberships available	TRAIN Tourist Railway Association, Inc.
P Bus/RV parking	🍽 Dining car	✉ Send S.A.S.E. for brochure	Amtrak service to nearby city
🎁 Gift, book, or museum shop	🔄 Excursions	NRHP National Register of Historic Places	VIA VIA service to nearby city
☕ Refreshments	TOUR Guided tours	VISA MasterCard DISCOVER AMERICAN EXPRESS Card	Credit cards accepted

OREGON

Baker City, OR

Sumpter Valley Railroad Restoration, Inc.

Train ride, Museum, Display
36" gauge

ADDRESS: PO Box 389 Baker City, OR 97814
TELEPHONE: (866) 894-2268
E-MAIL: svrydepotstaff@eoni.com
WEBSITE: www.svry.com

DESCRIPTION: 5- and 10-mile steam train rides run through Sumpter Valley with stops at McEwen and the historic gold mining town of Sumpter. Originally built beginning in 1890 to haul timber, the SVRy quickly became a common carrier transporting passengers, logs, lumber, livestock, mining equipment, gold, mail, and ore. Ceasing operations in 1947, the historic line is now being rebuilt and operated by dedicated volunteers.

SCHEDULE: Depart McEwen: 10 a.m., 12:30, 3 p.m. Depart Sumpter: 11:30 a.m., 2, 4:30 p.m. (final train of the day is one-way only).

ADMISSION/FARE: Round trip: Adults, $12.50; seniors, $11.50; children, $8; family, $30. One way: Adults, $9; seniors, $8; children, $5.50; family, $20. Children 5 and under, free.

LOCOMOTIVES/ROLLING STOCK: Sumpter Valley Railway Alco 2-8-2 no. 19; sister no. 20 is under restoration; WH Eccles Lumber Co. 2-truck Heisler no. 3; SVRy Coach no. 20; SVRy Cabooses no. 3 and 5; dozens of freight and passenger cars from the Sumpter Valley and other North American narrow gauge railroads.

SPECIAL EVENTS: Please call or visit online for information on specials and Night Trains, as well as holiday schedules.

NEARBY ATTRACTIONS: Oregon Interpretive Center/Museum, Oregon Trail Museum, camping at Phillips Lake, antique shop in Sumpter, and gold dredge.

DIRECTIONS: 22 miles southwest of Baker City on Hwy. 7.

Photo courtesy of Taylor Rush.

Canby, OR

Canby Depot Museum
Museum

SITE ADDRESS: 888 NE Fourth Ave. Canby, OR 97013
MAILING ADDRESS: Canby Historical Society, PO Box 160 Canby, OR 97013
TELEPHONE: (503) 266-6712
E-MAIL: depotmuseum@canby.com
WEBSITE: www.canbyhistoricalsociety.org

DESCRIPTION: In the early 1980s, the existing Canby Depot facility became available to the Canby Historical Society to house their museum. The Depot had been an active train station at the intersection of North First and Grant Sts. through most of the city's history, and later was moved to its present location near NE 4th and Pine Sts. adjacent to the Clackamas County Fairgrounds.

SCHEDULE: Thursday to Sunday, 1 to 4 p.m. Closed January and February.

ADMISSION/FARE: $2 donation requested.

LOCOMOTIVES/ROLLING STOCK: Caboose no. HMS7810M.

SPECIAL EVENTS: April and October, Flea Market and Antique Appraisals; July 4th, Pancake Breakfast; September, Open House.

NEARBY ATTRACTIONS: Clackamas County Fairgrounds (fair in August); Molalla River State Park, Canby Ferry Crossing, Willamette River; Flower Farmer Miniature Train Rides.

DIRECTIONS: Hwy. 99 East and Pine St., 7 miles south of Oregon City.

Photo courtesy of Bergman Photography.

Canby, OR

Phoenix & Holly Railroad, Inc.
Train ride
15" gauge

ADDRESS: 2512 N Holly St. Canby, OR 97013-9118
TELEPHONE: (503) 266-3581
E-MAIL: lgarre@canby.com
WEBSITE: www.narrowgaugerr.com

DESCRIPTION: Leo and Louis Garre first built the 700' loop of the Phoenix and Holly railroad in 1986 to enhance their fruit stand business. Soon, a group of railroad enthusiasts helped them expand. In 1995, the new 3,500' loop track was patterned after the Denver Rio Grande & Western of Colorado. Riders can see flowers, farm animals, and a gift shop. Mr. Garre has an extensive mechanical background in engineering, fabrication, and metallurgy, and is available at certain times of the year for consultation.

SCHEDULE: May to October: 11 a.m. to 6 p.m.

ADMISSION/FARE: Adults $4, seniors $3.50; children $3.50.

SPECIAL EVENTS: last Saturday, Sunday and Monday of August and September 2, 3, and 4, Summer Basil, Wine & Art festival; October, pumpkin patch; Christmas lighting display.

NEARBY ATTRACTIONS: Canby Ferry, Railroad Museum, Swan Island Dahlia Farm, Willamette River, antique shops, city park, and state parks.

DIRECTIONS: From south I-5 exit 278. I-5 north exit 282-A. 99 E from south: left on Elm, right on 4th, left on Holly. Go one mile. 99E from north: right on Territorial, right on Holly.

Photo courtesy of Flower Farmer.

Hood River, OR

Mount Hood Railroad and Dinner Train

EDITOR'S CHOICE

Train ride, Dinner train
Standard gauge

ADDRESS: 110 Railroad Ave. Hood River, OR 97031
TELEPHONE: (800) TRAIN-61 or (541) 386-3556
E-MAIL: mthoodrr@gorge.net
WEBSITE: www.mthoodrr.com

DESCRIPTION: Built in 1906, this historic railroad takes passengers on 4-hour tours from the Columbia Gorge to the foothills of Mt. Hood. The trip aboard the Excursion Train—comprised of 1910-20 Pullman coaches, concession car, and caboose—is narrated in one direction. The Dinner & Brunch Train offers excellent four-course dining.

SCHEDULE: April to December. Excursion Train: 10 a.m. and 3 p.m; Brunch Train: 11 a.m.; Dinner Train: Friday, 6:30 p.m., Saturday, 5:30 p.m. (4:30 p.m. October through December).

ADMISSION/FARE: Excursion: adults, $23; seniors, $21; children, $15; Brunch: $58; Dinner: $70; Murder Mystery and Comedy Dinner: $80.

LOCOMOTIVES/ROLLING STOCK: Two GP 9s; 1910 and 1920 Pullmans; 1940s dining cars.

SPECIAL EVENTS: Festivals, Train Robberies, Circus Train, Christmas Tree Trains, and Murder Mystery Trains.

NEARBY ATTRACTIONS: Mt. Hood, Columbia River National Scenic Area, and historic hotels.

DIRECTIONS: Sixty miles east of Portland on I-84, exit 63 right to Cascade St.

Lake Oswego, OR

Oregon Electric Railway Historical Society, Willamette Shore Trolley

EDITOR'S CHOICE

Trolley ride
Standard gauge

ADDRESS: Willamette Shore Trolley 311 N State St. Lake Oswego, OR 97304-3111
TELEPHONE: (503) 697-7436
WEBSITE: www.oregonelectricrailway.org

DESCRIPTION: Visitors can ride historic trolley cars on a scenic 6-mile historic rail line between Lake Oswego and Portland. Traveling along the Willamette River, the ride goes through parks, past mansions, over bridges, and through a tunnel.

SCHEDULE: Year-round: charters, excursions; May to October: scheduled trains. Call for full schedule timetable.

ADMISSION/FARE: Round trip: adults, $10; seniors 55+, $9; children 3-12, $6; one way: adults and seniors, $6; children, $4. Children 2 and under, free. Excursion fares vary.

LOCOMOTIVES/ROLLING STOCK: Portland Traction Brill master unit no. 813.

SPECIAL EVENTS: Fourth of July fireworks special; December (dates variable), Boat Light Parade specials.

NEARBY ATTRACTIONS: Tillamook Restaurant, Portland light rail lines, Portland Streetcar, vintage trolley, Washington Park, 30" zoo railway, old SP roundhouse (SP 4449 and SP & S 700), Union Station, Oregon Electric Railway Museum.

DIRECTIONS: Take I-5 to exit 292, and east 4 miles to Lake Oswego via Kruse Way to end, then left on Boones Ferry Rd. and right on Country Club Rd. which changes to A-Ave. In Lake Oswego, A-Ave. to end, then right on State St. (Hwy. 43), cross tracks and turn left on Foothills Rd. to enter parking lots. Depot is on the east side of State St., next to track.

Photo courtesy of Rod Cox.

Medford Railroad Park
Train ride, Museum, Display, Model train layout
7¹/₂" and standard gauge

SITE ADDRESS: 2222 Table Rock Rd. Medford, OR
MAILING ADDRESS: SOC-NRHS, PO Box 622 Medford, OR 97501
TELEPHONE: (541) 944-2230
E-MAIL: sorcnrhs@railfan.net
WEBSITE: http://sorcnrhs.railfan.net/medfordpark.htm

DESCRIPTION: Unique facility operated by five separate organizations working in cooperation to offer the following: a railroad museum, train rides on 7½ in. gauge track, an HO scale model railroad, live telegraph demonstrations, and a G-scale garden railroad.

SCHEDULE: April to October: second and fourth Sunday, 11 a.m. to 3 p.m.

ADMISSION/FARE: Donations are welcome.

LOCOMOTIVES/ROLLING STOCK: Medford Corporation No. 4 Willamette geared locomotive; SP caboose 1107; CB&Q caboose no. 14446; SP flanger no. SPMW 330; P&E hopper no. 74735 (ex-Great Northern); OC&E caboose no. 2001 (ex-SP no. 1000); BN caboose no. 11205 (ex GN no. X202); SP flat car no. 541254.

SPECIAL EVENTS: Labor Day Weekend, Live Steam Meet sponsored by the South Oregon Live Steamers.

NEARBY ATTRACTIONS: 2 hours from Crater Lake National Park, 20 miles from Ashland Shakespeare Festival, and 5 miles from Historic Jacksonville, Oregon.

DIRECTIONS: From Interstate 5, exit 30: take Hwy. 62 west; turn right on Hwy. 99; turn right on Table Rock Rd.; turn right on Berrydale Ave. Located behind the fire station.

Photo courtesy of Jerry Hellinga.

TRAVEL TIP: *Take your camera!*

It's traditional to get a snapshot of you and your family with the locomotive hauling your train. Don't be shy about asking the locomotive crew or the conductor to pose. They're especially good subjects in their uniforms.

Redmond, OR
Crooked River Dinner Train
Dinner train

ADDRESS: 495 NE O'Neil Way, PO Box 387 Redmond, OR 97756
TELEPHONE: (541) 548-8630
WEBSITE: www.crookedriverrailroad.com

DESCRIPTION: 3-hour, 38-mile round trip through Crooked River Valley on board a Western Theme Dinner Train, including a four-course meal. Year-round Murder Mystery. Sunday, Supper with Jesse James Train Robbery. Group rates and charters available.

SCHEDULE: Year-round, Thursday to Sunday.

ADMISSION/FARE: Adults, $65 to $78 per person; children 4-12, $39; children 3 and under, $20; seniors, $60-68.

LOCOMOTIVES/ROLLING STOCK: 1948 Milwaukee Road railcars, diesel over electric freight engine.

SPECIAL EVENTS: September, Railroad Days with Shay Steam Engine.

NEARBY ATTRACTIONS: Smith Rock State Park, Meadow Lake Gulf-Prineville Oregon, and Mt. Batchlor Ski Resort.

DIRECTIONS: 2 miles north of Redmond, ⅛ mile east of Hwy. 97.

Photo courtesy of Teri Hisaw.
Coupon available, see insert.

Rockaway Beach, OR
Oregon Coast Scenic Railroad
Train ride
Standard gauge

SITE ADDRESS: Hwy. 101 in Garibaldi and Rockaway Beach, OR
MAILING ADDRESS: 4421 Glenview Ave. Tillamook, OR 97141-2864
TELEPHONE: (503) 842-7972
E-MAIL: steamlokie@oregoncoast.com
WEBSITE: www.ocsr.net

DESCRIPTION: Train pulled by a Heisler locomotive. Passengers ride along the shores of Tillamook Bay and see the Pacific Ocean on a 10-mile, 1½-hour excursion. Operates in conjunction with the Port of Tillamook Bay Railroad.

SCHEDULE: Memorial Day to June and September: weekends; July and August: Friday to Sunday. Departs Garibaldi at 12, 2, and 4 p.m. Departs Rockaway Beach at 1 and 3 p.m.

ADMISSION/FARE: Adults, $13; children 3-10, $7; children under 3, free; cab rides, $30.

LOCOMOTIVES/ROLLING STOCK: The Curtiss Lumber Co. no. 2 1910 60-ton 2-truck Heisler locomotive; 1944 ex-Union Pacific caboose; open and covered cars.

SPECIAL EVENTS: July 4, Fireworks Spectacular; December, Santa Train.

NEARBY ATTRACTIONS: Blue Heron cheese and wine tasting and petting farm, Tillamook Cheese factory, Tillamook Air Museum, and Pacific Ocean.

DIRECTIONS: Rockaway Beach, 15 miles north of Tillamook on Hwy. 101. Garibaldi, 3rd St., 9 miles north of Tillamook on Hwy 101.

Tillamook, OR

Port of Tillamook Bay's Oregon Coast Explorer

Train ride, Dinner train
Standard gauge

ADDRESS: 4000 Blimp Blvd. Tillamook, OR 97141
TELEPHONE: (800) 685-1719
WEBSITE: www.potb.org/oregoncoastexplorer

DESCRIPTION: A 1950s vintage Rail Diesel Car travels along some of the scenic countryside of the Oregon coast. Passengers can see the Pacific from a whole new perspective. Train rides: local 1½-3 hours; dinner train, 3 hours; and canyon trips, 8 hours.

SCHEDULE: Memorial Day weekend to mid-November: passenger service; to mid-September, weekends, Heisler steam; July to second week in November: Salmonberry Canyon, Fall Foliage, brunch, and dinner trains. A variety of excursions are available with different running times on weekend. Private charters available during the week.

ADMISSION/FARE: Fare is from $13 to $110 depending upon the excursion.

LOCOMOTIVES/ROLLING STOCK: 1910 Heisler Steam Locomotive, 1953 BUDD Diesel Car.

SPECIAL EVENTS: Each town along the coast has fairs and festivals. The railroad is usually part of all of these fairs.

NEARBY ATTRACTIONS: Tillamook Air Museum, Tillamook Cheese Factory, Oregon Coast.

DIRECTIONS: All passenger rides start from depots along the coast at Garibaldi, Rockaway, Wheeler, and Banks Oregon on the east end of our rail line.

See ad on page A-27.

Wallowa, OR

Eagle Cap Excursion Train

Train ride, Dinner train
Standard gauge
Radio frequency: 160.560

SITE ADDRESS: 209 E First St. Wallowa, OR
MAILING ADDRESS: 102 Elm St. La Grande, OR 97850
TELEPHONE: (800) 848-9969 or (541) 886-3200
E-MAIL: maryann6972@eoni.com or visitlg@eoni.com
WEBSITE: www.eaglecaptrain.com

DESCRIPTION: Wallowa Union Railroad operates the Eagle Cap Excursion Train in the beautiful canyons and valleys of northeast Oregon. Various trips are available.

SCHEDULE: Call for free train schedule and visitor information.

ADMISSION/FARE: Varies from $45 to $80 depending on the excursion and the passenger's age.

LOCOMOTIVES/ROLLING STOCK: EMD-GP-7 no. 2085; EMD-GP-7 no. 2083; WURR baggage generator car no. 6741; WURR Pullman Standard Coach nos. 1120 & 3241; WURR Budd table coach car no. 2636; WURR 60' flat car no. 54526.

SPECIAL EVENTS: Watch the website for special holiday excursions.

NEARBY ATTRACTIONS: Wallowa Lake State park and resort area, Eagle Cap Wilderness, Hells Canyon NRA and National Scenic Byway, Eastern Oregon Fire Museum, Oregon Trail, museums, outdoor recreation, and much more.

DIRECTIONS: I-84 to La Grande, OR, then Hwy. 82 to Wallowa. Turn North on Story St.

Photo courtesy of Linda Eytchison.
See ad on page A-29.

TRAVEL TIP: *Rail and raft*

Several tourist railroads offer the option now of riding the train in one direction and then rafting back down an adjacent river. This is a good way to include a train ride on a summertime vacation when you want to both ride the rails and hit the water.

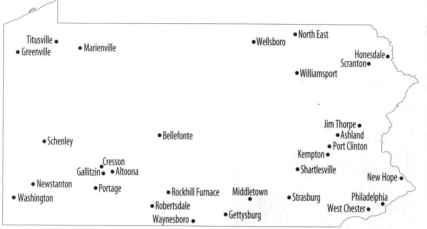

PENNSYLVANIA

Altoona, PA

Horseshoe Curve National Historic Landmark

EDITOR'S CHOICE

Museum, Display, Model train layout
HO scale

ADDRESS: 1300 Ninth Ave. Altoona, PA 16602
TELEPHONE: (888) 4ALTOONA or (814) 946-0834
E-MAIL: prdirector@railroadcity.com
WEBSITE: www.railroadcity.com

DESCRIPTION: Considered to be an engineering marvel, the Horseshoe Curve is celebrating more than 150 years of operation (1854-2006). Go trackside by way of the funicular (incline) for train watching during operating hours.

SCHEDULE: Sunday, 12 to 6 p.m.; Monday through Saturday, 10 a.m. to 6 p.m.

ADMISSION/FARE: Adults, $7.50; seniors, $6; youth 5-17, $5; toddlers 4 and under, free.

NEARBY ATTRACTIONS: Altoona Railroader's Memorial Museum, Allegheny Portage Railroad National Historic site, Gallitzin Tunnels, Lakemont Park, Altoona Curve Baseball, the Meadows Family Fun Center, Johnstown Flood Museum, Degrosso's Amusement Park, Servello Gallery of Art.

DIRECTIONS: From US22, Gallitzin exit and to Coupon Rd., right on Kittaning Point Rd.

Coupon available, see insert.

Altoona, PA

Railroaders Memorial Museum

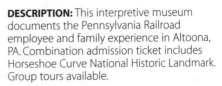

Museum

ADDRESS: 1300 Ninth Ave. Altoona, PA 16602
TELEPHONE: (888) 4ALTOONA or (814) 946-0834
E-MAIL: prdirector@railroadcity.com
WEBSITE: www.railroadcity.com

DESCRIPTION: This interpretive museum documents the Pennsylvania Railroad employee and family experience in Altoona, PA. Combination admission ticket includes Horseshoe Curve National Historic Landmark. Group tours available.

SCHEDULE: Please call or check website for hours and events.

ADMISSION/FARE: Adults, $7.50; seniors, $6; children 5-17, $5; children 4 and under, free.

LOCOMOTIVES/ROLLING STOCK: Charles Schwab's private car "Lorreto"; dining car, "Habor Springs;" and a variety of other historic and vintage rolling stock.

NEARBY ATTRACTIONS: Lakemont Park, Delgrosso's Amusement Park, Hollidaysburg Canal Basin Park, Altoona Curve Baseball, Boyer Candy, Southern Alleghenies Museum of Art, Altoona Heritage Discovery Center.

DIRECTIONS: Five minutes from the 17th St. exit off I-99. I-99 can be accessed from the Bedford exit of the Pennsylvania turnpike, or the Milesburg exit of I-80.

Photo courtesy of Peter D. Barton.
Coupon available, see insert.

Ashland, PA

Pioneer Tunnel Coal Mine and Steam Train

Train ride
Narrow gauge

ADDRESS: 19th & Oak St. Ashland, PA 17921
TELEPHONE: (570) 875-3850
WEBSITE: www.pioneertunnel.com

DESCRIPTION: Scenic ride along the Mahanoy Mountain is led by a steam locomotive of the 0-4-0T type built in 1927 by the Vulcan Iron Works of Wilkes-Barre, Pennsylvania. Guides tell the story of strip mining, bootlegging, and the Centralia Mine fire. Also available is a tour of a real anthracite coal mine in open mine cars pulled by a battery-operated mine motor, where mine guides tell the story of anthracite coal mining.

SCHEDULE: April: weekday mine tours, 11 a.m., 12:30, and 2 p.m. Memorial Day to Labor Day: daily mine tours and steam train, 10 a.m. to 6 p.m. May, September, October: weekday mine tours, 11 a.m., 12:30, and 2 p.m. Train tours for reserved groups only; weekend mine and train tours run continuously.

ADMISSION/FARE: Steam train: adults, $6; children under 12, $4.50. Mine: adults, $8; children under 12, $5.50. Group discounts.

LOCOMOTIVES/ROLLING STOCK: A "lokie" of the 0-4-0T type built by Vulcan Iron Works; two battery-powered mine motors.

SPECIAL EVENTS: August 19, Fourteenth Annual Pioneer Day: coal mine tours, steam train rides, large craft fair, ethnic foods, live music, and more.

NEARBY ATTRACTIONS: Pennsylvania Museum of Anthracite Mining and Knoebel's Park.

DIRECTIONS: I-81, exit 124B (Frackville). Route 61 north to Ashland.

Bellefonte, PA
Bellefonte Historical Railroad Society
Train ride, Dinner train
Standard gauge

ADDRESS: The Train Station, 320 High St. Bellefonte, PA 16823
TELEPHONE: (814) 355-2917
E-MAIL: query@bellefontetrain.com
WEBSITE: www.bellefontetrain.com

DESCRIPTION: 60-mile trips over the Nittany & Bald Eagle Railroad to Lemont, Pleasant Gap, Tyrone and Lock Haven. The Bellefonte Station, a restored former Pennsylvania Railroad structure built in 1888, houses historical photos and memorabilia of area railroading with an operating N gauge layout of the Bellefonte-Curtin Village route. A snowplow and caboose under restoration are displayed beside the station.

SCHEDULE: May through October: Sunday excursions depart Bellefonte Station at 2 p.m. Last Sunday of each month: dinner trains depart at 3 p.m.

ADMISSION/FARE: Adults, $12; children, $6; family membership, $40. Dinner train: adults, $55; children, $30.

LOCOMOTIVES/ROLLING STOCK: Budd RDC-1 9167, originally NYNH&H; Budd RDC-1 9153, originally Reading. Cars are air conditioned and can be configured for on-board meal service.

SPECIAL EVENTS: May and October, Railfan Days; Fall foliage and Christmas trains.

NEARBY ATTRACTIONS: Restored PRR passenger station, Bellefonte Central caboose and snow plow on static display. Downtown Victorian Bellefonte and Tallyrand Park, American Stamp Society Museum.

DIRECTIONS: Central Pennsylvania, less than 5 miles from exits 23 and 24 of I-80.

Photo courtesy of W.M. Rumberger.
Coupon available, see insert.

Cresson, PA
The Station Inn
Inn

ADDRESS: 827 Front St. Cresson, PA 16630
TELEPHONE: (800) 555-4757 or (814) 886-4757
E-MAIL: station.inn@verizon.net
WEBSITE: www.stationinnpa.com

DESCRIPTION: This historic trackside hotel was built in 1866 to serve salesmen and railroaders. Visitors can enjoy a restaurant with 1902 salon, rooms with private baths, railroad memorabilia, and a library.

SCHEDULE: Year-round, 7:30 a.m. to 11 p.m.

ADMISSION/FARE: Room rates $50-$99. Complimentary breakfast.

SPECIAL EVENTS: Altoona Railfest; first weekend in October, Cresson Heritage Days; Columbus Day weekend, East Broad Top Fall Extravaganza.

NEARBY ATTRACTIONS: Horseshoe Curve, Gallitzin Tunnels, Altoona Railroaders Museum, Allegheny Portage Railroad site, East Broad Top Railroad, Western Maryland Scenic Railroad, Potomac Eagle Railroad.

DIRECTIONS: Fifteen miles west of Altoona on US Route 22.

Photo courtesy of Thomas Davis.
See ad on page A-13.

Erie, PA

Museum of Erie GE History
Museum

ADDRESS: Bldg. 1-C, 2901 East Lake Rd. Erie, PA 16531
TELEPHONE: (814) 875-2494
E-MAIL: bakerie@aol.com
WEBSITE: www.members.aol.com/museriege

DESCRIPTION: GE in Erie, PA, has been the largest producer of locomotives for US and foreign railroads for many years. Ten years ago, a number of retired engineers and other employees made sure their memories and the plant history would be preserved by establishing a museum to commemorate the production of locomotives that began in 1913. An operating HO gauge model train layout represents the GE Erie factory and an adjacent town.

SCHEDULE: June to September: Saturday, 10 a.m. to 2 p.m.; October to May: first Saturday of the month, 10 a.m. to 2 p.m.

ADMISSION/FARE: Free.

NEARBY ATTRACTIONS: Beaches, water sports, indoor water parks, museums, historical sites, educational and tourist resources of Erie, PA, Lake Shore Railway Museum.

Gallitzin, PA

Allegheny Portage Railroad National Historical Site
Museum

ADDRESS: 110 Federal Park Rd. Gallitzin, PA 16641
TELEPHONE: (814) 886-6150
WEBSITE: www.nps.gov/alpo/

DESCRIPTION: This site preserves the remains of the Allegeny Portage Railroad, which operated from 1834 to 1854. The park also includes the Staple Bend Tunnel, the first railroad tunnel built in the country.

SCHEDULE: Year-round: daily, 9 a.m. to 5 p.m. Closed on winter holidays.

ADMISSION/FARE: Adults 17 and older, $4; national park passes honored.

NEARBY ATTRACTIONS: Gallitzin Tunnels, Horseshoe Curve, and Altoona Railroad Memorial Museum.

DIRECTIONS: US Route 22, Gallitzin exit, 10 miles west of Altoona.

Photo courtesy of National Park Service.

Gallitzin, PA

Tunnels Park Caboose & Museum

Museum

ADDRESS: 411 Convent St. Gallitzin, PA 16641-1295
TELEPHONE: (814) 886-8871
EMAIL: info@gallitzin.info
WEBSITE: www.gallitzin.info

DESCRIPTION: Adjacent to the Norfolk Southern's mainline, visitors can see the trains exit the Allegheny Tunnel. Trains run through the tunnels 24 hours a day. The park adjacent to the Gallitzin Tunnels exhibits a restored 1942 Pennsylvania Railroad N5C Caboose. The site also includes a railroad museum and theater.

SCHEDULE: Tuesday to Sunday, 11 a.m. to 5 p.m.; closed major holidays.

ADMISSION/FARE: Free.

LOCOMOTIVES/ROLLING STOCK: 1942 restored PRR caboose is open to the public in Tunnels Park.

SPECIAL EVENTS: August 20, Summer Fest; September 23 and 24, Tunnel Fest.

NEARBY ATTRACTIONS: Horseshoe Curve, Allegheny Portage Railroad National Historic Site.

DIRECTIONS: Gallitzin exit from Pennsylvania Route 22, then follow signs to the Tunnels.

Photo courtesy of Irene H. Szynal.

Gettysburg, PA

Pioneer Lines Scenic Railway

Train ride, Dinner train
Standard gauge

ADDRESS: 106 N Washington St. Gettysburg, PA 17325
TELEPHONE: (717) 334-6932
EMAIL: pioneerlines@innernet.net
WEBSITE: www.gettysburgrail.com

DESCRIPTION: A scenic excursion runs through the heart of Adams County, traveling through the north end of the battlefield at Gettysburg as the conductor gives a narrated history of the surrounding sites. The tour lasts approximately 1 hour and 15 minutes.

SCHEDULE: Year-round operation.

ADMISSION/FARE: Regular: adults, $15; children 4-12, $8; children 3 and under, free; Dinner train: $45; Murder Mystery Dinner, $65; Conductor Lunch: $25; Ghost train: $18.

LOCOMOTIVES/ROLLING STOCK: Two F7s and coaches.

SPECIAL EVENTS: Guided ghost trains, Murder Mystery Dinner trains, and several other specials. Call for details.

NEARBY ATTRACTIONS: Gettysburg Battlefield, Gettysburg Outlets, shops and attractions.

DIRECTIONS: Depot is one block north of Route 30.

Photo courtesy of J. C. Garner.

Greenville, PA
Greenville Railroad Park and Museum
Museum

ADDRESS: 314 Main St. Greenville, PA 16125
TELEPHONE: (724) 588-4009

DESCRIPTION: The railroad park and museum contains stationary railroad cars and reconstructions of a stationmaster's quarters and dispatcher's office.

SCHEDULE: May through September: weekends; June through August: daily, 1 to 5 p.m.; closed Mondays.

ADMISSION/FARE: Donations accepted.

LOCOMOTIVES/ROLLING STOCK: Static equipment: World's largest steam switching locomotive built in 1936 by Baldwin as an 0-10-2; antique Erie flatcar; B&LE iron ore car; UP caboose; Wheeling & Lake Erie caboose and B&LE caboose.

NEARBY ATTRACTIONS: Deer and Animal Park, Pymatuning State Park and Dam, Canal Museum, Thiel College, and Conneaut Lake Park.

DIRECTIONS: Fourteen miles east of I-79; 22 miles north of I-80.

Honesdale, PA
Stourbridge Line Rail Excursions
Train ride

ADDRESS: Wayne County Chamber of Commerce, 303 Commercial St.
Honesdale, PA 18431
TELEPHONE: (800) 433-9008 or (570) 253-1960
WEBSITE: www.waynecountycc.com

DESCRIPTION: Old-fashioned fun awaits the whole family aboard a restored BL2 diesel locomotive pulling five vintage cars. Scenic round-trip rides run from Honesdale to Hawley (24 miles) and Honesdale to Lackawaxen-on-the-Delaware (50 miles). The ride parallels the shimmering Lackawaxen River and closely follows the route of the Delaware & Hudson Canal.

SCHEDULE: Easter; summer Sundays: Great Train Robbery runs; August: Dinner Theater and Bavarian Fest; Autumn: fall foliage rides; Halloween and Christmas rides.

ADMISSION/FARE: Varies by ride.

LOCOMOTIVES/ROLLING STOCK: 1949 EMD BL2 no. 54, former Bangor & Aroostook.

SPECIAL EVENTS: Easter Bunny Run, Halloween Fun Run, and Santa Express. Call for dates.

NEARBY ATTRACTIONS: Claws 'n' Paws Wild Animal Park, Wayne County Historical Society and Museum Shop, Dorflinger Glass Museum, Lake Wallenpaupack, historic downtown Honesdale, D&H Gravity Railroad and Canal Exhibit, and Farmer's Market.

DIRECTIONS: Off Route 6 in historic Honesdale, birthplace of the American Railroad.

Jim Thorpe, PA
Lehigh Gorge Scenic Railway
Train ride
Standard gauge

SITE ADDRESS: Downtown Historic District, Broadway and Susquehanna Sts. Jim Thorpe, PA
MAILING ADDRESS: PO Box 91 Jim Thorpe, PA 18229
TELEPHONE: (570) 325-8485
WEBSITE: www.lgsry.com

DESCRIPTION: 1-hour, round-trip aboard old style passenger coaches from the 1920s. The 1850s formation of the Lehigh Valley Railroad brought prosperity to the area as it carried anthracite coal and other goods to market. The recently renovated former Central Railroad of New Jersey Station is the focal point of tourism in the town today. A new track was laid over an unused bridge just north of Jim Thorpe to create a direct rail-link to this line.

SCHEDULE: May 21 through December 18: weekends and Monday holidays, trains depart at 11 a.m., 1 and 3 p.m. Check website for additions to schedules.

ADMISSION/FARE: Adults, $11; children 12 and under, $8.

LOCOMOTIVES/ROLLING STOCK: SD50 diesel locomotives; 1920s-era open window passenger coaches.

NEARBY ATTRACTIONS: Mauch Chunk Lake Park, Lehigh Gorge State Park, Pocono Raceway.

DIRECTIONS: Historic Jim Thorpe, PA on PA Route 209. In close proximity to I-476, I-80.

Photo courtesy of Reading & Northern Archive Department.
See ad on page A-4.

Kempton, PA

Wanamaker, Kempton & Southern Railroad

Train ride
Standard gauge

ADDRESS: 42 Community Center Dr., PO Box 24 Kempton, PA 19529
TELEPHONE: (610) 756-6469
E-MAIL: info@kemptontrain.com
WEBSITE: www.kemptontrain.com

DESCRIPTION: A 6-mile, 40-minute round trip travels through scenic Pennsylvania Dutch country over part of the former Reading Company's Schuylkill & Lehigh branch. Restored stations were relocated from Joanna and Catasauqua, Pennsylvania. There are also original circa 1874 Wanamaker station and operating HO scale model layout (Sundays).

SCHEDULE: May to October, weekends. Call, write, or visit website for detailed schedule.

ADMISSION/FARE: Adults, $7; children 3-11, $3.50; children 2 and under, free.

LOCOMOTIVES/ROLLING STOCK: No. 2, 1920 Porter 0-4-0T, former Colorado Fuel & Iron; no. 65, 1930 Porter 0-6-0T, former Safe Harbor Water Power; no. 7258 1942 GE diesel-electric 45-ton, former Birdsboro Corp.; coaches nos. 1494 and 1474 and combine no. 408, all former Reading Company; coach no. 582, former Lackawanna; assorted freight cars and caboose, former Lehigh & New England; steel and wood cabooses, former Reading.

SPECIAL EVENTS: Mother's Day Special, Kids' Fun Weekend, Harvest Moon Special, Halloween Train, and Santa Claus Special. Write for schedule.

NEARBY ATTRACTIONS: Hawk Mountain, Crystal Cave, Roadside America, and Cabelas.

DIRECTIONS: Depot is located at Kempton just off Route 737 and Kistler Valley Rd., five miles north of I-78. The site is 20 miles west of Allentown.

Coupon available, see insert.

Middletown, PA

Middletown & Hummelstown Railroad
Train ride, Dinner train, Display

ADDRESS: 136 Brown St. Middletown, PA 17057
TELEPHONE: (717) 944-4435 ext. 0
WEBSITE: www.mhrailroad.com

DESCRIPTION: An 11-mile, 75-minute narrated train ride aboard 1920s vintage Delaware, Lackawanna and Western coaches. Trains depart from an 1891 Freight Station or Indian Echo Caverns Platform. The train follows the towpath of the historic Union Canal and alongside the peaceful Swatara, and crosses a 35-foot bridge above Swatara Creek. Displayed rolling stock includes: a trolley freight car built in Middletown in 1903; a wooden box car from the 1800s with link and pin couplers; a trolley snow sweeper; streetcars built in the 1930s and 40s; and a 1906 Convertible Trolley, which ran until 1947.

SCHEDULE: Memorial Day weekend through August: weekends; September: Sunday; October: weekends; December: weekends and special event trains.

ADMISSION/FARE: Regular train rides: adults, $10; children 2-11, $5; seniors 60+, $9. Check website for special event trains and pricing.

LOCOMOTIVES/ROLLING STOCK: Regular train consist: GE 65-ton nos. 1 and 2 with DL&W coaches; freight locomotives: Alco T6 no. 1016; WM Alco S6 no. 151; CN 2-6-0 no. 91; three SEPTA PCCs; and more.

SPECIAL EVENTS: April: Easter Bunny Express; May: Mother's Special Dinner Train; May, June, September, October, and November: Moonlight Dinner Trains with Sinatra Sounds and Murder Mystery Dinner Trains; Spring and Fall: Hobo Campfire Train; June: Dad's Special BBQ Train; July and August: Train Robbery Fund Raisers, Murder Mystery BBQ Express, and Hobo Sack Lunches on any 11 a.m. departures; last weekend in September: Civil War Reenactment; October: Fall Foliage Trains and Pumpkin Patch Ride; December: Santa's Surprise and Polar Bear Express; December 31 New Year's Celebration Train: 10 p.m. to 1 a.m. other events arranged by request to Passenger Marketing (ext. 18)

NEARBY ATTRACTIONS: Hersheypark: Chocolate World, outlets, Indian Echo Caverns; Harrisburg: State Capitol, Whitaker Center IMAX, State Museum, John Harris Mansion, Pride of the Susquehanna Paddleboat, Harrisburg Senators Baseball Games, Miniature Steam Train Rides, and Water Golf. PA National Fire Museum, the Governor's Residence, and the National Civil War Museum.

DIRECTIONS: From Harrisburg: I-83 south to I-283 south to I-283 east to Middletown/Hummelstown exit. Ramp goes into "Y"; stay right into Middletown. First light, turn right on Main St. Go one block, then left on Race St. Follow to tracks.

Photo courtesy of Middletown & Hummelstown Railroad.

New Hope, PA

New Hope & Ivyland Railroad

Train ride, Dinner train
Standard gauge

EDITOR'S CHOICE

ADDRESS: 32 W Bridge St. New Hope, PA 18938
TELEPHONE: (215) 862-2332
WEBSITE: www.newhoperailroad.com

DESCRIPTION: Visitors can travel into a scene from the past and enjoy a 45-minute, 9-mile round trip to Lahaska Station through the rolling hills and valleys of historic Bucks County on the ex-New Hope Branch of the Reading Company. The train goes along the same route that was filmed in the 1914 movie series "Perils of Pauline." Train tickets can be purchased in the authentic 1891 Reading Company "Witches Hat" train station which once was the location of the railroad telegraph operator who sent and received all messages for the town of New Hope.

SCHEDULE: Trains operate year-round. Schedule varies; visit website for a complete schedule.

ADMISSION/FARE: Holiday excursion: adults, $11; children, $7.75; children under 2, $2.

LOCOMOTIVES/ROLLING STOCK: No. 40, 2-8-0 ex-Cliffside; no. 3028, 4-8-4 ex-Mexican National Railroad; no. 1533, 4-6-0 ex-Canadian National; no. 9, 0-6-0 ex-Virginia Blue Ridge, ex-US Army; no. 2198, EMD GP30, ex-CR, ex-PC, ex-PRR; no. 7087, GE C30-7, ex-CSX; no. 531, GE C30-7, ex-UP; no. 7064, GE C30-7, ex-CSX. Ex-Reading Company, Canadian National & Long Island RR coaches. Various freight equipment.

SPECIAL EVENTS: Easter Bunny Express, Father's Day cab ride giveaways, song and story hour, fall foliage excursions to Ivyland, Halloween trains, Trick-or-treat trains, Railfan weekend, Santa trains, Polar Express trains, dinner trains.

NEARBY ATTRACTIONS: Downtown New Hope, Lambertville, Peddler's Village, Washington Crossing Park, and Sesame Place.

DIRECTIONS: Take I-95 to New Hope exit 51. Go north 10 miles into downtown New Hope. Turn left on Bridge St., go one block, and the driveway is on the right.

Coupon available, see insert.
See ad on page A-27.

North East, PA

Lake Shore Railway Museum

Train ride, Museum, Display
Standard and 7 ½" gauge

ADDRESS: 31 Wall St., PO Box 571 North East, PA 16428
TELEPHONE: (814) 725-1911
WEBSITE: http://lsrhs.railway.museum

DESCRIPTION: A restored New York Central passenger station built in 1899 by the Lake Shore & Michigan Southern houses an extensive collection of displays. The museum is adjacent to CSX and NS main lines. A passenger/freight station built in 1869 by the LS&MS is also on the grounds. There are demonstrations of Heisler fireless locomotive on selected weekends and a train ride on 7½" gauge.

SCHEDULE: May 31 to September 3: Wednesday to Sunday, 12 to 4 p.m.; April 22 to May 28, September, and October: weekends only, 12 to 4 p.m.

ADMISSION/FARE: Donations appreciated.

LOCOMOTIVES/ROLLING STOCK: NYC U25B no. 2500; CSS&SB no. 802 "Little Joe" electric locomotive; Illuminating Co. no. 6 Heisler fireless locomotive, Erie Dock Co. no. 7 ore hopper shunt; Pullman "NightStar;" CB&Q baggage car no. 1530; GN dining car no. 1251 "Lake Wenatchee;" GN sleeping car "Pend O'Reille River;" 18 additional passenger and freight cars, cabooses.

SPECIAL EVENTS: September 23 and 24, Wine Country Harvest Festival; November 25 and 26 and December 2 and 3, Christmas at the Station.

NEARBY ATTRACTIONS: Peek'n Peak Resort, Presque Isle State Park, Erie Zoological Society, Waldameer Amusement Park, Lake Erie nature walks, bicycling tours, beaches and marinas.

DIRECTIONS: Located at Wall and Robinson streets. Fifteen miles east of Erie, PA; two miles north of I-90, exit 41; three blocks south of US20.

Photo courtesy of Rodney E. Blystone III.
Coupon available, see insert.
See ad on page A-5.

Philadelphia, PA
Franklin Institute Science Museum
Museum

ADDRESS: 20th St. & the Ben Franklin Pkwy., 222 N 20th St. Philadelphia, PA 19103
TELEPHONE: (215) 448-1200
WEBSITE: www.fi.edu

DESCRIPTION: The Baldwin 60000 steam locomotive has become part of an exciting new attraction. "The Train Factory" transports visitors to an active turn-of-the-century train works where they feel the steam, hear the noise of the machines, and meet some of the people who worked to create America's locomotives. Visitors explore original and modern train technology as they journey through the sections of this exhibit, including The Machine Shop, The Track Shop, Research and Development, Accident Investigation, and the Baldwin 60000 test run.

SCHEDULE: Year-round: daily, 9:30 a.m. to 5 p.m.

ADMISSION/FARE: Call or check website for information.

LOCOMOTIVES/ROLLING STOCK: Baldwin 4-10-2 no. 60000.

DIRECTIONS: Center City Philadelphia, museum district.

Photo courtesy of The Franklin Institute Science Museum, The Ben Franklin National Memorial.

Portage, PA
Portage Station Museum
Museum

ADDRESS: Portage Area Historical Society, PO Box 45 Portage, PA 15946
TELEPHONE: (814) 736-9223 or (814) 736-8589

DESCRIPTION: Restored PRR train station built in 1926.

SCHEDULE: Wednesday and Saturday, 1 to 4 p.m.; or by appointment.

NEARBY ATTRACTIONS: Located next to the Pennsylvania Mainline.

DIRECTIONS: PA Route 53 into Portage and turn onto Lee St. Next to McDonald's.

Reading, PA

Reading Company Technical and Historical Society
Train ride

ADDRESS: PO Box 15143 Reading, PA 19612
TELEPHONE: (610) 372-5513
WEBSITE: www.readingrailroad.org

DESCRIPTION: The RCT&HS re-creates the old-fashioned "rail-ramble" excursion aboard preserved ex-Reading cars and locomotives. They travel along the former Pennsylvania Railroad Schuylkill Valley branch line through the scenic countryside of northern-central Berks County. These excursion trains are operated through the generosity of the Reading Blue Mountain & Northern Railroad Company.

SCHEDULE: Temple Station: Memorial Day to Labor Day, Saturday and Sunday, 12 to 5 p.m.; check website for excursions.

Robertsdale, PA

Friends of the East Broad Top Museum
Museum

SITE ADDRESS: Main St. Robertsdale, PA 16674
MAILING ADDRESS: PO Box 68 Robertsdale, PA 16674
TELEPHONE: (814) 625-2388
E-MAIL: febt@aol.com
WEBSITE: www.febt.org

DESCRIPTION: Located in two historic buildings at the former southern operating terminus of the East Broad Top Railroad. Exhibits and displays illustrate the history of the East Broad Top Railroad and the men and women who constructed, maintained, and operated the railroad.

SCHEDULE: June 4 to September 4: Saturday, 10 a.m. to 5 p.m.; Sunday, 1 to 5 p.m.

ADMISSION/FARE: Free. Donations appreciated.

LOCOMOTIVES/ROLLING STOCK: EBT maintenance-of-way handcar; EBT combination passenger-baggage cars nos. 16 and 18 (stored off-site); EBT baggage-express car no. 29 (stored off-site).

SPECIAL EVENTS: June 4 and 5, Summer Open House; August 13, EBT Rebirthday Celebration; October 8 and 9, Fall Open House and Reunion.

NEARBY ATTRACTIONS: East Broad Top Railroad, Broad Top Area Coal Miners Museum, Raystown Lake.

DIRECTIONS: Approximately 17 miles southwest of Orbisonia/Rockhill Furnace (EBT and US522), and 20 miles north of Breezewood (I-70, I-76, and US30).

Rockhill Furnace, PA

East Broad Top Railroad
Train ride

SITE ADDRESS: Route 994, Orbisonia Station Rockhill Furnace, PA 17249
MAILING ADDRESS: PO Box 158 Rockhill Furnace, PA 17249
TELEPHONE: (814) 447-3011
E-MAIL: ebtrr@innernet.net
WEBSITE: www.ebtrr.com

DESCRIPTION: The East Broad Top Railroad is an operating narrow gauge railroad that was chartered in 1856. The road hauled coal, freight, mail, express, and passengers for more than 80 years. Today it offers passengers a 10-mile, 60-minute ride through Aughwick Valley. On display is the railroad yard with shops, an operating roundhouse, and a turntable. Dates, times, and fares are subject to change. Call or write for latest information.

SCHEDULE: June through October: weekends, 11 a.m., 1, and 3 p.m.

ADMISSION/FARE: Adults, $10; children 2-11, $7.

LOCOMOTIVES/ROLLING STOCK: 1912 Baldwin locomotive 2-8-2 no. 14; 1914 Baldwin locomotive 2-8-2 no. 15.

SPECIAL EVENTS: Saturday, August 12, Appreciation Day: fares half-price, roundhouse and shop tours, special displays and activities, including Twilight Train. October 14 and 15, Fall Spectacular: extra train operating.

NEARBY ATTRACTIONS: Raystown Lake, Rockhill Trolley Museum.

DIRECTIONS: Pennsylvania Turnpike, exit Willow Hill or Fort Littleton. Also, US Route 22 to US Route 522. See the website for detailed directions and map.

Coupon available, see insert.

Rockhill Furnace, PA

Rockhill Trolley Museum
Trolley ride
Standard gauge

SITE ADDRESS: Meadow St. Rockhill Furnace, PA
MAILING ADDRESS: 1003 N Chester Rd. West Chester, PA 19380
TELEPHONE: (610) 692-5094 (Group Tours)
E-MAIL: info@rockhilltrolley.org
WEBSITE: www.rockhilltrolley.org

DESCRIPTION: A three-mile, 30-minute ride over the former Shade Gap branch of the East Broad Top Railroad aboard a restored trolley. A new 3,000-foot track extension takes riders into Blacklog Narrows. The collection has nine operational trolleys, including an operating open car, a Philadelphia PCC, high-speed interurban cars, and fascinating maintenance-of-way cars like a huge snowplow and a 106-year-old snow sweeper.

SCHEDULE: Memorial Day weekend through October: weekends. Weekday tours by arrangement. Trolley rides operate 11 a.m. to 4:15 p.m.

ADMISSION/FARE: Adults, $5; children, $2; group rates available; good for unlimited rides on day purchased, except for special events.

LOCOMOTIVES/ROLLING STOCK: York Railway's no. 163, 1924 Brill curveside; no. 1875 1912 open car; no. 311 Johnstown Traction Co. Birney car; Philadelphia and Western no. 205 Brill Bullet car; no. 172 single track semi-convertible car; many other trolleys on display; 100-year-old snowsweeper, snowplow, and more.

SPECIAL EVENTS: July 4th and Labor Day weekends, Ice Cream Night Trolley; Columbus Day weekend, Fall Spectacular; first Saturday in December, Santa's Trolley.

NEARBY ATTRACTIONS: East Broad Top Railroad, Raystown Lake, Swigart Antique Car Museum, Altoona Railroaders Museum, Horseshow Curve, and Altoona.

DIRECTIONS: Twenty miles north of exit 13 of Pennsylvania Turnpike, just off Route 522; opposite the East Broad Top Railroad.

Photo courtesy of Doug Peters
Coupon available, see insert.

Lackawanna County Electric City Trolley Station & Museum

Museum

ADDRESS: 300 Cliff St. Scranton, PA 18503
TELEPHONE: (570) 963-6590
WEBSITE: www.ectma.org or www.visitnepa.org

DESCRIPTION: The museum tells the story of electric traction in the Northeast. A one-hour ride highlights the north portal of Crown Ave. Tunnel, one of the longest interurban tunnels.

SCHEDULE: Museum: April 1 to December: daily, 9 a.m. to 5 p.m.; Ride: April 1 to October: Wednesday to Sunday; November and December, special events and rides.

ADMISSION/FARE: To be announced.

LOCOMOTIVES/ROLLING STOCK: 1926 Brill trolley car no. 76.

SPECIAL EVENTS: Thanksgiving weekend, Toys for Tots; first two December weekends, Santa visits.

NEARBY ATTRACTIONS: Steamtown National Historic Site, Lackawanna Coal Mine Montage, Red Barons AAA baseball.

DIRECTIONS: I-815 to exit 185; follow signs for Trolley Museum and Steamtown NHS.

Photo courtesy of American Views Claire Wagner.
See ad on page A-21.

Steamtown National Historic Site

Train ride, Museum, Display

SITE ADDRESS: Park entrance: Cliff St. from Lackawanna Ave. Scranton, PA 18503
MAILING ADDRESS: 150 S Washington Ave. Scranton, PA 18503
TELEPHONE: (570) 340-5200
WEBSITE: www.nps.gov/stea

DESCRIPTION: Visitors can experience the history of steam railroading through museum displays, multimedia exhibits, film, occasional excursions, and guided locomotive shop tours at the former DL&W Railroad Scranton yards.

SCHEDULE: Daily, year-round (winter hours may be in effect December 31 through mid-April). Closed Thanksgiving, Christmas, and New Year's Day.

ADMISSION/FARE: Prices vary. Check website for details.

LOCOMOTIVES/ROLLING STOCK: CN 2-8-2 no. 3254; CP 4-6-2 no. 2317; Baldwin Locomotive Works 0-6-0 no. 26; many more, including UP 4-8-8-4 "Big Boy" no. 4012, on static display.

SPECIAL EVENTS: April, National Park Week; October, Fall Foliage excursion rides; December, children's holiday event.

NEARBY ATTRACTIONS: Electric City Trolley Station & Museum, Everhart Museum, Anthracite Heritage Museum, Lackawanna Coal Mine, Scranton Iron Furnace State Park, Nay Aug Park, Lackawanna State Park, Lackawanna County Stadium, Montage Ski Resort.

DIRECTIONS: I-81 to exit 185, stay in the left lanes to downtown Scranton, left at first light. Lackawanna Ave. past Greyhound/Martz Bus Terminal, left on Cliff St.

Photo courtesy of NPS Photo.

Shartlesville, PA

Roadside America
Display, Model train layout

ADDRESS: 109 Roadside Dr. Shartlesville, PA 19554
TELEPHONE: (610) 488-6241
WEBSITE: www.roadsideamericainc.com

DESCRIPTION: More than 60 years in the making, this display includes 2,570 feet of track running O gauge trains, trolleys, and 250 railroad cars. This panorama of life in rural United States spans more than 200 years in time and shows, in exquisite miniature, how people lived and worked in pioneer days up to the present.

SCHEDULE: July 1 through Labor Day: weekdays, 9 a.m. to 6:30 p.m.; weekends to 7 p.m.; September 6 through June 30: weekdays, 10 a.m. to 5 p.m.; weekends to 6 p.m.

ADMISSION/FARE: Adults, $5; seniors, $4.50; children 6-11, $2.50; children under 6, free.

DIRECTIONS: Take I-78 to exit 23. Located at 109 Roadside Dr.

Strasburg, PA

Choo Choo Barn, Traintown U.S.A.®

Display, Model train layout
O, HO, and N scale

ADDRESS: Route 741 East Strasburg, PA 17579
TELEPHONE: (800) 450-2920 or (717) 687-7911
WEBSITE: www.choochoobarn.com

DESCRIPTION: This 1,700-square-foot miniature display of Lancaster County was built mostly by one family. It includes 22 O, HO, and N-gauge trains and more than 150 engines and vehicles. It was selected by Lionel Trains for participation in their Historic Layout Series.

SCHEDULE: April 1 to December 31: daily, 10 a.m. to 5 p.m.

ADMISSION/FARE: Adults, $5.50; children 5-12, $3.50; children under 5, free.

NEARBY ATTRACTIONS: Strasburg RR, RR Museum of PA, and National Toy Train Museum.

DIRECTIONS: Located along Route 741 east of Strasburg.

Photo courtesy of Fred M. Dole; coupon available, see insert.

KEY TO SYMBOLS

Handicapped accessible	Restaurant	Arts and crafts	Association of Railway Museums
Parking	Picnic area	Memberships available	Tourist Railway Association, Inc.
Bus/RV parking	Dining car	Send S.A.S.E. for brochure	Amtrak service to nearby city
Gift, book, or museum shop	Excursions	National Register of Historic Places	VIA service to nearby city
Refreshments	Guided tours	VISA MasterCard DISCOVER AMERICAN EXPRESS Card	Credit cards accepted

Strasburg, PA

National Toy Train Museum

Museum

ADDRESS: 300 Paradise Ln., PO Box 248 Strasburg, PA 17579-0248
TELEPHONE: (717) 687-8976
E-MAIL: nationaltoytrainmuseum@traincollectors.org
WEBSITE: www.traincollectors.org

DESCRIPTION: Five operating layouts feature toy trains from the mid-1800s to the present. The toy trains on display are presented in a colorful and exciting turn-of-the-century setting. The museum also has a vast collection of floor toys, electric trains, and train-related accessories. See Lionel, American Flyer, Marx, Marklin, LGB, and many others. The layouts are in standard, O, S, G, and HO gauges.

SCHEDULE: May 1 throgh October 31: daily; April, November, and December: weekends, 10 a.m. to 5 p.m. No one admitted ½ hour before closing.

ADMISSION/FARE: Adults, $4; senior citizens 65+, $3; children 6-12, $2; children under 5, free; family rate, $12.

DIRECTIONS: From US30: south on 896, east on 741, north on Paradise Ln.

Strasburg, PA

Railroad Museum of Pennsylvania

Museum

ADDRESS: Route 741, PO Box 125 Strasburg, PA 17579
TELEPHONE: (717) 687-8628
WEBSITE: www.rrmuseumpa.org

DESCRIPTION: A world-class collection of over 100 steam, electric, and diesel-electric locomotives and passenger and freight cars, as well as railroad-related art and artifacts. The 100,000-square-foot Rolling Stock Hall and outdoor restoration yard exhibit equipment dating from 1825 to 1992. Other features are the Stewart Junction interactive education center, Steinman Station replica depot, and Whistle Stop Shop museum store.

SCHEDULE: Monday to Saturday, 9 a.m. to 5 p.m.; Sunday, 12 to 5 p.m.

ADMISSION/FARE: Adults 18-59, $7; seniors 60+, $6; youth 6-17, $5; children under 6, free. Group rates available with advance reservation.

SPECIAL EVENTS: A variety of railroad-themed and holiday events, Members Day, children's days, workshops, educational lectures, museum rambles, and other activities.

NEARBY ATTRACTIONS: Strasburg Rail Rd., National Toy Train Museum, Choo Choo Barn, Pennsylvania Dutch attractions, and Lancaster County area museums and heritage sites.

DIRECTIONS: 10 miles east of Lancaster on Pennsylvania Route 741.

Photo courtesy of Railroad Museum of Pennsylvania, PHMC.

Strasburg, PA

Strasburg Rail Road

Train ride
Standard gauge

ADDRESS: Route 741 East, 301 Gap Rd., PO Box 96 Strasburg, PA 17579
TELEPHONE: (717) 687-7522
WEBSITE: www.strasburgrailroad.com

DESCRIPTION: A 45-minute ride aboard a shortline railroads goes through Amish farmland. Visitors can ride a vintage steam train to Groff's Grove for a picnic or dine aboard the Dining Car. They can also see the Cagney Steam Train (¼ the size of a standard train), try out the "people-powered" Pump Car, tour the mechanical shop, and see Reading car no. 10, a turn-of-the-century "mansion on wheels" for railroad tycoons and dignitaries.

SCHEDULE: Times and equipment may vary. See website for current schedule.

ADMISSION/FARE: Please see website for current rates. Group rates also available.

LOCOMOTIVES/ROLLING STOCK: No. 90, an ex-Great Western 2-10-0; no. 475, an ex-Norfolk & Western 4-8-0; no. 89, an ex-Canadian National 2-6-0; no. 31, an ex-Canadian National 0-6-0; no. 972, an ex-Canadian Pacific Railway 4-6-0; no. 4, an 0-4-0 camelback from the Reading; GE 44-tonner no. 9331; Plymouths nos. 1 and 2; early 20th-century wooden passenger cars; over a dozen early freight cars.

SPECIAL EVENTS: A Day Out with Thomas ™ events, Easter Bunny Trains, Trains & Troops Weekend; Santa Trains.

NEARBY ATTRACTIONS: Across the street from the Railroad Museum of Pennsylvania, near Cherry-Crest Farm's Amazing Maize Maze and Dutch Wonderland Amusement Park. Packages available.

DIRECTIONS: On Route 741 one mile east of Strasburg.

Oil Creek Railway Historical Society, Inc.

Train ride, Dinner train

SITE ADDRESS: 407 S Perry St. Titusville, PA 16354
MAILING ADDRESS: 7 Elm St. Oil City, PA 16301
TELEPHONE: (814) 676-1733
WEBSITE: octrr.clarion.edu

DESCRIPTION: Highlights include: a 27-mile, 2¹/₂-hour train ride that runs through "The Valley That Changed the World," rolling RPO with cancellation stamp, and Caboose Motel adjacent to Perry Street Station.

SCHEDULE: June and September departures: weekends only, 1 p.m. July and August departures: Wednesday through Sunday, 1 p.m. October departures: Wednesday, 11 a.m. and 1 p.m.; Thursday and Friday, 11 a.m.; weekends, 11 a.m. and 3 p.m.; special events train departures: 1 p.m. Halloween train departures: 6 p.m.

ADMISSION/FARE: Adults, $12; seniors 60+, $11; children 3-12, $8.

LOCOMOTIVES/ROLLING STOCK: 1947 Alco S-2 no. 75; 26-ton open gondola car, built 1944 for the Great Northern Railroad; Railway Post Office car, built 1927 by the Chesapeake & Ohio; multiple-unit coaches, built 1930.

SPECIAL EVENTS: February 11, Sweetheart Run; March 11, St. Patrick's Day Ride; April 8, Peter Cottontail Express; May 13, Mother's Day; November 11, Veterans' Day/Thanksgiving Express; August 12, Speeder Runs; select Saturdays in July and August, and September 9, 16, & 23, Murder Mystery Dinner Theater.

NEARBY ATTRACTIONS: DeBence Antique Music Museum; Drake Well Museum; Oil Creek State Park; Tyred Wheels Auto Museum; Venango Museum of Art, Science & Industry; and Two Mile Run County Park.

DIRECTIONS: Route 8 north or south to Titusville, watch for signs.

Photo courtesy of Betty Squire.
Coupon available, see insert.

Pennsylvania Trolley Museum

Trolley ride, Museum, Display
Standard and 5' 2½" gauge

ADDRESS: 1 Museum Rd. Washington, PA 15301
TELEPHONE: (724) 228-9256
WEBSITE: www.pa-trolley.org

DESCRIPTION: This 4-mile trolley ride has turning loops at both ends. The museum experience includes a video on the trolley era, a pictorial exhibit, the museum store, and a guided tour of the carbarn. A daily tour is available (for an additional fee of $2 for adults, $1 for children) of the new 28,000-square-foot Trolley Display Building, which includes 30 trolleys. This tour shows the cars in all conditions from "factory fresh" to "diamonds in the rough."

SCHEDULE: April through December: weekends, 11 a.m. to 5 p.m. Memorial Day through Labor Day: weekdays, 10 a.m. to 4 p.m. and weekends, 11 a.m. to 5 p.m. Last trolley leaves one hour before closing. Tour of the Trolley Display Building at 1:30 p.m. each day of operation (except during Bunny, Pumpkin, and Santa Trolleys).

ADMISSION/FARE: Adults, $6; seniors 65+, $5; children 3-15, $4.

LOCOMOTIVES/ROLLING STOCK: Streetcars from Pittsburgh, Philadelphia, Johnstown, Boston, and New Orleans. Armco Steel/Baldwin Westinghouse 1930 diesel switcher; PA Transformer/HK Porter 1942 diesel switcher.

SPECIAL EVENTS: April 14 and 15, Easter Bunny Trolley; June 24 and 25, Cruz'in with Trolleys; September 10, Antique Trucks & Trolleys; October 21, 22, 28, and 29, Pumpkin Patch Trolley; November 24 and 25, December 2, 3, 9, and 10, Santa Trolley; December 16, 17, and 27 through 30, Trolleys & Toy Trains.

DIRECTIONS: Thirty miles southwest of Pittsburgh. Take I-79 south to exit 41 Racetrack Rd., or I-79 north to exit 40 Meadowlands. Follow the museum signs 3 miles.

Photo courtesy of William M. Fronczek, Jr., M.D.
Coupon available, see insert.

Waynesboro, PA

Red Run Express-Washington Township
Train ride

ADDRESS: 13013 Welty Rd. Waynesboro, PA 17268
TELEPHONE: (717) 762-3128

DESCRIPTION: A miniature train ride around a 700-foot track and through tunnel building boards.

SCHEDULE: Memorial Day to Labor Day: weekends, 1 to 5 p.m.

ADMISSION/FARE: Free.

LOCOMOTIVES/ROLLING STOCK: Locomotive powered by Model A Ford engine, one coal car with one seat, one caboose, and two passenger cars (open).

SPECIAL EVENTS: Usually second weekend in December, Christmas Ride with Santa, free ride, refreshments. Call in early December to verify date.

NEARBY ATTRACTIONS: Hagerstown, MD Round House & Museum; Brunswick, MD Railroad Museum; and Martinsburg, WV Railroad Museum.

DIRECTIONS: US Route 15 north to Route 140, then Route 140 west to Penna Rd., which becomes Route 16. Follow Route 16 to Red Run Park.

Wellsboro, PA

Tioga Central Railroad *EDITOR'S CHOICE*
Train ride
Standard gauge

ADDRESS: PO Box 269 Wellsboro, PA 16901
TELEPHONE: (570) 724-0990
WEBSITE: www.tiogacentral.com

DESCRIPTION: A 90-minute excursion runs 24 miles round trip. A 42-mile round-trip train on Saturday evenings available in July and August.

SCHEDULE: May 8 to October 17: weekend departures at 11 a.m., 1 and 3 p.m.

ADMISSION/FARE: Adults, $12; seniors 60+, $11; children 6-12, $7. Children under 6, free with paying adult.

LOCOMOTIVES/ROLLING STOCK: Alco S2 no. 14; Alco RS1 no. 62; Alco RS3 no. 506.

SPECIAL EVENTS: October 21 through 23, Wellsboro Rail Days: special trains and longer runs for rail fans.

NEARBY ATTRACTIONS: Grand Canyon of Pennsylvania, Ives Run Recreation Area, many fine restaurants and Main St. shopping in beautiful Wellsboro.

DIRECTIONS: Three miles north of Wellsboro on SR287. Wellsboro is on US Route 6 east-west, and Pennsylvania Route 287 north-south; 35 miles south of Corning, NY.

Photo courtesy of Rich Stoving.

West Chester, PA

West Chester Railroad/4 States Railway Service Inc.

Train ride
Standard gauge
Radio frequency: 160.6050

SITE ADDRESS: 230 E Market St. West Chester, PA 19382
MAILING ADDRESS: PO Box 385 Yorklyn, DE 19736
TELEPHONE: (610) 430-2233
WEBSITE: www.westchesterrr.net

DESCRIPTION: A 16-mile round trip runs from West Chester to Glen Mills. This line is the unused portion of SEPTA's R-3 Elwyn line, which is very scenic as it follows Chester Creek in western Delaware County through eastern Chester County.

SCHEDULE: April to December, Sunday; call for information on special events.

ADMISSION/FARE: Adults, $10; children 2-12, $5.

LOCOMOTIVES/ROLLING STOCK: GP9 no. 6499; no. 1803 is DRS18U Alco former CP 1803; Reading Blue Liners coaches nos. 9114, 9124, 9117, 9107; baggage car former Pennsy B-60 7551; Alco C424 former CP 4230; and more.

SPECIAL EVENTS: Easter Bunny Express; third weekend in September, West Chester Restaurant Festival; October, Fall Foliage; November, Holiday Express; November and December, Santa Express.

NEARBY ATTRACTIONS: Valley Forge National Park, West Chester Restaurants, Chadds Ford, Brandywine Museum, and Winterthur Longwood Gardens.

DIRECTIONS: Hwy. 202, exit Gay St./West Chester. Follow Gay to Matlack turning left, one block to Market, left at railroad station, one block on right.

Coupon available, see insert.

PENNSYLVANIA

Williamsport

Williamsport, PA

Thomas T. Taber Museum of the Lycoming County Historical Society
Museum

ADDRESS: 858 W Fourth St. Williamsport, PA 17701
TELEPHONE: (570) 326-3326
WEBSITE: www.lycoming.org/lchsmuseum

DESCRIPTION: The model train exhibit features over 300 toy trains. There are also period rooms featuring furniture and machinery from the 19th century. Exhibits change often, keeping the Historical Society fresh and interesting for every visit.

SCHEDULE: Year-round: Tuesday through Friday, 9:30 a.m. to 4 p.m.; Saturday, 11 a.m. to 4 p.m.; Sunday, 1 to 4 p.m. November through April: closed Sunday. Major holidays: closed.

ADMISSION/FARE: Adults, $5; seniors (AARP/AAA), $4; children, $2.50.

SPECIAL EVENTS: November and Toy Train Expo. Area collectors have displays and layouts throughout the museum.

NEARBY ATTRACTIONS: Clyde Peeling's Reptile Land, Little League Museum.

Photo courtesy of Terry Wild Studio.
Coupon available, see insert.

KEY TO SYMBOLS

Handicapped accessible	Restaurant	Arts and crafts	Association of Railway Museums
Parking	Picnic area	Memberships available	Tourist Railway Association, Inc.
Bus/RV parking	Dining car	Send S.A.S.E. for brochure	Amtrak service to nearby city
Gift, book, or museum shop	Excursions	National Register of Historic Places	VIA service to nearby city
Refreshments	Guided tours	Credit cards accepted	

RHODE ISLAND

Newport, RI
Newport Dinner Train
Dinner train
Standard gauge

ADDRESS: 19 Americas Cup Ave.,
PO Box 1081 Newport, RI 02840
TELEPHONE: (800) 398-7427 or
(401) 841-8700
E-MAIL: info@newportdinnertrain.com
WEBSITE: ww.newportdinnertrain.com

Newport

DESCRIPTION: Rhode Island's only dinner train, traveling 22 miles round trip along scenic Narragansett Bay. Visitors can step back to a time when dining aboard a luxury train was a statement of elegance and privilege. The vintage rail cars have been meticulously restored to quietly bear the ambiance and aura of the golden age of railroading.

SCHEDULE: May through December. Please see website for schedule.

ADMISSION/FARE: Prices vary depending upon excursion. Please call or visit website for more information.

LOCOMOTIVES/ROLLING STOCK: Restored 1942-1944 Budd cars and two GE-44 ton locomotives.

SPECIAL EVENTS: Murder Mystery Trains, Cabaret Dining, Rail and Sail excursions.

TRAVEL TIP: *Streamliners*

You'll find many types of diesel locomotives on today's tourist and museum railroads, but among the most popular are streamlined units from the 1940s and 1950s. Built in an age when styling was king, these sleek and colorful locomotives are a pleasure to see in motion.

SOUTH CAROLINA

•Winnsboro

•Greenwood

Greenwood, SC
Railroad Historical Center
Museum, Display

ADDRESS: c/o the museum
908 S Main St., PO Box 3131
Greenwood, SC 29646
TELEPHONE: (864) 229-7093
E-MAIL: themuseum@greenwood.net

DESCRIPTION: Walk-through exhibit of steam engine, passenger cars, dining car, sleeper car, executive car, and caboose. This exhibit is a partnership of the Railroad Historical Center and the Museum (located four blocks to the north at 106 Main St.). There are no restroom facilities.

SCHEDULE: April through October: every third Friday, 10 am. to 4 p.m.; Saturday, 2 to 4 p.m., weather permitting.

ADMISSION/FARE: Adults, $2; children and seniors, $1; children under 6, free.

LOCOMOTIVES/ROLLING STOCK: Rockton & Rion 2-8-2 steam locomotive no. 19; no. 2102, a 1914 Southern Car Co.., steel trailer car built for the Piedmont & Northern Railway; no. 831, a 76-seat coach built in 1937 for the Seaboard Air Line Railroad; no. 746, a dining car built for the Delaware, Lackawanna & Western Railroad; no. 5, 1920s Pullman sleeper; P&N office car "Carolina"; caboose X23.

SPECIAL EVENTS: Free admission during the SC Festival of Flowers in June and the SC Festival of Discovery in July.

NEARBY ATTRACTIONS: The Museum, 106 Main St., Greenwood; Greenwood State Park; Ninety Six National Historic Site; Lauren's; Lyndley's Fort & the James Dunklin House; Historic Abbeville; Calhoun Falls State Park; Hickory Knob State Park; Table Rock State Park; Sumpter National Forest.

DIRECTIONS: On Main St. approximately three blocks from Uptown Greenwood, next to South Main Baptist Church.

Photo courtesy of Jimmy Wade.
Coupon available, see insert.

Lancaster & Chester Railway and Museum

Museum, Charter service

SITE ADDRESS: 512 S Main St., 2nd Floor Lancaster, SC 29721
MAILING ADDRESS: PO Box 1450 Lancaster, SC 29721
TELEPHONE: (803) 286-2100 or (803) 286-2102, schedule
WEBSITE: www.landcrailroad.com

DESCRIPTION: The L&C Railway is a privately owned short line railroad based in Lancaster. It provides rail freight service to connect its customers to the national rail network through both CSX and Norfolk Southern. The museum houses a scale model replica of the original 29-mile route of the L&C.

SCHEDULE: Every first and third Saturday of the month, 10 a.m. to 4 p.m., except some holidays; call for details.

ADMISSION/FARE: Free. Donations appreciated.

DIRECTIONS: Lancaster and Chester Counties, SC, 35 miles south of Charlotte, NC, on the I-77 corridor and 45 miles north of Columbia, SC.

See ads on page A-8 and A-12.

KEY TO SYMBOLS

Handicapped accessible	Restaurant	Arts and crafts	Association of Railway Museums
Parking	Picnic area	Memberships available	Tourist Railway Association, Inc.
Bus/RV parking	Dining car	Send S.A.S.E. for brochure	Amtrak service to nearby city
Gift, book, or museum shop	Excursions	National Register of Historic Places	VIA service to nearby city
Refreshments	Guided tours	VISA MasterCard DISCOVER AMERICAN EXPRESS Card	Credit cards accepted

Winnsboro, SC

South Carolina Railroad Museum, Inc.

Train ride, Museum, Display, Model train layout
Standard gauge
Radio frequency: 156.865

SITE ADDRESS: 110 Industrial Park Rd. Winnsboro, SC 29180
MAILING ADDRESS: PO Box 643 Winnsboro, SC 29180
TELEPHONE: (803) 635-4242
E-MAIL: info@scrm.org
WEBSITE: www.scrm.org

DESCRIPTION: This is a 10-mile round trip to Greenbrier and Rion. Trains travel over a portion of the former Rockton & Rion Railway. The route was built in the late 1800s as a quarry line to haul the world-famous Winnsboro Blue Granite from the quarries to the Southern Railway at Rockton. The museum also contains a static display train for tours, gallery, and gift shop.

SCHEDULE: June through October: first and third Saturday, 9 a.m. to 4 p.m.

ADMISSION/FARE: Museum and displays: free; train rides: 1st class, $14; lounge, $17; coach: adults, $10; children 1-11, $7; caboose: all, $11.

LOCOMOTIVES/ROLLING STOCK: US Army SW8's nos. 2015 and 2028; US Air Force RS4TCIAs nos. 1249 and 1275; Hampton and Branchville 4-6-0 No. 44 (static display); B&O caboose no. 903878, NKP caboose no. 465.

SPECIAL EVENTS: Two Saturdays prior to Easter, Easter Bunny Express Train; three Saturdays following Thanksgiving, Santa Trains.

NEARBY ATTRACTIONS: South Carolina State Museum, Riverbanks Zoo, Lake Wateree Park.

DIRECTIONS: I-77 exit 34, take SC 34 West 5 miles, the museum is on the left. From I-26, take SC 34 to Winnsboro and follow the brown signs to the museum.

Coupon available, see insert.

TRAVEL TIP: *Cab rides*

Many railroads offer the chance to ride the in the cab, the compartment where the engine crew rides. Here you'll get to see the engineer work the throttle and the brakes. If it's a steam engine you can watch the fireman manipulate the oil firing or shovel coal. Either way, you'll get a great view and be the envy of all your friends.

SOUTH DAKOTA

• Hill City
• Keystone

Madison •

Hill City and Keystone, SD

Black Hills
Central Railroad

Train ride

SITE ADDRESSES: 103 Winter St. Hill City, SD 57745 and
222 Railroad Ave. Keystone, SD 57751
MAILING ADDRESSES: PO Box 1880 Hill City, SD 57745
TELEPHONE: (605) 574-2222
E-MAIL: office@1880train.com

DESCRIPTION: A 20-mile trip on a vintage steam train. Located near Mt. Rushmore and Crazy Horse Memorial, the two-hour round-trip journey between Hill City and Keystone travels through the rugged landscape and offers a western experience steeped in history.

SCHEDULE: Early May through early October, daily. Departures added during summer season. Call, write, or e-mail for information.

ADMISSION/FARE: Adults, $19; children 4-14, $10; children 3 and under, free. Group rates available for parties of 20 and up.

LOCOMOTIVES/ROLLING STOCK: 1926 Baldwin 2-6-2 no. 104 saddle tank; 1919 Baldwin 2-6-2 no. 7; 1928 Baldwin 2-6-6-2 no. 110; 1880s-1910s passenger cars.

SPECIAL EVENTS: July, Fireworks Express; September, Wine Train.

NEARBY ATTRACTIONS: Mt. Rushmore, Crazy Horse Memorial, Custer State Park, the Badlands.

DIRECTIONS: Hwy. 16/385, 26 miles south of Rapid City. Tickets may be purchased at the Hill City Depot, 222 Railroad Ave., which is the truck bypass, or at the Keystone Depot, on the north end of Main St.

Photo courtesy of Rich W. Mills.

333

Madison, SD
Prairie Village
Train ride, Dinner train, Museum, Display
Standard gauge

SITE ADDRESS: Hwys. 34 & 81 Madison, SD 57042-0256
MAILING ADDRESS: PO Box 256 Madison, SD 57042
TELEPHONE: (800) 693-3644 or (605) 256-3644
E-MAIL: prairiev@rapidnet.com
WEBSITE: www.prairievillage.org

DESCRIPTION: Prairie Village is an assembly of turn-of-the-century buildings. There are steam traction engines, gas tractors, and displays of farm equipment. A two-mile loop of track is used for train rides. Buildings include the Wentworth Depot, Junius Depot, and roundhouse/turntable.

SCHEDULE: Museum: May through Labor Day: daily, 10 a.m. to 5 p.m., Sunday 11 a.m. to 4 p.m. Train rides: June through August: every Sunday during Railroad Days and Fall Jamboree.

ADMISSION/FARE: Museum: $5; train: $3.

LOCOMOTIVES/ROLLING STOCK: Duluth & North Eastern 0-6-0 no. 2; Kelly Island Lime & Transportation Co. 0-4-0T no. 11; Orrenstein & Koppel 0-4-0T "Wilhelmine"; Whitcomb 60-ton diesel; GE 80-ton diesel; Northern Pacific Russell snow plow; 4 Rock Island and Illinois Central cabooses.

SPECIAL EVENTS: June, Railroad Days; August, Car Show and Fall Jamboree.

NEARBY ATTRACTIONS: Restored Madison Milwaukee depot, Lake Herman State Park, and Smith-Zimmermann State Museum in Madison.

DIRECTIONS: Prairie Village is 2 miles west of Madison on Hwy. 34. From Sioux Falls, take I-29 north to the Madison/Colman exit, then travel west on Hwy. 34 to Madison.

Photo courtesy of Bill Nolan.

TRAVEL TIP: *Behind the scenes tours*

A great way to experience tourist railroading is to visit the repair shop, and many railroads have begun offering special behind-the-scenes tours that take you where the hard and heavy work takes place. You'll see locomotives and cars under restoration and get a feel for the work that goes into keeping the equipment roadworthy.

TENNESSEE

Chattanooga, TN

A.C. Kalmbach Memorial Library
National Model Railroad Association
Display, Model train layout, Library

ADDRESS: 4121 Cromwell Rd. Chattanooga, TN 37421
TELEPHONE: (423) 894-8144
E-MAIL: lib@hq.nmra.org
WEBSITE: www.nmra.org/library/

DESCRIPTION: Established in 1986, the Kalmbach Memorial Library offers research services. The library currently houses more than 7,000 books and manuals, more than 50,000 periodicals, and about 100,000 photographs of railroad history and modeling. In 2004, it was designated as the "Official Railroad Library of the State of Tennessee."

SCHEDULE: Year-round, Monday through Friday, 8:30 a.m. to 5 p.m.

ADMISSION/FARE: None.

SPECIAL EVENTS: Check the website for special programs and events.

NEARBY ATTRACTIONS: Tennessee Valley Railroad Museum, Lookout Mountain Incline Railway, Chattanooga Choo-Choo, Hamilton Place Mall, Tennessee Aquarium, Rock City, Ruby Falls.

DIRECTIONS: I-75 exit 4 onto Hwy. 153 to Jersey Pike (exit 3), turn left onto Jersey Pike then first right onto Cromwell Rd. NMRA building ¼-mile on right.

Chattanooga, TN
Chattanooga Choo-Choo
Museum, Display, Model train layout, Hotel
HO scale

ADDRESS: 1400 Market St. Chattanooga, TN 37402
TELEPHONE: (800) 872-2529 or (423) 266-5000
WEBSITE: www.choochoo.com

DESCRIPTION: Opened in 1909 as the Southern Railway's Terminal Station, this depot welcomed thousands of travelers during the golden age of railroads. Today, the restored station is the heart of the Chattanooga Choo Choo Holiday Inn, a 24-acre complex that houses 48 passenger cars. A special feature at the complex is the Model Railroad Museum. The HO gauge display is 174 feet long and 33 feet at its widest point. It has over 3,000 feet of track with up to eight trains running constantly on separate loops.

SCHEDULE: Summer, 10 a.m. to 8 p.m.; winter, 10 a.m. to 6 p.m.

ADMISSION/FARE: Adults, $3; children, $1.50; children under 3, free.

NEARBY ATTRACTIONS: Antique trolley ride, Tennessee Aquarium, Rock City, Ruby Falls, Creative Discovery Museum, Incline Railway, Bluff View Art District, Coolidge Park.

DIRECTIONS: Eastbound: I-24 to Lookout Mountain/Broad St. exit 178; S Broad St. split, then follow signs. Westbound: I-74 to exit 178; N Market St. turn, go 6 blocks.

Chattanooga, TN
Tennessee Valley Railroad
Train ride, Dinner train, Museum, Display
Standard gauge

ADDRESS: 4119 Cromwell Rd. Chattanooga, TN 37421-2119
TELEPHONE: (423) 894-8028
WEBSITE: www.tvrail.com

DESCRIPTION: A 45-minute round trip passes through pre-Civil War Missionary Ridge Tunnel. Daylong Dixie Land excursions run on select weekends; most with a dining car luncheon.

SCHEDULE: April to November: Saturday, 10 a.m. to 5 p.m.; Sunday, 11 a.m. to 5 p.m.; spring and fall: weekdays, 10 a.m. to 1 p.m.; summer: weekdays, 10 a.m. to 5 p.m.

ADMISSION/FARE: Adults, $12; children 3-12, $6; group rates/charters.

LOCOMOTIVES/ROLLING STOCK: US Army S-160 2-8-0 no. 610; Southern Railway 2-8-0 no. 630; SR 2-8-2 no. 4501; Kentucky & Tennessee 2-8-2 no. 10; Canadian National steam locomotive no. 5288; US Army Alco RSDI nos. 8669 and 8677; EMD GP7s nos. 1824 and 1829; Budd RDC nos. 20 and 22.

SPECIAL EVENTS: March, Spring Steam Up; October, Autumn Leaf Specials; November to December, Polar Express and Christmas.

NEARBY ATTRACTIONS: Hamilton Place Mall, Tennessee Aquarium, Rock City, Ruby Falls, Incline Railway, Chattanooga Choo Choo, NMRA headquarters, Kalmbach Memorial Library.

DIRECTIONS: I-75 exit 4 onto Hwy. 153 to Jersey Pike (fourth exit), follow signs ⅓ mile.

Photo courtesy of Steve Freer.

Cookeville, TN

Cookeville Depot Museum
Museum, Display, Model train layout

ADDRESS: 116 N Cedar Ave., PO Box 998 Cookeville, TN 38503
TELEPHONE: (931) 528-8570
E-MAIL: depot@cookeville-tn.com

DESCRIPTION: The railroad museum is housed in an old Tennessee Central Railway depot at the corner of Broad St. and Cedar Ave. Built in 1909, the building is listed on the National Register of Historic Places. You will find railway artifacts, old photos of the railroad in Putnam County, and a caboose with its original interior.

SCHEDULE: Tuesday through Saturday, 10 a.m. to 4 p.m.

ADMISSION/FARE: Admission free to self-guided museum.

LOCOMOTIVES/ROLLING STOCK: Louisiana & Arkansas 4-6-0 no. 509; Tennessee Central caboose no. 9828; L&N caboose no. 135.

SPECIAL EVENTS: First Saturday in May, Tennessee Central Rendezvous/Springfest.

NEARBY ATTRACTIONS: 3 lakes, 5 state parks, restaurants, malls, Tennessee Tech University.

DIRECTIONS: I-40 take exit 286 Willow Ave., north. Right on Broad St., depot is on right.

Photo courtesy of Cookeville Depot Museum.

Cowan, TN

Cowan Railroad Museum

Museum

ADDRESS: 108 S Front St. Cowan, TN 37318
TELEPHONE: (931) 967-3078
E-MAIL: commercialclub@yahoo.com
WEBSITE: www.visitcowan.com

DESCRIPTION: Railroad relics, photos, and a model railroad are inside a 100-year-old restored depot with an authentic steam locomotive, flatcar, and caboose.

SCHEDULE: May to October: Thursday to Saturday, 10 a.m. to 4 p.m.; Sunday 1 to 4 p.m.

ADMISSION/FARE: Free; donations are accepted.

LOCOMOTIVES/ROLLING STOCK: 1920 Porter-type 242, NC&StL caboose and flatcar.

SPECIAL EVENTS: September 17, Polly Crockett Days; September 25, Fall in Love with Cowan.

NEARBY ATTRACTIONS: Historic downtown Cowan, with fine dining and specialty shops and the Franklin-Pearson House, a restored railroad hotel.

DIRECTIONS: Hwy. 41A at the railroad track in Cowan.

Photo courtesy of Howard Coulson.

Jackson, TN

Casey Jones Museum and Train Store

Museum

SITE ADDRESS: 30 Casey Jones Ln. Jackson, TN 38305
MAILING ADDRESS: PO Box 11597 Jackson, TN 38308
TELEPHONE: (731) 668-1222
E-MAIL: ntaylor523@yahoo.com
WEBSITE: www.caseyjones.com

DESCRIPTION: Visitors are welcome at the home and railroad museum of Casey Jones. Casey was living in this home until his death in 1900. There are three layouts on display in the 1800s baggage car and a replica of no. 382, Casey's engine, along with a souvenir shop.

SCHEDULE: Year-round: seven days a week, 9 a.m. to 5 p.m.; closed major holidays.

ADMISSION/FARE: Adults, $4; seniors, $3.50; children 6-12, $3; children under 6, free. Lifetime passes available.

LOCOMOTIVES/ROLLING STOCK: Rogers 4-6-0 locomotive; 1800s Mobile & Ohio baggage car; Illinois Central caboose.

NEARBY ATTRACTIONS: State Park, Shiloh National Military Park, Home of Buford Pusser.

DIRECTIONS: Take I-40 exit 80A onto 45. Just off Hwy. 45. Look for the caboose in the sky.

Photo courtesy of Old Country Store.
Coupon available, see insert.

Jackson, TN

Nashville, Chattanooga, and St. Louis Depot and Railroad Museum

Museum, Model train layout
HO gauge

ADDRESS: 582 S Royal St. Jackson, TN 38301
TELEPHONE: (731) 425-8223
E-MAIL: thedepot@cityofjackson.net
WEBSITE: www.cityofjackson.net/departments/recpark/facilities/special/depot.html

DESCRIPTION: The restored NC&StL Depot features a museum that reflects Jackson's history as West Tennessee's railroad hub. A working scale model depicts local railroad heritage. An Amtrak dining car, which seats up to 48 diners, can be rented for catered parties.

SCHEDULE: Year-round: Monday through Saturday, 10 a.m. to 3 p.m.

ADMISSION/FARE: Free.

LOCOMOTIVES/ROLLING STOCK: Former Florida East Coast dining car, "Ft. Matanzas"; Southern Railway caboose X421; Chesapeake & Ohio caboose 3255.

NEARBY ATTRACTIONS: Brooks Shaw's Old Country Store, Historic Casey Jones Home and Railroad Museum, Pinson Mounds State Archaeological Area, Cypress Grove Nature Park, Chickasaw Rustic State Park, Pringles Park, home of West Tennessee Diamond Jaxx baseball.

DIRECTIONS: Turn off Hwy. 45 bypass onto Martin Luther King Dr. at the Jackson Main Post Office and go one block to S Royal St. Turn right, proceed one block, depot is on the left.

Photo courtesy of Moore Studios.

TENNESSEE Jackson

Knoxville, TN

Three Rivers Rambler

Train ride

SITE ADDRESS: Volunteer Landing on Neyland Dr. Knoxville, TN 37902
MAILING ADDRESS: L&N Station, 401 Henley St., Ste. 5 Knoxville, TN 37902
TELEPHONE: (865) 524-9411
WEBSITE: www.threeriversrambler.com

DESCRIPTION: A 1-hour and 20-minute round-trip excursion aboard a vintage train, which includes a restored 1925 steam engine "Lindy." The Three Rivers Rambler travels through east Tennessee farmland to the Three Rivers trestle, where the French Broad & Holsten Rivers meet to form the Tennessee River.

SCHEDULE: Summer: Saturday and Sunday, 2 and 5 p.m.; fall and spring rides available; first three weeks of December: Christmas train (reservations required).

ADMISSION/FARE: Coach: adults, $19; seniors 55+, $17; children 3-12, $11; children under 2, free. (Sales tax included.)

LOCOMOTIVES/ROLLING STOCK: 1925 Baldwin 2-8-0 no. 203, "Lindy"; two 1932 coaches, "Trustworthy" and "Intrepid"; 1940 open-air car "Dauntless"; caboose "Desire."

SPECIAL EVENTS: Football season, Railgates; December, Christmas Trains.

NEARBY ATTRACTIONS: Boat and paddleboat rentals, Star of Knoxville Riverboat, Women's Basketball Hall of Fame, Neyland Stadium, Thompson Boling, Downtown Knoxville, riverfront restaurants, and more.

DIRECTIONS: On I-40, take exit 386B to Neyland Drive. Turn left. Drive two miles to Tennessee Grill parking lot (C-18) on your left. After parking, cross Neyland Drive and proceed down sidewalk to train.

Photo courtesy of Richards Design Group.
Coupon available, see insert.

TRAVEL TIP: _Engineer for an hour_

Many tourist railroads and museums offer the chance to take the throttle and run a locomotive under supervision. These programs are often scheduled during the "off" season and include instruction, classroom training, and the chance to get to know the crews at the railroads. Many offer the chance to operate a real diesel locomotive, and some even offer the same for steam.

Nashville, TN

Tennessee Central Railway Museum
Train ride, Museum, Display, Model train layout

ADDRESS: 220 Willow St. Nashville, TN 37210-2159
TELEPHONE: (615) 244-9001
E-MAIL: hultman@earthlink.net
WEBSITE: www.tcry.org

DESCRIPTION: Offers an excursion train, hobby shop, railroad artifacts, modular HO and N scale model railroads, and museum room. The museum operates passenger excursions in Middle Tennessee. TCRM currently owns several passenger cars, cabooses, work/camp cars, boxcars, motorcars, baggage cars, locomotives, and a passenger business car. One of the main attractions is a fully restored Operation Lifesaver caboose, used to promote safety at railroad highway crossings. The caboose was built in 1974 for the Seaboard Coast Line Railroad and was donated to the museum by the CSX Railroad in 1991.

SCHEDULE: Tuesday through Saturday, 9 a.m. to 3 p.m.; early September, Day Out with Thomas™ event; 20 to 25 excursion trains operate each year.

ADMISSION/FARE: Museum: free; excursion train: varies.

LOCOMOTIVES/ROLLING STOCK: Several museum-owned and privately-owned EMD E8As; TC SW8 52; former Santa Fe coaches TCRX 4711, 4717, 4719, 4733, 4739; buffet-diners TCRX 3113, 3119; slumbercoach TCRX 2095; Pullman business car TC 102; Amtrak F40PHRs 258 and 375; Pullman standard sun lounge-sleeper "Hollywood Beach."

SPECIAL EVENTS: Excursion trains: Valentine's Day; Easter; Fall foliage; early September, A Day Out With Thomas™; Christmas/Santa; more.

NEARBY ATTRACTIONS: Tennessee Titans NFL football, downtown Nashville, Grand Ole Opry House, Opryland Hotel, Nashville Toy Museum, Music Row, Nashville Arena, and Opry Mills Shopping Mall.

DIRECTIONS: Take I-24/40 to eastbound exit 212, Fesslers Ln. Go left onto Fesslers Ln., ½ mile to left on Lebanon Rd., proceed 0.8 mile to right on Fairfield Ave., and follow signs to museum site.

Photo courtesy of Brent Gaddes.

Oak Ridge, TN

Southern Appalachia Railway Museum

Train ride, Dinner train, Display
Standard gauge
Radio frequency: 160.425

EDITOR'S CHOICE

SITE ADDRESS: The Heritage Center Hwy. 58 Oak Ridge, TN
MAILING ADDRESS: PO Box 5870 Knoxville, TN 37928
TELEPHONE: (865) 241-2140
WEBSITE: www.southernappalachia.railway.museum

DESCRIPTION: A 14-mile, 90-minute train ride aboard air-conditioned coaches with a dining car and caboose. The train travels a former Southern Railway branch line through the former Manhattan Project K-25 facility. There are a limited number of evening dinner trains. Additional shortline railroad charters are conducted across the United States.

SCHEDULE: Valentine's Day Dinner Trains, call for exact schedule; April to September: first and third Saturday, October, November, and December: additional weekends and Sundays; departures: 11 a.m., 1, and 3 p.m. Reservations recommended.

ADMISSION/FARE: Scenic train: adults, $13; children 12 and under, $9. Dinner trains and rare mileage excursions vary.

LOCOMOTIVES/ROLLING STOCK: US Atomic Energy Commission 1951 Alco RS-1 5310; Tennessee Valley Authority, formerly US Army, 1943 Alco S-2's nos 7100 and 7125; Central of Georgia 1947; coaches nos. 663, 664, and 665; Southern dining car 3164; SR caboose X261.

SPECIAL EVENTS: Valentine's Day Dinner Trains, Secret City Festival, photography weekend, Horn Honk, Halloween, Thanksgiving, Santa Trains.

NEARBY ATTRACTIONS: Big South Fork National River and Recreation Area, Oak Ridge Manhattan Project tours, American Museum of Science and Energy, and World of Model Trains Exhibit at Oak Ridge Children's Museum.

DIRECTIONS: Six miles north of I-40 exit 356 between Knoxville and Nashville at the East Tennessee Technology Park at Hwy. 58 and Hwy. 327. Because of a planned 2006 road construction project, they may be using a temporary boarding location. Call for updated information.

Photo courtesy of Joh Emory Humpfrey.

Pigeon Forge, TN

Dollywood Express Train

Train ride
Narrow gauge

ADDRESS: 1020 Dollywood Ln. Pigeon Forge, TN 37863-4101
TELEPHONE: (800) Dollywood or (865) 428-9488
WEBSITE: www.dollywood.com

DESCRIPTION: Located in the Village area of Dollywood, the train takes visitors on a 5-mile journey through this scenic park. As passengers ride on the authentic, coal-fired steam train, they can catch a glimpse of the different areas of Dollywood including: Rivertown Junction, The Village, and Craftsman's Valley. The Dollywood Express also takes visitors through replicas of a typical turn-of-the-century mountain village and logging community.

SCHEDULE: Thirty-minute rides every hour during park operating hours.

ADMISSION/FARE: Adults, $43.50; seniors, $40.15; children, $32.35. All-inclusive.

LOCOMOTIVES/ROLLING STOCK: "Klondike Katie," a 1943 Baldwin 2-8-2, former US Army no. 192; "Cinderella," a 1939 Baldwin 2-8-2, former US Army no. 70; open-air passenger cars.

SPECIAL EVENTS: Late March, Festival of Nations; June through August, Kidfest; late September through October, Harvest Celebration; November through December, Smoky Mountain Christmas Festival. School field trips. Special group rates.

NEARBY ATTRACTIONS: Numerous restaurants, lodging, shopping, and attractions in area.

DIRECTIONS: Call for directions.

Photo courtesy of Richards & Southern.

KEY TO SYMBOLS

♿ Handicapped accessible	🍴 Restaurant	🎨 Arts and crafts	arm Association of Railway Museums
P Parking	⛺ Picnic area	🏛 Memberships available	TRAIN Tourist Railway Association, Inc.
P Bus/RV parking	🍽 Dining car	✉ Send S.A.S.E. for brochure	AMTRAK Amtrak service to nearby city
🎁 Gift, book, or museum shop	Excursions	NRHP National Register of Historic Places	VIA VIA service to nearby city
☕ Refreshments	TOUR Guided tours	VISA MasterCard DISCOVER AMERICAN EXPRESS Card	Credit cards accepted

Townsend, TN

Little River Railroad and Lumber Co.

Museum, Display

SITE ADDRESS: 7747 E LaMar Alexander Pkwy., entrance to the Great Smoky Mountains National Park Townsend, TN 37882
MAILING ADDRESS: PO Box 211 Townsend, TN 37882
TELEPHONE: (865) 448-2211
E-MAIL: thurstonphoto@aol.com
WEBSITE: www.littleriverrailroad.org

DESCRIPTION: This organization offers a look at a restored Shay locomotive, depot, steam sawmill, and collection of railroad and lumber company artifacts and photographs. Interpretive displays tell the story of the community.

SCHEDULE: April, May, and September: weekends; June, July, August, and October: daily, 10 a.m. to 5 p.m.; November through March: by appointment only.

ADMISSION/FARE: Free. Donations appreciated.

LOCOMOTIVES/ROLLING STOCK: Little River 3-truck Shay no. 2147, made by the Lima Locomotive Works in 1909; Louisville & Nashville class NE "Little Woody" caboose; L&N steel frame flatcars; Frick portable steam engine.

SPECIAL EVENTS: First Saturday in May through last Saturday in September, Railroad Days, celebrating the heritage of the community: includes steam engine demonstration, music, and food.

NEARBY ATTRACTIONS: Great Smoky Mountains National Park.

DIRECTIONS: Located in Townsend, Tennessee, at the western entrance to the Great Smoky Mountains National Park.

Photo courtesy of Jim Thurston.

TRAVEL TIP: *Dining cars*

While many tourist railroads offer food and beverage services on site or nearby, some still equip their trains with authentic dining cars. This gives visitors the chance to experience a real "dinner in the diner," as it was prepared and served on board a moving train.

TEXAS

Arlington, TX

Six Flags Over Texas Railroad

Train ride
3' Narrow gauge

ADDRESS: PO Box 90191
Arlington, TX 76004-0191
TELEPHONE: (817) 530-6000
WEBSITE: www.sixflags.com

DESCRIPTION: This is a major theme
park with trains running along the
perimeter of the park.

SCHEDULE: Summer: daily; spring and fall: weekends. Call for schedule.

ADMISSION/FARE: $42.99; discounts for
guests under 48 inches and seniors.

LOCOMOTIVES/ROLLING STOCK: 1901 Dickson
0-4-0T converted 2-4-2 with tender, no. 1280;
1897 H.K. Porter 0-4-4T converted 2-4-2 with
tender, no. 1754.

SPECIAL EVENTS: September, Texas Heritage
Crafts Festival; October, Fright Fest; December,
Holiday in the Park.

NEARBY ATTRACTIONS: Texas Rangers baseball, Six Flags Hurricane Harbor Water Park,
Lone Star Park Racetrack, Texas Motor Speedway, Dallas, and Fort Worth.

DIRECTIONS: Located midway between Dallas and Fort Worth in Arlington at the
intersection of I-30 and Texas Hwy. 360.

Austin, TX

Austin Steam Train Association

Train ride
Steam train

ADDRESS: 610 Brazos, PO Box 1632 Austin, TX 78767
TELEPHONE: (512) 477-8468
WEBSITE: www.austinsteamtrain.org

DESCRIPTION: The Austin Steam Train Association provides year-round train excursions
through the Texas hill country and downtown Austin.

SCHEDULE: Year-round: weekends. Schedule changes seasonally. Please call for full details.

ADMISSION/FARE: Prices change seasonally. Please see website for details.

LOCOMOTIVES/ROLLING STOCK: Southern Pacific 2-8-2 no. 786, under restoration; A&TCR Alco RSD-15 no. 442; P-70 class coaches nos. 1699, 1731, 1646, 1658, 1726, 1730; Missouri Pacific lounge car no. 640; Santa Fe caboose no. 999418; Santa Fe Pullman no. 1343; Nickel Plate Pullman lounge 151.

SPECIAL EVENTS: Texas Hill Country Railfair and Festival, Day Out with Thomas™, and Twilight Flyers including Murder Mysteries scheduled throughout the year. Visit website or call the reservation line for dates/times.

DIRECTIONS: Cedar Park depot–US Hwy. 183 at RM 1431. Plaza Saltillo–E 5th St. and Comal St. Please visit our website for a map to our departure locations.

Photo courtesy of Austin Steam Train Association.

Dallas, TX
Age of Steam Railroad Museum
Museum
Standard gauge

ADDRESS: PO Box 153259 Dallas, TX 75315-3259
TELEPHONE: (214) 428-0101
WEBSITE: www.dallasrailwaymuseum.com

DESCRIPTION: A fine collection of steam and early diesel era railway equipment, including a complete heavyweight passenger train featuring restored Missouri-Kansas-Texas dining car and "Glengyle," the oldest all-steel, all-room Pullman.

SCHEDULE: Wednesday through Sunday, 10 a.m. to 5 p.m.

ADMISSION/FARE: Adults, $5; children 12 and under, $2.50; children 2 and under, free.

LOCOMOTIVES/ROLLING STOCK: Union Pacific "Big Boy" steam locomotive no. 4018 and "Centennial" no. 6913; Eagle-Picher Mining Co. 2-10-0 no. 1625; Santa Fe FP-45 no. 97; Pennsylvania Railroad GG-1 electric no. 4903; and more.

SPECIAL EVENTS: May, Dinner in the Diner; September 29 to October 22, Texas State Fair.

NEARBY ATTRACTIONS: The museum is located in Fair Park, a year-round collection of arts and cultural institutions housed in a restored art deco building originally constructed for the 1936 Texas centennial. The park is located in a historic district with eight museums, 1½ miles east of downtown Dallas.

DIRECTIONS: Two miles east of downtown; I-30 westbound, exit 47A right onto Exposition Ave., left on Parry Ave.

Photo courtesy of Age of Steam, Irwin Arnstein.

Dallas, TX

McKinney Avenue Transit Authority

Train ride
1:1 scale

ADDRESS: 3153 Oak Grove Ave. Dallas, TX 75204
TELEPHONE: (214) 855-0006
WEBSITE: www.mata.org

DESCRIPTION: McKinney Avenue Trolley operates a vintage fleet of streetcars that run on 3.6 miles of track in the Uptown area of Dallas. Trolley rides are free, but the cars are also available to charter for parties.

SCHEDULE: Weekdays, 7 a.m. to 10 p.m.; weekends, 10 a.m. to 10 p.m.

ADMISSION/FARE: Free.

LOCOMOTIVES/ROLLING STOCK: Stone & Webster type car no. 186, St. Louis Car Co. 1913, Melbourne W-2 no. 369 M&MTB 1926, Porto Portugal no. 122 J.G. Brill 1909, Birney Safety car no. 636 J.G. Brill 1920, P.C.C. no. 143 St. Louis Car Co. 1946, Interurban Dining car "Morning Star" no. 332 Northern TX Traction co, 1912.

SPECIAL EVENTS: The quarterly fundraiser, the "Trolley Dine-Around," incorporates the trolley and area restaurants into a progressive dinner. Call for schedule and reservations.

NEARBY ATTRACTIONS: Dallas Museum of Art, the Arts District, Gallery Walk District, Antique District, shopping, and over 80 unique restaurants.

DIRECTIONS: One mile north of Downtown in Uptown, along historic McKinney Ave.

Photo courtesy of Allan H. Berner.

Diboll, TX

The History Center

Museum, Display
Standard gauge

ADDRESS: 102 N Temple Diboll, TX 75941
TELEPHONE: (936) 829-3543
WEBSITE: www.thehistorycenteronline.com

DESCRIPTION: The Center maintains static displays and exhibits, including an archive and research collection pertaining to the history of central eastern Texas, especially logging railroads and area shortlines. It also holds the archives of the Texas South-Eastern Railroad.

SCHEDULE: Monday to Friday, 8 a.m. to 5 p.m.; Saturday, 9 a.m. to 1 p.m.; closed most major holidays.

ADMISSION/FARE: Free.

LOCOMOTIVES/ROLLING STOCK: Texas South-Eastern Railroad Baldwin 4-6-0 no. 13; Southern Pine Lumber Company log car no. 1893 (ca.1918); Texas South-Eastern Railroad caboose no. 6 (built by Santa Fe in 1948 as caboose no. 2246).

NEARBY ATTRACTIONS: Texas Forestry Museum in Lufkin and Texas State Railroad in Rusk.

DIRECTIONS: East side of US Hwy. 59 in downtown Diboll.

Photo courtesy of Johnathan Gerland.

Flatonia, TX

Flatonia Rail Park

SITE ADDRESS: I-10 halfway between San Antonio and Houston Flatonia, TX
MAILING ADDRESS: PO Box 66 Flatonia, TX 78941
TELEPHONE: (979) 743-5366
WEBSITE: https://home.comcast.net/~frhsnews

DESCRIPTION: For 35 years, the Flatonia Railroad Historical Society has welcomed everyone to join. The Photo Pavilion was constructed in 2001 so that railfans would have a safe, covered location to congregate, view passing trains, take photos, and relax. Visitors can see Southern Pacific's historic Tower no. 3 located in downtown Flatonia.

SCHEDULE: 24 hours, 7 days a week; guided tours by appointment.

LOCOMOTIVES/ROLLING STOCK: Southern Pacific caboose no. 4743.

SPECIAL EVENTS: FRHS meetings, one Saturday per month, 1 p.m.

NEARBY ATTRACTIONS: Original San Antonio and Arkansas Pass Freight Depot, E.A. Arnim Archives and Museum.

DIRECTIONS: I-10, halfway between San Antonio and Houston.

See ad on page A-35.

Fort Worth, TX
Forest Park Miniature Train
Train ride
24" gauge

SITE ADDRESS: 2116 Morning Glory Ave. Fort Worth, TX 76111
MAILING ADDRESS: Colonial Pkwy. in Forest Park, PO Box 183 Fort Worth, TX 76101
TELEPHONE: (817) 336-3328
WEBSITE: www.ledel.us/fpmt.htm

DESCRIPTION: This 40-minute, approximately five-mile round trip travels from Forest Park to the Duck Pond on Trinity Park and back.

SCHEDULE: March through October: Tuesday through Sunday, 11 a.m. to 5/6 p.m.; November through February: Saturday, Sunday, and selected holidays, 12 to 4/5 p.m.

ADMISSION/FARE: Adults 13+, $3; seniors 65+, $2.50; children 1-12, $2.50.

LOCOMOTIVES/ROLLING STOCK: Chance C.P. Huntington no. 102; no. 104; no. 105.

NEARBY ATTRACTIONS: Fort Worth Zoo, Log Cabin Village, and Fort Worth Botanic Garden.

DIRECTIONS: Across from Fort Worth Zoo on Colonial Pkwy.

Photo courtesy of David Ledel.

Galveston, TX

Galveston Railroad Museum
Museum

ADDRESS: 123 Rosenberg Ave. Galveston, TX 77550
TELEPHONE: (409) 765-5700
WEBSITE: www.galvestonrrmuseum.com

DESCRIPTION: With the generous support of the Moody Foundation, the museum acquired engines and rolling stock from various locations, including a vintage Houston and Texas Central (Southern Pacific) 4-6-0. In the gallery, full-sized figures, made from plaster molds of real persons, depict individuals who might have passed through the waiting room in 1932. Several pieces of railroad china are on display as well as a 700-square-foot HO-scale model railroad.

SCHEDULE: Seven days a week, 10 a.m. to 4 p.m.; January and February: closed Monday and Tuesday; also closed Thanksgiving, Christmas Eve & Day, New Year's Day, and during local Mardi Gras weekend.

ADMISSION/FARE: Adults, $5; children 4-12, $2.50; seniors 65+, $4.50.

LOCOMOTIVES/ROLLING STOCK: Three steam locomotives, four diesel electric locomotives, self propelled passenger car, four box cars, two flat cars, a gondola, refrigerator car, six tank cars, four cabooses, three maintenance-of-way cars, six baggage/express/railway post office cars, nine passenger/dining/business cars, and two Texas Limited cars.

DIRECTIONS: Located in downtown Galveston on the Strand.

Grapevine, TX

Grapevine Vintage Railroad
Dinner train

SITE ADDRESS: 705 S Main St. Grapevine, TX 76051
MAILING ADDRESS: One Liberty Park Plaza Grapevine, TX 76051
TELEPHONE: (817) 410-3123
WEBSITE: www.gvrr.com

DESCRIPTION: Tourist excursion train to Fort Worth and Trinity River Run. Steam and diesel engines pull passenger cars dating to the 1920s.

SCHEDULE: February to December. See website for dates, times, and current fares.

LOCOMOTIVES/ROLLING STOCK: Southern Pacific 1896 Cooke-built 4-6-0 steam locomotive no. 2248; 1953 GP7 diesel no. 2199; 1930s-style Victorian passenger coaches.

SPECIAL EVENTS: Polar Express Festival Short Runs, Summertime Train Robberies, Annual Jazz Wine Train. Also available: birthday party celebrations, group events, field trips, team-building outings, weddings, wine tasting, and much more.

NEARBY ATTRACTIONS: Stockyards Station Mall, Billy Bob's, Grapevine Mills Mall, Six Flags, Grapevine Historic Main St., Bass Pro Shop, and Gaylord Texan Resort.

DIRECTIONS: Grapevine: Hwy. 114 or 121, north on Main St. Stockyards: I35W to westbound NE 28th St. South on N Main St., left on Exchange St.

Houston, TX

Houston Railroad Museum
Museum

ADDRESS: 7390 Mesa Dr., PO Box 457 Houston, TX 77028
TELEPHONE: (713) 631-6612
WEBSITE: www.houstonrrmuseum.org

DESCRIPTION: The museum features a collection of locomotives, freight cars, and passenger cars with a Texas emphasis. It is operated by Gulf Coast Chapter, National Railway Historical Society, Inc.

SCHEDULE: First weekend in April to first weekend in November: Saturday, 12 to 4 p.m.; Sunday, 1 to 4 p.m.

ADMISSION/FARE: Adults, $4; children 12 and under, $2.

LOCOMOTIVES/ROLLING STOCK: Santa Fe Pullman "Verde Valley;" Santa Fe RPO 3401; Santa Fe Pullman end-door express car no. 1890; Missouri Pacific sleeper "Eagle Chasm;" Santa Fe Alco S2 diesel no. 2350; Santa Fe barber shop-lounge-dorm no. 1344; MKT cupola caboose no. 6; MKT coach "New Braunfels;" Kansas City Southern observer-lounge "Good Cheer;" Southern Pacific caboose no. 4696; Houston Belt & Terminal Also S2 no. 14; Texas-Mexican Baldwin DS44-750 no. 510; Spokane Portland & Seattle baggage no. 50; CSOX tank car 2198; MHAX helium car no. 1237.

SPECIAL EVENTS: First weekend in November, Open House and Railroad Photography Contest in recognition of National Model Railroad month; free admission.

NEARBY ATTRACTIONS: Astroworld Narrow Gauge Steam; Galveston Railroad Museum, Rosenberg Railroad Museum, NASA/Space Center Houston.

DIRECTIONS: From I-610 N Loop, exit McCarty, east to Mesa Rd., left on Mesa Rd.

Photo courtesy of Tom Marsh.

Houston, TX

Six Flags AstroWorld

Train ride
3' gauge

ADDRESS: 9001 Kirby Dr. Houston, TX 77054
TELEPHONE: (713) 799-8404
WEBSITE: www.sixflags.com

DESCRIPTION: Spanning 100 acres, the park features 33 exhilarating rides and other roller coasters, innovative entertainment, games, and WaterWorld. The train attraction is a complete two-mile trip around Six Flags AstroWorld. It lasts approximately 20 minutes. Guests hear history and view all of the attractions. The 610-limited train has been in continuous operation since the park opened in 1968.

SCHEDULE: 10 a.m. to closing; hours vary.

ADMISSION/FARE: General admission, $41.99; children under 48", $24.99; children 2 and under, free; seniors 55+, $26.99.

LOCOMOTIVES/ROLLING STOCK: Two diesel locomotives; converted ore car.

SPECIAL EVENTS: Fright Fest, Un Dia Padre, Gospel Celebration, Flag Day, concerts, Spirit Fest, 4th of July Celebration.

NEARBY ATTRACTIONS: Astrodome, Reliant Stadium.

DIRECTIONS: On I-610 exit Fannin; southwest of downtown, across from Reliant Park.

Marshall, TX

Historic Texas & Pacific Railway Museum

Museum, Display, Model train layout

ADDRESS: 800 N Washington Ave. Ste. 1 Marshall, TX 75670
TELEPHONE: (800) 513-9495 or (903) 938-9495
WEBSITE: www.marshalldepot.org

DESCRIPTION: Historic Texas & Pacific Railway Museum is housed in the Texas & Pacific Depot, built in 1912, and it contains artifacts and photos dating from the 1870s. The gift shop features Thomas the Tank Engine ™ toys and other memorabilia.

SCHEDULE: Tuesday through Saturday, 10 a.m. to 4 p.m. Other times by special request for groups of 12 or more.

ADMISSION/FARE: Adults, $2; students, $1; preschool children, free.

LOCOMOTIVES/ROLLING STOCK: Union Pacific caboose no. 25687.

SPECIAL EVENTS: Annual T&P employees' reunion; Thanksgiving through December, Wonderland of Lights in Marshall; First Saturday in December, Santa arrives by Amtrak.

NEARBY ATTRACTIONS: Marshall Pottery, Starr Family Historic Park, Caddo Lake and State Park, Harrison County Court House, Ginocchio Hotel, Harrison County Historical Museum, Michelson Art Museum, T. C. Lindsey store.

DIRECTIONS: I-20 to exit 617 north on US59, go 3.8 miles to US80, west one mile (three traffic lights) to N Washington Ave., then north three blocks. Enter through pedestrian tunnel.

Photo courtesy of Bill Robinson.

New Braunfels, TX
New Braunfels Railroad Museum
Museum

ADDRESS: 302 W San Antonio St., PO Box 310475 New Braunfels, TX 78131-0475
TELEPHONE: (830) 627-2447
WEBSITE: www.nbhrmsmuseum.org

DESCRIPTION: Housed in the restored 1907 International & Great Northern Depot next to Union Pacific main line. Displays include a steam locomotive, MP caboose, N and HO scale train layouts, and numerous railroad artifacts. The museum is run by the Bluebonnet Chapter, NRHS.

SCHEDULE: Thursday through Monday, 12 to 4 p.m.; closed Tuesday and Wednesday.

ADMISSION/FARE: Admission by donations.

LOCOMOTIVES/ROLLING STOCK: Lehigh Cement 0-6-0T Porter steam locomotive no. 7; Missouri Pacific caboose no. 13385.

SPECIAL EVENTS: Third Saturday in April, Annual Model Railroad Jamboree; early December, Wassailfest.

NEARBY ATTRACTIONS: Schlitterbahn Water Park, Landa Park Miniature Train Ride, Guadalupe and Comal Rivers, Historic New Braunfels and Gruene community, natural bridge caverns, Amtrak's Texas Eagle & Sunset limited service to nearby San Antonio.

DIRECTIONS: Downtown New Braunfels, 2 blocks south of the city's main plaza, at the Union Pacific railroad tracks.

Photo courtesy of Howard Harris, Jr.

Palestine and Rusk, TX

Texas State Railroad State Park

Train ride
Standard gauge

SITE ADDRESS: Park Rd. 70 in Palestine, TX and Park Rd. 76 in Rusk, TX
MAILING ADDRESS: PO Box 39 Rusk, TX 75785
TELEPHONE: (800) 442-8951 or (903) 683-2561
WEBSITE: www.texasstaterailroad.com

DESCRIPTION: Established in 1881, the Texas State Railroad carries passengers on a 4½-hour, 50-mile round trip across 25 bridges as it travels through east Texas pine and hardwood forest. Victorian-style depots are located in Rusk and Palestine.

SCHEDULE: March to November: weekend; June and July: Thursday to Sunday; first three Saturdays in December, Christmas runs.

ADMISSION/FARE: Round trip: adults, $16; children, $10; one way: adults, $11; children, $7. Air-conditioned coach: round trip: adults, $22; children, $14; one way: adults, $15, children, $11.

LOCOMOTIVES/ROLLING STOCK: No. 201, 1901 Cooke 4-6-0, former Texas & Pacific no. 316; no. 300, 1917 Baldwin 2-8-0, former Texas Southeastern no. 28; no. 400, 1917 Baldwin 2-8-2, former Magma Arizona no. 7; no. 500, 1911 Baldwin 4-6-2, former Santa Fe no. 1316; more.

SPECIAL EVENTS: Murder on the Dis-Oriented Express, Special Dogwood Excursion, living history re-enactments, Victoria Christmas train, the Gambler Train.

NEARBY ATTRACTIONS: In Rusk: one of the nation's longest foot bridges and Jim Hogg City Park; in Palestine: Museum of East Texas Culture and "Old Town" Palestine.

DIRECTIONS: Hwy. 84, two miles west of Rusk, three miles east of Palestine.

Photo courtesy of Bill Langford.

TRAVEL TIP: *Special events*

Most tourist and museum railroads offer a regular train trip, and many put on extra trains with a special flair during holidays like Easter, Mother's Day, Father's Day, Independence Day, Veterans Day, and Christmas. These themed events offer a way to combine the railroad experience with holiday flavor.

Panhandle, TX
Square House Museum
Museum

SITE ADDRESS: 5th St. and Hwy. 207 Panhandle, TX
MAILING ADDRESS: PO Box 276 Panhandle, TX 79068
TELEPHONE: (806) 537-3524
E-MAIL: shm@squarehousemuseum.org
WEBSITE: www.squarehousemuseum.org

DESCRIPTION: Museum dedicated to historical research and preservation of local artifacts and events. It started with the original Square House, a small house which was built in the late 1880s as the railroad reached the town of Panhandle.

SCHEDULE: Sunday, 1 p.m. to 5 p.m.; Monday through Saturday, 9 a.m. to 5 p.m.

ADMISSION/FARE: Free.

LOCOMOTIVES/ROLLING STOCK: 1928 caboose no. 1703R.

SPECIAL EVENTS: September 10, Museum Day; September and October, model train exhibit.

NEARBY ATTRACTIONS: Palo Puro Park, Lake Meredith, and Alibates National Monument.

DIRECTIONS: From I-40 take Hwy. 207 north to Panhandle, continue to 5th Ave.

Photo courtesy of Square House Museum.

San Angelo, TX
Historic Orient Santa Fe Depot
Museum

ADDRESS: 703 S Chadbourne San Angelo, TX 76903
TELEPHONE: (325) 486-2140
WEBSITE: www.railwaymuseumsanangelo.homestead.com

DESCRIPTION: Museum showing railroad significance in area, with several operating model trains. Static displays include two locomotives, a boxcar, and a caboose.

SCHEDULE: Saturday, 10 a.m. to 4 p.m.

NEARBY ATTRACTIONS: Fort Concho Museum, San Angelo Fine Arts Museum, Southwest Military Museum, San Angelo State Park.

DIRECTIONS: Downtown San Angelo on Chadbourne St.

San Antonio, TX

Texas Transportation Museum

Train ride, Museum, Display, Model train layout
HO, Lionel, and G scale

ADDRESS: 11731 Wetmore Rd. San Antonio, TX 78247
TELEPHONE: (210) 490-3554
E-MAIL: ttm1964@@sbcglobal.net
WEBSITE: www.txtransportationmuseum.org

DESCRIPTION: A short train ride in a converted caboose or flat car behind either a 1954 Baldwin RS4 or a 1925 Baldwin 0-4-0 steam switcher. Also massive indoor HO layout and huge G scale exterior layout.

SCHEDULE: Thursday, 9 a.m. to 4 p.m.; Saturday and Sunday, 10 a.m. to 5 p.m.; scheduled rides every 45 minutes, beginning 12 to 4:30 p.m.

ADMISSION/FARE: Adults $5, children 12 and under, $3; family rate (two adults, up to five children), $15.

LOCOMOTIVES/ROLLING STOCK: Moscow, Camden & San Augustine Railroad 2-8-0 no. 6; Comal Power 0-4-0T no. 1; GE Switcher, 1954 Baldwin RS4, Santa Fe Business Car 404, Pullman Sleeper McKeever, UP Cupola Caboose, MP Bay Window Caboose, MP Cupola & MP Transfer Caboose.

SPECIAL EVENTS: Three weekends before Christmas, Santa's Holiday Depot: slightly higher admission; whole park decorated, including nighttime train rides.

NEARBY ATTRACTIONS: San Antonio attractions.

DIRECTIONS: North of airport on Wetmore Rd., 2½ miles north of I-410. Map on website.

Photo courtesy of Texas Transportation Museum.

KEY TO SYMBOLS

♿ Handicapped accessible	🍽 Restaurant	🎨 Arts and crafts	arm Association of Railway Museums
P Parking	🪑 Picnic area	**MI** Memberships available	TRAIN Tourist Railway Association, Inc.
P Bus/RV parking	Dining car	✉ Send S.A.S.E. for brochure	AMTRAK Amtrak service to nearby city
🎁 Gift, book, or museum shop	Excursions	NRHP National Register of Historic Places	VIA VIA service to nearby city
☕ Refreshments	TOUR Guided tours	VISA MasterCard DISCOVER AMERICAN EXPRESS Card	Credit cards accepted

Railroad and Heritage Museum
Museum

ADDRESS: 315 W Ave. B Temple, TX 76501
TELEPHONE: (254) 298-5172
WEBSITE: www.rrhm.org

DESCRIPTION: Housed in the 1910 Gulf, Colorado & Santa Fe depot in downtown Temple, the museum features early Santa Fe and Missouri-Kansas-Texas station equipment and furniture, including a working telegraph for train orders. Observation alcoves with dispatch radios allow visitors to watch and listen to current BNSF operations just outside the museum. Exhibits focus on the effect of railroading on Texas and westward expansion, including a collection of railroad timetables, passes, photographs, and Santa Fe's engineer's tracings for the Southern Division. The archives are a repository for the Santa Fe Railway Historical and Modeling Society papers.

SCHEDULE: Year-round: Tuesday through Saturday, 10 a.m. to 4 p.m.; Sunday, 12 to 4 p.m.

ADMISSION/FARE: Adults, $4; seniors, $3; children 5 and under, $2.

LOCOMOTIVES/ROLLING STOCK: Santa Fe 4-6-2 no. 3423; no. 2301, a 1937 Alco HH600, the oldest surviving Santa Fe diesel; steel caboose no. 1556, former Gulf, Colorado & Santa Fe; and more.

SPECIAL EVENTS: Third weekend in September, Texas Train Festival; specials.

NEARBY ATTRACTIONS: Lake Belton, camping, fishing, large Whistle Stop playground.

DIRECTIONS: I-35 exit Adams/Central Ave. Go east on Central to Seventh St. Turn right and enter parking lot. Enter on trackside.

Coupon available, see insert.

Wichita Falls, TX

Wichita Falls Railroad Museum
Museum

ADDRESS: 500 Ninth St., PO Box 4242 Wichita Falls, TX 76308
TELEPHONE: (940) 723-2661
WEBSITE: www.wfrrm.com

DESCRIPTION: The museum is run by a non-profit group dedicated to the preservation of Wichita Falls-area railroad history. Their primary focus is the Missouri Kansas Texas Railway.

SCHEDULE: Tuesday through Saturday, 12 to 4 p.m.

UTAH

Farmington, UT

S&S Shortline Railroad Park and Museum

Train ride, Museum, Display,
Model train layout
7¹/₂" and 24"

ADDRESS: 575 N 1525 W, PO Box 604
Farmington, UT 84025
TELEPHONE: (801) 451-0222
WEBSITE: www.sssrr.8m.com

DESCRIPTION: This train park has 11,000
feet of 7¹/₂" gauge railroad and 5,000 feet
of 24" gauge rail. Here, there is something for the entire family: train rides, museum
exhibits, picnic and play areas, mini golf, gift shop, and snack bar.

SCHEDULE: Monday, 10 a.m. to 8 p.m.; Tuesday
through Saturday, 10 a.m. to 6 p.m.

ADMISSION/FARE: Museum: free; mini golf: $3.50;
rides range from $1.75 to $4.50, depending on ride.

SPECIAL EVENTS: Easter Egg Hunt, Quarterly Hobo
Dinners, Semi-Annual Train Meets, Christmas Tree
Train. See website for more details.

NEARBY ATTRACTIONS: Lagoon Amusement Park,
Davis County Fair Grounds.

DIRECTIONS: I-15 to Farmington exit, head west to
1525 West, turn right. Continue north ¹/₂ mile. They
are on the west side of the road.

TRAVEL TIP: *Dining cars*

While many tourist railroads offer
food and beverage services on site
or nearby, some still equip their
trains with authentic dining cars.

This gives visitors the chance to
experience a real "dinner in the
diner," as it was prepared and served
on board a moving train.

Heber Valley Historic Railroad [EDITOR'S CHOICE]

Train ride, Dinner train
Standard gauge
Radio frequency: 150.995

ADDRESS: 450 S 600 W Heber, UT 84032
TELEPHONE: (435) 654-5601 or (801) 581-9980
E-MAIL: reservations@hebervalleyrr.org
WEBSITE: www.hebervalleyrr.org

DESCRIPTION: Steam and diesel powered scenic train excursions operate year-round through Heber Valley with wide-open views of the Wasatch Mountains and majestic Mt. Timpanogos at 12,000 feet in elevation, then descend into glacier-carved Provo Canyon. Evening excursions include food, fun, and entertainment. Adventure packages offer summertime fun combining river rafting and train rides, and wintertime fun combining snow tubing and train rides. Special events are held throughout the year. Train also available for private functions.

SCHEDULE: Schedule varies throughout the year; check website.

ADMISSION/FARE: Fares vary by excursion and event; check website.

LOCOMOTIVES/ROLLING STOCK: 1907 Baldwin steam 2-8-0s nos. 618 from the Union Pacific and 75 from the Great Western; MRS1 no. 1813; no. 1218, a Davenport 44-ton switcher; Lackawanna coaches nos. 250 and 270; Clinchfield no. 248; open-air cars nos. 365, 366, 501, 504; UP caboose 3768 no. 3700; DRGW coaches 7508 and 7510; Colorado & Southern 7593; and more.

SPECIAL EVENTS: A Day Out with Thomas™, Cinco De Mayo, Pioneer Day, Halloween Haunted Canyon, The Polar Express; Night Trains: Comedy Murder Mystery, Sunset BBQ Special, Heber Valley Hoedown, Ol' West Casino Train; Adventure Packages: Raft 'n' Rails, Tube 'n' Train.

NEARBY ATTRACTIONS: Aero Museum, Hot Springs Crater, 2002 Olympics venues, Cascade Springs, Robert Redford's Sundance Resort, Wasatch Mountain and Jordanelle State Parks, Timpanogos Cave, golfing, fly fishing, rafting, hiking, biking, camping, boating, horseback riding, hot air ballooning, snow tubing, skiing, snowmobiling, snowshoeing, and sleigh rides.

DIRECTIONS: 45 minutes from downtown Salt Lake City and 20 minutes from Park City. Take Hwy. 40 to Heber City, and 300 South six blocks west to the train depot.

Photo courtesy of Diane Dray.
See ad on page A-37.

Helper, UT

Western Mining and Railroad Museum

Museum

SITE ADDRESS: 296 S Main Helper, UT 84526
MAILING ADDRESS: PO Box 221 Helper, UT 84526
TELEPHONE: (435) 472-3009
E-MAIL: helpermuseum@helpercity.net
WEBSITE: www.wmrrm.org

DESCRIPTION: Railroad and coal mining museum features exhibits from the 1800s though 1950s. Exhibits focus on the Denver & Rio Grand Western and Utah railways. The museum is two hours southeast of Salt Lake City. The Denver and Rio Grande Railroad established the town when the railroad came through the area and coal—which was needed to fuel the steam engines—was found. As more coal mines were opened, it became the railroad center and the "hub" for coal miners and their families from the many mining camps. The museum is housed in the Old Helper Hotel building, built in 1913-1914.

SCHEDULE: May 1 through September 30: Monday through Saturday, 10 a.m. to 5 p.m.; October 1 through April 30: Tuesday through Saturday, 11 a.m. to 4 p.m.

ADMISSION/FARE: Admission by donation.

LOCOMOTIVES/ROLLING STOCK: Utah Railway caboose no. 55; D&RGW Spreader 044.

SPECIAL EVENTS: First week in June, Heritage Week; third weekend in August, Helper Arts Festival; mid-November to early December, Utah's Christmas Town.

NEARBY ATTRACTIONS: Price River Pkwy., coal mining ghost towns, rock art, hiking and biking on old railroad grades. Train viewing in the historic Helper railroad yard and in scenic Price Canyon to the ghost town of Soldier Summit.

DIRECTIONS: Six miles north of Price on Hwy. 6. Located on historic Helper Main St.

Photo courtesy of Western Mining and Railroad Museum/Darrin Teply.

Ogden, UT

Ogden Union Station

Museum

ADDRESS: 2501 Wall Ave. Ste. 100 Ogden, UT 84401
TELEPHONE: (801) 393-9886
E-MAIL: keri@theunionstation.org
WEBSITE: www.theunionstation.org

DESCRIPTION: Home to Utah State Railroad Museum and Eccles Rail Center. Other features include John M. Browning Firearms Museum, classic cars, natural history museum, and an art gallery.

SCHEDULE: Monday through Saturday, 10 a.m. to 5 p.m.

ADMISSION/FARE: Adults, $5; seniors 62+, $4; children 2-12, $3.

LOCOMOTIVES/ROLLING STOCK: Union Pacific 4-8-4 no. 833; X-26 gas turbine locomotive; restored American Red Cross hospital car; restored RPO car; Olympic torch car from the 2002 winter Olympics.

SPECIAL EVENTS: First weekend of March, annual model train show.

NEARBY ATTRACTIONS: Historic 25th St. shops and restaurants, Hill Aerospace Museum, Eccles Dinosaur Park.

DIRECTIONS: I-15 exit 344A, left at Wall Ave., north to Union Station.

KEY TO SYMBOLS

Handicapped accessible	Restaurant	Arts and crafts	arm Association of Railway Museums
Parking	Picnic area	Memberships available	Tourist Railway Association, Inc.
Bus/RV parking	Dining car	Send S.A.S.E. for brochure	Amtrak service to nearby city
Gift, book, or museum shop	Excursions	National Register of Historic Places	VIA service to nearby city
Refreshments	Guided tours	VISA MasterCard DISCOVER AMERICAN EXPRESS Card	Credit cards accepted

Promontory, UT

Golden Spike National Historic Site

Museum, Display

SITE ADDRESS: Promontory, UT
MAILING ADDRESS: PO Box 897 Brigham City, UT 84032
TELEPHONE: (435) 471-2209, ext. 29
E-MAIL: gosp_interpretation@nps.gov
WEBSITE: www.nps.gov/gosp/

DESCRIPTION: The famous Golden Spike ceremony took place here May 10, 1869, marking completion of the nation's first transcontinental railroad. Operating replicas of the original locomotives are on display. The locomotives run from May 1 to Labor Day for display. The site does not offer train rides. The locomotives operate between 10 a.m. and 4:30 p.m. The Visitor Center offers color movies and exhibits, with park rangers on hand.

SCHEDULE: Visitor Center: May 1 through September 30, daily; October 1 through April 30, 9 a.m. to 5 p.m.; closed Monday and Tuesday; closed New Year's Day, Thanksgiving, and Christmas. Outside attractions are open during daylight hours.

ADMISSION/FARE: May 1 through Labor Day, $7 per vehicle; rest of year, $5 per vehicle.

LOCOMOTIVES/ROLLING STOCK: Full-sized operating replicas of Union Pacific 4-4-0 no. 119, a coal-fired locomotive; and Central Pacific 4-4-0 no. 60, the "Jupiter," a wood-fired locomotive.

SPECIAL EVENTS: May 10, anniversary celebration of Golden Spike Ceremony; second Saturday in August, Railroader's Festival; Winter Steam Demonstration; call Visitor Center for further information.

DIRECTIONS: 32 miles west of Brigham City, via Hwys. 13 and 83 through Corinne.

TRAVEL TIP: *Photo outings*

Many railroads offer a railfan event that includes special trains, unusual equipment, and the chance to get great photos of your favorite railroad. Be sure to check the special events listings of your favorite line to see if they schedule a photography weekend or a photo freight that will provide a glimpse into the past.

VERMONT

Bellows Falls, VT
Green Mountain Railroad
Train ride

ADDRESS: 54 Depot St., PO Box 498
Bellows Falls, VT 05101
TELEPHONE: (802) 463-3069
WEBSITE: www.rails-vt.com

DESCRIPTION: Three scenic rail excursions. The Green Mountain Flyer is a 2-hour round trip from Bellows Falls to Chester Depot; it travels along the Connecticut and Williams Rivers, past two covered bridges, and Brockways Mills Gorge. White River Valley Flyer travels from White River Junction to Thetford and Montshire Museum of Science. Champlain Valley Flyer is a 1-hour round trip from Burlington to Shelburne.

SCHEDULE: Late June through mid-October; summer: closed on Monday.

ADMISSION/FARE: Varies with location and length of trip.

LOCOMOTIVES/ROLLING STOCK: No. 405, a former Rutland Alco RS-1; GP40s nos. 302, 304 and 305; GP9s nos. 803 and 804; S3 no. 3050.

SPECIAL EVENTS: Easter Bunny Express, Mother's Day Excursion, Fireworks Special, Santa Express, Rutland Limited, Fall Ludlow Limited.

NEARBY ATTRACTIONS: Bellows Falls: Basketville, Santa's Land, Vermont Country Store. Whiteriver Junction: Montshire Museum of Science, Billings Farm Museum, Vins, Quechee Gorge Village. Burlington: Echo, Lake Champlain Ferries, Shelburne Museum.

DIRECTIONS: I-91 exit 5 to Bellows Falls, take Route 5 north three miles.

Shelburne, VT

Shelburne Museum

Museum

ADDRESS: PO Box 10 Shelburne, VT 05482
TELEPHONE: (802) 985-3346
WEBSITE: www.shelburnemuseum.org

DESCRIPTION: Art and Americana, includes a steamship, train station, "Locomotive 220," and the rail car Grand Isle (interior pictured), which was built by the Wagner Palace Car Company c. 1890. Visitors can operate an American Flyer toy train layout.

SCHEDULE: May to October, 10 a.m. to 5 p.m.

ADMISSION/FARE: Please call for rates.

DIRECTIONS: Take exit 13 off I-89. Go five miles south on US Route 7.

White River Junction, VT

New England Transportation Museum

Museum, Display, Model train layout
N scale

ADDRESS: 100 Railroad Row White River Junction, VT 05001
TELEPHONE: (802) 291-9838 or (802) 295-5036
WEBSITE: www.newenglandtransportationmuseum.org or www.glorydaysoftherailroad.org

DESCRIPTION: The museum in the downtown Amtrak station celebrates the Upper Valley's 400 years of transportation history with exhibits and annual "Glory Days of the Railroad" festival. The campus and facilities occupy restored historic railroad and commercial properties in the neighboring communities of the Connecticut River.

ADMISSION/FARE: Adults, $3; children, $1.

LOCOMOTIVES/ROLLING STOCK: B&M 4-4-0 no. 494; B&M wooden caboose built by Laconia Car Co.

SPECIAL EVENTS: September 9, 14th annual Glory Days of the Railroad; October, Hobo Halloween; December, Santa by Train (Amtrak).

NEARBY ATTRACTIONS: Claremont Concord Railroad; NECR Railroad; Amtrak Green Mountain Railroad; CV Roundhouse; B&M Westboro Yard, Roundhouse, and Sand House.

DIRECTIONS: One mile from I-91 and I-89 intersection.

VIRGINIA

Carson, VA

Appomattox Regional Library System, Carson Branch
Museum

Fairfax Station
Parksley
•Staunton
Richmond•
•Roanoke
Carson•
Fort Eustis / Portsmouth
Suffolk

ADDRESS: 16101 Halligan Park Rd. Carson, VA 23860
TELEPHONE: (804) 458-0860
E-MAIL: ckoutnik@arls.org
WEBSITE: www.arls.org

DESCRIPTION: Renovated caboose and depot features exhibits depicting local railroad history.

SCHEDULE: Monday through Thursday, 3 to 7 p.m.; Friday 3 to 6 p.m.; Wednesday, also open 10 a.m. to 12 p.m. and by appointment.

ADMISSION/FARE: Free.

LOCOMOTIVES/ROLLING STOCK: Norfolk & Western caboose no. 583286.

NEARBY ATTRACTIONS: Museum of the Civil War Soldier, Petersburg National Battlefield, Williamsburg, Jamestown, Yorktown, Petersburg Siege Museum, and Old Dominion Railroad Museum.

DIRECTIONS: Take I-95 south from Petersburg, VA 13 miles to exit 37. Turn left onto Route 301, and right onto Halligan Park Rd.

Fairfax Station, VA

Fairfax Station Railroad Museum
Museum

ADDRESS: 11200 Fairfax Station Rd., PO Box 7 Fairfax Station, VA 22039
TELEPHONE: (703) 425-9225
WEBSITE: www.fairfax-station.org

DESCRIPTION: Restored Southern Railway depot is rich in Civil War and local history. American Red Cross founder Clara Barton was a nurse here after the Second Battle of Manassas.

SCHEDULE: Year-round: Sunday, 1 to 4 p.m.; model train layouts: third Sunday of every month, 1 to 4 p.m. and Labor Day, 12 p.m. to 5 p.m.

ADMISSION/FARE: Adults, $2; children 3-10, $1. December Model Train Show: Adults, $3; children, $1.

LOCOMOTIVES/ROLLING STOCK: Caboose N&W no. 518606.

SPECIAL EVENTS: Third Sunday each month, model train layouts; first December weekend, annual Model Train Display; Quarterly Forums; historic tours and more.

NEARBY ATTRACTIONS: Washington, D.C., museums, Manassas Museum, and Fairfax City Museum.

DIRECTIONS: Three miles south of Fairfax. Located ¼ mile from the corner of Route 123 (Ox Rd.) and Fairfax Station Rd.

Fort Eustis, VA

US Army Transportation Museum
Museum

ADDRESS: Besson Hall, 300 Washington Blvd. Fort Eustis, VA 23604-5260
TELEPHONE: (757) 878-1115
E-MAIL: david.hanselman@us.army.mil
WEBSITE: www.transchool.eustis.army.mil/museum/museum.html

DESCRIPTION: This military history museum displays transportation artifacts dating from 1776 to the present. Inside the 30,000-square-foot museum are dioramas and exhibits; on five acres outside are rail rolling stock, trucks, jeeps, amphibious marine craft, helicopters, aircraft, and an experimental hovercraft.

SCHEDULE: Year-round: Tuesday to Sunday, 9 a.m. to 4:30 p.m.; closed Mondays and federal holidays.

ADMISSION/FARE: Free.

LOCOMOTIVES/ROLLING STOCK: 2-8-0 steam locomotive no. 607; 0-6-0 steam locomotive no. V-1923; ambulance ward car no. 87568; steam wrecking crane; 40-ton and 50-ton flatcars; cabooses; Berlin duty train cars.

NEARBY ATTRACTIONS: Yorktown, Jamestown, Colonial Williamsburg, Busch Gardens, and Water Country.

DIRECTIONS: From I-64 exit 250A. Drive two miles into Fort Eustis—museum on left.

Eastern Shore Railway Museum
Museum, Display

ADDRESS: 18468 Dunne Ave., PO Box 135 Parksley, VA 23421
TELEPHONE: (757) 665-RAIL

DESCRIPTION: A restored 1920s Pennsylvania Railroad station houses a museum and several train cars, including two cabooses, a baggage car, a Pullman sleeper, a Budd dining car, and a touring car.

SCHEDULE: Wednesday through Sunday, 12 to 4 p.m.; closed Monday and Tuesday.

ADMISSION/FARE: $2; under 12, free.

LOCOMOTIVES/ROLLING STOCK: 1920s RF&P post office car; 1962 NKP caboose no. 473; 1949 Wabash caboose no. 2783; Seaboard Air Line dining car no. 8011; 1927 Pullman parlor-observation "Diplomat;" more.

SPECIAL EVENTS: First Saturday in June, Parksley Spring Festival.

NEARBY ATTRACTIONS: Chincoteague Island, Kiptopeke State Park, and Ocean City.

DIRECTIONS: Midway between Chesapeake Bay Bridge Tunnel and Salisbury, MD. From Route 13, it is two miles west on SR176.

Photo courtesy of Robert J. Lewis.

Portsmouth, VA

Lancaster Antique Train & Toy Collection
Museum, Model train layout
O, HO, N, and G scale

ADDRESS: Children's Museum, 221 High St. Portsmouth, VA 23704
TELEPHONE: (757) 393-5397
E-MAIL: www.childrensmuseumva.com/lancaster.html

DESCRIPTION: This private collection publicly displays over 5,000 trains. A.J. "Junie" Lancaster collected antique toys and model trains from all over the country for 35 years. He and his wife wanted to share their love of trains with a new generation, so they donated the collection to the Children's Museum of Virginia in 1995. A large part of the museum's second floor is dedicated to the collection that features four working layouts: a G gauge called Candy Land, an HO gauge of harbor town, an O gauge of a 1950s mining town, and a combined N and HO gauge.

SCHEDULE: Monday through Saturday, 9 a.m. to 5 p.m.; Sunday, 11 a.m. to 5 p.m.

ADMISSION/FARE: $6 per person.

SPECIAL EVENTS: One weekend each month, a toy train show is held that features several of the local clubs.

NEARBY ATTRACTIONS: Naval Shipyard Museum, Fine Arts Gallery, Lightship Museum, Museum of Military History, and Nauticus.

DIRECTIONS: I-264 to Portsmouth, take the Effingham St. exit, go to High St. and turn right. Go down to the 200 block. We are on the right.

Richmond, VA

Old Dominion Railway Museum
Museum, Display, Model train layout
Standard gauge

ADDRESS: 102 Hull St., PO Box 8583 Richmond, VA
TELEPHONE: (804) 233-6237
WEBSITE: www.odcnrhs.org

DESCRIPTION: The Old Dominion Railway Museum tells the story of Virginia's railroading heritage through artifacts, videos, static displays, and an HO layout. It is located within a few blocks of the 1831 birthplace of Virginia railroad operations.

SCHEDULE: Year-round: Saturday, 11 a.m. to 4 p.m.; Sunday, 1 to 4 p.m.; closed some holidays; group tours by appointment.

ADMISSION/FARE: Free. Donations requested.

LOCOMOTIVES/ROLLING STOCK: RF&P express car 185; David M. Lea & Co. 0-4-0T no. 2; SCL caboose 21019; Seaboard System boxcar 111935; Fairmont motor car.

SPECIAL EVENTS: Second Sunday of each month, 2 p.m., Floodwall Guided Walking Tours.

NEARBY ATTRACTIONS: Tripple Crossing, downtown Richmond tourist area, Richmond Floodwall Promenade, James River recreation, and Manchester Art Studios.

DIRECTIONS: Take I-95 to exit 73 (Maury St.). Turn right onto Maury St., go two blocks. Turn left onto W Second St., then right on Hull St., to museum on right.

Photo courtesy of Old Dominion Railway Museum.

Roanoke, VA

O. Winston Link Museum

Museum

ADDRESS: 101 Shenandoah Ave., NE Roanoke, VA 24016
TELEPHONE: (540) 982-LINK
E-MAIL: coordinator@linkmuseum.org
WEBSITE: www.linkmuseum.org

DESCRIPTION: Only two photographers in America have museums dedicated to their work: Ansel Adams and O. Winston Link. Link's N&W Railway photographs are housed in downtown Roanoke's restored N&W passenger station, designed by the famous industrial designer Raymond Loewy in 1947. Also in the museum: artifacts, Link's photo equipment, and sound recordings.

SCHEDULE: Year-round: Monday through Saturday, 10 a.m. to 5 p.m.; Sunday, 12 to 5 p.m. Closed New Year's Day, Easter, Thanksgiving, and Christmas.

ADMISSION/FARE: Adults, $5; seniors, $4; children, $3.

SPECIAL EVENTS: Early Summer, Festival at the Station; early Fall, Norfolk Southern Calendar Show; December, Santa by Rail. See website for additional events and programs.

NEARBY ATTRACTIONS: Visitors center (on site), Virginia Museum of Transportation, Historic Farmer's Market, cultural center, Blue Ridge Pkwy., restaurants, and shopping.

DIRECTIONS: I-81 to 581 south, exit 5 (Williamson Rd.) to Shenandoah Ave. 581 north from 220 to exit 6, left on Elm Ave., right on Williamson Rd., left on Wells Ave., left on Jefferson Ave., and left on Shenandoah Ave.

Photo courtesy of O. Winston Link Museum.

Roanoke, VA

Virginia Museum of Transportation Inc.

Museum, Display, Model railroad layout
Standard gauge

ADDRESS: 303 Norfolk Ave. SW Roanoke, VA 24016
TELEPHONE: (540) 342-5670
E-MAIL: info@vmt.org
WEBSITE: www.vmt.org

DESCRIPTION: Exhibits include a large collection of rolling stock, carriages, antique automobiles, trucks, a trolley, a rocket, and a transportation play area. In the historic freight station, find a four-tier O gauge model train, a model circus train, an African American Rail Heritage exhibit, and more.

SCHEDULE: Monday to Friday, 11 a.m. to 4 p.m.; Saturdays, 10 a.m. to 5 p.m.; Sundays, 1 to 5 p.m. Closed Thanksgiving, Christmas Eve and Day, New Year's Eve and Day, Easter, Labor Day, Memorial Day, and Mondays in January and February.

ADMISSION/FARE: Adults, $7; seniors 60+, $6; children 3-11, $5; plus 5 percent Roanoke City admission tax.

LOCOMOTIVES/ROLLING STOCK: N&W A class 2-6-6-4 no. 1218; N&W J class 4-8-4 no. 611; N&W GP9 no. 521; Virginian Class C10 electric no. 321; Panama Canal electric locomotive no. 686, more.

SPECIAL EVENTS: February, African American Heritage Celebration; April, Gathering of the Eagles; July, Star City Motor Madness; October, Haunted Railyard; call for rail special events.

NEARBY ATTRACTIONS: Blue Ridge Pkwy., Explore Park, Mill Mountain Zoo, O. Winston Link Museum, natural bridge, and many more.

DIRECTIONS: The museum is located in downtown Roanoke between 2nd St. and 5th St. SW, beside the Norfolk Southern main line.

Photo courtesy of Virginia Museum of Transportation.

Staunton, VA

Gypsy Express, Inc.
Train ride
16" gauge

ADDRESS: PO Box 1313 Staunton, VA 24401-1313
TELEPHONE: (540) 885-4518
E-MAIL: gypsyexpress@hotmail.com

DESCRIPTION: Volunteer non-profit organization provides 16" gauge mini train ride on replica of Santa Fe Super Chief F3.

SCHEDULE: Mid-April to Labor Day: Saturday, 12 to 6 p.m.; Sunday, 1 to 5 p.m.; rides for organizations can be arranged at other times.

ADMISSION/FARE: $1 per person. Children under 6 must ride with an adult. Donations accepted.

LOCOMOTIVES/ROLLING STOCK: Replica of EMD F3 Phase I; three smooth-sided, 8-wheel passenger cars similar to ones built by Budd & Pullman (one is wheelchair accessible).

SPECIAL EVENTS: July 4th, free rides; Halloween; call or e-mail for Christmas specials.

NEARBY ATTRACTIONS: Black Friar Shakespeare Theater, Frontier Farm Museum, and Woodrow Wilson Birthplace and Museum.

DIRECTIONS: Located in Gypsy Hill Park. Follow signs for VA route 250 West from US I-81.

Photo courtesy of Gypsy Express, Inc.

Suffolk, VA
Suffolk Seaboard Station Railroad Museum
Museum

ADDRESS: 326 N Main St. Suffolk, VA 23434
TELEPHONE: (757) 923-4750
E-MAIL: snhs@exis.net
WEBSITE: http://kelsey3.tripod.com

DESCRIPTION: The restored 1885 station features an award-winning HO scale model layout depicting Suffolk in 1907, railroad memorabilia, seasonal exhibits, a caboose, and a gift shop.

SCHEDULE: Wednesday through Saturday, 10 a.m. to 4 p.m.; Sunday, 1 to 4 p.m.

ADMISSION/FARE: Donations gratefully accepted. Admission for group tours: Adults, $2; children 12 and under, $1.

LOCOMOTIVES/ROLLING STOCK: Bay Window caboose no. 557593, built for the Nickel Plate Railroad in 1962.

SPECIAL EVENTS: April, Civil War Weekend; June through August, Spectacular Storytime; October, Harvest Days; December, Candlelight Tour.

NEARBY ATTRACTIONS: 1839 Riddick's Folly House Museum, Historic Prentis House & Visitor Center circa 1800, Suffolk Art Museum, Nansemond Indian Museum, Dismal Swamp National Wildlife Refuge, and Peanut Festival.

DIRECTIONS: Hampton Roads region, off Hwy. 58 Bypass in downtown Suffolk on Hwy. 13/460.

Photo courtesy of Tim Rudziensky, VirginiaImages.com.

WASHINGTON

Carnation, WA

Remlinger Farms'
Tolt River Railroad

Train ride
2' gauge

- Wickersham
- Carnation
- Snoqualmie
- Cashmere
- Renton
- Chehalis
- Elbe
- Toppenish
- Pasco
- Dayton

SITE ADDRESS: 32610 NE 32nd St.
Carnation, WA 9801
MAILING ADDRESS: PO Box 177
Carnation, WA 98014
TELEPHONE: (425) 333-4135
E-MAIL: info@remlingerfarms.com
WEBSITE: www.remlingerfarms.com

DESCRIPTION: Remlinger Farms Country Fair Fun Park features the Tolt River Railroad, powered by a half-sized steam locomotive. This 10-minute train ride covers a mile of track, including a 120-foot tunnel, which winds across this charming working farm.

SCHEDULE: May through October: weekends, 11 a.m. to 5 p.m.; mid-June through Labor Day: daily, 11 a.m. to 5 p.m.

ADMISSION/FARE: Country Fair Family Fun Park: people 12 months to 64 years, $9; 65+ and handicapped, $8; October Harvest Festival: $12.

LOCOMOTIVES/ROLLING STOCK: Two American Standard 4-4-0 highly modified Crown Metal Works, Wyano, PA. Four passenger cars were constructed for the farm in 1994 by Jack Hamilton of North Bend, WA. Each car is 24 feet long and can carry up to 40 adults. One car is wheelchair accessible. Three Crown passenger cars.

NEARBY ATTRACTIONS: The Family Fun Park offers a lot for young families, from pony rides to a mini roller coaster. The farm also has a country restaurant and farm market.

DIRECTIONS: 45 minutes east of Seattle in Carnation, WA. Visit website for directions.

Photo courtesy of Remlinger Farms.

Cashmere, WA
Chelan County Historical Society and Pioneer Village
Display

ADDRESS: 600 Cotlets Way, PO Box 22 Cashmere, WA 98815
TELEPHONE: (509) 782-3230
E-MAIL: info@cashmeremuseum.com
WEBSITE: www.cashmeremuseum.com

DESCRIPTION: The village features a caboose, dining car, and section house with railroad artifacts, ticket office, 20 pioneer cabins, and a museum.

SCHEDULE: March through October 31: daily, 9:30 a.m. to 4:30 p.m.

ADMISSION/FARE: Adults, $4.50; students and seniors, $3.50; children 5-12, $2.50; children under 5, free; family, $10.

LOCOMOTIVES/ROLLING STOCK: 1907 Great Northern caboose.

SPECIAL EVENTS: First October weekend, Apple Days.

NEARBY ATTRACTIONS: Liberty Orchards.

DIRECTIONS: Located right off Hwy. 2 in Cashmere, WA.

Chehalis, WA
Chehalis-Centralia Railroad Association
Train ride, Dinner train
Standard gauge

SITE ADDRESS: 1101 SW Sylvenus St. Chehalis, WA 98532
MAILING ADDRESS: 1945 S Market Blvd. Chehalis, WA 98532
TELEPHONE: (360) 748-9593
WEBSITE: www.ccrra.com

DESCRIPTION: Two excursions are available: a 13-mile, 1¼-hour round trip or a 19-mile, 1¾-hour round trip over former Weyerhaeuser (Chehalis Western) trackage, once part of the Milwaukee Road, from South Chehalis to Millburn or Ruth.

SCHEDULE: Memorial Day to September: Saturday and Sunday departures to Millburn, 1 and 3 p.m.; Saturday departure to Ruth, 5 p.m.; dinner trains to Ruth: select Saturday departures, 5 p.m. Call for information and to request pre-paid reservations.

ADMISSION/FARE: Milburn: adults, $10; children 4-16, $7. Ruth: adults, $13, children, $10. Dinner trains: call for prices. Prices subject to change without notice.

LOCOMOTIVES/ROLLING STOCK: No. 15, a 1916 Baldwin 90-ton 2-8-2 (formerly Cowlitz, Chehalis & Cascade). This engine was displayed for 33 years in a local park; restoration was completed in 1989 at Mt. Rainier Scenic Railway shop by volunteers from Lewis County; Milwaukee Z-frame 40-foot wood boxcar no. 711018, used as shop/supply car; also Milwaukee steel rib-side 40-foot boxcar, 2 open cars, 2 former UP cabooses, more.

SPECIAL EVENTS: October Halloween events: October 8, Haunted Dinner Train, October 15, Pumpkin Train and Dinner Train.

NEARBY ATTRACTIONS: Veteran's Museum, Historical Museum, motels, restaurants, outlet mall, and antique stores. One hour from Mt. Rainier Scenic Railroad's steam operation.

DIRECTIONS: Midway between Seattle, Washington, and Portland, Oregon on I-5 at exit 77. Turn West to first street (Riverside). Turn left and proceed approximately ½ mile to Sylvenus St. Turn left and proceed to train yard.

Photo courtesy of David LaClair.

Dayton, WA

Dayton Historical Depot Society
Museum

ADDRESS: 222 Commercial St., PO Box 316 Dayton, WA 99328
TELEPHONE: (509) 382-2026
WEBSITE: www.historicdaytondepot.org

DESCRIPTION: This train depot is fully restored and on the National Register of Historic Places. It houses train memorabilia and artifacts (mostly photos) from early Columbia County history.

SCHEDULE: Winter: Tuesday to Saturday, 10 a.m. to 5 p.m.; Sunday and Monday, by appointment; summer: Tuesday to Thursday, 11 a.m. to 5 p.m.; Friday and Saturday, 10 a.m. to 5 p.m.; Sunday, 1 to 4 p.m.

ADMISSION/FARE: $3 per person.

LOCOMOTIVES/ROLLING STOCK: UP caboose 25219 built in 1952.

NEARBY ATTRACTIONS: Three historic districts nearby.

DIRECTIONS: Through Dayton on Hwy. 12, turn north on Second St., go one block.

Elbe, WA

Mount Rainier Scenic Railroad
Train ride

ADDRESS: Mountain Hwy., PO Box 921 Elbe, WA 9833
TELEPHONE: (888) steam11 or (360) 569-2351
WEBSITE: www.mrsr.com

DESCRIPTION: An extensive collection of logging locomotives includes Shay, Heisler, and Climax engines as well as rod logging engines. The regular scenic excursion is 1½-hours. Special event trains every month.

SCHEDULE: Memorial Day to July 4th, weekends only; July 4th to Labor Day, daily; Labor Day to October, weekends only. Pumpkin Express, Ghost Train, Snowball Express, BBQs. Departure times, 11 a.m., 1:15 and 3:30 p.m.

ADMISSION/FARE: Adults, $15; seniors, $14; children 4-12, $10; children 3 and under, free.

LOCOMOTIVES/ROLLING STOCK: 2-8-2T no. 17 ; 3-truck Climax no. 100; 3-truck Shay no 11; 3-truck Heisler no. 91; assorted rolling stock.

SPECIAL EVENTS: Valentine's Special, Easter Egg Express, Mother's Day Tea, Father's Day Barbeques, Halloween Trains, Fall foliage trains, History in Motion, and Tacoma Railfest.

NEARBY ATTRACTIONS: Thirteen miles from Mount Rainier National Park.

DIRECTIONS: Take Hwy. 12 to SR7 from Tacoma or SR706 from Olympia to Elbe.

Photo courtesy of Martin Hansen.

Pasco, WA

Washington State Railroads Historical Society Museum
Museum

ADDRESS: 122 N Tacoma Ave., PO Box 552 Pasco, WA 99301
TELEPHONE: (509) 543-4159
WEBSITE: www.wsrhs.org

DESCRIPTION: The museum collects and displays artifacts and photos of the railroads that built the state of Washington, including: the Great Northern Railway, Milwaukee Railroad, the Northern Pacific, Union Pacific, SP&S Railway, and more.

SCHEDULE: April through December: Saturday, 9 a.m. to 3 p.m.

ADMISSION/FARE: Free. Donations appreciated.

LOCOMOTIVES/ROLLING STOCK: Main rolling stock in Port of Pasco.

NEARBY ATTRACTIONS: BNSF hump yard and refueling facilities nearby; Franklin County History Society Museum.

DIRECTIONS: Take 4th Ave. exit south from I-182 in Pasco. Turn east on Clark to Tacoma St. Turn south to 122 N Tacoma Ave.

Renton, WA

Spirit of Washington Dinner Train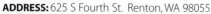

Dinner train

ADDRESS: 625 S Fourth St. Renton, WA 98055
TELEPHONE: (800) 876-7245
E-MAIL: customerservice@swdtrain.com
WEBSITE: www.spiritofwashingtondinnertrain.com

DESCRIPTION: Travelers can experience the nostalgia of passenger rail as they ride and dine in a luxurious, vintage rail car. From Renton to Woodinville, the 3¼-hour, 44-mile round-trip journey travels along Lake Washington and over historic Wilburton Trestle (102 feet high, 975 feet long). The trip includes a gourmet meal and a 45-minute stop at Columbia Winery.

SCHEDULE: Year-round; October to May: Tuesday to Friday, 6:30 p.m.; Saturday, 12 and 6:30 p.m.; Sunday, 11 a.m. and 5:30 p.m. June to September: also Monday, 6:30 p.m.

ADMISSION/FARE: Parlor: dinner, $59.99; lunch/brunch, $49.99. Dome: dinner, $74.99; lunch/brunch, $64.99. Mystery events: parlor seating only, $79.99. Group rates available.

LOCOMOTIVES/ROLLING STOCK: Two F9 locomotives, 7 vintage dining cars, 1 power car.

SPECIAL EVENTS: Year-round, Murder Mystery Trains; July 4, Fireworks Train; November through April, children ride free; New Year's Eve celebration.

NEARBY ATTRACTIONS: Boeing plant, Lake Washington, Renton, Mercer Island, Wilburton Trestle, and Columbia Winery.

DIRECTIONS: From I-5 (north or south) or I-405 (southbound): exit 2 (Rainier Ave.), go south. Turn right on 3rd St. Turn right on Burnett Ave. Travel south to train depot.

Waterfront Streetcar
Trolley ride
Standard gauge

ADDRESS: Seattle Metro 821 Second Ave. Seattle, WA 98104-1598
TELEPHONE: (206) 684-2100

DESCRIPTION: The Waterfront Streetcar travels 1.8 miles southbound and back. It passes Ivars and other restaurants as well as waterfront activities and shops.

SCHEDULE: Year-round.

ADMISSION/FARE: Normal hours, $1; rush hour, $1.50.

LOCOMOTIVES/ROLLING STOCK: W-2 class streetcars from Melbourne, Australia, nos. 272, 482, 512, 518, and 605.

NEARBY ATTRACTIONS: Puget Sound, many restaurants, sporting events at the major stadiums, downtown Seattle, Space Needle, Spaghetti Factory.

DIRECTIONS: I-5 exit at Mercer St., head west to Broad St. Streetcar's first stop at the north end is at Broad St. and Alaskan Way.

Photo courtesy of Donald E. Kelly.

Snoqualmie, WA

Northwest Railway Museum
Train ride, Museum
Standard gauge
Radio frequency: 1.6135/1.61385

ADDRESS: 38625 SE King St., PO Box 459 Snoqualmie, WA 98065
TELEPHONE: (425) 888-3030
WEBSITE: www.trainmuseum.org

DESCRIPTION: This operating railway museum features exhibits at the restored 1890 Queen Anne-style Snoqualmie Depot. It offers 10-mile round-trip train excursions to Snoqualmie Falls on restored heavyweight passenger coaches pulled by first-generation diesel locomotives.

SCHEDULE: Train: April to October, Saturday, Sunday, Memorial Day, July 4, Labor Day, some weekdays; museum and gift shop: year-round, daily, 10 a.m. to 5 p.m.

ADMISSION/FARE: Train: adults, $9; seniors 62+, $8; children 2-12, $6. Museum: free.

LOCOMOTIVES/ROLLING STOCK: Kennecott Copper RSD-4 no. 201; Weyerhaeuser Timber H12-44 no. 1; Spokane, Portland & Seattle Railway Barney and Smith steel coaches nos. 272 and 276; more.

SPECIAL EVENTS: May 6 and 7, Mothers Ride Free; June 17 and 18, Pops on Us; July 7 to 9 and 14 to 16, Day out with Thomas™; August 4 to 12, Snoqualmie Railroad Days; September 9 and 10, Grandparents' Grand Excursion; November 25 and 26, December 2, 3, 9, and 10, Santa Train.

NEARBY ATTRACTIONS: Snoqualmie Falls.

DIRECTIONS: I-90, eastbound exit 27 or westbound exit 31.

Toppenish, WA

Northern Pacific Railway Museum
Train ride, Dinner train, Display

ADDRESS: 10 Asotin Ave., PO Box 889 Toppenish, WA 98948
TELEPHONE: (509) 865-1911
WEBSITE: www.nprymuseum.org

DESCRIPTION: Tourist train on the former Northern Pacific White Swan branch line. Passenger excursions are 20-mile round trips from Harrah to White Swan. The 1911 former NP railroad depot in Toppenish serves as the museum and gift shop. The freight house has been converted to an engine house and the former NP section foreman's house is adjacent to the depot.

SCHEDULE: September and October: every Saturday.

ADMISSION/FARE: Train: adults, $5; children, $3; depot: adults, $3; children under 12, $2.

LOCOMOTIVES/ROLLING STOCK: NP GP9 no. 316; two heavyweight former Pennsylvania Railroad coaches.

SPECIAL EVENTS: Third weekend in August, Transportation Day and open house; rides and railroad memorabilia swap meet.

NEARBY ATTRACTIONS: The only Hop museum in the United States, Indian Museum, more than 50 murals throughout the town.

DIRECTIONS: 20 minutes south of Yakima; next to tracks in the center of town.

Photo courtesy of Harold K. Chandler.

Wickersham, WA

Lake Whatcom Railway

Train ride
Standard gauge

SITE ADDRESS: NP Rd. Wickersham, WA
MAILING ADDRESS: PO Box 91 Acme, WA 98220
TELEPHONE: (360) 595-2218
WEBSITE: www.lakewhatcomrailway.com

DESCRIPTION: This 6½-mile round-trip train ride goes through the woods of Whatcom County. Visitors can ride the authentic, full-sized old Northern Pacific train, see a steam engine that is almost 100 years old, ride a vintage hand car or little railroad work speeder along the shore of Lake Whatcom, and eat at the train's coffee shop car. The passenger coaches date to the early 1900s and were used for many years on the Northern Pacific passenger trains out of Seattle. Some ancient wooden freight cars from the Great Northern Railway are also on the premises.

SCHEDULE: July and August: Saturday and Tuesday, 9:30 a.m., 12 and 2:30 p.m. Special events trains preceding Christmas and Easter: advance reservations required.

ADMISSION/FARE: Adults 18 and up, $14; children 2-17, $7; babies, free.

LOCOMOTIVES/ROLLING STOCK: Alco S-1 diesel locomotive built 1940, no. 30; Pullman built (former Northern Pacific) heavyweight passenger coaches nos. 627 and 634; steam locomotive built 1907, former Northern Pacific 0-60 no. 1070; other cars from NP and GN Railways.

SPECIAL EVENTS: Saturday before Easter weekend, Easter Trains; October, Autumn Train; December Saturdays before Christmas, Christmas Trains. Call for schedule and reservations.

NEARBY ATTRACTIONS: San Juan Islands, Mt. Baker, North Cascade Mountains (RV parks), and restaurants in nearby towns.

DIRECTIONS: Take I-5 to Burlington, WA (exit 230). Go east 6 miles on Hwy. 20 to Arco Gas Station in Sedro Woolley. Turn north at the traffic light there. Go 10 miles on Hwy. 9. Turn onto NP Rd.

Photo courtesy of Chris Camp.

WEST VIRGINIA

Belington, WV

New Tygart Flyer, West Virginia Central Railroad

Train ride, Dinner train
Standard gauge
Radio frequency: 160.455

Wheeling
Parkersburg
Belington
Harpers Ferry
Cheat Bridge
Cass
Durbin
Huntington

SITE ADDRESS: Belington, WV
MAILING ADDRESS: WVCRR, PO Box 44 Durbin, WV 26264
TELEPHONE: (304) 456-4935
E-MAIL: ticketinfo@mountainrail.com
WEBSITE: mountainrail.com

DESCRIPTION: Passengers can have a choice of 24-, 46-, 62-, or 102-mile excursions through two river valleys, over mountains, through a unique S-curve tunnel, and into two remote canyon areas with many scenic views.

SCHEDULE: May through October; winter: excursions are scheduled; call for dates.

ADMISSION/FARE: Rates start at $15 and vary according to choice of excursion. Lounge car service is available.

LOCOMOTIVES/ROLLING STOCK: FP7A no. 67; FP7B no. 415; FA-2 no. 303; BL-2 no. 82; all in WM speed lettering. Train is climate-controlled with dinette, snack coach, lounge car, and coaches.

SPECIAL EVENTS: Mid-July, Civil War re-enactments in Belington and Beverly; first week of October, Elkins Forest Festival.

NEARBY ATTRACTIONS: Monongahela National Forest, Davis and Elkins College, Canaan Valley resort area, and Cheat Mountain Salamander railbus ride.

DIRECTIONS: Belington is located on US Route 250, 5 miles north of US33. Elkins is located at the intersection of US33, Route 219, and Route 250 in east central WV.

Photo courtesy of Lars O. Byrne.

Cass, WV
Cass Scenic Railroad State Park
Train ride, Dinner train, Museum, Display, Model train layout
Standard gauge
Radio frequency: low band

ADDRESS: Route 66 Main St., Depot, PO Box 107 Cass, WV 24927
TELEPHONE: (800) 225-5982 or (304) 456-4300
E-MAIL: cassrr@sunlitsurf.com
WEBSITE: www.cassrailroad.com

DESCRIPTION: This railroad park has a large roster of Shay steam locomotives and examples of a Hisler and a Climax, all three once used extensively in the state on logging railroads. Visitors can experience the past with an excursion on a Shay steam locomotive. Visitors also can stay in a turn-of-the-century two-story logging house with all the modern conveniences and enjoy the country store, museum, dinner train series, walking tours, and other special activities.

SCHEDULE: May 27 through September 5 departures from Cass to: Whittaker Station: daily, 12 and 2:30 p.m.; Spruce: Friday, 10:30 a.m.; Bald Knob: Tuesday, Wednesday, Thursday, Saturday, and Sunday, 10:30 a.m.; also departs at 10:30 a.m. on these Mondays: May 30 (Memorial Day), July 4 (Independence Day), and Sept. 5 (Labor Day). Special Fall schedule is available. Friday of Memorial Day weekend through last Sunday in October: Mountain train rides; call for daily departure times and destinations.

ADMISSION/FARE: Prices vary with event, and reservations are recommended. Group rates are available. Call or check our website for details.

LOCOMOTIVES/ROLLING STOCK: No. 2, a 1928 Pacific Coast-type Shay; no. 4, a 1922 70-ton Shay; no. 5, a 1905 90-ton Shay; Western Maryland no. 6, a 150-ton locomotive built in 1945 as the last Shay constructed; no. 11, a 1923 110-ton Shay; Heisler no. 6, formerly of Meadow River Lumber Company.

SPECIAL EVENTS: Spring Birding Train, Summer Dinner Train, Murder Mystery Train, and Fall Harvest Train.

NEARBY ATTRACTIONS: Green Bank National Radio Astronomy Observatory, Snowshoe Resort, The Durbin and Greenbrier Valley Railroad and the Potomac Eagle.

DIRECTIONS: SR28/92 between Dunmore and Green Bank in Pocahontas County, eastern WV.

See ad on pages A-11 and A-28.

Cheat Bridge, WV

Cheat Mountain Salamander Rail Ride

Train ride
Standard gauge
Radio frequency: 160.455

SITE ADDRESS: Red Run Rd. Cheat Bridge, WV
MAILING ADDRESS: PO Box 44 Durbin, WV 26264
TELEPHONE: (877) 686-7245 [877-MTN-RAIL]
E-MAIL: ticketinfo@mountainrail.com
WEBSITE: www.mountainrail.com

DESCRIPTION: Passengers can enjoy a 34-, 42-, or 76-mile mountain wilderness ride on top of Cheat Mountain through the spectacular Monongahela National Forest. The self-propelled railbus crosses a 4,066-foot mountain pass and stops at the inspirational High Falls of the Cheat River, where it meets the New Tygart Flyer excursion train.

SCHEDULE: April to October, 11 a.m. and 2:30 p.m.; call for details.

ADMISSION/FARE: Adults, $22; seniors, $20; children 4-11, $15.

LOCOMOTIVES/ROLLING STOCK: No. M-3, a self-propelled 50-passenger Edwards Railway Company motor coach.

SPECIAL EVENTS: Fall foliage trips.

NEARBY ATTRACTIONS: Durbin & Greenbrier Valley Scenic Railroad and New Tygart Flyer Excursion Train.

DIRECTIONS: 28 miles south of Elkins or 7 miles north of Durbin on US Route 250.

Photo courtesy of Lars O. Byrne.

Durbin, WV

Durbin & Greenbrier Valley Railroad

Train ride
Standard gauge
Radio frequency: 160.455

ADDRESS: 3 E Main St., PO Box 249 Durbin, WV 26264
TELEPHONE: (877) 686-7245
E-MAIL: ticketinfo@mountainrail.com
WEBSITE: www.mountainrail.com

DESCRIPTION: This 10½-mile, 2-hour round trip along the upper Greenbrier River travels the former Chesapeake & Ohio Railroad Greenbrier Division. The Durbin Rocket is powered by a rare Climax steam locomotive, one of only three in operation today.

SCHEDULE: May to October, 11 a.m. and 3 p.m.; moonlight excursions; call for details.

ADMISSION/FARE: Adults, $16; seniors, $14; children 4-11, $10.

LOCOMOTIVES/ROLLING STOCK: 55-ton Climax no. 3, ex-Moore-Keppel Co., built in 1910; 20-ton Whitcomb gas/mechanical "Little Leroi," built in 1940; 45-ton GE sideroad center cab, built in 1941.

SPECIAL EVENTS: Annual "Highballin' for History" Railfan event, moonlight train rides with home-cooked meals; call for details.

NEARBY ATTRACTIONS: Monongahela National Forest, New Tygart Flyer Excursion Train, Gaudineer Scenic Area, Cheat Mountain Salamander Railbus ride, Rail and Trail Store.

DIRECTIONS: 35 miles south of Elkins on US Route 250 in east central WV.

Photo courtesy of Lars O. Byrne.

Harpers Ferry, WV

Harpers Ferry Toy Train Museum & Joy Line Railroad

Miniature/park train ride, Display, Model train layout
16" gauge

SITE ADDRESS: 937 Bakerton Rd. Harpers Ferry, WV 25425
MAILING ADDRESS: Route 3 Box 315 Harpers Ferry, WV 25425
TELEPHONE: (304) 535-2291 or (304) 535-2521
E-MAIL: hfttm@aol.com

DESCRIPTION: One-half mile of 16" gauge track and a collection of antique toy trains.

SCHEDULE: April through October: weekends and holidays, 9 a.m. to 5 p.m.

ADMISSION/FARE: Adults, $1.50.

LOCOMOTIVES/ROLLING STOCK: Two miniature train G-16s; S-16; homebuilt 2-4-4T; four M.T. passenger cars; six freight cars; caboose; snowplow; work crane.

NEARBY ATTRACTIONS: Harpers Ferry National Park.

DIRECTIONS: Take 340 west one mile past Harpers Ferry and turn right onto Bakerton Rd. (Route 27), continue one mile and turn left.

Huntington, WV

Collis P. Huntington
Railroad Historical Society, Inc.

Train ride, Museum, Display
Standard gauge

EDITOR'S CHOICE

SITE ADDRESS: 1323 8th Ave. Huntington, WV
MAILING ADDRESS: New River Train Excursions P.O. Box 451 Kenova, WV 25530
TELEPHONE: (866) 639-7487 or (304) 523-0364
E-MAIL: newrivertrain@aol.com
WEBSITE: www.newrivertrain.com

DESCRIPTION: The New River Train excursions travel through New River Gorge in southern West Virginia. During the peak autumn foliage of mid- to late October, the train traverses the former Chesapeake & Ohio mainline from Huntingon to Hinton. Since 1959, the outdoor and indoor museums and rail excursions have been offering a well-rounded educational and fun experience for all.

SCHEDULE: Museum: Memorial Day through late September: Sunday, 2 to 5 p.m.; excursions in October, also by appointment year-round.

ADMISSION/FARE: Museum: donations appreciated; excursions: from $115.

LOCOMOTIVES/ROLLING STOCK: C&O Mallet steam locomotive no. 1308, now on National Register of Historic Places; C&O and Virginian cabooses; operating hand-pump car; boxcar; baggage car; concession car; former Reading RS3 diesel locomotive; New York Central lounge car no. 38; Operation Lifesaver caboose; lounge/parlor car no. 190.

SPECIAL EVENTS: Four 1-day, 300-mile round trips; March, Tri-State Railroad Days at Greenbo State Resort Park near Ashland, Kentucky; October, Annual New River Train Excursions, Hinton Railroad Days; Thanksgiving weekend, model railroad show.

NEARBY ATTRACTIONS: Radio Museum, Heritage Museum, Highlands Museum and Discovery Center, Huntington Museum of Art, Blenko Glass, CSX, NS main lines, Greenbo Lake State Resort Park.

DIRECTIONS: Excursions: 7th Ave. and 19th St., Huntington; museum: 14th St. W and Ritter Park, Huntington; office and indoor museum: 1323 8th Ave.

Photo courtesy of Greig A. Goodall.
Coupon available, see insert.

Potomac Eagle Scenic Railroad

Train ride
Standard gauge

ADDRESS: 2306 35th St. Parkersburg, WV 26104
TELEPHONE: (304) 424-0736
E-MAIL: corbittdavid@hotmail.com
WEBSITE: www.potomaceagle.info

DESCRIPTION: A 40-mile, 3½-hour ride travels along the South Branch of the Potomac River on the South Branch Valley Railroad. Potomac Eagle passengers see the "trough," a beautiful forested canyon. Some 70-mile, all-day trips are available each month.

SCHEDULE: May through October.

ADMISSION/FARE: Three-hour trip: coach: adults, $24; children 6-16, $10; first-class club car: $54; all-day trip: coach: adults, $40; children 6-16, $20; first-class club car: $99.

LOCOMOTIVES/ROLLING STOCK: Baltimore & Ohio GP9 6604; Chessie System GP9 6240; Potomac Eagle F7 no. 722; Chesapeake & Ohio F3 no. 8016; mid-20s coaches; 1950 lounge cars; open-air sight-seeing cars.

SPECIAL EVENTS: Various special trains are available for home tours, Railfan Day, all-day and evening trips. Call, write, or check the website.

NEARBY ATTRACTIONS: Western Maryland Scenic Railroad; C&O Canal.

DIRECTIONS: Take Route 50 east or west to Route 28 north.

Photo courtesy of D.W. Corbitt.

TRAVEL TIP: *Photo outings*

Many railroads offer a railfan event that includes special trains, unusual equipment, and the chance to get great photos of your favorite railroad. Be sure to check the special events listings of your favorite line to see if they schedule a photography weekend or a photo freight that will provide a glimpse into the past.

Wheeling, WV

Benedum Science Center

Display, Model train layout
O scale

ADDRESS: Route 88 N Oglebay Resort Wheeling, WV 26003
TELEPHONE: (800) 624-6988 or (304) 243-4100
E-MAIL: smitch@oglebay-resort.com
WEBSITE: www.oglebay-resort.com/goodzoo/train.htm

DESCRIPTION: A 1,200-square-foot O gauge model railroad and village is located within the children's zoo, part of 1,800-acre family resort. CP Huntington replica train ride available around the zoo.

SCHEDULE: Daily, 11 a.m. to 4 p.m.; June, July, and August, 11 a.m. to 5 p.m.

ADMISSION/FARE: Adults, $6.25; children $5.25; children 2 and under, free.

SPECIAL EVENTS: January 14 and 15, 2006, 16th annual model railroad show.

NEARBY ATTRACTIONS: Oglebay Resort: 210-room rustic lodge, restaurant, 45 cabins, 4 golf courses, children's zoo, tennis, historic mansion museum, gardens; Kruger Street Toy & Train Museum; Marx Toy Museum, Cabella's Outdoor Megastore 15 minutes away.

DIRECTIONS: From I-70 east or west to Wheeling, West Virginia. Follow Route 88 north 4 miles to Oglebay Park. Layout is located at zoo building.

Photo courtesy of Steven Mitch.

KEY TO SYMBOLS

Handicapped accessible	Restaurant	Arts and crafts	Association of Railway Museums
Parking	Picnic area	Memberships available	Tourist Railway Association, Inc.
Bus/RV parking	Dining car	Send S.A.S.E. for brochure	Amtrak service to nearby city
Gift, book, or museum shop	Excursions	National Register of Historic Places	VIA service to nearby city
Refreshments	Guided tours	Credit cards accepted	

Kruger Street Toy and Train Museum

Museum, Display, Model train layout
Various gauges; O, HO, and G scale

ADDRESS: 144 Kruger St. Wheeling, WV 26003
TELEPHONE: (304) 242-8133
E-MAIL: museum@toyandtrain.com
WEBSITE: www.toyandtrain.com

DESCRIPTION: The museum houses a wide variety of toys, dolls, games, trains of all types, and playthings from all eras. The collections are housed in a restored 24,000-square-foot vintage 1906 Victorian schoolhouse. Several operating train layouts and a gift shop are also available on site.

SCHEDULE: January to Memorial Day, Friday to Sunday; Memorial to Labor Day, 7 days a week; Labor Day to October 31, 6 days a week, closed Tuesday; November 31 to December 31, 7 days a week. Hours are always 9 a.m. to 5 p.m.

ADMISSION/FARE: Adults, $8; seniors 65+, $7; students 10-18, $5; children under 10, free with adult.

LOCOMOTIVES/ROLLING STOCK: Restored B&O caboose C-2019, an I-5 type caboose built in 1926.

SPECIAL EVENTS: Last Saturday in April, Wheeling Caboose Day; June, host site for the Marx Toy and Train Collectors National Convention and Mego collectors; contact the museum for details.

NEARBY ATTRACTIONS: Oglebay Resort and Conference Center, Wheeling Island Racetrack and Gaming Center, Jamboree USA, and Cabela's. The Pennsylvania Trolley Museum is ½ hour away in Washington, Pennsylvania.

DIRECTIONS: From I-70 or I-470, take exit 5. Turn left at bottom of exit ramp. Go to first traffic signal and turn left again onto Kruger St. Museum is about 100 yards up Kruger St. on the right-hand side.

Photo courtesy of Thomas Pollard.
Coupon available, see insert.

WISCONSIN

Brodhead Historical Society Depot Museum
Museum

SITE ADDRESS: 1108 First Center
Brodhead, WI 53520
MAILING ADDRESS: 310 N SR104
Brodhead, WI 53520-9040
TELEPHONE: (608) 897-4150
E-MAIL: wawalters@ckhweb.com

DESCRIPTION: This restored Chicago, Milwaukee & St. Paul depot was built in 1881 and houses a permanent railroad display with rotating historical displays. Milwaukee Road switch engine no. 781 and caboose no. 1900 stand alongside the depot.

SCHEDULE: Memorial weekend through September: Wednesday, Saturday, Sunday, and holidays, 1 to 4 p.m.; and appointment.

ADMISSION/FARE: Donations accepted.

LOCOMOTIVES/ROLLING STOCK:
Milwaukee Road Fairbanks-Morse switch engine no. 781; Milwaukee road caboose no. 1900.

SPECIAL EVENTS: April, Depot Days.

NEARBY ATTRACTIONS: Veteran's Memorial Park, Sugar River State Trail, Rustic Road, Amish attractions, antique shops, campsites, and apple orchards.

DIRECTIONS: Take Hwy. 11 to Brodhead. Hwy. 11 is 1st Center Ave. in Brodhead.

Photo courtesy of Brodhead Independent Register.

Colfax Railroad Museum, Inc.
Museum
Standard and 3' gauge

ADDRESS: 500 Railroad Ave., PO Box 383 Colfax, WI 54730
TELEPHONE: (715) 962-2076
E-MAIL: colfaxrr@wwt.net

DESCRIPTION: A large collection of railroad memorabilia, an extensive reference library and an outdoor collection of locomotives and rolling stock.

SCHEDULE: May and September: weekends, 11 a.m. to 4 p.m.; June, July and August: Thursday through Sunday, 11 a.m. to 4 p.m.

ADMISSION/FARE: Adults $2.50, children 6 to 14 $1.00; children under 6, free.

LOCOMOTIVES/ROLLING STOCK: Soo Line GP30 no. 703; Soo Line wooden cabooses nos. 256 and no. 273; DSS&A caboose no. 580; Milwaukee Road caboose no. 992154; Soo Line Coach no. 991; Omaha Route mail car no. 301; NP wooden coach no. 950; Milwaukee Road flanger no. 00931; two GE 3' gauge electric locomotives; two CN speeders; Velocipede; Soo Line outside bracer wooden boxcar no. 33400.

SPECIAL EVENTS: Mid-June, Colfax Free Fair; mid-September, Twister Run; Red Cedar River and Trail.

NEARBY ATTRACTIONS: Red Cedar River and Trail.

DIRECTIONS: Exit 52 off I-94 to Chippewa Falls. After about ¾ mile, go north on Hwy. 40 for 8 miles to Colfax. First right after the railroad tracks, go one block. Museum is on the right.

Photo courtesy of Herbert Sakalaucks.

East Troy, WI

East Troy Electric Railroad

EDITOR'S CHOICE

Train ride, Dinner train, Museum
Standard gauge

ADDRESS: 2002 Church St. East Troy, WI 53120
TELEPHONE: (262) 642-3263 or (262) 642-3077
WEBSITE: www.easttroyrr.org

DESCRIPTION: The East Troy Electric Railroad was built in 1906-7 by the Milwaukee Electric Railway and Light Company, as part of its 200-mile system of streetcar and interurban service. The scenic 11-mile round trip of restored electric trolley cars runs from East Troy to Mukwonago in southeast Wisconsin and operates in interchange with Canadian National. The line roughly follows old Wisconsin Hwy. 15, now County ES, which is paralleled by Interstate 43. Much of the mainline is original 80-pound rail, which was laid in 80-foot lengths with parallel joints. It is completely electrically operated. The original Milwaukee Electric 500KW rotary convertor motor-generator set, still capable of operation, is on display in the depot. There is also a gift shop and main ticket agent, as well as a five-track yard and 60' x 250' car barn.

SCHEDULE: May through October: weekends and holidays, 11:30 a.m. to 4 p.m.; mid-June through August: Wednesday through Friday, 10 a.m., 12 p.m., and 2 p.m.

ADMISSION/FARE: Trolley ride: adults, $9; children 3-11, $5.

LOCOMOTIVES/ROLLING STOCK: CSS&SB 9, 13, 21, 24, 25, 30, 111; CTA 28, 35, 45, 4420, 4453; Minneapolis Streetcar 1583; P&W 64; ETER 21; TMER&L 200, D23, L6, L8, and L9; CNS&MRR 228 and 761; SEPTA PCC 2185; TTC PCC 4617; WP&L 26 and TE-1; Milwaukee Streetcar 846.

SPECIAL EVENTS: May 20 and 21, Railroad Days; October 14 and 15, Fall Color Spectacular.

NEARBY ATTRACTIONS: Many nearby historic attractions and other family activities.

DIRECTIONS: One mile off I-43, north on Hwy. 120; 20 minutes north of Lake Geneva and 35 minutes southwest of Milwaukee.

Photo courtesy of Scott Patrick.

Green Bay, WI

National Railroad Museum
Train ride, Museum
Standard gauge

ADDRESS: 2285 S Broadway Green Bay, WI 54304
TELEPHONE: (920) 437-7623
WEBSITE: www.nationalrrmuseum.org

DESCRIPTION: Visitors can sit in the cab of the Union Pacific Big Boy, view General Eisenhower's WWII command train, examine the future of railroading in the sleek 1955 General Motors Aerotrain, enjoy a train ride aboard vintage rolling stock with historical narrative provided by the conductor, and more. Admission includes train ride, all exhibits, model railroad layout, theater presentation, and 85-foot observation tower.

SCHEDULE: Monday through Saturday, 9 a.m. to 5 p.m.; Sunday, 11 a.m. to 5 p.m.

ADMISSION/FARE: Adults, $7; seniors, $6; children 4-12, $5; 3 and under, free.

LOCOMOTIVES/ROLLING STOCK: Union Pacific Big Boy no. 4017; Pennsylvania Railroad GG1 no. 4890; General Motors Aerotrain; Eisenhower's WWII command train.

SPECIAL EVENTS: Many events throughout the year. See website or call for details.

DIRECTIONS: Hwy. 41 or 172 to Ashland Ave. exit, go north to Cormier Ave. then east 3 blocks.

Hartford, WI

1003 Operations

Museum
Standard gauge

SITE ADDRESS: Wisconsin Automotive Museum, 147 N Rural Hartford, WI 53027
MAILING ADDRESS: 3466 RFD Long Grove, IL 60047
TELEPHONE: (262) 673-7999

DESCRIPTION: 1003 Operations, LLP, maintains this locomotive for periodic use.

SCHEDULE: Special events are scheduled one to two times per year in conjunction with area festivals and celebrations. Soo Line steam locomotive no. 1003 appears with caboose and/or other equipment. Locomotive may be viewed at Hartford Automotive Museum when not operating.

ADMISSION/FARE: Admission to museum is $7.

LOCOMOTIVES/ROLLING STOCK: Soo Line 2-8-2 class LI steam locomotive no. 1003; Soo Line caboose no. 268; Milwaukee Road caboose no. 02012.

NEARBY ATTRACTIONS: Milwaukee area attractions, Green Bay National Railway Museum.

DIRECTIONS: Hartford, WI is approximately 30 miles northwest of Milwaukee on Route 60.

Laona, WI

Camp Five

Train ride, Museum
Standard gauge

ADDRESS: 5480 Connor Farm Rd. Laona, WI 54541
TELEPHONE: (800) 774-3414 or (715) 674-3414
E-MAIL: mverich@camp5museum.org
WEBSITE: www.camp5museum.org

DESCRIPTION: Visitors ride the Lumberjack Special steam train (2.5 miles one way) to the museum complex, then a guided surrey tour through forests managed on a perpetual-cycle basis. A hayrack/pontoon ride on the Rat River is also available. The logging museum features an early-transportation wing and an active blacksmith shop, 1/2-hour steam engine video, a large outdoor display of logging artifacts, petting corral, and more.

SCHEDULE: June 23 through August 27.

ADMISSION/FARE: Adults, $16; children 4-12, $6; children 3 and under, free.

LOCOMOTIVES/ROLLING STOCK: 1916 Vulcan 2-6-2; three cupola cabooses; two passenger coaches.

SPECIAL EVENTS: September 30, October 7 and 14, Fall Festival.

DIRECTIONS: West of Laona on Hwy. 8.

Coupon available, see insert.

Manitowoc, WI
Pinecrest Historical Village
Museum

SITE ADDRESS: 924 Pine Crest Ln. Manitowoc, WI
MAILING ADDRESS: Manitowoc County Historical Society, 1701 Michigan Ave. Manitowoc, WI 54220
TELEPHONE: (920) 684-4445
WEBSITE: www.mchistsoc.org

DESCRIPTION: This is an open-air museum of Manitowoc County history.

SCHEDULE: May 1 through October 24: daily, 9 a.m. to 4 p.m.

ADMISSION/FARE: Adults, $6; children $4; families, $15; MCHS members, free.

LOCOMOTIVES/ROLLING STOCK: 1896 Collins Depot, Wisconsin Central Railway steam locomotive 0-6-0 steam locomotive no. 321, tender, flatcar, Wisconsin Central Railway caboose no. 99006.

SPECIAL EVENTS: Third weekend in July, German Fest; Third weekend in September, Fall Harvest Festival; Second weekend in December, A Holiday in History.

NEARBY ATTRACTIONS: Wisconsin Maritime Museum.

DIRECTIONS: 1-43, exit CTH JJ. Go west 3 miles to Pinecrest Lane.

Marshall, WI

Whiskey River Railway

Train ride
16" gauge

ADDRESS: 700 E Main St. Marshall, WI 53559
TELEPHONE: (888) 607-7735
E-MAIL: gardyloo@jvlnet.com
WEBSITE: www.littleamerricka.com

DESCRIPTION: A 2-mile scenic ride travels through the Wisconsin countryside. The Whiskey River Railway is a ⅓ size railroad operating an array of steam and diesel engines and prototypical freight and passenger cars with over three miles of track on the ground. The location is also the home of Merrick Light Railway Equipment. Visitors can see the shops where ⅓ size steam, diesel, and car equipment are still being built.

SCHEDULE: Diesel: Monday through Friday; steam: Saturday and Sunday; visit their website for a full schedule of dates and times of operation.

ADMISSION/FARE: $4.50 per ride. Unlimited rides: under 42" tall, $10; 42" and up, $13.

LOCOMOTIVES/ROLLING STOCK: 1919 Pacific, Gene Autrey's 1956 Pacific, Oakland Acorn Pacific, Norm Gracey Atlantic, 1996 & 1997 GPs, Santa Fe Switch Locomotive.

DIRECTIONS: Located ¼ mile east of Hwy. 73 on Hwy. 19 in Marshall.

Photo courtesy of D. Klompmaker Collection.

Milwaukee, WI

Zoofari Express Milwaukee County Zoo

Train ride
15" gauge
Radio frequency: 458.525 3 Z and 458.9125 3 Z

ADDRESS: 10001 W Bluemound Rd. Milwaukee, WI 53226
TELEPHONE: (414) 771-3040
WEBSITE: www.milwaukeezoo.org

DESCRIPTION: The railroad has operated at the Milwaukee County Zoo since 1958, carrying over 13 million riders. The 1.25 mile trip across the zoo lasts about 8 minutes.

SCHEDULE: May through September: daily, 10 a.m. to 4 p.m.; March, April, and October: weekends only, 10 a.m. to 4 p.m.

ADMISSION/FARE: Zoo admission: adults, $9.75; children 3-12, $6.75. Train ride: adults, $2.50; children, $1.50. Parking: $8.

LOCOMOTIVES/ROLLING STOCK: Sandley Light locomotives and rolling stock: coal-fired steam locomotive 4-6-2 no. 1924, coal-fired steam locomotive 4-4-2 no. 1916, diesel hydraulic switcher no. 1958, F2 diesel hydraulic no. 1992, 16-passenger day coach, and OS 1080-1096.

NEARBY ATTRACTIONS: Mitchell Park Domes, Milwaukee Public Museum, Miller Park, Bradley Center, Wehr Nature Center, and Boerner Botanical Gardens.

DIRECTIONS: Located 8 miles west of downtown Milwaukee at the intersection of I-94, I-894, and Hwy. 45.

Monroe, WI

Green County Welcome Center

Museum, Display

ADDRESS: 2108 Seventh Ave. Monroe, WI 53566
TELEPHONE: (608) 325-4636
E-MAIL: info@greencountywelcomecenter.org
WEBSITE: http://lorenzo.uwstout.edu/cheese/cheese.htm

DESCRIPTION: Features a restored Milwaukee Road Depot and Ribsider.

SCHEDULE: Daily, 9 a.m. to 4 p.m. Winter: December, Friday, 11 a.m. to 3 p.m; closed January and February.

ADMISSION/FARE: $2 donation to museum.

LOCOMOTIVES/ROLLING STOCK: Milwaukee Road Ribsided Caboose no. 992094.

SPECIAL EVENTS: Green County Depot Days; call or check website for details.

DIRECTIONS: Located on WI69 S (south edge of Monroe).

New London, WI

New London Historical Society
Museum

SITE ADDRESS: 900 Montgomery St. New London, WI 54961
MAILING ADDRESS: 101 Beckert Rd., Apt. 204 New London, WI 54961-2500
TELEPHONE: (920) 982-5186 or (920) 982-8557

DESCRIPTION: Features a restored CNW depot, complete with railroad artifacts.

SCHEDULE: June to August: first and third Sundays, 1 to 4 p.m. or by appointment.

ADMISSION/FARE: Donations appreciated.

LOCOMOTIVES/ROLLING STOCK: US Army no. 4555, renumbered US Army no. 7436, built by Vulcan Iron Works 1941, sold to Laona & Northern Railway October 1948 to become engine no. 101; Soo Line caboose no. 138; CNW caboose no. 11153; Soo Line boxcar no. 75618.

SPECIAL EVENTS: First Sunday in August, Rail Fest Days.

NEARBY ATTRACTIONS: Mosquito Hill Nature Center, and Memorial Park.

DIRECTIONS: Route 45 north to Business 45, High St. east to railroad tracks, north to depot.

North Freedom, WI

Mid-Continent Railway Historical Society
Train ride, Dinner train, Museum
Standard gauge

SITE ADDRESS: E8948 Diamond Hill Rd. North Freedom, WI 53951
MAILING ADDRESS: PO Box 358 North Freedom, WI 53951-0358
TELEPHONE: (800) 930-1385 or (608) 522-4261
E-MAIL: inquiries@midcontinent.org
WEBSITE: www.midcontinent.org

DESCRIPTION: A seven-mile, 50-minute diesel-powered ride travels through a rural setting. Trains depart from a restored 1894 C&NW depot. On display is an extensive collection of early 1900s-era vintage freight, passenger, and company-service equipment, including newly restored wooden coaches MLS&W 63 and CR 60. Caboose and cab rides are offered. Dinner and first-class services operate on select dates. Call or visit website for details.

WISCONSIN

North Freedom – Osceola

SCHEDULE: May 6 through October 22: weekends; May 15 through September 4: daily. Train operates: 10:30 a.m.; 12:30, 2, and 3:30 p.m.

ADMISSION/FARE: Adults, $12; seniors, $11; children 3-12, $7; children under 3, free; cab ride: $30; caboose: adult, $14; child, $8; first class: $25; dinner train: $70. Reservations required. Extra fare for Snow Train and Santa Express.

LOCOMOTIVES/ROLLING STOCK: Alco S1 diesel no. 7; Chicago & North Western 4-6-0 no. 1385; Polson Logging Co. 2-8-2 no. 2; WC&C 4-6-0 no. 1; Delaware Lackawanna & Western combine and coaches; more.

SPECIAL EVENTS: February, Snow Train; October, Autumn Color Weekends and Pumpkin Special; November, Santa Express.

NEARBY ATTRACTIONS: Circus World Museum, International Crane Foundation, Devils Lake State Park, and Wisconsin Dells.

DIRECTIONS: State Hwy. 136 west to County Hwy. PF to North Freedom. Follow signs.

Photo courtesy of Paul Swanson.
Coupon available, see insert.

Osceola, WI

Osceola & St. Croix Valley Railway (Minnesota Transportation Museum) EDITOR'S CHOICE

Train ride, Dinner train, Museum
Standard gauge
Radio frequency: 161.295

ADDRESS: PO Box 176 Osceola, WI 54020
TELEPHONE: (715) 755-3570
WEBSITE: www.trainride.org

DESCRIPTION: Passengers can enjoy the scenic St. Croix River Valley on a 90-minute round trip between Osceola and Marine-on-St. Croix, Minnesota, or a 45-minute round trip through rural Wisconsin between Osceola and Dresser. Visitors can see the restored Osceola Historical Depot, featuring exhibits about railroading and the Osceola area, and the US Railway Post Office exhibits aboard Northern Pacific triple combine no. 1102.

SCHEDULE: Saturday, Sunday, and Holidays, 11 a.m., 1, and 2:30 p.m.; weekday appointments. Holidays: dinner and pizza Saturday, 5:30 p.m.; Sunday brunch, 10 a.m., opposite weekends.

ADMISSION/FARE: Marine: $7 to $14; Dresser: $5 to $10; Meal and first class: $25-$45 more.

LOCOMOTIVES/ROLLING STOCK: Soo Line GP7 no. 559; three Great Northern streamlined coaches; nos. 2604 and 2608 cars, former Rock Island; NP triple combine car no. 1102; DL&W no. 2232 commuter coach; BN 6234-SD 9 Road Switcher, GN 138660 Box Car in Big Sky Blue Colors.

SPECIAL EVENTS: Mother's and Father's Day Brunch, Dinner and Pizza Train, Fireworks Express, Park Naturalist Trips, and Fall Color Trips.

NEARBY ATTRACTIONS: Cascade Falls, St. Croix River, St. Croix Art Barn, William O'Brien Park.

DIRECTIONS: I-35W to Forest Lake, Hwy. 97 east to Hwy. 95, north to I-243 East across St. Croix River to Hwy. 35S, to Depot Rd.

Photo courtesy of Osceola & St. Croix Valley Railway.
Coupon available, see insert.

Platteville, WI
Mining Museum & Rollo Jamison Museum
Train ride
24"

SITE ADDRESS: 405 E Main St. Platteville, WI
MAILING ADDRESS: City of Platteville-Museum Dept., PO Box 780 Platteville, WI 53818-0780
TELEPHONE: (608) 348-3301
E-MAIL: museums@platteville.org

DESCRIPTION: Visitors tour an 1845 lead mine and ride a 1931 mine locomotive. They can also tour home and farm exhibits in Rollo Jamison Museum. The train ride is part of the mine tour and takes 3 to 5 minutes.

SCHEDULE: Train usually available May to October: daily, 9 a.m. to 5 p.m.; self-guided exhibits: November to April: Monday to Friday, 9 a.m. to 4 p.m.; group tours year-round.

ADMISSION/FARE: Adults, $7; seniors, $6.30; children 5-15, $3.

LOCOMOTIVES/ROLLING STOCK: Whitcomb Co., Rochelle, Illinois, 1931 locomotive.

NEARBY ATTRACTIONS: First Capital Historic Site, University of Wisconsin-Platteville.

DIRECTIONS: Corner of Main S and Virgin Ave., three blocks north of Business Hwy. 151.

Coupon available, see insert.

Sparta, WI

Little Falls Railroad and Doll Museum, Ltd.

Train ride, Museum, Model train layout
12" gauge

ADDRESS: 9208 County Hwy. II Sparta, WI 54656-6485
TELEPHONE: (608) 272-3266
E-MAIL: raildoll@centurytel.net
WEBSITE: www.raildoll.org

DESCRIPTION: Located in Cataract, WI, this three-acre campus houses a doll museum, a train museum, a picnic area, swings, a 12"-gauge train with 300 feet of track, 2500-square foot garden railroad, and a 40' kids' play train in the picnic area.

SCHEDULE: April 1 to November 1: Thursday to Monday, 1 to 5 p.m., or by appointment. (Closed Tuesday and Wednesday.)

ADMISSION/FARE: Both museums, $5. Train ride, $2.

LOCOMOTIVES/ROLLING STOCK: Milwaukee smooth side bay window caboose no. 992175.

NEARBY ATTRACTIONS: Fort McCoy, Wegner grotto, and Elroy-Sparta bike trail.

DIRECTIONS: Halfway between Sparta and Black River Falls, 1.8 miles east of Cataract on County Hwy. II. Take County Hwy. B to 11.

Photo courtesy of Dr. Jim Brown.

Spooner, WI

Railroad Memories Museum

Museum, Display, Model train layout
G and HO gauge

SITE ADDRESS: 424 Front St. Spooner, WI 54801
MAILING ADDRESS: 1011 Huron St. Spooner, WI 54801
TELEPHONE: (715) 635-3325, when closed (715) 635-2752
WEBSITE: www.spoonerwi.com/railroadmuseum/

DESCRIPTION: This historical, educational museum covers all aspects of railroading, including tools, equipment, track vehicles, memorabilia, history from the 1800s, many station signs, books, art, and rare uniforms. Also available: guided tours, videos, model trains, eleven large rooms, and an 8 x 12-foot scale diorama of the Spooner yard and complex from the years when Spooner was a big, busy terminal.

SCHEDULE: Memorial to Labor Day weekend: daily, 10 a.m. to 5 p.m. Group appointments.

ADMISSION/FARE: Adults, $4; children 6-12, $0.50; children under 6, free.

LOCOMOTIVES/ROLLING STOCK: 1896 track bicycle, Velocipede, four-man pumper, and track derreck.

NEARBY ATTRACTIONS: Namekagon Scenic River System, Bulik's Amusement Park, Museum of Wood Carving, Heart O' North Rodeo, State Fish Hatchery, family restaurants, and antique stores.

DIRECTIONS: Two blocks from Hwys. 70 and 63; in old CNW depot at Walnut and Front Sts. In 1902 Omaha/CNW depot. See Wisconsin Heritage Site signs on Hwy. 70 and Front St.

Photo courtesy of Carl Schult.

Trempealeau, WI

Inn on the River

ADDRESS: 11321 Main St., P.O. Box 335 Trempealeau, WI 54661
TELEPHONE: (608) 534-7784
WEBSITE: www.innontheriverwisconsin.com

DESCRIPTION: For those who have a passion for trains, the Inn on the River offers a spectacular view of the BNSF, CP, Amtrak, and ICE railroad lines that run on both sides of the Mississippi River. Visitors can sit back and enjoy the show from a balcony. Two Amtrak stations are located within 20 miles.

SCHEDULE: Open year-round.

ADMISSION/FARE: $59 to $99 for two people.

DIRECTIONS: Located on Hwy. 35 between LaCrosse, WI and Winona, MN.

Wisconsin Dells, WI

Riverside & Great Northern Railway

Train ride, Museum
15" gauge

ADDRESS: N115 CRN Wisconsin Dells, WI 53965
TELEPHONE: (608) 254-6367
WEBSITE: www.randgn.com

DESCRIPTION: The R&GN is a living museum preserving miniature steam equipment and the facilities of the Sandley Light Railway Equipment Works, makers of narrow gauge railroads for over 30 years. Passengers can experience a breathtaking view from the new 210'-long, 43'-high bridge. They can also enjoy a scenic, 3-mile round-trip journey on a railroad dating back to the 1850s, through rock cuts and thick forest just north of Wisconsin Dells.

SCHEDULE: Memorial Day to Labor Day: daily, 9:30 a.m. to 5:30 p.m., trains run every 45 minutes; April to May and Labor Day to December: weekends, 10 a.m. to 4 p.m., trains run on the hour. Weather permitting and schedule subject to change; please call ahead.

ADMISSION/FARE: Adults, $9; seniors 62+, $8; children 3-15, $7; children 2 and under, free; family pass, $50. Prices subject to change.

LOCOMOTIVES/ROLLING STOCK: No. 82, 1957 4-4-0 steam engine, former Milwaukee County Zoo; 0-4-0 vertical boiler "Tom Thumb" steam engine; 95 SW style diesel engine.

SPECIAL EVENTS: Two weekends before Halloween, Pumpkin Trains; November and December weekends only, Santa/Snow Trains.

NEARBY ATTRACTIONS: Wisconsin Dells, in Lake Delton area.

DIRECTIONS: West on 90/94 to exit 87, turn left on 12 west, right on CRA, then left under the bridge.

Photo courtesy of Marshall L. "Pete" Deets.
Coupon available, see insert.

TRAVEL TIP: *Volunteers*

Many museum and tourist railroads rely on volunteers for their restoration and operating workers. If you like what you see at a railroad, inquire as to volunteer opportunities. You might find yourself working on your favorite locomotive one day, or even better, running it!

WYOMING

Cheyenne, WY

Cheyenne Depot Museum & Gift Shop
Museum

ADDRESS: 121 W 15th St.
Cheyenne, WY 82001
TELEPHONE: (307) 632-3905, depot
or (307) 638-6338, gift shop
E-MAIL: depoorter11@hotmail.com or pam@cheyennedepotmuseum.org
WEBSITE: www.cheyennedepotmuseum.org

Douglas•

•Evanston   Cheyenne•

DESCRIPTION: The Cheyenne Depot Museum captures the essence of Cheyenne's railroad history, including the history of the Union Pacific Depot. The railroad museum and gift shop are located in the historic Union Pacific Depot in downtown Cheyenne. The depot was built in 1886. Major renovations were completed in 2004, with many new projects scheduled for the next few years.

SCHEDULE: Year-round, 7 days a week: weekdays, 9 a.m. to 5 p.m.; Saturday 10 a.m. to 5 p.m.; Sunday, 11 a.m. to 5 p.m. Extended hours during summer months.

ADMISSION/FARE: Museum, $4; children 12 and under, free.

LOCOMOTIVES/ROLLING STOCK: Big Boy steam locomoitve no. 4004 is about 11 blocks from the Cheyenne depot. It is in a permanent location in Holliday Park.

SPECIAL EVENTS: June 8-11, Depot Days; Annual July 4 celebration in plaza; Last 10 days of July, Frontier Days include free pancake breakfast; free entertainment every Friday evening during the summer; August through September, every Saturday, Farmer's Market.

NEARBY ATTRACTIONS: Seven museums, state and national parks are within 20 miles of Cheyenne. Several historic districts in downtown Cheyenne. See www.cheyenne.org.

DIRECTIONS: The Cheyenne Depot Museum and Cheyenne Visitor Center are located in the Cheyenne Depot in downtown Cheyenne.

Photo courtesy of Candi Homan.

Cheyenne, WY

Union Pacific Railroad

Main line excursions, Displays

DESCRIPTION: The Union Pacific is the only Class I railroad that still maintains its own steam locomotoives for use on excursions and for displays. Locomotives include 4-8-4 no. 844 and 4-6-6-4 no. 3895 as well as historic E9 diesels nos. 951, 949 and 963B, and DD40X diesel no. 6936. Locomotives are based in Cheyenne but not available for viewing there except for special events.

SCHEDULE: The UP usually runs a special from Denver to Cheyenne in conjunction with the Denver Post for the annual Frontier Days rodeo in July. Other outings are announced during the year. Check www.uprr.com in the "general public" area; click on "special trains."

ADMISSION/FARE: Varies.

LOCOMOTIVES/ROLLING STOCK: Locomotives as listed above. Historic lightweight passenger cars from an extensive pool mainained by the UP for special trains. Consists are drawn from the following: Baggage cars: "Council Bluffs," "Pony Express;" Business cars: "Arden," "Cheyenne," "Feather River," "Kenefick," "North Platte," "Selma," "Shoshone," "St. Louis." Club lounge car: "Sun Valley." 44-seat coaches: "City of Salina," "Katy Flyer," "Portland Rose," "Sunshine Special," "Texas Eagle." Concession car: "Sherman Hill." Crew car: "Cabarton." Crew sleepers: "Columbia River," "Little Rock." Deluxe sleepers: "Green River," "Lake Bluff," "Lake Forest," "Omaha," "Portola," "Powder River," "Wyoming." Diners: "City of Denver," "City of Los Angeles," "Overland." Dome coaches: "Challenger," "Columbine." Dome diners: "City of Portland," "Colorado Eagle," "Missouri River Eagle." Inspection cars: "Fox River," "Idaho." Kitchen cars: "Pacific Limited." Dome lounge cars: "City of San Francisco," "Harriman," "Walter Dean." Museum car: "Promontory." Power cars: nos. 205, 207, and 208.

Photo courtesy of Union Pacific Railroad.

Cheyenne, WY

Wyoming Transportation Museum

Museum

ADDRESS: PO Box 704 Cheyenne, WY 82003
TELEPHONE: (307) 637-3376

DESCRIPTION: This museum is housed in the old Cheyenne Union Pacific depot, built in 1886. The exhibits display artifacts relating to the history of travel in the region.

SCHEDULE: Please call or write for more information on schedule, admission/fare, special events, nearby attractions, and directions.

Douglas Area Chamber of Commerce
Museum

ADDRESS: 121 Brownfield Rd. Douglas, WY 82633
TELEPHONE: (307) 358-2950
WEBSITE: www.douglaschamber.com

DESCRIPTION: The Douglas Railroad Interpretive Center has a total of eight vehicles that were donated by railroads. The Depot Building houses the Chamber of Commerce, which has information available for local and statewide attractions.

SCHEDULE: All train cars can be freely viewed from the exterior, seven days a week, 24 hours a day. A Douglas Railroad Interpretive Center Visitors Guide is available for self-guided tour of the inside of the cars during regular business hours: Monday to Friday, 9 a.m. to 5 p.m.

ADMISSION/FARE: Free.

LOCOMOTIVES/ROLLING STOCK: Chicago Burlington & Quincy 4-8-4 no. 5633; CB&Q dining car no. 196; Union Pacific stock car no. 483300; Great Northern sleeper no. 1182; UP baggage car no. 1897; Chicago & North Western coach no. 1886; CB&Q caboose no. 14140; Fairmont motorcar.

SPECIAL EVENTS: June, High School Rodeo finals; Jackalope Days; August, Wyoming State Fair; Labor Day Weekend, Laramie Peak Blue Grass Festival; October, Octoberfest; First December Saturday, Holiday Winter Fest and Lighting of Jackalope Square.

NEARBY ATTRACTIONS: Wyoming Pioneer Memorial Museum, Wyoming State Fair Park, Riverside Park, North Platte River walking and bike path, Douglas Motorsports Park, and Fort Fetterman State Historic Site.

DIRECTIONS: From I-25 take exit 140 and drive the Yellowstone highway into Douglas for one mile to the intersection of Center St. and Brownfield Rd.

See ad on page A-5.

TRAVEL TIP: *Steam locomotives*

Once numbering in the thousands when they were in regular use, only about 150 steam locomotives are still active in the United States on tourist and museum railroads. Union Pacific Railroad's No. 844 is the only main line steam locomotive that has never been retired. It still pulls occasional public trips on the UP system.

Evanston, WY

Roundhouse Restoration, Inc.

Historic roundhouse and railyard

ADDRESS: 1200 Main St. Evanston, WY 82930
TELEPHONE: (307) 783-6320 or (307) 789-8248
E-MAIL: rrinc@allwest.net

DESCRIPTION: Historic Roundhouse and Railyard includes a 28-bay roundhouse, working turntable, and renovated machine shop. Nearby, Historic Depot Square includes a restored 1900 depot, replica Chinese Joss House, and museum.

SCHEDULE: Winter: Monday to Friday, 8 a.m. to 5 p.m.; summer: Monday to Friday, 9 a.m. to 9 p.m.; Saturday, 9 a.m. to 7 p.m.; and Sunday, 12 to 6 p.m. Call to arrange tours.

ADMISSION/FARE: Free.

SPECIAL EVENTS: Second weekend in August, Roundhouse Festival: model train show, art and quilt shows, and tours.

NEARBY ATTRACTIONS: Wyoming Downs horse racing and Purple Sage Golf Course, summer months. Uinta Mountains, camping, hiking, winter sports, Bear Parkway. Very close to Park City and Salt Lake City, Utah. South of Jackson Hole and Yellowstone Park. Close to Heber Valley Railroad, Utah.

DIRECTIONS: On I-80, 1440 Main St., Front & 10th St., 85 miles east of Salt Lake City.

Photo courtesy of Rick Lunsford.

KEY TO SYMBOLS

Handicapped accessible	Restaurant	Arts and crafts	arm Association of Railway Museums
P Parking	Picnic area	IMI Memberships available	TRAIN Tourist Railway Association, Inc.
P Bus/RV parking	Dining car	Send S.A.S.E. for brochure	Amtrak service to nearby city
Gift, book, or museum shop	Excursions	NRHP National Register of Historic Places	VIA VIA service to nearby city
Refreshments	TOUR Guided tours	VISA MasterCard DISCOVER AMERICAN EXPRESS Card	Credit cards accepted

CANADA

Prince Rupert
Prince George
Revelstoke
Jasper
Edmonton
Squamish
Kamloops
Vancouver
Calgary
Saskatoon
Victoria
Surrey
Regina
Winnipeg
Komoka
Huntsville
Osoyoos
Cranbrook
Cochrane
Capreol
Tottenham
Summerland
Fort Steele
Moose Jaw
Carlyle
Sault Ste. Marie
Orangeville
Ottawa
Gatineau
Smith Falls
Clinton
Milton
Brighton
Uxbridge
Chatham
Aberfoyle
Fort Erie
Elmira
Corner Brook
Vallee-Jonction
Thetford Mines
St. Constant

ALBERTA

Calgary, AB
Heritage Park Historical Village

Train ride, Museum, Display

EDITOR'S CHOICE

ADDRESS: 1900 Heritage Dr. SW Calgary, AB T2V 2X3
TELEPHONE: (403) 268-8500
E-MAIL: reception@heritagepark.ab.ca
WEBSITE: www.heritagepark.ca

DESCRIPTION: The past comes to life right in front of your eyes in this living historical village. This first-class summer tourist attraction also serves as a year-round catering and convention facility.

SCHEDULE: Mid-May through Labor Day: daily, 9 a.m. to 5 p.m.; weekends until Canadian Thanksgiving.

ADMISSION/FARE: Call, write, or see website.

LOCOMOTIVES/ROLLING STOCK: 1905 CPR 0-6-0 steam no. 2018; 1942 PT 0-6-0 steam no. 2023; 1944 PT 0-6-0 steam no. 24; 1949 PT 2-10-4 steam no. 5931 "Selkirk"; 1944 CPR Diesel no. 7019; 1882 CPR Construction car no. 76; 1901 CPR York Car no. 100; 1902 CPR Rupertsland no. 5; c. 1885 MF&M passenger car no. 5; c. 1885 MF&M passenger car no. 62; 1912 CPR colonist car no. 2658; 1907 CPR suburban coach; 1912 CPR caboose no. 436209; 1949 CPR caboose no. 437358; c. 1920 CPR Tank car CGTX no. 6010; 1913 CPR box car no. 19752; 1973 flat car no. 221 replica; MF&M flat car no. 53; 1918 CPR RPO no. 3774 (404901); 1923 CPR box car no. 404687; 1912 CPR flat car no. 418181; 1923 CPR service car no. 412409; c. 1923 NAR cattle car no. 20006; 1920 CPR wrecking crane no. 414328; 1907 CPR wrecking crane tender no. 415722; 1911 CPR snow plow no. 400884; 1913 CPR Jordan spreader no. 402829.

SPECIAL EVENTS: May, Opening weekend, Festival of Quilts; June, Railway Days and Father's Day; July, Canada Day; August, Rural Roots; September, Old Time Fall Fair and Fall Harvest Sale; October, October West. Call or visit website for information.

NEARBY ATTRACTIONS: Calgary Zoo, Olympic Park, Glenbow Museum, Fort Calgary, Telus World of Science, and Chinook Mall.

DIRECTIONS: Follow Heritage Dr. west.

Photo courtesy of Heritage Park Historical Village.

Calgary, AB

Royal Canadian Pacific

Train ride, Dinner train

ADDRESS: 133 Ninth Ave. SW Calgary, AB T2P 2M3
TELEPHONE: (877) 665-3044 in North America or (403) 508-1400 outside North America
WEBSITE: www.royalcanadianpacific.com

DESCRIPTION: The Royal Canadian Pacific offers luxury, all-inclusive rail tour packages beginning and ending in Calgary. These six-day, five-night excursions take guests through the Canadian Rockies, Columbia River Valley, and Alberta Prairies. Guests enjoy gourmet meals and luxury *en suite* guest rooms. Tours include: Royal Canadian Rockies Experience, Royal Clubhouse Golf Excursion, Royal Fly-Fishing Adventure, and Royal Culinary, Wine, & Music Experience. Custom private charters also available.

SCHEDULE: May through November: excursions; please call or visit website for more information.

ADMISSION/FARE: Fares vary per excursion; please call or visit website for information.

LOCOMOTIVES/ROLLING STOCK: Locomotives and 10 vintage business cars 1916-1931.

Photo courtesy of Canadian Pacific Railway.

Edmonton, AB

Alberta Railway Museum

Train ride, Museum

ADDRESS: Londonderry Postal Outlet Box 70014 Edmonton, AB T5C 3R6
TELEPHONE: (780) 472-6229
WEBSITE: railwaymuseum.ab.ca

DESCRIPTION: The collection of railway equipment has an emphasis on the cars and locomotives of the Canadian National Railways and the Northern Alberta Railways. Passenger rides are available in the summer on select weekends.

SCHEDULE: Museum: Victoria Day to Labour Day weekend: daily, 10 a.m. to 5 p.m. Passenger trains: Victoria Day, Canada Day, Heritage Day, and Labour Day.

ADMISSION/FARE: Adults, $4; students and seniors, $2.50; children 3-12, $1.25; under 3, free. Train rides $3.

SPECIAL EVENTS: Visit the website or call for special events.

Edmonton, AB

Edmonton Radial Railway Society, Bridge and Park

Trolley ride
Standard gauge

SITE ADDRESS: Strathcona Barn, 84th Ave., 103rd St., and 143 St. Edmonton, AB T6H 5Y1
MAILING ADDRESS: PO Box 45040 Lansdowne PO Edmonton, AB T6H 5Y1
TELEPHONE: (780) 437-7221 or (780) 496-1464
E-MAIL: info@edmonton-radial-railway.ab.ca
WEBSITE: www.edmonton-radial-railway.ab.ca

DESCRIPTION: Streetcar (tram) operation from historic Old Strathcona, across the North Saskatchewan River and over the high level bridge, includes access to the Provincial Legislature, and ends at Jasper Terminal. The Park Division operates a 1.1-mile streetcar ride within historic Fort Edmonton Park.

SCHEDULE: Park: May 20 to September 5, daily; September 9 to October 17, weekends only. Bridge: May 22 to June 30, daily, 10 a.m. to 4 p.m.; July 1 to September 5, 10 a.m. to 6 p.m.

ADMISSION/FARE: Park: Round trip, $3; family round trip, $10; one-way and group rates are available; bridge: included in admission to Fort Edmonton Park.

LOCOMOTIVES/ROLLING STOCK: Park: Hankai Tramway 247 (1921); bridge: 5 different cars in operation at Fort Edmonton Park. The car in the photo is Edmonton Car #42, built in 1912 by the St. Louis Car Company.

SPECIAL EVENTS: Bridge: last weekend in August, Harvest Festival.

NEARBY ATTRACTIONS: Old Strathcona, C&E railway station, Provincial Legislature, Streetcar Operation within Historic Fort Edmonton.

DIRECTIONS: Park: Grandin subway station is one block west of the north terminal. The south terminal is at 85th Ave. and 103rd St. Bridge: Located in the park at the corner of Whitemud Dr. and Fox Dr.

Photo courtesy of W.L. Shearer.

Edmonton, AB

Fort Edmonton Park **EDITOR'S CHOICE**

Train ride, Museum

ADDRESS: Fox Dr. and Whitemud Dr. Edmonton, AB
TELEPHONE: (780) 496-8787 or (780) 496-7227, Hotel Selkirk
WEBSITE: www.edmonton.ca/fort

DESCRIPTION: Nestled in Edmonton's river valley, Fort Edmonton Park is brought to life by costumed staff reenacting life as it was in Edmonton at the 1846 fur trading fort and in the streets of 1885, 1905, and 1920. The train transports visitors through the park. The train station is the first stop for guests staying at the new Hotel Selkirk.

SCHEDULE: May 21 to September 4, daily; September, Sunday.

ADMISSION/FARE: Adults, $9.25; seniors and youth 13-17, $7; children 2-12, $4.75; families, $29.50. Price includes train ride.

LOCOMOTIVES/ROLLING STOCK: 1919 Baldwin 2-6-2 no. 107, former Oakdale & Gulf Railway (restored to a 1905 appearance).

SPECIAL EVENTS: Call, write, or check website for information.

NEARBY ATTRACTIONS: Downtown Edmonton, West Edmonton Mall, and Valley Zoo.

Edmonton, AB

Fun Train Canada
Train ride

ADDRESS: Ste. 903, 11830 Kingsway Ave. Edmonton, AB T5G 0X5
TELEPHONE: (866) 688-9999
E-MAIL: funtrain@telusplanet.net

DESCRIPTION: This five-hour scenic family rail excursion features a round trip from Edmonton on restored railcars from the Super Continental cross-country passenger train.

SCHEDULE: May, June, September, and October: Saturday and Sunday; July and August: Thursday through Sunday; trains depart at 5 p.m.

ADMISSION/FARE: Theme car: $99 (Canadian) per person plus GST; day coach:$69 (Canadian) per person plus GST.

LOCOMOTIVES/ROLLING STOCK: 1954 CN Super Continental train cars.

Jasper, AB

The Skeena—VIA Rail Canada
Train ride

SITE ADDRESS: VIA Station 607 Connaught Dr. Jasper, AB
MAILING ADDRESS: VIA Rail Canada, Marketing, 1150 Station St., Ste. 300
Vancouver, BC V6A 4C7
TELEPHONE: (888) 842-7245
E-MAIL: literature@viarail.ca
WEBSITE: www.viarail.ca/skeena

DESCRIPTION: VIA's train "The Skeena" is a two-day land cruise through the Canadian Rockies and Northern British Columbia between Jasper, Prince George, and Prince Rupert. Totem Class offers comfortable seating, at-seat meal service, and access to the Park Car lounges and dome. Totem Deluxe Class offers the features of Totem Class, and confirmed seating in the Panorama Dome car.

SCHEDULE: Mid-May to September 30: four days a week from Jasper, AB or Prince Rupert, BC on the north Pacific Coast. For specific schedules, please visit VIA's website.

ADMISSION/FARE: Fares vary by season and class.

LOCOMOTIVES/ROLLING STOCK: "Park" Lounge Dome Observation car, Budd/AMF; "Panorama" Dome, Colorado Railcar; "Totem Class" Club Galley, Budd/AMF.

NEARBY ATTRACTIONS: Jasper, Banff, Yoho National Parks; BC Ferries from Prince Rupert to Vancouver Island; and Alaska State Ferries from Prince Rupert to Alaska.

DIRECTIONS: Maps, driving directions and other information for VIA's stations in Jasper, Prince George, and Prince Rupert are available on VIA's website.

See ad on page A-3.

Stettler, AB

Alberta Prairie Railway Excursions

Train ride, Dinner train
Standard gauge

ADDRESS: 4611 47th Ave., PO Box 1600 Stettler, AB T0C 2L0
TELEPHONE: (403) 742-2811
E-MAIL: info@absteamtrain.com
WEBSITE: www.absteamtrain.com

DESCRIPTION: Round-trip tours of several different types are featured from Stettler to Big Valley, a distance of 21.2 miles. The five- to six-hour excursions are operated on a former Canadian National branch line through picturesque parkland and prairies in central Alberta. All excursions include full-course roast beef dinner and on-board entertainment and commentary. Five-course meals are served on fine dining excursions to Big Valley.

SCHEDULE: Late May to August: weekends and selected weekdays. September to mid-October: weekends. Fine dining: November to April, select dates.

ADMISSION/FARE: Varies; call for complete schedule and fare information.

LOCOMOTIVES/ROLLING STOCK: No. 41, a 1920 Baldwin 2-8-0, former Jonesboro Lake City & Eastern; no. 41, former Frisco; no. 77, former Mississippian; coaches; more.

SPECIAL EVENTS: Murder Mysteries, Canada Day, Limiteds, Train Robberies.

NEARBY ATTRACTIONS: Ol' MacDonald's Resort, museum, Rochon Sands Provincial Park.

DIRECTIONS: A 2½-hour drive from Edmonton or Calgary; one hour east of Red Deer in central Alberta.

KEY TO SYMBOLS

Handicapped accessible	Restaurant	Arts and crafts	Association of Railway Museums
Parking	Picnic area	Memberships available	Tourist Railway Association, Inc.
Bus/RV parking	Dining car	Send S.A.S.E. for brochure	Amtrak service to nearby city
Gift, book, or museum shop	Excursions	National Register of Historic Places	VIA service to nearby city
Refreshments	Guided tours	VISA MasterCard DISCOVER AMERICAN EXPRESS Card	Credit cards accepted

BRITISH COLUMBIA

Cranbrook, BC

Canadian Museum of Rail Travel
Museum

SITE ADDRESS: 57 Van Horne St. S Cranbrook, BC V1C 1Y7
MAILING ADDRESS: Box 400 Cranbrook, BC V1C 4H9
TELEPHONE: (250) 489-3918
E-MAIL: mail@trainsdeluxe.com
WEBSITE: www.trainsdeluxe.com

DESCRIPTION: The museum collects and restores vintage CPR passenger trains as well as business cars and cars of state. Now located at its new, larger site, which includes the historic 1898 Freight Shed and the Royal Alexandra Hall—formerly the 1906 Grand Café from the Royal Alexandra Hotel (CPR) of Winnipeg. The museum will expand from its current 9 cars on tour to the full 28 in late 2006.

SCHEDULE: Open year-round. Early April to mid-October: daily, 10 a.m. to 6 p.m.; winter: Tuesday through Saturday, 10 a.m. to 5 p.m.

ADMISSION/FARE: Current prices subject to change at AGM February 2006.

LOCOMOTIVES/ROLLING STOCK: Trans-Canada Limited (1929), complete set; Soo-Spokane Train Deluxe (1907); CP "Strathcona" (1927); business car "British Columbia" (1928); "Redvers" (1929); 17 other cars and locomotives coming soon.

SPECIAL EVENTS: December, Museum Centennial Heritage Christmas Dinner.

DIRECTIONS: Located downtown Cranbrook on Hwy. 3/95 next to the Prestige Inn Hotel and CP Rail offices.

Fort Steele, BC

Fort Steele Steam Railway
Train ride

ADDRESS: 9851 Hwy. 93/95 Fort Steele, BC V0B 1N0
TELEPHONE: (250) 426-7352 or (250) 417-6000
E-MAIL: info@fortsteele.bc.ca
WEBSITE: www.fortsteele.bc.ca

DESCRIPTION: Fort Steele Heritage Town is a restored 1890s Pioneer Boomtown that runs the railway. Located outside the historic park, the railway runs alone or as part of an all-inclusive ticket. A Montreal Locomotive Works 2-6-2 Prairie-type locomotive pulls passengers around a 2.5-mile loop of track with a stop at a lookout point to explain the view and local railroad history.

SCHEDULE: July 1 through Labor Day: daily, 12, 1, 2, 3:15, 4, and 5 p.m.; Father's Day, 11 a.m. to 4 p.m.

ADMISSION/FARE: Adults, $6; seniors 65+, $5; youth 13-18, $3; children 6-12, $2; children 5 and under, free, train only. Call for details on all-inclusive attraction ticket.

LOCOMOTIVES/ROLLING STOCK: Montreal Locomotive Works 2-6-2 Prairie-type no. 1077, built in 1923; Shay class 90 Pacific Coast no. 115, built in 1934; Dunrobin, Sharp & Stewart 2-4-0 side tank engine, built in 1895.

SPECIAL EVENTS: Father's Day, dads ride free; plus displays of other gas and steam engines, roundhouse tours, entertainment, concession and farmer's market.

NEARBY ATTRACTIONS: Fort Steele Heritage Town, Fairmont and Radium Hot Springs, Provincial Parks and Camping, and Canadian Museum of Rail Travel in Cranbrook.

DIRECTIONS: Southeast corner of British Columbia, 16 kilometers northeast of Cranbrook, BC, on Hwy. 93/95.

Photo courtesy of Fort Steele Steam Railway.

Kamloops, BC

Kamloops Heritage Railway Society

Train ride, Dinner train

ADDRESS: #6 510 Lorne St. Kamloops, BC V2C 1W3
TELEPHONE: (250) 374-2141
E-MAIL: info@KamRail.com
WEBSITE: www.KamRail.com

DESCRIPTION: The 182km round trip goes between Campbell Creek and Armstrong on the "Armstrong Explorer," which has restored and custom cars. This full-day trip allows two hours in Armstrong for lunch. Passengers can also travel into history on a 75-minute steam train experience starting from a 1927 CN Station, crossing the South Thompson River, past historic buildings, and finishing with the reenactment of the Bill Miner Train Robbery on every trip.

SCHEDULE: Spirit of Kamloops: end of June to Labor Day weekend, Friday to Monday, evening trips; Saturday, additional morning trip; June and September, limited departures. Armstrong Explorer: May, June, September, and October. Ghost Train: late October departures. Spirit of Christmas: mid-December.

ADMISSION/FARE: Adults, $14; seniors 60+, $11.75; youth 6-18, $9.50.

LOCOMOTIVES/ROLLING STOCK: 1912 ex-CNR 2141 2-8-0 built by the Canadian Locomotive Company in Kingston, Ontario; 1930 ex-CNR 4893 parlour car Georgian Bay, now KHRX 406 Pioneer Park; 1937 ex-BCR 990243 coach, now KHRX 401 Riverside Park; 1954 KHRX 402 Monte Lake cafe-lounge car, ex-CNR/VIA 0755; more.

SPECIAL EVENTS: Father's Day, Christmas Lights Trips, Canada Day, BC Day, Labour Day, Kamloops Railway Day.

NEARBY ATTRACTIONS: Kamloops Wildlife Park, BX Stagecoach rides, museums, art gallery, Music in the Park, First Nation Museum, beaches, water parks, golf, horseback riding, fishing, more.

DIRECTIONS: Located in downtown Kamloops, 355 kilometers NE of Vancouver, on Hwy. 5 or Hwy. 1 Trans Canada. Crossroads of Yellowhead and Trans Canada Hwys.

Photo courtesy of Kamloops Heritage Railway.

Kelowna, BC
Okanagan Valley Wine Train
Train ride

SITE ADDRESS: Kelowna, BC
MAILING ADDRESS: Ste. 903, 11830 Kingsway Ave. Edmonton, AB T5G 0X5
TELEPHONE: (866) 688-9999
E-MAIL: funtrain@telusplanet.net
WEBSITE: www.okanaganvalleywinetrain.com

DESCRIPTION: This five-hour scenic family rail excursion features a round trip from Kelowna to Vernon on restored railcars from the Super Continental cross-country passenger train.

SCHEDULE: July through October: Wednesday and Saturday, trains depart at 5 p.m.

ADMISSION/FARE: Theme car: $79.95 (Canadian) per person plus GST; day coach: $29.95 (Canadian) per person plus GST.

LOCOMOTIVES/ROLLING STOCK: 1954 CN Super Continental train cars.

Osoyoos, BC

Osoyoos Desert Model Railroad

Display, Model train layout

ADDRESS: Buena Vista Industrial Park 11611-115 St. Osoyoos, BC V0H 1V5
TELEPHONE: (250) 495-6842
E-MAIL: pedersen@vip.net
WEBSITE: www.osoyoosrailroad.com

DESCRIPTION: Privately owned, this railroad is 2,000 square feet of family fun featuring a miniature world with more than 4,000 hand-painted people. The details depict all aspects of real life such as an amusement park with working Ferris wheel and working ski lift on the ski hill. This Marklin train layout has multiple rail lines and European-style houses and towns. It's not just a railroad; it's a fantasy world.

SCHEDULE: Year-round: Monday through Saturday, 10 a.m. to 5 p.m.; closed Sunday.

ADMISSION/FARE: Adults, $5; children 2-12, $3.50; children under 2, free.

LOCOMOTIVES/ROLLING STOCK: 20 European Marklin trains.

DIRECTIONS: Frontage on Hwy. no. 3 West.

Photo courtesy of Jenifer Sander.

Port Alberni, BC

Alberni Pacific Railway

Train ride, Display
Standard gauge

ADDRESS: 3100 Kingsway Ave. Port Alberni, BC V9Y 3B1
TELEPHONE: (250) 723-1376
E-MAIL: info@alberniheritage.com
WEBSITE: www.alberniheritage.com

DESCRIPTION: This railway offers six-mile steam train rides from Port Alberni Railroad Station to McLean Mill National Historic Site, a stage show, and a steam-powered saw mill demonstration. There is also a return trip to Port Alberni Railroad Station.

SCHEDULE: 35 minutes each way: depart Port Alberni Station, 10 a.m.; depart McLean Mill, 1 p.m.; depart Port Alberni Station, 2 p.m.; depart McLean Mill, 5 p.m.

ADMISSION/FARE: Adults, $26; seniors and students, $19.50; children 6 and under, $5.

LOCOMOTIVES/ROLLING STOCK: 1929 Baldwin 2-8-2T, 1954 Alco RS3. In storage: 1912 42-ton Shay, 1942 42-ton General Electric, and two gasoline-powered locomotives, five passenger cars, and other assorted cars.

NEARBY ATTRACTIONS: Roundhouse tours, Heritage Truck Museum tours.

DIRECTIONS: Located at the foot of Argyle St. in Port Alberni.

Prince George, BC
Prince George Railway and Forestry Museum
Museum

ADDRESS: 850 River Rd. Prince George, BC V2L 5S8
TELEPHONE: (250) 563-7351
E-MAIL: trains@pgrfm.bc.ca
WEBSITE: www.pgrfm.bc.ca

DESCRIPTION: The museum presents the history of the area in a park-like setting, where visitors are encouraged to have a hands-on experience. The varied collections range from 1899 to the 1960s, and include a building, a locomotive, structures, rail cars, and artifacts related to the forest industry, fire fighting, and early communication equipment.

SCHEDULE: Mid-May through mid-October.

ADMISSION/FARE: Adults, $6; seniors and students, $5.

LOCOMOTIVES/ROLLING STOCK: Steam locomotive 1520; 1990 65-ton diesel locomotive 101; Russell wooden snow plow; more.

SPECIAL EVENTS: Forest Tree Fest, Tree & Tier Dog Day, Friends of Thomas Days, Steam Days, Hogwarts Festival.

NEARBY ATTRACTIONS: The Exploration Place, Two Rivers Art Gallery, Huble Homestead.

DIRECTIONS: At the east end of 1st Ave., turn left on River Rd. Follow River Rd. to the park. Next to Cottonwood Island Park.

Prince Rupert, BC

Kwinitsa Railway Station Museum

Museum

SITE ADDRESS: Prince Rupert waterfront next to Rotary Waterfront Park
Prince Rupert, BC V8J 1A8
MAILING ADDRESS: 100-1st Ave. W Prince Rupert, BC V8J 1A8
TELEPHONE: (250) 624-3209
E-MAIL: mnbc@citytel.net
WEBSITE: www.museumofnorthernbc.com

DESCRIPTION: This restored station house was originally located half way between Terrace and Prince Rupert. In 1985, Kwinitsa was transported down the Skeena River to its present location on the waterfront. Kwinitsa depicts the life of early station agents and linemen who worked for the Grand Trunk Railway at the turn of the century. Photographs, video, and detailed restorations depict how the arrival of the railway affected Prince Rupert.

SCHEDULE: Mid-June through early September: daily, 9 a.m. to 12 p.m. and 1 to 5 p.m.

ADMISSION/FARE: Donations accepted.

NEARBY ATTRACTIONS: Kwinitsa Railway Station Museum is located next to Rotary Waterfront Park overlooking the Prince Rupert waterfront a short distance to additional museums and the downtown shopping district.

DIRECTIONS: Located at the Prince Rupert waterfront next to Rotary Waterfront Park. When entering the city on Hwy. 16, continue to the bottom of McBride St. and turn left on 1st Ave. Follow 1st Ave. one block and turn right on Bill Murray Way.

Photo courtesy of Museum of Northern British Columbia.

Revelstoke, BC

Revelstoke Railway Museum

Museum

ADDRESS: 719 Track St. W, PO Box 3018 Revelstoke, BC V0E 2S0
TELEPHONE: (877) 837-6060, toll-free in North America or (250) 837-6060
E-MAIL: railway@telus.net
WEBSITE: www.railwaymuseum.com

DESCRIPTION: The history of the Canadian Pacific Railway is presented from construction to present day, and focuses on western Canada. Visitors can learn about the building of the railway and the challenges of keeping the railway working. They can also find out how the early railway builders solved some of the quandaries of the Canadian Pacific Railway in British Columbia, walk through the cars on display, and see the many artifacts.

SCHEDULE: Year-round: July and August, 9 a.m. to 8 p.m.; December to March, 1 to 5 p.m.; April to June and September to November, 9 a.m. to 5 p.m.

ADMISSION/FARE: Adults, $6; seniors, $5; youth, $3; children 6 and under, free; family, $13. Group rates available.

LOCOMOTIVES/ROLLING STOCK: CP steam locomotive 5468; business car no. 4; caboose no. 437477; road repair car no. 404116; 40-foot flatcar no. 421237; service flanger no. 400573; Jordan spreader no. 402811; wedge plow no. 401027; baggage car no. 404944.

SPECIAL EVENTS: January 8, 2006, "Mail, Rail, Retail: Connecting Canadians" special exhibition on display; third weekend in August, Revelstoke Railway Days.

NEARBY ATTRACTIONS: Revelstoke Hydroelectric Dam, Mt. Revelstoke and Glacier National Parks, British Columbia Interior Forestry Museum, City Museum, and Canyon Hot Springs.

DIRECTIONS: In downtown Revelstoke, at Victoria Rd. along the tracks.

Coupon available, see insert.

Squamish, BC
West Coast Railway Heritage Park
Train ride, Museum, Display
7½" and Standard gauge

SITE ADDRESS: 39645 Government Rd. Squamish, BC
MAILING ADDRESS: PO Box 2790 Station Main Vancouver, BC V6B 3X2
TELEPHONE: (604) 898-9336
E-MAIL: manager@wcra.org
WEBSITE: www.wcra.org

DESCRIPTION: This large heritage railway collection is located in a beautiful 12-acre mountain valley setting. A mini rail (7½" gauge) ride circles the park. Visitors can tour authentic railway equipment in various stages of restoration, set amid some of the most beautiful scenery in Canada. An early 20th century station and town are also featured. Train rides on Budd RDC are available during summer.

SCHEDULE: Year-round: daily, 10 a.m. to 5 p.m.; closed Christmas and New Year's Day.

ADMISSION/FARE: Adults, $10 (Canadian); seniors, $8.50; children, $5; children under 5, free. Family rate (5 people), $34.

LOCOMOTIVES/ROLLING STOCK: Canadian Pacific Royal Hudson no. 2860; Canadian Pacific FP7A no. 4069; Pacific Great Eastern 2-6-2 no. 2; Pacific Great Eastern RDC's; 1890 business car British Columbia, RPO, plus 65 other pieces of heritage rolling stock from five major railways that served western Canada.

SPECIAL EVENTS: July 1, Canada Day; December, Christmas Lights at the Park.

NEARBY ATTRACTIONS: 40 miles north of Vancouver, on the way to Whistler resort area.

DIRECTIONS: Hwy. 99 north from Vancouver; follow signs from to Heritage Park.

Photo courtesy of Don Evans.
Coupon available, see insert.

Summerland, BC
Kettle Valley Steam Railway Society
Train ride
Standard gauge

SITE ADDRESS: 18404 Bathville Rd. Summerland, BC V0H 1Z0
MAILING ADDRESS: PO Box 1288 Summerland, BC V0H 1Z0
TELEPHONE: (877) 494-8424
E-MAIL: kvr@telus.net
WEBSITE: www.kettlevalleyrail.org

DESCRIPTION: Passengers can enjoy a journey overlooking the beautiful orchards and vineyards of the scenic Okanagan Valley. Narrated with a historical commentary, the 1-hour and 45-minute ride travels through orchards, vineyards, and natural landscapes, and includes a trip onto the Trout Creek trestle/bridge (circa 1913). The locomotive, a 1924 Shay steam engine, pulls two 1950s passenger coaches and the open air Kettle and McCulloch Cars.

SCHEDULE: May through October: 10:30 a.m. and 1:30 p.m.; Spring (May long weekend and June), Saturday through Monday; Summer (June through August), Thursday through Monday; Fall (September and October), Saturday through Monday.

ADMISSION/FARE: Adults, $17; seniors, $16; teens, $15; children 3-12, $11.

LOCOMOTIVES/ROLLING STOCK: 1924 Shay no. 3 locomotive; 1912 Consolidation locomotive no. 3716; two vintage coaches, and three open-air cars.

SPECIAL EVENTS: Easter; Mother's Day; Father's Day; June to September: nine events of barbecues and The Great Train Robberies; Christmas trains.

NEARBY ATTRACTIONS: Giants Head Mountain Park, Summerland Ornamental Gardens, Summerland Museum, Nixsdorf Car Museum, fruit stands, campgrounds, and beaches.

DIRECTIONS: 6km off Hwy. 97, 45km south of Kelowna, 16km north of Penticton.

Photo courtesy of David Layland.

Surrey, BC

Bear Creek Park Train
Train ride
15" gauge

ADDRESS: 13750 88th Ave. Surrey, BC V3W 3L1
TELEPHONE: (604) 501-1232
E-MAIL: david@bctrains.com
WEBSITE: www.bctrains.com

DESCRIPTION: A ⅝-mile ride goes into the park's forest and gardens, through a tunnel with displays that change every two months, and over a trestle.

SCHEDULE: Year-round: daily, 10 a.m. to sunset; October 13 through 31, Halloween: 10 a.m. to 10 p.m.; December 10 through 26, Christmas: 10 a.m. to 10 p.m.

ADMISSION/FARE: Adults, $3.50; seniors, $3; children 2-12, $2.50. Special events may have additional fee.

LOCOMOTIVES/ROLLING STOCK: 1992 Alan Keef "Tank Engine" diesel locomotive; 1968 Van Heiden Welsh mining steam locomotive; Welsh Mines covered coaches; two Alan Keef open touring coaches.

SPECIAL EVENTS: Easter Festival, Spring Break, Canada Day, Summer Train Camp, Halloween Festival, and Christmas Festival.

NEARBY ATTRACTIONS: Free swimming pool and water park, youth athletic park, Bear Creek Gardens, and Art Gallery.

DIRECTIONS: 30 minutes from US border via Hwy. 99; 40 minutes from downtown Vancouver via Hwy. 1 and Port Mann Bridge.

Coupon available, see insert.

Vancouver, BC

Granville Island Model Train Museum

Museum, Display, Model train layout
Various gauges

ADDRESS: 1502 Duranleau St., Granville Island Vancouver, BC V6H 3S4
TELEPHONE: (604) 683-1939
E-MAIL: staff@granvilleislandmuseums.com
WEBSITE: www.granvilleislandmuseums.com

DESCRIPTION: The museum has an operating layout with thousands of model and toy trains by Lionel, Marx, Hornby, Dorfan, and American Flyer.

SCHEDULE: May 1 through October 1: daily, 10 a.m. to 5 p.m.; October 2 through April 30, closed Monday.

ADMISSION/FARE: Adults, $7.50; seniors, $6; children, $4; family, $20.

DIRECTIONS: Below the Granville St. Bridge.

Vancouver, BC

Rocky Mountaineer Vacations

Train ride

ADDRESS: 100-1150 Station St. Vancouver, BC V6A 2X7
TELEPHONE: (800) 665-7245
E-MAIL: brochure@rockymountaineer.com
WEBSITE: www.rockymountaineer.com

DESCRIPTION: Rocky Mountaineer Vacations has grown from a small, entrepreneurial dream to a successful company with 400 employees and sales representation in 18 countries. The original two-day rail tour is now just one of the 70 independent vacation options that include city stops, sightseeing tours, rail and drive programs, and year-round, destination-based vacations.

SCHEDULE: Mid-April through mid-October: please visit website for departure dates and times. Winter departures also available in December.

ADMISSION/FARE: Please visit website for fare information.

LOCOMOTIVES/ROLLING STOCK: Five General Motors GP40-2 locomotives and 33 passenger cars; 12 bi-level Dome coaches which seat 70 guests each, built by Colorado Rail Car. Four Electric Generator Cars built in the 1950s by National Steel Car. Two Electric Generator Cars built by Pullman Standard in 1948.

NEARBY ATTRACTIONS: The Westcoast Railway Heritage Park, in Squamish.

DIRECTIONS: Rocky Mountaineer train station, 1755 Cottrell St., Vancouver, BC. East on Terminal Ave., south on Cottrell St., located beside the Home Depot store.

Photo courtesy of Rocky Mountaineer Vacations.

Vancouver, BC

Vancouver's Downtown Historic Railway
Train ride
Standard gauge

SITE ADDRESS: 1601 Ontario St. Vancouver, BC V5Z 2N5
MAILING ADDRESS: 949 West 41st Ave. Vancouver, BC V5Z 2N5
TELEPHONE: (604) 665-3903
E-MAIL: dale@trams.ca
WEBSITE: www.trams.ca

DESCRIPTION: The railway takes passengers on a 3km ride along the south side of False Creek.

SCHEDULE: Mid-May through mid-October: weekends and holidays, 12:30 to 5 p.m.

ADMISSION/FARE: Adults, $2; seniors and children, $1. Charters, $150 per hour.

LOCOMOTIVES/ROLLING STOCK: BCER interurban no. 1207 built in 1905 all-wood passenger car; BCER interurban no. 1213 built in 1913 steelside passenger car; BCER all wood interurban passenger car no. 1207 built in 1905; BCER steel side interurban passenger car no. 1231 built in 1912.

NEARBY ATTRACTIONS: Granville Island Public Market at west end of line. Science World (Omnimax theatre) at east end of line. VIA Rail/Amtrak station at east end of line, walking distance to Chinatown.

DIRECTIONS: Car barn at First Ave. and Ontario St., two blocks southwest of Skytrain's Main St. Station. Free parking.

Photo courtesy of Tim Chaput.

Victoria, BC

The Malahat—VIA Rail Canada

Train ride

SITE ADDRESS: VIA Rail Canada Victoria Train Station, 450 Pandora Ave. Victoria, BC
MAILING ADDRESS: VIA Rail Canada Marketing, 1150 Station St., Ste. 300
Vancouver, BC V6A 4C7
TELEPHONE: (888) 842-7245
E-MAIL: literature@viarail.ca
WEBSITE: www.viarail.ca/malahat

DESCRIPTION: VIA's train The Malahat, popularly known as the "E&N Railiner," is a lovely day excursion on Vancouver Island. Passengers should be sure to bring walking shoes, a camera, and plenty of film. Some of the most beautiful countryside to be seen is on Vancouver Island between Victoria, at the southern tip of the island, and Courtenay, at the northern end.

SCHEDULE: One daily morning departure Northbound from Victoria to Nanaimo and Courtenay. Schedule permits same day return trips to various "Up Island" points. For schedules and further information, please visit VIA's website.

ADMISSION/FARE: Various fares based on advance purchase and seasonality.

NEARBY ATTRACTIONS: Fairmont's Empress Hotel, Chemainus artist community, Native Heritage Center in Duncan, BC Forestry Museum in Hayward, "Bungy Zone" near Cassidy, Nanaimo's beautiful harbour front, beautiful sandy beaches at Qualicum Beach.

DIRECTIONS: Maps, driving directions and other information for stations in Victoria, Nanaimo, and Courtenay are available on VIA's website.

See ad on page A-3.

KEY TO SYMBOLS

Handicapped accessible	Restaurant	Arts and crafts	Association of Railway Museums
Parking	Picnic area	Memberships available	Tourist Railway Association, Inc.
Bus/RV parking	Dining car	Send S.A.S.E. for brochure	Amtrak service to nearby city
Gift, book, or museum shop	Excursions	National Register of Historic Places	VIA service to nearby city
Refreshments	Guided tours	Credit cards accepted	

MANITOBA

Winnipeg, MB
Prairie Dog Central Railway
Train ride

ADDRESS: RPO Polo Park, PO Box 33021 Winnipeg, MB R3G 3N4
TELEPHONE: (204) 832-5259
E-MAIL: gpauln@escape.ca
WEBSITE: www.pdcrailway.com

DESCRIPTION: Special event and round trip excursion trains stop at Grosse Isle and Warren.

SCHEDULE: May, June, and September: Sunday; July and August: Saturday and Sunday; trains depart at 10 a.m. and 3 p.m.

ADMISSION/FARE: Adults 17+, $15; children 2-16, $10; special prices for Mother's Day and Father's Day trains.

LOCOMOTIVES/ROLLING STOCK: American Standard 4-4-0, built by Dubs and Co. of Glasgow for the CNR in 1882. Ex-Grand Trunk GP9 no. 4138, built by GM Electro-Motive division, 1958. Bunk car, boxcar, hopper, caboose, coach cars and more.

SPECIAL EVENTS: Murder Mysteries, Western Dinner and Dance, Family Days, Howlin' Halloween, Santa Train and more. See website for details.

Winnipeg, MB
Vintage Locomotive Society, Inc.
Train ride, Museum
Standard gauge

SITE ADDRESS: 1 mile west of Route 90 and Inkster Blvd. on Prairie Dog Trail Winnipeg, MB R3G 3N4
MAILING ADDRESS: PO Box 33021, RPO Polo Park Winnipeg, MB R3G 3N4
TELEPHONE: (204) 832-5259
E-MAIL: info@pdcrailway.com
WEBSITE: www.pdcrailway.com

DESCRIPTION: Visitors can experience the living history of the prairies on an 18-mile trip from Winnipeg, northwest to Warren. Throughout the year, there are special trips for family days, Halloween, Christmas, murder mystery, fall foliage viewing, and more. The train consists of five fully restored coaches—all built between 1901 and 1913—that hold 300 passengers. Canadian Northern Railway built the railway line in 1905 and the station in 1910. The Vintage Locomotive Society, Inc. acquired both in 1999.

SCHEDULE: Call for an updated schedule.

ADMISSION/FARE: Rates vary. Call for updates.

Winnipeg, MB

Winnipeg Railway Museum

Museum

ADDRESS: 123 Main St. Box 48 Winnipeg, MB R3C 1A3
TELEPHONE: (204) 942-4632
WEBSITE: www.icenter.net/~prs/

DESCRIPTION: This railroad history museum has a variety of railroad cars and locomotives on display.

SCHEDULE: Summer: June through September, Friday through Sunday, 11 a.m. to 5 p.m.; winter: September through June: weekends, 12 to 4 p.m.

Photo courtesy of Ron Einarson.

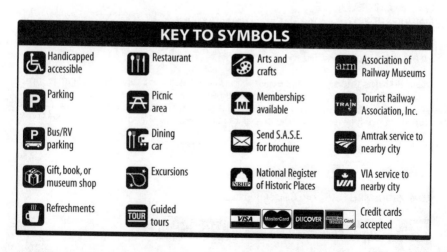

KEY TO SYMBOLS

Handicapped accessible	Restaurant	Arts and crafts	Association of Railway Museums
Parking	Picnic area	Memberships available	Tourist Railway Association, Inc.
Bus/RV parking	Dining car	Send S.A.S.E. for brochure	Amtrak service to nearby city
Gift, book, or museum shop	Excursions	National Register of Historic Places	VIA service to nearby city
Refreshments	Guided tours	VISA MasterCard DISCOVER AMERICAN EXPRESS Card	Credit cards accepted

NEWFOUNDLAND

Corner Brook, NF
Railway Society of Newfoundland
Museum

SITE ADDRESS: Station Rd. Corner Brook, NF A2H 6G1
MAILING ADDRESS: PO Box 673 Corner Brook, NF A2H 6G1
TELEPHONE: (709) 634-2720

DESCRIPTION: A 100-year-old freight shed, converted into a museum, contains historic artifacts and a display of locomotives and rail cars.

SCHEDULE: June to August, 9 a.m. to 9 p.m.

ADMISSION/FARE: $2 membership fee; children under 17, free; group rate, $20.

LOCOMOTIVES/ROLLING STOCK: Baldwin steam locomotive no. 593 built in 1920; NF box baggage car no. 1598 built in 1954; steel baggage car no. 1900 built in 1943; steel passenger coach no. 758 built in 1949; steel diner coach no. 10 built in 1943; diesel locomotive no. 931 built in 1956; caboose no. 6072 built in 1956.

NEARBY ATTRACTIONS: Marbe Mountain Ski Lodge, Corner Brook Museum, and Captain Cook site.

DIRECTIONS: Intersection of Riverside Dr. and Station Rd.

TRAVEL TIP: *Membership*

Many museum railroads offer membership packages that provide train rides, gift shop discounts, and other perks like members-only events. Some memberships even provide unlimited train rides. Check out this feature if you think you'll be visiting often.

ONTARIO

Aberfoyle, ON

Aberfoyle Junction Model Railway, Inc.

Model train layout
O scale

SITE ADDRESS: 128 Brock Rd. S Aberfoyle, ON N1H 6H1
MAILING ADDRESS: 257 Broadway Ave. Hamilton, ON L8S 2W7
TELEPHONE: (905) 527-5474
WEBSITE: www.aberfoylejunction.com

DESCRIPTION: A 1,500-square-foot, fully scenicked, O scale model railway depicts Southern Ontario c. 1957. Canadian Pacific and Canadian National are featured in mainline, branch, and yard operation, plus a 10-minute dawn to dusk sequence.

SCHEDULE: First two weekends in May and three weekends in October following Canadian Thanksgiving (US Columbus Day), 10 a.m. to 4:30 p.m. Private showings by appointment.

ADMISSION/FARE: Adults, $6; seniors and students, $4; children, $3 (Canadian).

LOCOMOTIVES/ROLLING STOCK: A large variety of scratchbuilt models of both CN and CP steam and diesel locomotives and passenger and freight equipment.

SPECIAL EVENTS: Private showings for groups (seniors, church, model railroad, etc.) can be arranged by contacting the Aberfoyle Junction Group.

NEARBY ATTRACTIONS: Halton County Radial Railway (street car museum), ½ hour drive; South Simcoe Railway (steam train rides), 1 hour drive.

DIRECTIONS: In the village of Aberfoyle, 1½ miles north of Hwy. 401, exit 299 on regional road 46. In a Quonset hut on the east side, no. 128.

Photo courtesy of Craig Webb.

Brighton, ON

Memory Junction Museum

Train ride, Museum, Display

SITE ADDRESS: 60 Maplewood Ave. Brighton, ON
MAILING ADDRESS: 27 Maplewood Ave., PO Box 294 Brighton, ON K0K 1H0
E-MAIL: banger@sympatico.ca
WEBSITE: www.memoryjunction.netfirms.com

DESCRIPTION: Memory Junction features many railway and area artifacts, memorabilia, and historic pieces. From the station, you can view the busy main line with more than 75 trains passing daily. On the three acres stands the original Grand Trunk Station, a baggage shed, and the Morow building, which was originally used in the early 1900s as a Ford unloading depot. The 1857 Grand Trunk Railway and later CNR Station houses a number of artifacts. On the rail sidings, you can view several fully restored rail cars.

SCHEDULE: May 24 to mid-October: daily, July, 10 a.m. to 4 p.m.; closed Tuesday and Friday.

LOCOMOTIVES/ROLLING STOCK: 1906 steam engine no. 2834, 1929 caboose, two metal cabooses, 1954 boarding car, 1913 box car, flatbed, 1898 Velocipede, three speeders.

NEARBY ATTRACTIONS: Presquile Provincial Park Air Force Museum, Trenton, swimming, golfing, and Proctor House Museum.

DIRECTIONS: 401 cut off no. 509, follow signs.

Capreol, ON
Northern Ontario Railroad Museum
Museum

ADDRESS: 26 Bloor St. Capreol, ON P0M 1H0
TELEPHONE: (705) 858-5050
E-MAIL: normhc@vianet.ca
WEBSITE: www.NorthernOntarioRailroadMuseum.ca

DESCRIPTION: The Northern Ontario Railroad Museum and Heritage Centre emphasizes railroading history in northern Ontario and the impact railroads had on mining and lumbering; also, early settlements in the area and how they came about because of the railroads.

SCHEDULE: June 1 through August 31: Tuesday through Sunday, 11 a.m. to 4 p.m.; September to May, by appointment only.

ADMISSION/FARE: Donation.

LOCOMOTIVES/ROLLING STOCK: CN no. 6077 Mountain-type steam locomotive (4-8-2) built by MLC; velocipede; four-man handcar; gas car; wooden caboose no. 77562; rules instruction car no. 15019; early INCO slagpot car. A newly acquired exhibit includes two INCO electric locomotives (not yet on display); a wooden CN snowplow car; and a metal caboose.

SPECIAL EVENTS: July, Garden tour with blueberry tea; August, Capreol Daze; November, Remembrance displays. Call or write for dates.

NEARBY ATTRACTIONS: Numerous lakes in area for fishing, camping, boating; Science North and Dynamic Earth, Sudbury. Contact the City of Greater Sudbury Regional Development Corporation for information on tourism: (705) 671-CITY.

DIRECTIONS: Located 40km (25 miles) northeast of Sudbury. Take Regional Rd. 80 from Sudbury, then Regional Rd. 84 to Capreol.

Photo courtesy of Bob Michelutti.

Chatham, ON
Chatham Railroad Museum
Museum

ADDRESS: 2 McLean St., PO Box 434 Chatham, ON N7M 5K5
TELEPHONE: (519) 352-3097
E-MAIL: ckrailmuseum@yahoo.ca
WEBSITE: www.geocities.com/ckrailmuseum/

DESCRIPTION: The Chatham Railroad Museum is a retired Canadian National baggage car built in 1955 in Hamilton, Ontario. It has exhibits on local, national, and international railroad history.

SCHEDULE: May 1 to September 1: Monday to Friday, 9 a.m. to 4 p.m.; Saturday, 11 a.m. to 4 p.m.

ADMISSION/FARE: Free. Donations accepted.

LOCOMOTIVES/ROLLING STOCK: CNR Baggage Car 9626

DIRECTIONS: Located across from the Chatham VIA Rail Station.

Photo courtesy of Gary Shurgold.

Clinton, ON
Original CNR School on Wheels 15089
Museum, Display

SITE ADDRESS: 76 Victoria Terrace Clinton, ON N0M 1L0
MAILING ADDRESS: Victoria Terrace, PO Box 488 Clinton, ON N0M 1L0
TELEPHONE: (519) 482-3997

DESCRIPTION: This museum allows modern children and nostalgic seniors to visit one of the seven schools on wheels that taught children along the northern Ontario railways. Railway schools were used as a successful method of reaching and teaching the isolated children and adults of Northern Ontario wilderness. Car 15089 was thought to have been scrapped years ago, until it was found abandoned in the Toronto/Mississauga CNR rail yard in 1982, and it is possibly the last remaining of the original seven schools on wheels.

SCHEDULE: May, Victoria Day weekend to end of September: Thursday to Sunday and holidays, 11 a.m. to 5 p.m.

ADMISSION/FARE: Free. Donations.

LOCOMOTIVES/ROLLING STOCK: Canadian National 15089.

NEARBY ATTRACTIONS: Campgrounds, state parks, 10 minutes from Lake Huron.

DIRECTIONS: Off Hwy. 4 near London, Ontario.

Cochrane, ON

Cochrane Railway and Pioneer Museum
Museum

ADDRESS: 210 Railway St., PO Box 490 Cochrane, ON P0L 1C0
TELEPHONE: (705) 272-4361
E-MAIL: towncoch@puc.net
WEBSITE: www.town.cochrane.on.ca

DESCRIPTION: This museum preserves a three-dimensional picture of the pioneer railway and homesteading days as a tribute to the men and women who opened northern Ontario. A model train display aboard a former Canadian National coach introduces the main railway exhibits, which include a telegraph operator's corner, a ticket office, a document display, an insulator collection, and uniforms. A large, varied display of photographs is also featured. Many of the pictures, for which the museum is now trustee, are from the large collection assembled around 1912 by the Rev. W. L. Lawrence. Train "Tim" Horton Memorial Museum contains a display of hockey artifacts.

SCHEDULE: June 23 through September 3: daily, 8:30 a.m. to 8 p.m.

ADMISSION/FARE: Adults, $2; seniors, $1; students/children, $1.50; families, $5. Group rates available.

LOCOMOTIVES/ROLLING STOCK: No. 137 2-8-0, former Temiskaming & Northern Ontario.

SPECIAL EVENTS: August, Museum Days.

Cochrane, ON

Polar Bear Express—Ontario Northland

Train ride

SITE ADDRESS: 200 Railway St. Cochrane, ON P0L 1C0
MAILING ADDRESS: 555 Oak St. E North Bay, ON P1B 8L3
TELEPHONE: (800) 268-9281 or TTY (866) 472-3865
E-MAIL: choochoo@polarbearexpress.ca
WEBSITE: www.polarbearexpress.ca

DESCRIPTION: Summer excursion train travels to the edge of the Arctic on a 186-mile train ride operating between Cochrane and Moosonee, Ontario.

SCHEDULE: Late June to Labor Day: Tuesday to Sunday, depart Cochrane 8:30 a.m., arrive Moosonee 12:50 p.m.; depart Moosonee 6:00 p.m., arrive Cochrane 10:05 p.m.

ADMISSION/FARE: Adults, $97.90; seniors 60+, $88.10; students, $83.20; children 2-11, $48.95; under 2, free. Family plan (7% GST included) and Day and Multi-Day packages available. Prices subject to change.

NEARBY ATTRACTIONS: Gold Mine Tour, Hunta Museum, Shania Twain Centre, Pulp and Paper Tours.

DIRECTIONS: Take Hwy. 11 north through North Bay past New Liskeard to Cochrane.

Photo courtesy of Ontario Northland.

Fort Erie, ON

Fort Erie Railroad Museum

Museum

SITE ADDRESS: 400 Central Ave. Fort Erie, ON
MAILING ADDRESS: PO Box 339 Ridgeway, ON L0S 1N0
TELEPHONE: (905) 894-5322
WEBSITE: www.museum.forterie.ca/railroad.html

DESCRIPTION: This museum features the steam engine 6218, a 4-8-4 northern. Also on display are railroad-related exhibits in two train stations, maintenance-of-way equipment, a caboose, and a fireless engine.

SCHEDULE: Victoria Day to Labor Day: daily, 9 a.m. to 5 p.m.; Labor Day to Thanksgiving: weekends, 9 a.m. to 5 p.m.

ADMISSION/FARE: Adults, $2; children under 13, $.50.

LOCOMOTIVES/ROLLING STOCK: No. 6218, former Canadian National 4-8-4; Porter fireless locomotive.

NEARBY ATTRACTIONS: Niagara Falls, Fort Erie Historical Museum, Historic Fort Erie, and Mahoney Dolls House Gallery.

DIRECTIONS: On Central Ave. between Gilmore Rd. and Wintemute St., north of the west end of the Peace Bridge.

Huntsville, ON

Huntsville & Lake of Bays Railway
Dinner train, Display, Model train layout
42" gauge

SITE ADDRESS: 88 Brunel Rd. Huntsville, ON P1H 1R1
MAILING ADDRESS: 26 Centre St. N Huntsville, ON P1H 1X4
TELEPHONE: (705) 789-7576
E-MAIL: nicholls@vianet.ca
WEBSITE: www.portageflyer.org or www.muskokaheritageplace.org

DESCRIPTION: Approximately ¾-mile train ride has a turn table at each end. Steam operates through July and August. Operations include a "live" telegraph operation Wednesdays in July and August.

SCHEDULE: July and August: Tuesday to Saturday, 12:01, 1, 2, and 3 p.m.; September to early October: weekdays, limited operation.

ADMISSION/FARE: Train: $5+tax; train and Muskoka Heritage Place Museum: $11+tax.

LOCOMOTIVES/ROLLING STOCK: MLW 0-4-0 ST no. 1 17-ton, coal fired (static display); MLW 0-4-0 ST no. 2 21-ton, oil fired, both units built in 1926. GE diesel-electric 26-ton switch engine, plus an 8-ton Brookville gas-powered switch engine used for track repair. Two 1900 vintage open-sided coaches, Velocipede. 4-man pump cab. Fairmont motor car.

SPECIAL EVENTS: May and June: long weekends, Canada Day, special runs for wedding groups; July and August: every Wednesday, live telegraph demonstrations.

NEARBY ATTRACTIONS: Algonquin Provincial Park, Lion's Look-out, Ragged Rapids Park, Dyer Memorial Park, golf courses, lakes, and rivers.

DIRECTIONS: 200 miles north of Toronto on Hwys. 400 and 11, to Huntsville, Ontario. The Muskoka Heritage Place Steam Train and Pioneer Village is located right in the town, along the north branch of the Muskoka River.

Photo courtesy of Russ Nicholls Collection.

Huntsville, ON

Muskoka Heritage Place
Steam Train & Pioneer Village

Train ride
42" narrow gauge

ADDRESS: 88 Brunel Rd. Huntsville, ON P1H 1R1
TELEPHONE: (705) 789-7576
E-MAIL: village@muskokaheritageplace.org
WEBSITE: www.muskokaheritageplace.org

DESCRIPTION: The Portage Flyer is a fully restored 1902 steam train. The complete trip takes about 45 minutes, including the tour of the Steam Museum. Passengers board the train at the Rotary Village Station & Steam Museum, then travel alongside Muskoka River and Fairy Lake (1.8 km). The train stops at Fairy Lake Station at Camp Kitchen, when passengers unload so the engine can turn around. Passengers then re-board for return trip.

SCHEDULE: May 20 to October 7: daily, 10 a.m. to 4 p.m.; July and August: Tuesday to Saturday; May, June, September, and October, 1 p.m only; Portage Flyer Steam Train: Tuesday through Saturday, 12, 1, 2, and 3 p.m.

LOCOMOTIVES/ROLLING STOCK: Montreal Locomotive Works no. 2, 1926 steam oil 21½-ton; Montreal Locomotive Works no. 1, 1926 coal fired 17 ton; GE Diesel Locomotive, 1949 no. 3; gas power Brookville no. 4.

SPECIAL EVENTS: July 1, Celebrate Canada Day; October 7, Thanksgiving Festival; October 31, The Great Pumpkin Train; December 23, A Portage Flyer Christmas.

NEARBY ATTRACTIONS: Restaurants, shopping, golf, and Lion's Lookout.

DIRECTIONS: Two hours north from Toronto and one hour south from North Bay. From Hwy. 11, exit on Ravenscliffe. Northbound drivers turn right at stop sign, southbound turn left. Continue through the light at Tim Horton's (unless you're ready for a coffee) and watch for the blue Muskoka Heritage Place signs on the right side of the street. Pass through the second set of lights at Centre St. The next set of lights is Main St. Turn right and cross over the swing bridge. The first lights are Brunel Rd., turn left and to approximately 1 km. Just past the Huntsville High School on the left is Park Dr. and Muskoka Heritage Place parking.

Photo courtesy of Muskoka Heritage Place Archives.

Komoka, ON

Komoka Railway Museum

Museum

ADDRESS: 133 Queen St., PO Box 22 Komoka, ON N0L 1R0
TELEPHONE: (519) 657-1912
E-MAIL: komokarailmuseum@aol.com
WEBSITE: www.komokarail.ca

DESCRIPTION: Visitors can relive railroad history at this restored railroad station, letting imaginations run down the tracks as they examine early railway equipment. The museum is home to an extensive collection of books, photos, and artifacts that rail enthusiasts of all ages can enjoy.

SCHEDULE: June to August: Friday to Monday, 9 a.m. to 4 p.m.; September to May: Saturday, 9 a.m. to 12 p.m.

ADMISSION/FARE: Adults, $4; seniors, $3; children under 5, free; families of five or fewer, $12. Group tours must be booked in advance.

LOCOMOTIVES/ROLLING STOCK: 1913 Shay logging locomotive; 1939 CN baggage car no. 8731; 1972 GTW caboose no. 79198; collection of maintenance jiggers (speeders).

NEARBY ATTRACTIONS: Delaware Speedway, Little Beaver Restaurant, Komoka Provincial Park, and Belamere Farm Market and Winery.

DIRECTIONS: Eight miles west of London on Glendon/Commissioners Rd.

Photo courtesy of Pierre Ozorak.

Milton, ON

Halton County Radial Railway Museum

Train ride, Museum
1.5m gauge

SITE ADDRESS: 13629 Guelph Line Milton, ON
MAILING ADDRESS: PO Box 578 Milton, ON L9T 5A2
TELEPHONE: (519) 856-9802
E-MAIL: streetcar@hcry.org
WEBSITE: www.hcry.org

DESCRIPTION: Founded in 1953, this operating electric railway museum is situated at Stop 92 on the former right-of-way of the Toronto Suburban Railway. It offers a trip down memory lane with rides on a variety of restored street cars, radial and work cars, through two kilometers of scenic woodlands. There are various railway-related items displayed inside the 1912 former Rockwood Station, including cast iron stoves that emit the smell and warmth of a wood fire when they are used to heat the station on cool days.

SCHEDULE: May, June, September, and October: weekends and holidays; July and August: daily.

ADMISSION/FARE: Adults, $9.50 plus tax; seniors, $8.50 plus tax; youth, $6.50 plus tax; children 3 and under, free.

LOCOMOTIVES/ROLLING STOCK: Open car no. 327; Peter Witt no. 2424; London & Port Stanley interurban no. 8; Montreal & Southern Counties no. 107; PCC no. 4600; maintenance equipment.

SPECIAL EVENTS: Wildflower weekend; July 1, Streetcar Heritage Day; August, Ice Cream and Starlight Evening; Fall Trolley Festival, Halloween Fright Night; December, Holly Trolley.

NEARBY ATTRACTIONS: Conservation areas, Mohawk Race Track, Halton Region Museum, Lion Safari, Royal Botanical Gardens, and Canadian Warplane Museum.

DIRECTIONS: Hwy. 401 to exit 312 (Guelph Line), north for 9 miles, or Hwy. 7 to Guelph Line, south for 3 miles.

Photo courtesy of J.D. Knowles.
Coupon available, see insert.

Orangeville, ON
Credit Valley Explorer Tour Train
Train ride, Dinner train
Standard gauge

ADDRESS: Orangeville-Brampton Railway Townline Rd. Orangeville, ON L9W 2Z7
TELEPHONE: (866) 708-6279
E-MAIL: info@creditvalleyexplorer.com
WEBSITE: www.creditvalleyexplorer.com

DESCRIPTION: This unique, half-day rail tour travels through the Forks of the Credit and the Hills of Headwaters, which are known for rolling hills, deep valleys, unsurpassed fall colors, and being the headwaters for four major river systems. The 70km adventure aboard classic rail cars with spacious first-class seating and large picture windows, is sure to be a memorable experience.

SCHEDULE: Tours operate year-round. For current tour schedule, please visit the website.

ADMISSION/FARE: Fares vary depending on tour type and date.

LOCOMOTIVES/ROLLING STOCK: GP9 locomotives; refurbished, air-conditioned classic rail cars with reclining seats and large picture windows.

SPECIAL EVENTS: Please see the website for details.

NEARBY ATTRACTIONS: Hills of Headwaters tourism region. Numerous nearby attractions catering to many tastes. For detailed information visit www.thehillsofheadwaters.com.

DIRECTIONS: Located near the intersection of Hwys. 9 and 10 in Orangeville, just an hour north of Metro Toronto. Take Hwy. 10 north from Hwy. 401, or Hwy. 9 west from Hwy. 400; head into downtown Orangeville on Hwy. 9/Broadway. Turn left on Townline Rd., go approximately 1km to railway yard.

Photo courtesy of Steve Bradley.

Ottawa, ON

Canada Science and Technology Museum

Museum

ADDRESS: 1867 St. Laurent Blvd., PO Box 9724, Station T Ottawa, ON K1G 5A3
TELEPHONE: (613) 991-3044
E-MAIL: cts@technomuses.ca
WEBSITE: www.sciencetech.technomuses.ca

DESCRIPTION: This museum features all types of transportation, from Canada's earliest days to the present time. On display in the Locomotive Hall are four huge locomotives, a CNR narrow gauge passenger car from Newfoundland, and a caboose. Visitors have access to two of the cabs, where sound effects give the feeling of live locomotives. The engines are meticulously restored, with polished rods and lighted number boards and class lights.

SCHEDULE: Museum: May 1 to Labor Day, daily, 9 a.m. to 5 p.m.; Labor Day through April, Tuesday through Sunday, 9 a.m. to 5 p.m.; closed Monday and Christmas Day. Free train ride with admission: July through August, Wednesday and Sunday.

ADMISSION/FARE: Adults, $6; seniors and students, $5; children 4-14, $3; children under 4, free; family of two adults/three children, $14. Group rates available.

LOCOMOTIVES/ROLLING STOCK: 1923 Shay steam locomotive no. 3; CN 4-8-4 no. 6400; CP 4-6-0 no 926; CP 4-6-4 no. 2858, a Royal Hudson; CP 4-8-4 no. 3100; CNR business car "Terra Nova"; CNR 76109 caboose.

SPECIAL EVENTS: August 5 and 6, railway weekend: ride a Shay steam locomotive, tour the museum's railway treasures, explore locomotive and railway engineering feats.

DIRECTIONS: Queensway (Hwy. 417) exit St. Laurent south for 2.6km, left at Lancaster Rd.

Photo courtesy of Shay steam locomotive, Canada Science and Technology Museum, Ottawa, Canada.

ONTARIO

Sault Ste. Marie, ON

Algoma Central Railway/CN

Train ride
Standard gauge

ADDRESS: 129 Bay St., PO Box 130 Sault Ste. Marie, ON P6A 6Y2
TELEPHONE: (800) 242-9287 or (705) 946-7300
E-MAIL: kelly.booth@cn.ca
WEBSITE: www.algomacentralrailway.com

DESCRIPTION: Tour trains take passengers on a one-day wilderness excursion to Agawa Canyon Park. The regular passenger train provides service to Hearst and access to a variety of wilderness lodges. Private Car and Camp Car rentals are available.

SCHEDULE: Passenger service: year-round, seasonally; Agawa Canyon Tour: mid-June through mid-October, daily; snow train: January through mid-March, weekends. Group rates available.

ADMISSION/FARE: Varies, call for information.

LOCOMOTIVES/ROLLING STOCK: CN Rail GP40s; SD50s; refurbished 1950s VIA coaches.

NEARBY ATTRACTIONS: Depot is located downtown close to hotels, restaurants, shopping and attractions.

DIRECTIONS: Located in downtown Sault Ste. Marie, minutes from International Bridge. Follow Train Tour attraction signs.

Photo courtesy of ACR/Elmer Kars.

Smiths Falls, ON

Smiths Falls Railway Museum

Museum

ADDRESS: 90 William St. W, PO Box 962 Smiths Falls, ON K7A 5A5
TELEPHONE: (613) 283-5696
E-MAIL: sfrmchin@superaje.com
WEBSITE: www.sfrmeo.ca

DESCRIPTION: Smiths Falls Railway Museum of Eastern Ontario is a restored Canadian Northern Railway Station/National Historic Site, which offers exhibitions, special events, and a children's area.

SCHEDULE: June and August: daily, 10 a.m. to 4 p.m. Check website for September to May schedule. Open year-round by appointment for groups.

ADMISSION/FARE: Adults, $5; seniors 65+, $3; students 12+, $3; children 6-11, $2; under 6, free.

LOCOMOTIVES/ROLLING STOCK: Canadian northern no. 1112, 4-6-0; CPR S-3 no. 6591, railway dental car; CP Cadillac inspection car; two Wickham track inspection vehicles; boxcars; cabooses; velocipede; handcars.

SPECIAL EVENTS: Please check their website for an up-to-date schedule.

NEARBY ATTRACTIONS: Heritage House Museum, Rideau Canal and Rideau Canal Museum, and Hershey's Canada plant.

DIRECTIONS: From Ottawa: Hwy. 416 south, exit Roger Stevens Dr. west at North Gower. From Montreal, Ogdensburg NY: Hwy. 401 west, exit. Hwy. 29 north at Brockville. From Toronto: Hwy. 401 west exit Hwy. 15 north at Kingston.

St. Thomas, ON

Elgin County Railway Museum
Museum

ADDRESS: 255 Wellington St., PO Box 20062 St. Thomas, ON N5P 4H4
TELEPHONE: (519) 637-6284
E-MAIL: thedispatcher@ecrm5700.org or tours@ecrm5700.org
WEBSITE: www.ecrm5700.org

DESCRIPTION: The museum has ongoing restoration and display of engines, rolling stock, and artifacts, and model train layout.

SCHEDULE: Summer: daily, 10 a.m. to 4 p.m.; remainder of year: Monday, Wednesday, and Saturday, if staff is available.

ADMISSION/FARE: By donation.

LOCOMOTIVES/ROLLING STOCK: CN 4-6-4 no. 5700; London & Port Stanley Railway electric coach no. 14 electric coach; L&PS electric freight locomotive; CP RSD17 no. 892; more.

SPECIAL EVENTS: First May weekend, Nostalgia Days; last August weekend, Heritage Days.

NEARBY ATTRACTIONS: Elgin Pioneer Museum, statue of "Jumbo," elephant killed by a train in St. Thomas; Elgin Military Museum; village of Port Stanley; and city of London.

DIRECTIONS: From Hwys. 401 or 402, south on Hwy. 4, Wellington Rd. or Highbury Ave.

Tottenham, ON

South Simcoe Railway

Train ride, Museum

ADDRESS: Mill St. W, PO Box 186 Tottenham, ON L0G 1W0
TELEPHONE: (905) 936-5815
E-MAIL: info@steamtrain.com
WEBSITE: www.steamtrain.com

DESCRIPTION: Passengers can enjoy a scenic journey through the Beeton Creek Valley aboard South Simcoe Railway's vintage steam trains. Excursions are just under an hour and are highlighted by the friendly and informative commentary of the conductor. It's a unique trip into the past that the whole family can enjoy!

SCHEDULE: Mid-May through mid-October: Sunday and holiday Mondays, departures at 10:30 a.m., 12, 1:30, and 3 p.m. Other special excursions operate through the year. Please call or visit their website for full schedule.

ADMISSION/FARE: Adults, $12; seniors, $10; children, $7 (taxes included).

LOCOMOTIVES/ROLLING STOCK: Rogers Locomotive Works 4-4-0 no. 136 (built 1883); Montreal Locomotive Works 4-6-0 no. 1057 (built 1912); vintage open-window day coaches dating from the 1920s.

NEARBY ATTRACTIONS: Nearby family attractions: The Falconry Centre; Puck's Farm; Gould's Apple Orchard; large Conservation Park with swimming, camping, and picnic pavilions; and nearby restaurants and shopping.

DIRECTIONS: From Hwy. 400, take Hwy. 9 west 20km to Tottenham Rd., turn north. Turn left at first traffic lights in Tottenham, follow signs to free parking.

Photo courtesy of Edward Wakeford.

KEY TO SYMBOLS

♿ Handicapped accessible	🍴 Restaurant	🎨 Arts and crafts	arm Association of Railway Museums
P Parking	🪑 Picnic area	M Memberships available	TRAIN Tourist Railway Association, Inc.
P Bus/RV parking	Dining car	✉ Send S.A.S.E. for brochure	Amtrak service to nearby city
Gift, book, or museum shop	Excursions	NRHP National Register of Historic Places	VIA VIA service to nearby city
Refreshments	TOUR Guided tours	VISA MasterCard DISCOVER AMERICAN EXPRESS Card	Credit cards accepted

York Durham Heritage Railway
Train ride

SITE ADDRESS: Railway St. Uxbridge, ON
MAILING ADDRESS: PO Box 462 Stouffville, ON L4A 7Z7
TELEPHONE: (905) 852-3696
E-MAIL: kendra5@sympatico.ca

DESCRIPTION: Twelve-mile train ride from Uxbridge and Stouffville. The association began operating this tourist train in the fall of 1996.

SCHEDULE: Call or write for information.

ADMISSION/FARE: Adults, $18; seniors, $15; students 13-18, $15; children 2-12, $9; people under 2 and over 90, free; family (2 adults and 3 children ages 2-12), $50.

LOCOMOTIVES/ROLLING STOCK:
No. 3612 Alco RS11; no. 1310 Alco RS3; nos. 3209 and 3232 cafe cars, former VIA; 1920s heavyweight 4960; former rules instruction car; caboose; flatcar.

SPECIAL EVENTS: Father's Day, Teddy Bear Day, Murder Mystery Trains, Halloween Spook Trains, and Christmas Trip (weather permitting). Call or write for dates.

NEARBY ATTRACTIONS: Sales Barn, Uxbridge Scott Museum, Lucy Maude Montgomery Home, restaurants, gift shops.

DIRECTIONS: Thirty minutes northeast of Toronto, Ontario. Take Hwy. 404 to Bloomington Sideroad, go east on the Bloomington Sideroad, which becomes Hwy. 47 into Uxbridge.

Photo courtesy of John Skinner, Eagle Vision Photography.

TRAVEL TIP: *Best place to ride*

What's the best place to ride on a tourist train? It all depends on what you like. Many lines offer open-air cars so you can enjoy the scenery, but remember, these are subject to the whim of weather.

Closed-window cars offer climate control. And some railroads offer an open car with no top, where all can enjoy the scenery. Be sure and ask what's available before you make your reservations.

PRINCE EDWARD ISLAND

Elmira, PE

Elmira Railway Museum
Train ride, Museum

ADDRESS: 457 Elmira Rd. Elmira, PE C0A 1K0
TELEPHONE: (902) 357-7234
E-MAIL: info@elmirastation.com
WEBSITE: www.elmirastation.com

DESCRIPTION: The museum offers a 12-minute, 1.6km train ride and a collection of HO scale model trains. Elmira Station became an important part of railroading on the Island in the early 1900s, when it was known as the end of the line for those traveling east on Prince Edward Island. The original wooden station house, platform, freight shed, and master's office have been re-created, along with maps and artifacts. The original two waiting rooms in the station now house thematic displays that illustrate various facets of railway life. Since opening the station as a museum in 1975, the building has expanded and undergone extensive renovations to offer visitors more than just a historical experience.

SCHEDULE: Mid-June through September, daily.

ADMISSION/FARE: Museum and model train viewing under separate admission from train ride. See website for details.

SPECIAL EVENTS: Fourth Sunday in July, Strawberry social.

KEY TO SYMBOLS

Handicapped accessible	Restaurant	Arts and crafts	Association of Railway Museums
Parking	Picnic area	Memberships available	Tourist Railway Association, Inc.
Bus/RV parking	Dining car	Send S.A.S.E. for brochure	Amtrak service to nearby city
Gift, book, or museum shop	Excursions	National Register of Historic Places	VIA service to nearby city
Refreshments	Guided tours	VISA MasterCard DISCOVER AMERICAN EXPRESS Card	Credit cards accepted

QUEBEC

Gatineau, QC

Hull-Chelsea-Wakefield Steam Train

Train ride, Dinner train
Standard gauge

ADDRESS: 165 Deveault St. Gatineau, QC J8Z 1S7
TELEPHONE: (800) 871-7246 or (819) 778-7246
E-MAIL: info@steamtrain.ca
WEBSITE: www.steamtrain.ca

DESCRIPTION: Half-day excursions are available aboard a 1907 steam train in a climate-controlled Voyager coach or 1940s Club Riviera car. The award-winning Sunset Dinner Train offers fine regional cuisine and live musical entertainment as it travels through Gatineau Hills

LOCOMOTIVES/ROLLING STOCK: 1907 Swedish locomotive class 2-8-0 no. 909; European GM diesel no. 244 (1962); 8 passenger cars (1940); first-class luxury dinner/parlour car (1940), Swedish built by SJ (Swedish national railway).

NEARBY ATTRACTIONS: Canadian Parliament buildings, 8 national museums, national park, 2 major casinos, wildlife park, water slide amusement park, and national heritage sites.

DIRECTIONS: 2 hours west of Montreal; 5 hours east of Toronto; 10 minutes from Ottawa.

Photo courtesy of Andrew Van Beek.

St. Constant, QC

Exporail, the Canadian Railway Museum   EDITOR'S CHOICE

Museum

ADDRESS: 110 Saint-Pierre St., PO Box 148 St. Constant, QC J5A 1G7
TELEPHONE: (450) 632-2410
E-MAIL: mfcd@exporail.org
WEBSITE: www.exporail.org

DESCRIPTION: Exporail has a large collection of railway equipment with more than 162 vehicles. Visitors can tour the new exhibit pavilion which hosts 45 vehicles and a double observation pit, and ride vintage streetcars and a miniature railway.

SCHEDULE: May to Labor Day: daily, 10 a.m. to 6 p.m.; Labor Day to October: Wednesday to Sunday, 10 a.m. to 5 p.m.; November to May: weekends and holidays, 10 a.m. to 5 p.m.

ADMISSION/FARE: Adults, $12; seniors, $9.50; youth 13-17, $7; children 4-12, $6; family (2 adults and 2 children), $30. All rates in Canadian dollars with taxes included.

LOCOMOTIVES/ROLLING STOCK: 164 vehicles, including 50 locomotives such as CPR 144, CPR 5335, CNR 77, CNR 4100, and more. See website for full list of rolling stock report.

SPECIAL EVENTS: June through October, special weekend activity every month.

DIRECTIONS: Hwy. 15 south to Route 132 west (exit 42) toward Chateauguay, then Route 209 south.

Photo courtesy of Kevin Robinson.

Vallee-Jonction, QC

Centre d'Interpretation Ferroviaire de Vallee-Jonction

Museum

ADDRESS: 397 Boul. J. M. Rousseau Vallee-Jonction, QC G0S 3J0
TELEPHONE: (418) 253-6449
E-MAIL: garevalleejonction@globetrotter.net
WEBSITE: www.garevalleejonction.ca

DESCRIPTION: This museum relates the history of the Quebec Central Railway.

SCHEDULE: April to November; June 24 to September 1: daily.

ADMISSION/FARE: Adults, $4. Rebates for groups, seniors, and children.

LOCOMOTIVES/ROLLING STOCK: Steam locomotive CN no. 46 4-6-4t; ex. caboose no. 434065; CPR tank car; CPR 40' boxcar.

SPECIAL EVENTS: August, Railway Festival.

NEARBY ATTRACTIONS: Trains Touristiques de Chaudiere-Appalaches (train excursions), historic old Quebec City, Cabane a Pierre traditional maple sugar camp, and Cache a Maxime winery.

DIRECTIONS: 30 minutes south of Quebec Bridge (and junction with trans-Canada Hwy. 20) on Hwy. 73 south exit 81, Vallee-Jonction.

Vallee-Jonction, QC

Trains Touristiques de Chaudiere-Appalaches
Train ride
Standard gauge

SITE ADDRESS: Galeries de Thetford, 520 Boul. Frontenac W Thetford Mines, QC G0S 3J0
MAILING ADDRESS: 399 Boul. Rousseau Vallee-Jonction, QC G0S 3J0
TELEPHONE: (418) 338-6071 or (877) 642-5580
E-MAIL: info.beaucerail@globetrotter.net
WEBSITE: www.beaucerail.ca

DESCRIPTION: Visitors can enjoy French Canadian hospitality on scenic excursions in the mines and lakes region of Thetford-Mines. Bilingual guides and musicians entertain guests on trips lasting two to three hours.

SCHEDULE: April to June 24, weekends; June 24 to Labor Day, six days a week; September to November, weekends, some weekdays. Call for details and reservations.

ADMISSION/FARE: Regular adult fares vary, $23.95 to $28.95 (taxes included), depending on trip. Rebates for groups and children; children 5 and under, free. Prices are subject to change.

LOCOMOTIVES/ROLLING STOCK: TTCA no.1301 GMDD FP7-A; TTCA power car no. 616; TTCA Pullman coach nos. 2722, 2709, and 2841.

SPECIAL EVENTS: All-day excursions to Sherbrooke, Sugar Bush specials, Fall Foliage, Halloween, and Santa Claus Trains.

NEARBY ATTRACTIONS: Mineralogical and Mining Museum and mine visits, Historical Quebec City, Frontenac Provincial Park, and Vallee-Jonction Railway Museum.

DIRECTIONS: From Montreal: Trans-Canada Hwy. 20 east to exit 228, Route 165 south to Thetford-Mines. From Quebec City: Trans-Canada Hwy. 20 west to exit 305, Route 269 south to Thetford-Mines.

Photo courtesy of Martin Laflamme.

TRAVEL TIP: *Caboose rides*

Who hasn't wanted to go for a ride in a little red caboose? Many tourist railroads and museums offer that opportunity, either on regularly-scheduled trains or during special events. Some lines even offer the chance to rent a caboose for exclusive use during a trip. Check the offerings at the lines you'd like to visit; you might just get your chance.

SASKATCHEWAN

Carlyle, SK

Rusty Relics Museum
Museum

ADDRESS: 306 Railway Ave. W Carlyle, SK S0C 0R0
TELEPHONE: (306) 453-2266
E-MAIL: mwhume@sk.sympatico.ca

DESCRIPTION: A museum housed in a 1910 CNR station contains early CNR and CPR artifacts. A Canadian Pacific Railway caboose is out front.

SCHEDULE: June through Labor Day: Monday through Saturday, 9 a.m. to 5 p.m.

ADMISSION/FARE: Adults, $2; children, $1; preschool children free.

LOCOMOTIVES/ROLLING STOCK: 1948 CPR caboose containing all original furnishings and tools.

NEARBY ATTRACTIONS: Kenosee Lake Provincial Park Waterslides, golf courses, and White Bear Lake.

DIRECTIONS: Two hours north of Minot, North Dakota.

Moose Jaw, SK

Western Development Museum
Museum

ADDRESS: 50 Diefenbaker Dr. Moose Jaw, SK S6J 1L9
TELEPHONE: (306) 693-5989
E-MAIL: moosejaw@wdm.ca
WEBSITE: www.wdm.ca

DESCRIPTION: Displays in air, water, land, and rail galleries. Visitors can hop on board the WDM Shortline narrow gauge railway and tour the track outside the museum.

SCHEDULE: Daily, 9 a.m. to 5 p.m.; January through March, closed Monday.

ADMISSION/FARE: Adults, $7.25; seniors, $6.25; students, $5.25; children $2; preschool, free; family (2 guardians, children under 18), $16.

LOCOMOTIVES/ROLLING STOCK: Vulcan 0-4-0 no. 2265; DS-6F no. 6555; G20 no. 2634; CPR coach no. 95; CPR caboose no. 6139; combination no. 3321; 1934 inspector's Buick M-499.

SPECIAL EVENTS: May long weekend through Labor Day: weekends and holidays, weather permitting; shortline railway 1914 Vulcan runs on museum grounds.

NEARBY ATTRACTIONS: Museums, historic sites, camping, a mineral spa, and a variety of cultural and sporting events.

DIRECTIONS: Junction of Hwys. 1 and 2.

Saskatoon, SK

Saskatchewan Railway Museum
Museum
Standard gauge

SITE ADDRESS: Hwy. 60 Pike Lake Rd. Saskatoon, SK
MAILING ADDRESS: PO Box 19, Site 302 RR 3 Saskatoon, SK S7K 3J6
TELEPHONE: (306) 382-9855
E-MAIL: srha@saskrailmuseum.org
WEBSITE: www.saskrailmuseum.org

DESCRIPTION: This museum has static displays and ½-mile motor car rides. Guided and self-tours of the museum are available; and a minimum of one hour should be allowed to tour the museum. There is also a significant collection of buildings, including a station, express shed, interlocking tower, tool sheds, etc.

SCHEDULE: May and September: weekends, 1 to 6 p.m.; June to August: daily, 1 to 6 p.m.

ADMISSION/FARE: Adults, $4; children over 6, $2. Please call for group rates.

LOCOMOTIVES/ROLLING STOCK: CP S-3 no. 6568; Saskatchewan Power GE 23-ton; for cabooses; several freight cars; Saskatoon Street Cars 40, 51 and 203; two snow plows; Jordan Spreaders; 12-1 sleeping car.

SPECIAL EVENTS: Late June, Railway Heritage Day; late August, Great Garage Sale.

NEARBY ATTRACTIONS: Western Development Museum, Pike Lake Provincial Park, Forestry Farm Park and Zoo, and Wanuskewin Heritage Park.

DIRECTIONS: Southwest of Saskatoon on Hwy. 60, approximately 4 miles from city limits.

Photo courtesy of P.J. Kennedy.